OXFORD STUDIES IN AFRICAN AFFAIRS

General Editors

JOHN D. HARGREAVES *and* GEORGE SHEPPERSON

CHURCH AND STATE IN ETHIOPIA 1270–1527

A reproduction of a fifteenth-century original portrait of an Ethiopian monarch

Mrs. E. Moore of the Institute of Ethiopian Studies (Addis Ababa) made the drawing on the basis of some fifteenth-century diptychs now in the collection of the Museum of the Haile Sellassie I University

CHURCH AND STATE IN ETHIOPIA

1270–1527

BY

TADDESSE TAMRAT

OXFORD
AT THE CLARENDON PRESS
1972

Oxford University Press, Ely House, London W. 1

GLASGOW NEW YORK TORONTO MELBOURNE WELLINGTON
CAPE TOWN IBADAN NAIROBI DAR ES SALAAM LUSAKA ADDIS ABABA
DELHI BOMBAY CALCUTTA MADRAS KARACHI LAHORE DACCA
KUALA LUMPUR SINGAPORE HONG KONG TOKYO

Printed in Great Britain
at the University Press, Oxford
by Vivian Ridler
Printer to the University

TO THE MEMORY OF
MY FATHER

PREFACE

THIS book is based on the research I undertook for a Ph.D. thesis at the School of Oriental and African Studies of the University of London between 1965 and 1968. Besides the Ethiopic collections at the British Museum, the Bodleian, and the Cambridge University libraries, and the Bibliothèque Nationale (Paris), I also made use of the rich manuscript collections of some medieval monasteries in central Ethiopia during a five-months' study tour in the spring of 1966.

I am very grateful to the British Council who sponsored my studies in London. They also co-operated with Haile Sellassie I University to facilitate my field-work in Ethiopia. During my visits to some of the medieval monasteries in Ethiopia, the officials of the Ethiopian Church were very helpful. I specially acknowledge the encouragement I received from His Holiness, Abunä Baslyos, the late Patriarch, and from the head of the Menelik Memorial Church, Līqä-Līqawnt Hailä-Mäsqäl.

Professor Roland Oliver supervised my research in London. He was a very patient guide and his unfailing interest in every state of my work has been a source of much encouragement. Inter-departmental co-operation is one of the best qualities of the School of Oriental and African Studies and acknowledgement of every assistance received will make this Preface too long. I must, however, thank in particular Professor Edward Ullendorff, Dr. A. H. Irvine, and Dr. J. Wansbrough, who have made themselves easily accessible every time I required their help and advice. At the Haile Sellassie I University I thank the President, Dr. Aklilu Habte, for his encouragement and support; Professors Richard Pankhurst and Stanislaw Chojnacki, and Mrs. E. Moore of the Institute of Ethiopian Studies; and all my colleagues in the Department of History, particularly Professor Sven Rubenson, to whom I owe my first introduction to the study of Ethiopian history. Mr. R. Schneider of the Ethiopian Institute of Archaeology was of great help to me whenever I asked for his advice. Mrs. Diana Spencer has let me use her unique pictures of Amba Gishän in Chapter VIII. Lastly, my gratitude is due to my wife, Almaze Seyoum, who, as a patient and devoted companion, has also made a vital contribution to the production of this book.

Haile Sellassie I University
Addis Ababa, 1970

TADDESSE TAMRAT

CONTENTS

LIST OF MAPS AND PLAN

LIST OF PLATES

ABBREVIATIONS

AÉ	*Annales d'Éthiopie.*
AÉO	*Archives d'études orientales.*
ARIV	*Atti del Reale Istituto Veneto.*
BIÉ	*Bulletin de l'Institut d'Égypte.*
BO	*Bibliotheca Orientalis.*
BSAC	*Bulletin de la Société d'archéologie copte.*
BSGI	*Bollettino della Società Geografica Italiana.*
BSOAS	*Bulletin of the School of Oriental and African Studies.*
CAA	*Cahiers de l'Afrique et l'Asie.*
CÉA	*Cahiers d'études africaines.*
CHÉ	*Cahiers d'histoire d'Égypte.*
CSCO	*Corpus Scriptorum Christianorum Orientalium.*
GJ	*Geographical Journal.*
GSAI	*Giornale della Società Asiatica Italiana.*
JA	*Journal asiatique.*
JES	*Journal of Ethiopian Studies.*
JRGS	*Journal of the Royal Geographical Society.*
JSS	*Journal of Semitic Studies.*
MRAL	*Memorie della Reale Accademia dei Lincei.*
MSOS	*Mitteilungen des Seminars für orientalische Sprachen.*
OCA	*Orientalia Cristiana Analecta.*
OCP	*Orientalia Cristiana Periodica.*
OM	*Oriente moderno.*
PO	*Patrologia Orientalis.*
ROC	*Revue de l'Orient chrétien.*
ROL	*Revue de l'Orient latin.*
RRAL	*Rendiconti della Reale Accademia dei Lincei.*
RS	*Revue sémitique.*
RSE	*Rassegna di studi etiopici.*
RSO	*Rivista degli studi orientali.*
SNR	*Sudan Notes and Records.*
ZA	*Zeitschrift für Assyriologie.*
ZDMG	*Zeitschrift der Deutschen Morgenländischen Gesellschaft.*
ZS	*Zeitschrift für Semitistik.*

TRANSLITERATION

Vowels:

The seven different sounds of an Ethiopic letter are respectively represented as follows:

ä; u; ī; a; é; i; and o.

Explosives:

I have used the following equivalents for the five explosives in Ethiopic and Amharic:

q = the explosive form of 'k'.
ṭ = the explosive form of 't'.
p = the explosive form of 'p'. No other special symbol has been used for the letter 'p' because it only occurs here in its explosive form.
ṣ = the explosive form of 's'.
ch̲ = the explosive form of 'ch'.

CHAPTER I

Introduction

MORE than three hundred years of European scholarship has produced an extensive literature on the languages, history, and cultures of the Ethiopian peoples. Yet Conti Rossini's *Storia d'Etiopia*—written more than forty years ago—still remains a unique contribution in the specific field of the critical study of Ethiopian history. Ullendorff has recently furnished the book with a much-needed index which has made it more accessible to the student. But the absence of a bibliography, and of the copious annotations so characteristic of Conti Rossini's other writings, is still a serious handicap. More important still, successive volumes to *Storia d'Etiopia* are yet to be written.

The date 1270, with which Conti Rossini ends his book, has provided the starting-point for my attempt in this book to reconstruct the more limited story of the development of Church and State in Ethiopia until the wars of Gragn. The nature of the material which I have utilized—consisting mainly of hagiographical traditions and the available royal chronicles—was a major factor in determining the title of the book.

Ever since 1896, when Ignazio Guidi and Conti Rossini simultaneously published *Gädlä Arägawī* and *Gädlä Täklä-Haymanot*, respectively, the value of the lives of the local saints for the study of Ethiopian history has been increasingly recognized. Introducing Conti Rossini's *Il 'Gadla Takla-Haymanot'* Guidi had the following to say on the subject:

> A class of sources very important for the history of Abyssinia are the lives of those saints who had some influence on the events and the development of that country: neither should this cause any surprise if one considers the more or less theocratic nature of the government and the power of the clergy.[1]

Following this judicious statement, many of the lives of the saints available in the Ethiopic manuscript collections of European libraries

[1] *MRAL*, ser. 5, vol. ii (1896), p. 97.

have been published, translated, and annotated. It now seems that European libraries can yield little more of the hagiographical traditions. In Ethiopia, however, the resources of the church in this respect are almost untouched. This has already been indicated by G. Ellero,[1], A. Mordini,[2] and R. Schneider[3] for the province of Tigré. More recently Dr. Sergew Hable-Selassie of the Haile Sellassie I University has been engaged in a survey of the historical sources available in the libraries of the Ethiopian Church. This has taken him to many of the monasteries in the provinces of Tigré, Gojjam, and Shäwa. His still unpublished list of the new documents he has uncovered includes many lives of saints which still await a critical study. My own short tour of a selected group of medieval monasteries in central Ethiopia has also been very encouraging. I have listed in the bibliography only a selection of the unpublished material I was able to consult in these distant libraries.

The most searching analytical study of the Ethiopic hagiographical literature in general was made by Conti Rossini.[4] Apart from the translated lives of the saints and martyrs of the early Christian church, the hagiographies of the Ethiopian church consist of two major divisions, namely those dealing with the local saints (*a*) of the Aksumite period, and (*b*) of the late medieval period. All the hagiographies falling under this second category belong to the period after 1270, and it is with them that we are mainly concerned. To determine the historical value of such hagiographical works, Conti Rossini has proposed a simple general rule: 'Their value as a contribution for the reconstruction of the political and ecclesiastical history [of Ethiopia] is inversely proportional to the distance, in time, of the saint whom they intend to celebrate.'[5]

The date of the composition of a *Gädl* is thus a crucial factor. But it is often very difficult to establish precisely. The hagiographical traditions about a local saint generally consist of four essential parts:

(*a*) the story of his life: his evangelical work and/or his monastic pursuits in an isolated hermitage;

(*b*) the *Kīdan*, or pact, which he receives from God in return for his endeavours. According to this the saint receives God's forgiveness for the sins of whoever prays and is charitable to the poor and to the Church in his name;

[1] *BSGI*, ser. 7, vol. iv (1939); *RSE*, i (1941).
[2] *RSE*, xii (1953).
[3] *Tarik*, Addis Ababa, vol. ii (1963).
[4] *ARIV*, vol. 96, pt. 2 (1937).
[5] Ibid., p. 404 n. 2.

(*c*) the miracles attributed to him both in his lifetime and after his death; and

(*d*) his *Mälk*, or the short hymns composed in praise of his holy life.

Each of these sections, in part or as a whole, may be written at different periods of time and thus complicate the problem of fixing the date of the *Gädl*. Generally, the *Mälk* and many of the miracles attributed to the saint after his death are written much later. The major purpose of a *Gädl* being to edify the congregation to whom it is read, and to increase the prestige of the community to which the saint belonged, the narrative of the post-mortem miracles is often paraphrased, amplified, and occasionally re-edited. This also seems to apply, to a lesser extent, to the *Kīdan*.

But to try to determine the chronological context of a local saint, only the story of his life and the traditions about the miracles in his own lifetime may be taken as the basic parts of the *Gädl*. Additional help is sometimes provided by the hagiographer, who says whether he is writing from a personal acquaintance with the saint, or from information gathered from others, or by divine inspiration. The value of these indications by the author(s) only lies in helping one to form an initial assessment of the work. By far the most final bases of determining the date of a *Gädl* are its own internal evidence and the corroboration which its story may receive from other independent sources.

Conti Rossini has divided the medieval lives of saints at his disposal —most of which are now published—into three categories:

(*a*) The hagiographies which are more or less biographical in character, and which have much historical significance as such. Among some others he included *Gädlä Fīlipos and Yohannis* (Bīzän), and *Gädlä Abäkäräzun*, in this category. Of the unpublished hagiographies which I have listed in the bibliography Nos. 7, 8, 9, 10, and 11, and all the Stephanite ones belong to this major division;

(*b*) those which have important traditions, but which are greatly affected by their narrative of wondrous tales about the life of the saint. He included in this category *Gädlä Täklä-Haymanot*, and *Gädlä Ewosṭatéwos*. Nos. 3, 4, 5, 6 in the bibliography seem to belong here; and

(*c*) those which are written many years after the event they describe and tend to be without much significance. Conti Rossini has *Gädlä*

Lalībäla, and *Gädlä Gäbrä-Mänfäs-Qidus* in this division, to which Nos. 1 and 2 of my bibliography also seem to belong.

For the religious and political history of the country in the middle of the fifteenth century, Zär'a-Ya'iqob's *Mäṣhafä-Birhan* and *Mäṣhafä-Mīlad* occupy an outstanding place in a class of their own. From these two compositions of the scholar king, it is possible to reconstruct the major aspects of his religious policy and to obtain intimate details of political and military events which are only given an incidental mention in the official chronicle of the reign.

The very few royal chronicles available are an obviously more important source of medieval Ethiopian history. For the whole period covered by this book only the chronicles of Amdä-Ṣiyon (1314–44), Zär'a-Ya'iqob (1434–68), Bä'idä-Maryam (1468–78), and much shorter entries about the following reigns until the wars of Gragn have come down to us. These have all been published and translated during the last hundred years. All my attempts to obtain other chronicles for this purpose during my short visits to Hayq, Gishän, Lalībäla, Dīma, Däbrä-Wärq, and some of the island monasteries of Lake Ṭana have been in vain. But I was able to gather a number of small isolated notes, particularly in the form of land grants, from early manuscripts of the Four Gospels, similar to those in Conti Rossini's 'L'evangelo d'oro'. These notes have been of great help in forming a more complete picture of the medieval period, and they shed fresh light particularly on the chronology of the kingdom.

A brief look at the bibliography shows how the student of Ethiopian history is indebted to the many European scholars who have devoted lifetime efforts to the study of Ethiopian culture. Thanks to this, we have a large body of Ethiopic texts published and translated into European languages with annotations and scholarly comments. I have made extensive use of this large collection of printed primary source material, besides the new unpublished historical documents which are listed in the bibliography. There is no doubt that a more complete picture of the story of Church and State in Ethiopia can only be formed after a much closer investigation of the traditions of the peoples and of the churches considered in this book. No study comparable to Conti Rossini's 'Studi su popolazioni . . .', Kolmodin's *Traditions*, and many of the other monographs dealing with the tribal groups in Eritrea, is yet available for the whole area south of and including the province of Tigré. Until this is done, the increasingly well-known history of the late medieval period will always look like a clear incident in a hazy background.

Sabeanization of northern Ethiopia

The ultimate origins of the Ethiopian State lie in the remote past, when Sabean settlements were established in northern Ethiopia, and a brief recapitulation of the major lines of development in the early history of the Ethiopian region is very essential here. South Arabian immigrants began to settle in the hinterland of Adulīs as far inland as the surroundings of Aksum before the fifth century B.C.[1] From then on, their settlements became the spearhead of a long process of semitization in the Ethiopian region. The extensive area of north-east Africa, between the Red Sea and the Nile as far north as the First Cataract and including the whole of the Ethiopian region, is still predominantly inhabited by a large family of people known to anthropologists and linguists as the Kushites.[2] Already at the time of the south Arabian immigration it seems that the Kushites of the Ethiopian plateau consisted of three distinctive linguistic groups. The area north of the Barka-Ansaba basin was the homeland of the Béja pastoralists.[3] South of the Märäb and Bäläsa rivers, and probably extending as far south as the Jäma river, and from the edge of the plateau in the east to the valley of the river Täkäzé in the west, there lived the Agäw.[4] The narrow wedge on the Eritrean plateau between the Béja and the Agäw was apparently occupied by the Kunama-Barya group, whose linguistic features represent a cross between Kushitic and a more ancient language spoken in the area.[5]

[1] Conti Rossini, 'Sugli Habasat' in *RRAL*, ser. 5, vol. xv (1906), pp. 45–9. Id., 'Expéditions et possessions des Habeshat en Arabie', in *JA*, ser. 11, vol. xviii (1921), pp. 6–10. Id., *Storia d'Etiopia* (1928), pp. 102, 109.

[2] Ibid., pp. 68–9. Id., *Etiopia e genti d'Etiopia* (1937), pp. 123–4. Baumann, H., and Westermann, D., *Les Peuples et les Civilisations de l'Afrique* (1962), pp. 274–5, 466–7.

[3] Conti Rossini, *Storia d'Etiopia*, pp. 74–5. Id. 'Schizzo etnico e storico delle popolazioni eritree', in *L'Eritrea economica* (1913), pp. 65, 71–2. Cohen, M., *Études d'éthiopien méridional* (1931), p. 44. Here Cohen makes the point that one of the Semitic languages of Ethiopia, *Tigré*, which developed after the south Arabian migration, has *Béja* substrata. Ullendorff, E., *The Semitic Languages of Ethiopia* (1955), p. 20.

[4] Conti Rossini, 'Schizzo etnico', p. 64; *Storia d'Etiopia*, p. 74. Cohen, op. cit., p. 44: Ge'ez Tigrigna and Amharic (particularly northern Amharic) have Agäw substrata. Ullendorff, op. cit., p. 28.

[5] Conti Rossini, 'Schizzo etnico', pp. 64, 69–70. Id., 'Studi su popolazioni dell'Etiopia: iv. Antiche popolazioni Nuba-etiopiche', in *RSO*, vi (1913), pp. 138–41 (extract). Id., *La Langue des Kemant en Abyssinie* (1912), p. 39. Here Conti

The third major group of Kushites, namely the Sīdama, probably occupied the extensive area south of the Jäma river, the plateau of Shäwa,[1] Harär,[2] and Balī,[3] and extended right across the basins of the Rift Valley lakes and the Omo valley[4] as far west as the left bank of the Blue Nile and beyond the river Didéssa.[5]

It was on this Kushitic population of the Ethiopian plateau that the south Arabian settlers[6] began to exert their pressure and to usher in an intensive cultural and political development, of which the Christian kingdom in 1270 was only part of the result. Nothing

Rossini demonstrates that the earliest contact made by the settlers from south Arabia must have been with non-Agäw speakers and probably with the Kunama or the Barya. Following Conti Rossini, Cohen also concludes that this must have protected Ge'ez from early 'couchitization', op. cit., p. 44. Cf. also Conti Rossini, 'Per la conoscenza della lingua cunama' in *GSAI*, xvi (1903), pp. 190–1. Pollera, A., *I Baria e i Cunama* (1913), pp. 11–14.

[1] Conti Rossini, 'Studi su popolazioni dell'Etiopia: v. Appunti di lingua Gonga', in *RSO*, vi (1913), p. 153 (extract). Id., *Storia d'Etiopia*, p. 75. Cohen, op. cit., pp. 44–5. Leslau, W., 'The Influence of Sidamo on the Ethiopic Languages of Guragé' in *Language*, xxviii (1952), pp. 63–5.

[2] Cohen, op. cit., p. 45. More recently Cerulli has concluded that the Semitic language, Harari, has developed on Sīdama substrata and that it was through the latter that it received other Kushitic influences, *Studi etiopici*: i. *La lingua e la storia di Harar* (1936), pp. 440–2. He closes the book with the following authoritative and cautious remarks: '. . . in the areas where the language we now call Harari was spoken, the Semites were superimposed on the preexisting Sidama populations.'

[3] Cerulli, E., *Studi etiopici*: ii. *La lingua e la storia dei Sidamo* (1938), pp. 1–2, 31–3.

[4] Today the lake region and the middle Omo basin are the last stronghold of the Sīdama, forming three major linguistic sub-groups, viz. eastern, central or Ometto, and western Sīdama, Cerulli, E., 'Note su alcune popolazioni Sidama dell'Abissinia meridionale', in *RSO*, x (1925), pp. 597–8; xii (1929), pp. 1–3. Id., *Studi etiopici*: ii, pp. 242, 248; iii, p. 215; iv, pp. 5–10, 523, 525–6. Conti Rossini, 'Contributi per la conoscenza della lingua haruro' in *RRAL*, ser. 6, vol. xii (1936), p. 625. Id., 'Studi su popolazioni dell'Etiopia: vi. I bambala di Amarr Burgi e il loro linguaggio', in *RSO*, vi (1913), pp. 160–7 (extract).

[5] Grottanelli, V. L., 'Gli Scinascia del Nilo Azzurro ed alcuni lessici poco noti della loro lingua', in *RSE*, i (1941), pp. 235–6. Id., 'I Niloti dell'Etiopia', in *BSGI*, xx (1941), pp. 572, 574–5. Cerulli, *Etiopia occidentale*, ii (1933), pp. 87–91.

[6] Conti Rossini had long proposed that these settlers predominantly consisted of *Habashat* tribes whose original homeland he traced back to the south-western corner of the south Arabian peninsula, 'Sugli Habasat', pp. 39–55; 'Expéditions', pp. 6–7; *Storia d'Etiopia*, p. 109. His location of the area whence the major south Arabian influence came to Ethiopia is still generally considered valid. But his identification of *Habashat* tribes in south Arabia has been contested recently in the light of much more epigraphical material than he had at his disposal, Irvine, A. K., 'On the identity of the Habeshat in the South Arabian Inscriptions', in *JSS*, x (1965), pp. 178–96. Drewes, A. J., *Inscriptions de l'Éthiopie antique* (1962), pp. 2–5, 89–93.

precise is known about the nature of the initial confrontation between these settlers and the indigenous peoples of northern Ethiopia. It is apparent however that the arrival of a settler population from across the Red Sea was only the last decisive phase of the long intercourse between the Ethiopian region and the ancient civilizations of Egypt and Arabia.[1] Strongly motivated, no doubt, by their knowledge of the terrain and of its potential resources and probably also making use of the long amicable relations they had already established with the local people, intrepid individuals or groups of individuals from south Arabia trickled on for centuries until they finally gained a permanent foothold in what are today the highland districts of northern Tigré and southern Eritrea. Ancient hunting stations on the African coast between the straits of Bab-el-Mandeb and the Dahlak islands probably served them as a spring-board for an effective penetration of the interior. From the epigraphical and archaeological findings it would appear that the route from the coast leading to Adulīs, Mäṭara, and Yéha was their most important highway.[2] They probably came in different dialectal groups.[3] At first each group probably consisted of a small number of individuals who set out for Africa with specific hunting or commercial interests, only expecting to stay there for a short time. It is most likely that it was during these

[1] Conti Rossini, 'Egitto ed Etiopia nei tempi antichi e nell'età di mezzo', *Aegyptus*, iii (1922), pp. 3–8; *Storia d'Etiopia*, pp. 39–54, 66; *Etiopia e genti d'Etiopia*, pp. 25–31. Doresse, J., *L'Empire du Prêtre-Jean*, i (1957), pp. 4–67. Leroy, J., 'Les "Éthiopiens" de Persépolis' in *AÉ*, v (1963), pp. 293–7. Playne, B., 'Suggestions on the Origin of the "False Doors" of the Axumite Stele', in *AÉ*, vi (1965), pp. 279–80. Cf. also Leclant, J., 'Note sur l'amulette en cornaline', *AÉ*, vi (1965), pp. 86–7.

[2] Contenson, H. de, 'Les principales étapes de l'Éthiopie antique', *CÉA*, nos. 5–8 (1961), p. 12.

[3] Conti Rossini, *Storia d'Etiopia*, p. 109. Id., *Etiopia e genti d'Etiopia*, pp. 126–7. Ullendorff, *The Semitic Languages of Ethiopia*, pp. 7–8. The problem of the origin (or origins) of the modern Semitic languages is also relevant for the direction of both the initial south Arabian migration and the eventual expansion of the kingdom of Aksum and its medieval counterpart. The view generally accepted is that the earliest immigrants probably spoke different dialects of a common south Arabian language of which the modern Semitic languages of Ethiopia are the distant offspring. This implies that the spread of Semitic influence in the Ethiopian region originally had northern Ethiopia as a single point of departure. While accepting this as 'la plus vraisemblable' in the case of Amharic at least, Cohen has long drawn attention to the *possibility* that other ports like Raheita and Zeila may have also been used by south Arabian immigrants to move over to the regions of Amhara, Shäwa, and Harär, *Études*, pp. 3–4, 38–40, 46–52. Cf. also his review of Ullendorff, *The Semitic Languages*, in *BO*, xiii (1956), pp. 14–15, 20. Cerulli has proposed a compromise solution, *Studi etiopici*: i. *La lingua e la storia di Harar* (1936), pp. 441–2.

early visits that they first established direct contacts with the local people. The identity and the way of life of these natives can only be surmised at this stage. Some isolated linguistic data seem to indicate that the earliest people they met in the Eritrean plateau were the non-Kushitic ancestors of the Kunama-Barya people.[1] But it was with the Agäw group of the Kushitic peoples of northern Ethiopia that the south Arabian immigrants established a lasting relationship, and it was among them that their cultural and political impact was most deeply felt.[2] It is most likely that at the time of their earliest contact with the south Arabians the native people were in a primitive stage of material culture, and lived in small isolated clans or groups of clans with no state or political organizations.[3] This must have given the immigrants an excellent opportunity to assert themselves and easily reduce the local population to a position of political vassalage. The immigrants themselves probably consisted of small tribal groups, each constituting a different political unit of its own. Thus the political system they introduced from the very beginning was not characterized by a large unitary State and only consisted of small units based on tribal groupings. This characteristic organization left an indelible mark on the political developments which their arrival in Africa must have initiated among the local people, and we shall have much occasion to see it at work in the course of this study. Each of these groups probably imposed itself on the section of the local people in whose neighbourhood it happened to settle, and began to integrate them into its superior cultural and political system. It is thus possible to imagine that by the middle of the fifth century B.C.—to which period the earliest epigraphical material seems to belong—the Agäw population of northern Tigré had already been organized into small political units with the settler population as nuclei.[4] The formation of these units probably followed both the clan groups of the native peoples and the tribal or dialectal divisions of the immigrants.

Conti Rossini had envisaged the possibility of an initial period of

[1] Conti Rossini, *La Langue des Kemant en Abyssinie* (1912), p. 39. Cohen, *Études*, p. 44.

[2] Conti Rossini, 'Notes sur l'Abyssinie avant les Sémites', in *Florilegium de Vogüé* (1909), pp. 139–40.

[3] Ibid., pp. 148–9.

[4] Conti Rossini, 'Sugli Habasat', p. 57; Caquot, A., and Drewes, A. J., 'Les monuments recueillis à Maqallé (Tigré)', *AÉ*, i (1955), pp. 26, 30; Drewes, 'Les inscriptions de Melazo', *AÉ*, iii (1959), p. 84; 'Nouvelles inscriptions de l'Éthiopie' in *BO*, xiii (1956), p. 180 n. 15.

direct political control of these settlements by a south Arabian kingdom.[1] This postulate does not seem to be necessary for the reconstruction of the history of this early period and, among the increasing amount of epigraphical material since discovered in Ethiopia, not a single sign of such a direct south Arabian rule has been procured. This seems to indicate that the south Arabian settlements were primarily private in origin, and did not represent an official act of political expansion and conquest by any state in the Arabian peninsula. Nevertheless, contacts between the two sides of the Red Sea were clearly frequent; the settler population probably continued to receive a regular flow of new immigrants, and by the mid-fifth century B.C. an independent political structure had already evolved in northern Ethiopia. By then also the political leadership was probably no longer purely south Arabian.[2]

The existence of such an early political organization in northern Tigré is attested by the recent epigraphical discoveries at Azbī-Déra and Hawiltī.[3] The earliest indication of a kingdom in this region is obtained from the Azbī-Déra inscription on a stone altar dedicated to the south Arabian god Almouqah. The anonymous king of this inscription bore a long title styling himself 'King of Sr'n, Ygzyan, Mkrb of D'mt and SB . . .'[4] The twin titles of *Mlkn* (= King) and *Mkrb* which this sovereign held at this early stage are most significant, not only in showing the south Arabian origin of the organization of state but also in pointing to the direction of the future development of the institution of kingship in Ethiopia. *Mkrb* was the title held by the supreme ruler of Saba in south Arabia between the ninth and the end of the fifth centuries B.C., and it meant 'Prêtre-Prince, Prince-Sacrificateur'.[5] By the end of the fifth century, it was no longer in use there, and the rulers of Saba began to assume the title of 'King of Saba'.[6] On the Tigrean plateau, however, the kings apparently continued to use it together with the new title of *Mlkn*. It is not known exactly when the practice started nor when it was discontinued. But

[1] Op. cit., pp. 57–8.

[2] Cf. Drewes, *Inscriptions de l'Éthiopie antique* (1962), pp. 94–7.

[3] Doresse, op. cit., i (1957), pp. 78–83; Caquot and Drewes, op. cit., pp. 26, 30; Schneider, R., 'Inscriptions d'Enda Çerqos', *AÉ*, iv (1961), pp. 62–5.

[4] Doresse, op. cit., pp. 81–3. Caquot and Drewes, op. cit., p. 30; Drewes, *Inscriptions de l'Éthiopie antique*, p. 97.

[5] Ryckmans, J., *L'Institution monarchique en Arabie méridionale avant l'Islam* (1951), pp. 51–3.

[6] Ibid., p. 101.

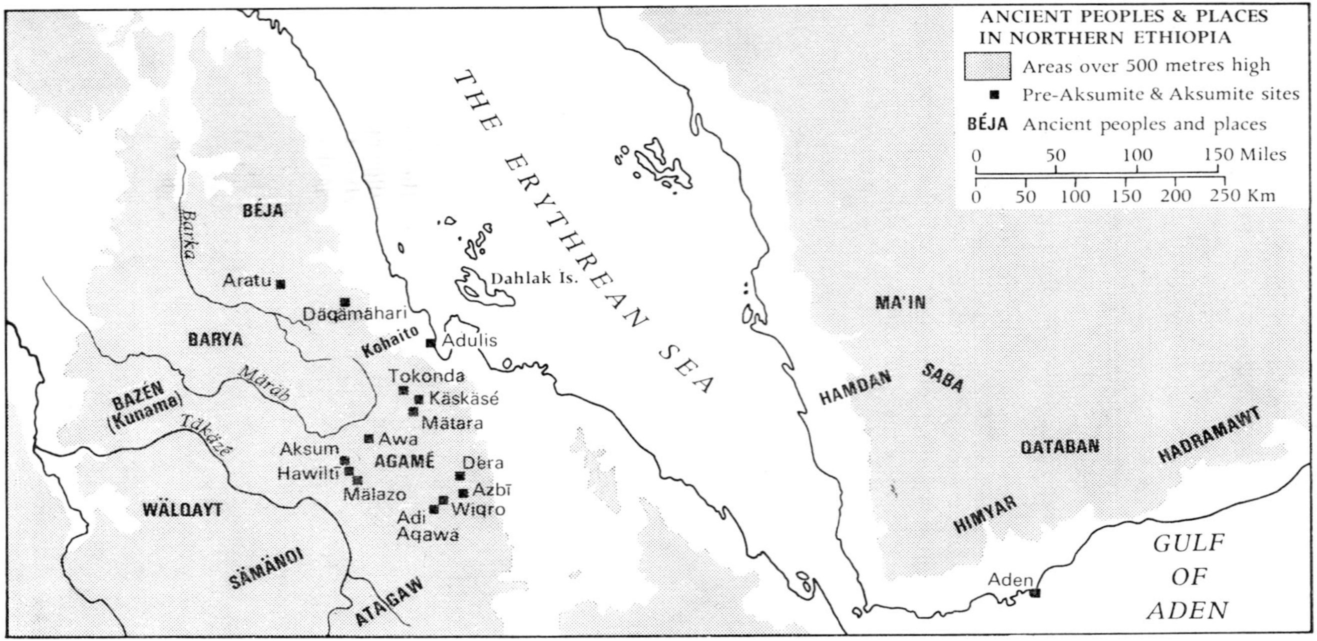
ANCIENT PEOPLES & PLACES
IN NORTHERN ETHIOPIA
Areas over 500 metres high
Pre-Aksumite & Aksumite sites
BÉJA Ancient peoples and places
0 50 100 150 Miles
0 50 100 150 200 250 Km
THE ERYTHREAN SEA
Dahlak Is.
BÉJA
Barka
Aratu
Däqämähari
BARYA
Kohaito
Adulis
Märäb
BAZÉN
(Kunama)
Täkäzé
Tokonda
Käskäsé
Mätara
Awa
Aksum
AGAMÉ
Hawilti
Mälazo
Dera
Azbī
Wiqro
Adi
Aqawä
WÄLQAYT
SÄMÄNOI
ATAGAW
MA'IN
HAMDAN
SABA
QATABAN
HADRAMAWT
HIMYAR
Aden
GULF
OF
ADEN

MAP I

the king of the Azbī-Déra inscription appears to be neither the first nor the last to bear the title, and two other inscriptions found at Hawiltī and at another unknown place probably belonged to his own sons.[1] From the epigraphic remains of the period it is apparent that the territory over which these kings maintained a political supremacy largely consisted of the triangle between Adulīs on the coastal strip, the eastern edge of the Tigré plateau around Azbī-Déra, and the surroundings of Hawiltī and Aksum.[2] Its centre of gravity probably lay in the region of Shīmäzana and southern Akälä-Guzay.[3] There is no need to imagine at this stage a strong unitary state. Neither the apparent dialectal fragmentations of the first south Arabian settlers (probably also augmented by their contending economic and commercial interests), nor the clan groupings of the local people on which they were superimposed, would seem to warrant such an early political development. What seems to be most likely is that there were a number of small autonomous political units sharing the same social and cultural heritage, among which one unit may have won sufficient economic and military prestige to enable its leader to assume royal titles such as those of the Azbī-Déra inscription. It is in fact very significant that two of the tribal groups mentioned in this Sabean inscription as the subjects of the king—namely Sr'n and Ygzyan—also appear many centuries later in two Ethiopic inscriptions as being engaged in rebellious military hostilities against King Ezana.[4] If the dating of the Azbī-Déra king (*c.* 450 B.C.) is correct, eight centuries separate him from Ezana, and the feeling of self-identity and independence of the peoples of his 'kingdom' could have only been much stronger. This picture of small political units, vying among themselves, may also provide at least part of the explanation for the

[1] Only one letter of the king's name is intact in the Azbī-Déra inscription. However, from the two other inscriptions referred to above, Schneider has proposed a reconstruction of the name, and even suggests that the authors of the two inscriptions were probably the sons of the Azbī-Déra king, op. cit., p. 65.

[2] The first inscription discovered by the German expedition at Däbrä Päntäl-léwon near Aksum seems to have a special relation with the Azbī-Déra one, Littmann, *Deutsche Aksum-Expedition*, iv (1913), p. 1; Caquot and Drewes, op. cit., pp. 30–2; Contenson, H. de, 'Les Principales Étapes de l'Éthiopie antique', p. 13.

[3] Conti Rossini describes the area as 'centro d'intesa vita nell'antichita', *Storia d'Etiopi*, p. 109. Much has been found since to confirm his verdict, Franchini, V., 'Ritrovamenti archeologici in Eritrea', *RSE*, xii (1953), pp. 8, 23–8. Drewes, 'Nouvelles Inscriptions de l'Éthiopie', p. 182.

[4] Littmann, op. cit., pp. 24–32. Cf. also Doresse, op. cit., i, pp. 82–3.

long silence of the classical writers about any state organization in the region.

Nevertheless, continuously inspired by their close contacts with the Arabian peninsula, the peoples of the region seem to have gradually made their impact felt among their neighbours. The annals of this period are completely shrouded in uncertainty and a full reconstruction of its history must await further archaeological discoveries in the area. But there can be no doubt that it was a crucial formative period in which the activities of the sabeanized inhabitants of northern Ethiopia must have produced a chain of political and social developments further inland in various directions. Hunting, or commercial interests, as well as deliberate attempts at territorial expansion must have spurred groups of individuals to push on into the interior. Already in the middle of the fourth century B.C. King Harsiotef (*c.* 404–369 B.C.) of Meroe claimed to have sent a successful expedition against a town called Habasa (?Habasi = Hebsi). The inhabitants of the town are called Metit and are said to have agreed to pay tribute to Meroe.[1] A variant of the name Metit is also found in one of Ezana's inscriptions,[2] and with additional material from the classical writers and local tradition Conti Rossini has proposed an identification with an ancient people in the Barya-Kunama area of south-western Eritrea.[3] The leaders of the Metit people are called Baruga and Semnasa in Harsiotef's inscription. These are south Arabian names[4] and may very well represent the spearhead of the commercial and political activities of the residents of northern Ethiopia at the time. It is especially significant that individuals bearing south Arabian names should be mentioned as the leaders of the local Metit people. It is precisely in this characteristic pattern of a few south Arabian or sabeanized individuals moving far into the interior and assuming political and cultural leadership among the Kushitic people of the Ethiopian region that one can best envisage the origin and the eventual expansion of the embryonic state organization long established in northern Ethiopia.[5] A fragment of a Sabean inscription

[1] Cf. Budge, E. A. W., *Annals of Nubian Kings* (1912), pp. 117–39. Another campaign was also conducted by King Nastasen (336–315 B.C.). For the dates see Arkell, A. J., *A History of the Sudan to 1821* (ed. 1961), pp. 155–6.

[2] Littmann, op. cit., Inscription 8.

[3] 'Studi su popolazioni dell'Etiopia: iv. Antiche popolazioni Nuba-etiopiche', pp. 138–40.

[4] Conti Rossini, *Storia d'Etiopia*, p. 107. Doresse, op. cit., p. 94.

[5] Essentially, the same pattern will also be seen at work in the medieval as well as the relatively modern periods of Ethiopian history.

recently found at Hawiltī makes a vague reference to 'the red and the black'.[1] This clearly ethnic description is probably a reference to the crucial process of the confrontation between the culturally superior, south Arabian (or sabeanized) groups and the natives of the interior. It is impossible to say exactly how far inland this cultural influence was felt before the rise of Aksum. But the time difference between the earliest Sabean inscriptions in Ethiopia (fifth century B.C.) and the first mention of the kingdom of Aksum by classical writers (second century A.D.) seems to suggest that during the long interval new ideas of social and political reorganization had been percolating slowly among the Kushitic tribes further west and south, beyond the sabeanized triangle of northern Ethiopia. The extensive sphere of influence of the kingdom of Aksum soon after its full emergence in documentary history is otherwise inexplicable.

Pre-Christian Aksum

Despite the clear evidence of the inscriptions for the early existence of a kingdom in northern Ethiopia, there is no mention of an organized state in the area by the classical writers until the middle of the second century of our era. Ptolemy was the first to make an unequivocal reference to 'Axume where is the King's palace'.[2] Conti Rossini has already shown the limitations of the knowledge of these writers concerning the inhabitants of even the coastal areas,[3] and their long silence about the political situation further inland cannot be taken as absolute negative evidence. Moreover it is very clear from the compilations of both Strabo (d. A.D. 24) and Pliny (d. A.D. 79) that trade between Ptolemaic Egypt and the Ethiopian region was of very long standing. This trade was most active between Ptolemais (founded in about 269–264 B.C.),[4] and the straits of Bab-el-Mandeb, where a town called Deire is located by Strabo on the authority of Artemidorus (second century B.C.), and Eratosthenes (d. 192 B.C.).[5] Another

[1] Schneider, 'Inscriptions d'Enda-Čerqos', p. 62. See, however, Drewes's reservations as to this interpretation, *Inscriptions de l'Éthiopie antique*, p. 98 n. 2.

[2] *The Geography of Claudius Ptolemy*, ed. and tr. E. Luther Stevenson (1932), p. 108. Cf. Contenson, 'Les premiers rois d'Axoum', p. 80.

[3] 'Commenti e notizie di geografi classici sovra il Sudan egiziano e l'Etiopia', in *Aegyptus*, vi (1925) pp. 9–10.

[4] Ibid., pp. 5–6. Crowfoot has identified Ptolemais with Aqiq to the north of the site of medieval Badi, 'Some Red Sea Ports in the Anglo-Egyptian Sudan', *GJ*, vol. 37 (1911), pp. 534–7.

[5] Conti Rossini, 'La città di Deire e i due laghi di Strabo XVI, 14', *RRAL*, xxix (1920), pp. 291, 295. Strabo mentions a stela erected here with hieroglyphic

port, probably near the present site of Assab,[1] was called Arsinoe after the sister of Ptolemy II Philadelphus (*c.* 284–247 B.C.), who is described by Pliny as the monarch of Egypt 'who first thoroughly explored the cave-dweller country'.[2]

The port of Saba, mentioned by Artemidorus and Ptolemy, which was probably the same as the fifteenth-century site of Girar just to the north of Miṣiwwa, was probably founded by Sabean traders in pre-Hellenic times.[3] Archaeological studies of Adulīs, first mentioned by Pliny, also indicate a much earlier, pre-Hellenic date for the establishment of the site.[4] This coastal strip between Ptolemais and Deire, which classical documentary material shows to have been studded with hunting and trading stations by the middle of the third century B.C., served the rich hinterland of the highland areas of northern Ethiopia and probably also the regions further south. Pliny's description of Adulīs suggests a strong tradition of commerce in the area and the commodities are reminiscent of later, medieval times: 'Here is a very large trading centre of the cave-dwellers and also of the Ethiopians . . .: they bring into it a large quantity of ivory, rhinoceros horns, hippopotamus hides, tortoise shells, apes and slaves.'[5]

Somewhere between Adulīs and another site he calls Isis, Pliny also speaks of 'a bay in the coast that has not been explored, which is surprising, in view of the fact that traders ransack *more remote districts* . . .'.[6] These 'remote districts' are certainly the country of 'the numerous tribes of Asachae who are said to be five days' journey from the sea; they live by hunting elephants'.[7] The coastal market towns and the interior which they served had been visited by south

inscriptions commemorating the conquests of Sesostries, i.e. Ramses II, king of Egypt about 1333 B.C. Pliny takes the conquests of the same king as far as Mossylites Cape and Harbour, the last place he mentions near Cape Guardafui, *Natural History*, vi. 32. 174.

[1] Conti Rossini, *Storia d'Etiopia*, p. 60.

[2] vi. 32. 168.

[3] Conti Rossini, 'Commenti e notizie di geografi classici', pp. 15–17.

[4] Ibid., pp. 17–18. Here the author identifies Adulīs with Melinos Limni; Littmann, op. cit. i, p. 42. Pliny attributed the origin of the town to runaway slaves from Egypt. He did this by attaching a Greek meaning (*a-doulus* = non-slave, free) to the name Adulīs, which may have only been Kushitic in origin, Conti Rossini, *Storia d'Etiopia*, pp. 104–6.

[5] vi. 34. 172.

[6] Ibid., para. 173.

[7] vi. 35. 191. The distance from the sea, and the name Asachae which has a slight onomatopoeic connection with Aksum, or Aksumites have to some suggested that Pliny may have been referring to the latter. Contenson, 'Les premiers rois d'Axoum', p. 77. Conti Rossini only takes the Asachae as one of the tribes in northern Ethiopia of south Arabian origin, 'Commenti e notizie di geografi classici', pp. 14–15; Id., *Storia d'Etiopia*, p. 63.

Arabian merchants for centuries, and the Greco-Egyptian explorer-traders of the coastal areas were only following in their footsteps. Even here, however, they never replaced the local merchants. It is probably owing to the economic strength of the local traders that the direct knowledge of the classical writers concerning the region long remained defective and superficial.

But in the long run the revival of direct Egyptian interest in the Red Sea and in the eastern trade opened a new chapter in the history of the Ethiopian region, and had far-reaching consequences in the political and economic development of nothern Ethiopia. Before the advent of the Hellenic traders, the Ethiopian region had been a huge reserve for the economic activities of south Arabian merchants, and Ethiopian commerce had been only a small appendage to Arabian trade. The curiosities and products of the African side of the Red Sea reached the eastern Mediterranean and even Alexandria and lower Egypt via the land routes of the Arabian peninsula.[1] Local participation in international trade could have only been minimal. The hunter-traders who had settled in the Ethiopian region had only acted as distant suppliers of their African products to the agents of the commercial magnates of Arabia. Imports from Mediterranean and eastern countries could have only come through Arab middlemen and both their volume and quality were doubtless determined by them. Thus both for its cultural inspiration and its economic development the Ethiopian region had depended entirely on south Arabia. Conti Rossini's oft-quoted generalization that 'la civiltà etiopica non è se non un riflesso della civiltà sud-arabica'[2] is perhaps true only up to this point. The reopening of direct contacts between Egypt and the Red Sea area under the Ptolemies drastically changed the situation. Its effects were not immediate, and much of the African trade followed the ancient Arabian routes long after the advent of the Greco-Egyptian traders.[3] But part of the trade soon began to be diverted in the direction of Egypt, whose merchants came to the African coast and made direct transactions with the local people. They brought with them Egyptian and other Mediterranean products in exchange. The items of export from Adulīs listed by Pliny are repeated almost verbatim by the anonymous author of the *Periplus*

[1] Préaux, C., 'Sur les communications de l'Éthiopie avec l'Égypte hellénistique', in *Chronique d'Égypte*, xviii, no. 53 (1952), pp. 258, 275–8.

[2] *Storia d'Etiopia*, p. 106.

[3] Préaux, op. cit., pp. 274–5.

about the end of the second or the beginning of the third century A.D.[1] Probably, the imports were also similar at the times of the two authors. According to the *Periplus*, these included brass and copper objects, iron bars for making spears, and weapons such as axes, adzes, and swords. The supply of these valuable goods, which helped to revolutionize their military and economic power, and the creation of an alternative market for their products no doubt impressed the local people, and probably encouraged the emergence of a new class of merchants fully committed to the development of direct trade with Egypt. This was also reflected in the economic and political life of the people, and the Ethiopian region set out on a fresh development of its own completely independent of, and often antagonistic to, its ancient south Arabian partners. If the early history of northern Ethiopia owed a great deal to south Arabia, the new source of cultural and political inspiration was certainly the Greco-Roman world of the eastern Mediterranean. Aksum rose and flourished with a Mediterranean orientation, and even when the spread of Islam interrupted its lines of communication, it was the legacy of this early cultural association which continued to give the Ethiopian region a special Christian identity throughout the medieval period.

No absolute dates are yet available for the beginning of Aksum as a political and cultural centre. As we have already seen above, Ptolemy was the first to mention the kingdom of the 'Axoumites' with the royal court at 'Axume', and his work is attributed to about the mid-second century A.D.[2] Together with Adulīs, which is also

[1] *The Periplus of the Erythrean Sea*, tr. and annotated by Schoff, W. H. (1912), p. 24. For the problems of the dating of the *Periplus* see ibid., pp. 290–3; Pirenne, J., *Le Royaume Sud-Arabe de Qataban* (1961), pp. 161–201. Id., 'La date du Périple de la mer Érythrée', *JA*, vol. 249 (1961), pp. 450–5. Cf. also Ryckmans, J., *La Chronologie des rois de Saba et du Raydan* (1964). The new dating seems to have been reluctantly accepted by some scholars who are currently in very close touch with the study of the kingdom of Aksum, Contenson, 'Les premiers rois d'Axoum', pp. 75–80. Cf. also Leclant's review of Pirenne's book, *Le Royaume Sud-Arabe de Qataban*, in *AÉ*, v (1963), pp. 301–3. Drewes, *Inscriptions de l'Éthiopie antique* (1962), p. 102.

[2] See p. 13 n. 2. The chronology of the kingdom of Aksum had been based on the early date given to the *Periplus*. Very serious problems have been raised recently which lower the date of the work by about two centuries, cf. n. 1 above. Thus we only have Pliny and Ptolemy as points of departure for the chronology of Adulīs and Aksum. About a hundred years separate Ptolemy's work from Pliny who only mentions Adulīs and 'the tribes of Asachae . . . five days from the sea'. It is not certain if the rise of Aksum can be dated within this period separating the two authors. Ptolemy only represents perhaps the progress of Greco-Roman geographical knowledge about north-east Africa in general, and

mentioned by Pliny before him, Ptolemy refers to two other towns, Coloe and Maste. It is however in the *Periplus* that we begin to see a clear term of reference for the territorial limits of the Aksumite kingdom. On the coast it extended from Ptolemais in the north to the straits of Bab-el-Mandeb.[1] The most striking difference between the writers before him (Strabo, Pliny, and Ptolemy) and the author of the *Periplus* is that, except for the islands of Alalai (Dahlak), he does not mention coastal towns other than Ptolemais and the port of Adulīs. Apparently, he had a direct personal knowledge of the Aksumite coast, and it is very significant that he should omit many of the sites reported in their works. It is most likely that this represents the growing power of the rulers of Aksum over the entire coast and the emergence of Adulīs as their major port at the expense of the other coastal settlements. It is also apparent that the hinterland served by these settlements had similarly passed over into the growing political and economic sphere of influence of the kingdom of Aksum. Compared with the pre-Aksumite (Sabean) period referred to above, there seems to have taken place a tremendous development, not only in the consolidation of the power of the kings, but also in their effective control of large territories.

The *Periplus* is not as useful in determining the territorial limits of the kingdom in the interior. Nevertheless it seems to offer valuable guide-lines:

> . . . from [Adulīs] is a three-days' journey to Coloe, an inland town and the first market for ivory. From that place to the city of the people called Axsumites there is a five-days' journey more; to that place all the ivory is brought from the country beyond the Nile through the district called Cyeneum, and thence to Adulīs.[2]

In this passage and in the Adulīs inscription 'the Nile' seems to be a reference to the river Täkäzé,[3] and Cyeneum has been identified

the development of closer contacts with the Aksumite region in particular. Conservative estimates recently advanced place the foundation of Aksum between the middle of the first and the beginning of the second century A.D., Contenson, op. cit., p. 80. Id., 'Les principales étapes de l'Éthiopie antique', p. 19.

[1] The wording in the *Periplus* is '. . . from the Calf-Eaters to the other Berber country' § 5. The Calf-Eaters are elsewhere identified as one of the people who live behind the coastal strip between Berenice and Ptolemais which is also called 'the country of the Berbers' §§ 2, 3. 'The other Berber country' is a reference to the coastal region of the Horn of Africa beyond the straits of Bab-el-Mandeb, § 7. See also the notes of the editor.

[2] Schoff, op. cit., p. 23.

[3] McCrindle, *The Christian Topography of Cosmas Indicopleustes*, p. 61 and n. 3. Ezana refers to the river by its present name, Littmann, op. cit., Inscription 11.

with the region of Sennaar in the eastern Sudan.[1] From these indications it seems that Zoskales,[2] the king of Aksum at the time of the *Periplus*, was at the head of a large empire extending to the straits of Bab-el-Mandeb in the south-east and beyond the Täkäzé river in the west. No specific estimates of the southern frontiers can be given at this stage of the history of Aksum; but it must be said that it was only natural for a growing kingdom in northern Tigré, which had already taken full control of the seaboard and had pushed its political and economic frontiers beyond the Täkäzé, to try to expand southwards and secure a dominant position also in the region of the sources of the same river, and even further south. In his description of what can be called 'the arms trade' of Adulīs, the author of the *Periplus* reports in particular that the imported iron which was made into spears was used by the Aksumites 'against the elephants . . . and in their wars'.[3]

These armed conflicts probably included wars of conquest undertaken by the Aksumite kingdom in the interior. The *Monumentum Adulitanum*,[4] and three of the inscriptions of King Ezana[5] are particularly concerned with such military expeditions in the region south and south-west of Aksum. The local resistance put up against the Aksumite attempts at expansion was strongly organized and suggests a fairly high degree of political evolution. It was a far cry from the weak, disorganized clan groups which the first south Arabian settlers must have encountered in northern Ethiopia.[6] In the Adulīs inscription strong tribal leaders are presented as resisting the Aksumite advances, and were only reduced to tributary status by the military

[1] Schoff, *The Periplus*, p. 61.

[2] The dates for this king necessarily depend on the dating of the *Periplus*. There have been attempts to identify the king with Zä-Haqle, who appears in the traditional lists of the kings of Aksum, and to use his reign for dating the *Periplus*, Schoff, op. cit., pp. 66–8. But these lists are a much later compilation and are of little or no chronological help, Conti Rossini, 'Les listes des rois d'Aksoum', in *JA*, ser. 10, vol. xiv (1909), pp. 313–20. Zoskales is certainly a predecessor of the king of the Adulīs inscription.

[3] Schoff, op. cit., p. 24.

[4] For the text and description of this inscription see McCrindle, op. cit., pp. 54–66. Conti Rossini, 'Expéditions', pp. 18–25. The name of the king is missing and no satisfactory identifications have been proposed as yet. His dates are however estimated to have been between A.D. 250 and 285, Contenson, 'Les premiers rois d'Axoum', p. 82. Drewes's recent attempt to identify him with Shamr Yuharish of south Arabia is extremely arbitrary, *Inscriptions de l'Éthiopie antique*, pp. 106–7.

[5] Littmann, op. cit., Inscriptions 8, 9, 10.

[6] Conti Rossini, 'Notes sur l'Abyssinie avant les Sémites', pp. 148–9.

superiority of the kingdom: 'Upon their submission I restored their territories to them, subject to the payment of tribute. Many other tribes besides these submitted of their own accord, and became likewise tributary.'[1] According to his inscriptions Ezana also ruled over a number of tributary kings and vassal chiefs. His military expeditions were undertaken to reduce the rebellious among them and to make fresh conquests of other neighbouring territories. Many of the peoples and regions thus conquered are named in both the *Monumentum Adulitanum* and in Ezana's inscriptions and indicate an intensive programme of territorial expansion during these reigns.[2] It is unfortunate that these names are still mostly unidentifiable, but there seems to be no doubt that many of them refer to areas south of the Aksumite region.

As has already been suggested above, the slow penetration of social and cultural influences into these southern areas must have started in the pre-Aksumite period. It is in fact apparent that the Aksumite conquests were only a second major wave of 'Semitic' expansion into the interior of the Ethiopian highlands. With the introduction of the Church into Aksum, this process of expansion got yet another dimension, and it continued throughout the early and the late medievial period. The next chapter recapitulates the broad outlines of the history of the Christian period until the end of the thirteenth century, when the nature of our sources begins to enable us to examine the Christian kingdom of Ethiopia in much greater detail.

The thirteenth century ushered in an active development in both Church and State in the Christian kingdom of Ethiopia. The process had already started in the Zagwé period, but it was considerably intensified with the rise of the new dynasty founded by Yikunno-Amlak

[1] McCrindle, op. cit., p. 64.

[2] Cf. Littmann, op. cit., Inscription 8 which mentions: SWSWT, king of the Aguezat and his people; SBL, king of Gabaz; and the king of Wylq. This place is mentioned immediately after a people called Samen, no doubt the same Samenoi whose inaccessible, cold, mountainous country is aptly described in the Adulīs Inscription, McCrindle, op. cit., pp. 61–2. Wylq (= Wälqayt) and Samen (= Simén) still keep their ancient appellation and are side by side just across the Täkäzé from Shiré. Inscription 9: major conflict with Abaliqiwo, king of Aguezat, who was captured with 'the bearer of his throne'. His territory seems to have adjoined that of Atagau, also mentioned in the Adulīs inscription. It apparently bordered on Erg, also mentioned in what appears to be the first Ge'ez inscription by Gdr, king of Aksum, Drewes, 'Problèmes de paléographie éthiopienne, in *AÉ*, i (1955), pp. 123–6. Inscription 10: campaigns against what seems to mean 'the kingdom of Afan', and the people called Ṣerene, who also appear in the Azbī-Déra inscription, cf. p. 9 n. 4 above.

in 1270. This development manifested itself in various ways in the period with which this book is mainly concerned. Within the kingdom itself, the power of the king over his vassal chiefs, his army, and his wealth all greatly increased. The literary reawakening of the Church led to the revival of monasticism and brought in a series of reform movements initiated by the new monastic leaders of the country. Of much more importance to the history of the whole area of the Horn of Africa was the rapid expansion of the territorial limits of the Christian kingdom, and the evangelization of many of the conquered areas.

These outward movements of both Church and State were most active in the reigns of Amdä-Ṣiyon (1314–44) and Yishaq (1413-30), who were the most outstanding military leaders of the kingdom in the whole of the period covered by this book. Their campaigns pushed the Christian frontiers far into the heart of the Muslim-dominated areas beyond the Awash in the east, the rich Sīdama country between the left bank of the Abbay and the Lake region of the Rift Valley in the south, and the Agäw and Fälasha country consisting of Gojjam and what is today the province of Bägémdir in the west and in the north-west.

The literary and religious activities of Zär'a-Ya'iqob (1434–68) were essentially an attempt to stabilize these manifold conquests of his predecessors, and to give a sound institutional basis for both Church and State in the whole of the Christian empire. The relatively radical programmes which he rigorously put into effect during his reign were not continued by his successors, and with the reigns of a series of minor kings the diverse regional and religious interests fully reasserted themselves. The absence of a strong, united leadership for half a century (following Bä'idä-Maryam's reign) sapped the Christian kingdom of much of its political and military strength, and led in the end to the brilliant successes of Imam Ahmad ibn Ibrahim, otherwise known as Gragn.

CHAPTER II

The Legacy of Aksum and Adäfa

The establishment of the Church in Aksum

AKSUM was at the height of its power in the middle of the fourth century. Its military interventions in the Nile valley had already given the tottering kingdom of Meroe the *coup de grâce*,[1] and had brought the former provinces of its old rival under its own sphere of influence. More than a century of direct participation in the local struggle for power among the south Arabian kingdoms had also brought Aksum into its first period of political supremacy in the Arabian peninsula.[2] Its port of Adulīs had developed into the most important centre of international trade on the African coast of the Red Sea, and with the decline of the land routes of Arabia much of the eastern trade was handled by Roman maritime traders with whom Aksum was on friendly terms.[3]

It is quite clear that, from the start, these economic contacts with the eastern Mediterranean were also accompanied by a strong cultural influence. Already at the time of the author of the *Periplus* we are told that King Zoskales of Aksum was 'acquainted with Greek literature'. No doubt this was also true of his courtiers, many of

[1] Sayce, A. H., 'A Greek inscription of a King (?) of Axum found at Meroe', *Proceedings Soc. Biblical Archaeology*, xxxi (1909), pp. 189–203; Littmann, op. cit., iv, pp. 32–42; Kammerer, A., *Essai sur l'histoire antique d'Abyssinie*, pp. 67–83; Conti Rossini, *Storia d'Etiopia*, p. 201; Doresse, J., *L'Empire du Prêtre Jean*, i, pp. 94–8, 145–9; Kirwan, L. P., 'A Survey of Nubian Origins', in *SNR*, xx (1937), pp. 49–52; Arkell, op. cit., pp. 170–3; Shinnie, P. L., 'The Fall of Meroe' in *Kush*, iii (1955), pp. 82–5; id., *Meroe, a Civilization of the Sudan* (1967), pp. 52–7.

[2] Conti Rossini, 'Expéditions', pp. 25–6; Kammerer, op. cit., pp. 39–43; Conti Rossini, *Storia d'Etiopia*, pp. 131–9; Ryckmans, *L'Institution monarchique en Arabie méridionale avant l'Islam* (1951), pp. 304–17; Doresse, op. cit., pp. 120–8; id., 'L'Éthiopie et l'Arabie méridionale aux 3e et 4e siècles d'après les découvertes récentes', *Kush*, v (1957), pp. 52–8. The chronology of these events has been drastically modified in more recent works, Drewes, *Inscriptions de l'Éthiopie antique* (1962), pp. 101–6; Ryckmans, J., *La Chronologie des rois de Saba et du Raydan*, pp. 19–22.

[3] Charlesworth, M. P., *Trade-Routes and Commerce of the Roman Empire* (1924), pp. 58–67; Hitti, P. K., *History of the Arabs* (1961 edn.), pp. 58–60. Cf. also Hourani, G. F., 'Did Roman Commercial Competition ruin South Arabia?', *Journal of Near and Middle East*, xi (1952), pp. 291–5.

whom were probably themselves Greeks, Hellenized Egyptians, or Syrians. It is most likely that such foreign advisers, who knew the king's personality at a very close range, provided the author of the *Periplus* with his description of Zoskales as '. . . miserly in his ways and always striving for more, but otherwise upright'.[1] This characteristic pattern of resident merchants of Mediterranean provenance exercising a strong, permanent influence has been recently demonstrated in the case of south Arabia and the eastern coast of the Red Sea.[2] The Ethiopian region seems to have had its full share of this Mediterranean impact since the advent of the Ptolemies in Egypt. In many ways, Ezana's conversion to Christianity in the middle of the fourth century was the climax of this cultural influence.[3]

It is probable that there were some Christians among the foreign residents of Adulīs, Coloe, and Aksum even before the conversion of the king.[4] They may have also had a few converts among their Aksumite servants and commercial associates long before they could exert any influence on the royal family. Their religious propaganda must have gathered momentum with the growing prestige of the Christian Church in the Roman empire, and with the final success of the Emperor Constantine (312–37) against his anti-Christian rivals. It is precisely in the last decade of the reign of Constantine that the traditions seem to place the first arrival of Frémnaṭos in Aksum.[5] The triumphant establishment of the Christian Church in the Roman empire gave an impetus to the religious efforts of the

[1] *The Periplus*, p. 23. It seems that the passage has also been interpreted as signifying heavy custom duties (levied by the kingdom of Aksum), Charlesworth, op. cit., p. 64.

[2] Pirenne, J., 'La Grèce et Saba; une nouvelle base pour la chronologie sud-arabe', in *Mémoires Acc. Inscr. Belles-Lettres de l'Institut de France*, t. xv, 1ère partie (1960), pp. 116–20, 131, 176–91.

[3] Kammerer, op. cit., pp. 99–106; Conti Rossini, *Storia d'Etiopia*, pp. 145–56; Doresse, op. cit., pp. 136–9, 149–53.

[4] Guidi, I., 'La Chiesa abissina', in *OM*, ii (1922), p. 124.

[5] According to these traditions Frémnaṭos first stayed in Aksum as a court official for some years before his return to his country, Syria. On his way there he called at Alexandria and told Patriarch Atnatéwos (328–73) of the excellent prospects of the Church in Aksum, appealing to him to send a bishop to guide the small congregation. The patriarch saw the enthusiasm of the young Syrian and appointed him the first bishop of the Aksumite kingdom, Conti Rossini, 'A propos des textes éthiopiens concernant Salama (Frumentius)', in *Aethiops*, i (1922), pp. 2–4, 17–18; Kammerer, op. cit., p. 101. Patriarch Atnatéwos suffered a number of exiles in his term of office because of the Arian controversy, and it appears that it was on his second return to his seat (346–57) that Frémnaṭos was ordained. Lagier, Mgr. C., *L'Orient chrétien*, i (1935), p. 138.

Christians in Aksum, and Ezana's conversion may not have been totally free of diplomatic and political considerations.[1]

Despite its virtue, the king's conversion does not seem to have opened the whole of his kingdom to the proselytizing influence of the Christian zealots at his court. In fact, if one were to judge from his first non-pagan inscription, his own acceptance of the new religion was extremely equivocal and he may have had to contend with anti-Christian conservative forces in the kingdom.[2] It seems therefore that at first Bishop Frémnaṭos's congregation consisted only of a section of the royal court and the foreign resident merchants and their households. In Aksum and other centres of population along the major routes to the coast former temples were converted into churches,[3] and new places of Christian worship erected. Because of the lack of books in Ethiopic at the time, Greek was probably the major language of the Church. Most of the clergy may also have been of foreign provenance. Thus, although its position as the royal cult may have added much prestige to Christianity in the country, its scope for expansion after Ezana's conversation was extremely limited. It is in fact more than a century after Ezana's conversion, with the advent of groups of Syrian missionaries—the *Ṣadqan*, and the Nine Saints—that the traditions of the Church show definite signs of progress in the kingdom of Aksum.[4]

The episode of the *Ṣadqan* and the Nine Saints is placed towards the end of the fifth century, and may have been connected with anti-monophysite persecutions in the Byzantine empire after the Council of Chalcedon.[5] Before the advent of these clerics in Ethiopia, it seems that the effective sphere of influence of the Church was limited to a narrow corridor between Adulīs and Aksum along the main caravan routes. But they established permanent outposts beyond these frontiers

[1] Halévy, J., 'L'alliance des Sabéens et des Abyssiniens contre les Himyarites', *RS*, iv (1896), p. 64; Guidi, I., 'Bizanzio e il regno di Aksum', in *Studi bizantini* (1924), p. 137; Kammerer, op. cit., pp. 102–3.

[2] Cerulli, *Storia della letteratura etiopica* (1956), pp. 20, 21.

[3] Doresse, op. cit., pp. 190, 230–9.

[4] The hagiographical traditions about these early missionaries have been studied by various authors, *Gädlä Arägawī*, ed. and tr. in part, Guidi, I., in *MRAL*, ser. 5, vol. ii, pt. 1 (1896), pp. 54–96; Conti Rossini, 'L'omelia di Yohannes vescovo di Aksum, in onore di Garima,' in *Actes du XI Congrès intern. des orient.* (1897), pp. 139–77; id., *Acta Yared e Pantalewon*, in *CSCO*, Script. Aeth., series altera, t. xvii (1904); id., *Storia d'Etiopia*, pp. 156–63; Doresse, op. cit., i, pp. 182–9.

[5] Guidi, 'La Chiesa abissina', p. 126; Kammerer, op. cit., p. 104; Conti Rossini, *Storia d'Etiopia*, pp. 162–3.

and the monastic communities attributed to the Nine Saints alone extend from the river Märäb north of Aksum as far as the district of Gär'alta in central Tigré.[1] The other group, collectively known as *Ṣadqan*, are said to have settled and taught in the district of Shimäzana.[2] A much more productive career seems to have been that of Abba Mäṭa, who is renowned for his evangelical activities in the region of Baqla in northern Eritrea, in Sära'é and Shimäzana, where his famous church of Däbrä Lībanos was still the centre of a powerful community in the fourteenth century.[3]

The efforts of these men brought the Church deep into the interior, and the traditions of their conflicts with the local people[4] probably represent pagan resistance to the fresh incursions of the new religion. It seems that the importance of these communities lay, more than in anything else, in serving as permanent centres of Christian learning. No doubt the first thing these Syrian monks set out to do was to translate the Bible and other religious books into Ethiopic.[5] Although Ethiopic was already in use as a written language,[6] their literary activities further enhanced its development and facilitated the teaching of the Christian religion in the country. Many of the local people joined the communities, received enough religious training, and provided a growing number of recruits for the Church. Many of them opened their own little schools in their parishes and offered educational facilities for the members of their congregation who cared to send their children to school. The kings watched the development very closely and encouraged it. This gave much prestige and economic benefit to the clerical profession and no doubt attracted many individuals to it. Two basic problems—lack of trained candidates for the services of the Church, and the absence of books in Ethiopic—had

[1] The most northerly community was Abba Aléf's at Bi'isa, overlooking the Märäb river from the south; Yim'ata went southwards, crossed the river Wär'i and established himself in Gär'alta. The rest of the group settled between these limits: Līqanos and Pänṭälléwon near Aksum, Afṣé at Yéha, Arägawī at Däbrä Damo; and Gärīma north of Adwa, Conti Rossini, *Storia d'Etiopia*, pp. 158-61; Doresse, op. cit. i, p. 185.

[2] Ibid., p. 187; Conti Rossini, op. cit., pp. 156–7; Anfray and Schneider, loc. cit.

[3] Conti Rossini, op. cit., pp. 157–8; id., 'L'evangelo d'oro di Dabra Libanos', *RRAL*, ser. 5, vol. x (1901), pp. 177–80; Doresse, J., op. cit., pp. 187–8.

[4] *Gädlä Arägawī*, p. 64.

[5] Cerulli, *Storia della letteratura etiopica* (1956), pp. 23–33. The translation of the Gospel of St. Matthew is especially attributed to Abba Mäṭa, Conti Rossini, *Storia d'Etiopia*, pp. 157–8.

[6] See Drewes, *Inscriptions de l'Éthiopie antique*, pp. 94–7, 101–3.

faced the Church in its programme of evangelization. The initiative generally attributed to the Syrian monks seems to have done a great deal to alleviate these problems and to strengthen the position of the Church in the country.

Christian expansion in the Agäw interior

Except for hagiographical traditions—which in their written form cannot be dated earlier than the thirteenth century—there are practically no contemporary sources for the story of the evangelization of the kingdom of Aksum. It is quite clear, however, that by the beginning of the sixth century the Church had made tremendous progress, and Cosmas included the kingdom among the countries where 'there are everywhere churches of the Christians, and bishops, martyrs, monks and recluses by whom the Gospel of Christ is proclaimed'.[1] This was no doubt true of northern Ethiopia, including much of the province of Tigré, the whole of the Eritrean plateau, and the coastal settlements.[2] The effect of these developments must have also been felt in the more distant parts of the kingdom, particularly along the major trade routes and wherever military outposts had been established. It may be that Cosmas was also making a reference to the interior districts of the Aksumite empire when he reported that Christianity had spread 'in Ethiopia and Axom, *and in all the country about it*'. Such active expansion of the Church into the Aksumite interior tallies very well with the strong position held by the kingdom in the sixth century as a champion of Christianity in the whole of the Red Sea area. The crusading activities of King Kaléb against the persecutions of Christians in south Arabia, and the second Aksumite occupation of the peninsula that followed his military intervention, are very well documented.[3] It is also apparent that within his own kingdom his reign was marked by major progress in the spread of the Christian religion among the Agäw tribes of what are today the districts of Wag and Lasta. Local traditions collected at Lalībäla

[1] McCrindle, op. cit., p. 120.

[2] Conti Rossini, *Storia d'Etiopia*, p. 163.

[3] McCrindle, op. cit., p. 55; Moberg, A., *The Book of the Himyarites* (1924), pp. 134–5, 138, 140–2; Procopius, *History of the Wars*, tr. and ed. Dewing, H. B. (1914), i, pp. 179–95; *Gädlä Pänṭälléwon*, ed. Conti Rossini, pp. 52–6 (text); Halévy, 'L'alliance des Sabéens et des Abyssiniens contre les Himyarites', *RS* (1896), p. 86; Kammerer, op. cit., pp. 107–17; Ryckmans, *Institution monarchique*, pp. 320–5; Doresse, op. cit., pp. 154–97.

attribute a number of churches to him in the region of the sources of the river Täkäzé.[1]

At the time of Kaléb's expedition to south Arabia the region of Wag and Lasta was already an integral part of the Aksumite kingdom. Cosmas provides an important documentary confirmation for this. He makes a reference to the 'governor of Agau', who was entrusted by the king with the protection of the vital long-distance caravan routes to the gold mines of Sassou.[2] These gold mines have been identified with the region of Fazogli on the Blue Nile just to the west of the present border between the Sudan and Ethiopia.[3] If this is correct, the caravan routes from Aksum probably ran southwards to the present district of Wag, where they crossed the Täkäzé, and then proceeded in a south-westerly direction across Dämbya, north and west of Lake Ṭana to the gold-producing area of Fazogli. In the region west of Lake Ṭana the territory traversed by these routes is dissected by many rivers flowing westwards to join the Blue Nile and Cosmas's geographical notes on the region tend to make the above identification very secure: '. . . the sources of the river Nile lie somewhere in these parts, and in winter, on account of the heavy rains, the numerous rivers which they generate obstruct the path of the traveller.'[4]

Apart from showing the extensive sphere of Aksumite commercial activities in the reign of Kaléb, these notes of Cosmas are also invaluable as providing the earliest account of the western limits of the Kushitic peoples of the Ethiopian plateau. In the late medieval period much of the area through which Cosmas's caravan routes passed

[1] The churches include Iyäla Mīka'el, Dibisa Giyorgis, and Marora Maryam. My informant was Mägabī Tägägn, an elderly member of the community of Lalībäla, who was especially recommended to me by the abbot, Mämhir Afä-Wärq. Presented to him by the Mämhir, I found Mägabī Tägägn an inexhaustible source of oral traditions about his native province of Lasta in particular. His traditions about Kaléb, as well as the Zagwé dynasty have a definite local orientation. According to him, for instance, Kaléb was a man of Lasta and his palace was at Bugna where it is known that Lalībäla had later established his centre. The relevance of this tradition for us is the mere association of the name of Kaléb with the evangelization of this interior province of Aksum. Cf. Alvarez, *The Prester John of the Indies*, i, pp. 200–1.

[2] McCrindle, op. cit., pp. 52–3.

[3] Conti Rossini, 'Notes sur l'Abyssinie avant les Sémites', pp. 147–8. He seems to have changed his views later in favour of a more untenable identification in Wäläga, *Storia d'Etiopia*, p. 169; Wainwright, G. A., 'Cosmas and the Gold Trade of Fazogli', in *Man*, vol. 42 (1942), no. 30, pp. 52–8; Arkell, A. J., 'Cosmas and the Gold Trade of Fazogli', in *Man*, vol. 44 (1944), no. 24, pp. 30–1.

[4] McCrindle, op. cit., p. 53.

was inhabited predominantly by the Agäw,[1] and even nowadays the district of Agäw-midir has a dwindling minority of Agäw-speaking families. Cosmas's mention of the 'governor of Agau' as being in charge of the caravans strongly indicates that already at the beginning of the sixth century, the western frontiers of the Agäw people extended towards the region of Lake Ṭana and the sources of the Blue Nile. His description of the 'silent trade' also indicates that a major linguistic frontier had to be crossed before reaching the gold-mining areas.

There are local traditions of Agäw migrations from north-east into the rich country of Gojjam south of Lake Ṭana: the Awīya-speaking tribes of Agäw-midir derive their origin from Lasta. The original inhabitants of the area appear to have been ancestors of the Gumuz, who still occupy the territory west of Achäfär and Agäw-midir and extend beyond the Ethiopian-Sudanese frontier.[2] The Agäw call them 'Shanqilla' and relate that they originally conquered the land from them.[3] No chronological deductions can be made from these traditions as such, but Cosmas's report of the caravan routes protected by the Agäw implies that the migrations into this area were well under way by the first half of the sixth century. Between this date and the beginning of the fourteenth century (when hagiographical traditions become available) the process was already complete, and Agäw predominance in Dämbya and east of the headwaters of the Dinder, Balasa, and Dura rivers in Gojjam was a *fait accompli*. It is apparent that, in the end, it was not the Shanqilla but the unfavourable climatic conditions of the regions further west which put a limit to this continuous process of territorial expansion which had already started before the time of Kaléb's 'governor of Agau'.

The Agäw language and people consist of a number of dialectal groups at present found in small pockets spread over a vast territory extending from Bogos in Eritrea to Agäw-midir in Gojjam.[4] In all

[1] See pp. 196–202.

[2] Conti Rossini, 'Popoli dell'Ethiopia occidentale: i Gunza ed il loro linguaggio', in *RRAL*, xxvii (1919), pp. 252–4; Grottanelli, 'I Niloti dell'Etiopia allo stato attuale delle nostre conoscenze', *BSGI* (1941), pp. 567–8; Cerulli, *Peoples of South-West Ethiopia and its Borderlands* (1956), p. 12.

[3] Beke, C. T., 'Abyssinia, Being a Continuation of Routes in that Country', *JRGS*, xiv (1844), p. 10; Conti Rossini, 'Appunti sulla lingua Awiya del Danghela', *GSAI*, xviii (1905), pp. 122–3; id., 'Popoli dell'Etiopia occidentale: i Gunza', p. 257.

[4] Conti Rossini, *La Langue des Kemant en Abyssinie* (1912), pp. 25–34; Tubiana, J., 'Note sur la distribution géographique des dialectes Agaw', in *CAA*, no. 5 (1955), pp. 3–12.

their traditions of origin they indicate Lasta as the area of dispersal.[1] Conti Rossini has explained this as being a general tendency of the Agäw to show a common origin, and to associate themselves with the political fortunes of the Zagwé dynasty.[2] His explanation is quite acceptable in the case of the lesser, and relatively more recent migrations such as those of the Zagwa and Adkämä-Mälga of Eritrea.[3] For the western and southern Agäw, however, the insistence of their traditions of Lasta origin seems to refer to a period much earlier than the Zagwé dynasty. Aksumite attempts to expand southwards had been long and persistent, and were most active in the second half of the third and the beginning of the fourth centuries of our era. Both the *Monumentum Adulitanum* and one of the inscriptions of Ezana make a clear reference to the people of Ath-*agau*,[4] and both seem to locate them in the region east of the river Täkäzé. In these documents the Agäw are presented as the object of intensive wars of conquest led from the north against them, and it is apparent that by the middle of the fourth century, already before Ezana's conversion to Christianity, a decisive break-through had been achieved by the kingdom of Aksum into the very heart of their country east of the river Täkäzé. Naturally the Aksumite pressure was strongest on the frontier districts of Abärgälé, Séloa, and Bora, and the centre of

[1] Conti Rossini, 'Racconti e canzoni bileni', *Actes du XIVe Congrès intern. des orient.* (1907), pp. 332–4; id., 'Studi su popolazioni dell'Etiopia', pp. 53–4, 82 (extract).

[2] 'Appunti sulla lingua Khamta dell'Averghelle', in *GSAI*, xvii, pt. 2 (1905), p. 190; id., 'Appunti sulla lingua Awiya del Danghela', *GSAI*, xviii (1905), p. 122.

[3] On the Zagwa and the Adkämä-Mälga see p. 63 n. 4, and p. 67 n. 2. It is very unlikely that any migrations from the south were at all involved in the case of the Bilén (Bogos). Conti Rossini has taken the legendary episode of Gudīt (10th C.) as a point of departure for their migration northwards from Lasta, 'Note etiopiche', *GSAI*, x (1897), pp. 153–6; 'Racconti e canzoni bileni', pp. 336–7; *Storia d'Etiopia*, p. 286. But he himself has suggested a Damoti (Sīdama) origin for the queen whose anti-Christian activities in the 10th C. are attested by Christian and Muslim sources. It is most improbable that the actions of this queen of the south could have resulted in such a major population movement in the northern part of the kingdom, cf. pp. 65–70. Unlike the Zagwa and the Adkämä-Mälga who have lost their language in the process of their migrations northwards, the Bilén still speak a dialect of Agäw which, Conti Rossini has himself shown, preserves many archaic forms, *La Langue des Kemant*, p. 27. It is more likely that the Bilén are the descendants of the original Agäw inhabitants of northern Ethiopia who, in the period of the early south Arabian migrations, were pushed northwards and isolated from their southern kinsmen by an expanding 'Semitic' wedge which stretched from the coast to the region of Aksum.

[4] McCrindle, op. cit., p. 61; Littmann, op. cit. iv, pp. 24–8. For the identification of the name with Agäw see Conti Rossini, 'Appunti sulla lingua Khamta', p. 183 n. 1.

Agäw resistance seems to have moved to the area south of the river Ṣälläri, in Wag and Lasta. Two centuries after Ezana's conquest, when the region was well established as a tributary province, Kaléb's 'governor of Agau' probably had his seat of government in this area (which also served later as the cradle of the Zagwé dynasty). From here he protected the caravan routes west of the Täkäzé, where some Agäw tribes may have already begun to settle. Probably subsequent migrations also followed the same direction, thus giving rise to the Awīya tradition of Lasta origin.[1]

The traditions of vigorous evangelical activities by the Aksumite church in the interior, during the reign of King Kaléb, only reflect a general phenomenon of the sixth century, which was marked by an active expansion of the Christian Church in north-east Africa. The three pagan kingdoms of Nobatia, Mukurra, and Aloa were converted between the years 543 and 580, and the temple of Isis on the island of Philae was at last converted into a church.[2] It was apparently an official policy of the Byzantine empire to evangelize these areas in an attempt to stop the recurrent border clashes on the southern frontier of Egypt.[3] A similar programme preoccupied the minds of the Christian kings of Aksum. It has always been assumed that the original group of Syrian missionaries[4] came to the kingdom on their own initiative, or, as the hagiographers have it, by divine inspiration. It is more likely that there was an official encouragement of clerical immigrants in Aksum, possibly accompanied also by a programme of careful recruitment and selection by the (Monophysite) patriarchate of Alexandria. In those days, when religious controversies ran high, it is unlikely that the patriarch would have allowed the prosperous diocese of Aksum to slip out of his hands. Indeed, even in the very early history of the Church, it is a sign of the great influence of the

[1] Conti Rossini sees a possible reference to this Lasta origin in the name *Dehema* or *Dahma* given to the Agäw by the Gumuz of western Gojjam; the name may be a derivation from *Dahna*, a place-name which he locates in western Lasta, 'Popoli dell'Etiopia occidentale: I Gunza', p. 258. Dähana is today one of the three districts of Wag, *Journal of the Ministry of Interior*, i, no. 3 (1961), p. 8. The Chronicler of Amdä-Ṣiyon also makes a reference to the 'governor of Dahna' next to the 'governor of Wag', *Histoire des guerres d'Amde-Siyon, roi d'Étiopie*, ed. and tr. Perruchon, J., in *JA*, ser. 8, vol. xiv, pp. 293, 384.

[2] Kirwan, L. P., 'A Contemporary Account of the Conversion of the Sudan to Christianity' in *SNR*, xx (1937), pp. 289–95; Monneret de Villard, U., *Storia della Nubia cristiana* (1938), pp. 53–70; Latourette, K. S., *A History of the Expansion of Christianity*, i (1953), p. 194.

[3] Arkell, A. J., *A History of the Sudan to 1821* (ed. 1961), pp. 179–81.

[4] See p. 23 n. 4 above.

patriarch that there is a Byzantine tradition of a vain attempt by the Emperor Constantius (337–61) to convert the Aksumite Church to his Arian persuasions.[1] The dangers were as great in the sixth century. John of Ephesus's story of the intrigues and intensive competition between the Jacobite and Orthodox factions in Constantinople on the occasion of the conversion of Nubia[2] was characteristic of the whole period. Aksum seems to have participated actively in this struggle for episcopal influence, and the earliest Christian missionaries in the kingdom of Aloa are believed to have been Aksumite.[3] Within the realm of Aksum itself, it is very clear that, from the start, the kings and bishops encouraged the advent and settlement of Christian missionaries. The programme was probably intensified towards the end of the fifth century, when, as we have seen above, the traditions place the advent of the Nine Saints and the *Ṣadqan*. In these traditions the kings are closely associated with the conduct of the religious activities of the period. They assigned the new arrivals to suitable areas, they made generous endowments to the communities and to the religious schools established by them, and protected them from local anti-Christian ill-treatment.[4] They probably made recruits from among the young students of these communities, had them ordained, and sent them to staff new parishes established further afield. Similar encouragement was probably practised at the local level in the courts of the king's officials. This probably continued until the prestige of the Church was sufficiently established for the local people to enter the ministry of their own accord. We have practically no documentation for the details of the life of the Church in this period. But it is quite clear that the essential doctrinal and liturgical traditions were securely established in the first four centuries of the history of the Aksumite Church. It is indeed due to the strength of these traditions that the Ethiopian Church was able to survive a long period of only intermittent contacts with Alexandria.[5]

[1] Kammerer, op. cit., pp. 105–6.

[2] Kirwan, op. cit., pp. 290–4. Monneret de Villard, op. cit., pp. 60–4. The latter author challenges the story of early monophysite successes in Nubia reported by John of Ephesus.

[3] Ibid., p. 69; Doresse, op. cit., p. 193.

[4] *Gädlä Pänṭälléwon* (text) ed. Conti Rossini, pp. 44, 52–6, 59; *Gädlä Arägawī*, ed. Guidi, pp. 68–9, 74. There is an echo of the royal protection given to these early missionaries against local ill feeling in the legendary campaigns conducted by Kaléb in the district of Bur in support of the *Ṣadqan*, Schneider, 'Une page du Gadla Sadqan', *AÉ*, v (1963), pp. 168–9.

[5] Commenting on the obscure period of Ethiopian history before the 13th

Islam and the decline of Aksum

Kaléb's intervention in south Arabia was mainly undertaken at the invitation of the patriarch of Alexandria and the Emperor Justinian. However, Byzantine interest in the peninsula was not limited to the establishment of the Church there. The protection of the eastern trade from Persian monopoly constituted a major factor in Justinian's policy of securing the alliance of Aksum and her south Arabian dependencies.[1] Aksumite readiness to co-operate in this was half-hearted, and proved completely ineffective against the superior economic and military prowess of the Persian empire. But it probably gave the Persians and their allies enough reason to strike hard at the maritime trade of Aksum in the Red Sea. Local traditions among the inhabitants of the islands and coastal settlements—formerly under Aksumite rule—refer to a period when they were dominated by a people called *Furs*, to whom many wells are attributed. This is probably a reference to the Persians.[2] It is apparent that the first serious blow to Aksumite economic and political interests in the Red Sea was inflicted by the Persians during their ephemeral success over the Byzantine empire. Nascent Islam continued on this course, and in time ensured a more permanent withdrawal of effective Christian power from the coastal areas.

The amicable relations between the Prophet and the kingdom of Aksum during the period of his flight which have been preserved in Muslim traditions[3] were only short-lived, and hostilities seem to have already started before his death in 632. Many incidents of maritime conflict between the Aksumites and the Muslims marked the whole of the seventh century. At first their longer experience in naval warfare apparently gave the Aksumites an advantage over their adversaries. It was not until the advent of the Umayyads and Mu'awiyya's

century, Cerulli makes the following valuable remark: '. . . it seems to me, that this vacuum of centuries, which divides the inscriptions of King Daniel and the works of the early thirteenth century, is only apparent; and it only indicates a lacuna in the transmission of MSS. [from that period] . . .', *Storia della letteratura etiopica*, p. 35.

[1] Procopius, *History of the Wars*, i. 20. 9–10; cf. also Smith, S., 'Events in Arabia in the Sixth Century A.D.', in *BSOAS*, xvi (1954), pp. 425–7.

[2] D'Abbadie, A., *Géographie de l'Éthiopie* (1890), ii, pp. 24, 328; Basset, R., 'Les Inscriptions de l'île de Dahlak' in *JA*, ser. 9, vol. i (1893), pp. 85–6; Conti Rossini, *Storia d'Etiopia*, pp. 196–201; Doresse, *L'Empire du Prêtre Jean*, i, pp. 193–5; Trimingham, J. S., *Islam in Ethiopia* (ed. 1965), p. 42.

[3] Conti Rossini, *Storia d'Etiopia*, pp. 207–11; Trimingham, op. cit., pp. 44–6; Doresse, op. cit. ii, pp. 3–5.

organization of a strong Muslim naval force that the balance of power began to change in favour of the Muslims.[1] Soon afterwards, at the beginning of the eighth century, the Dahlak islands were annexed, and began to serve as a distant place of political exile for prominent prisoners of state during both the Umayyad and Abbasid caliphates.[2] Even after this major defeat, however, the Aksumites seem to have continued the struggle and we have references to maritime conflicts as late as A.D. 770.[3] But this was a hopeless struggle. During the period between the beginning of the seventh and the middle of the eighth centuries the Christians seem to have gradually lost their control of the maritime trade. The Byzantine merchants who resided in the Aksumite kingdom,[4] on whom much of the international trade depended, probably left in the early stages of the conflict. The coastal settlements and other centres of trade declined, and the Aksumite kings seem to have stopped issuing coins towards the middle of the eighth century.[5] Once again, the control of international trade in the Ethiopian region passed into the hands of the dominant group in the Red Sea area. Only this time it was the Muslim merchants who benefited by the change of the political situation.

There are no historical documents which can help us study what exactly was the effect of this development on the kingdom of Aksum itself. It is apparent, however, that, despite the reverses suffered on the coast, the kingdom held its own on the mainland. It is significant that the earliest tradition of a Muslim exile in the Red Sea area is that of Abu Mihgan banished to the port of Basa' (= Baḍi) by

[1] For these early conflicts see Conti Rossini, op. cit., pp. 211–14; Trimingham, op. cit., pp. 46–7. Yusuf Faḍl Ḥasan, *The Arabs and the Sudan* (1967), p. 30.

[2] Basset, R., 'Les inscriptions de l'île de Dahlak', pp. 89–90; Rossi, E., 'Sulla storia delle isole Dahlak (Mar Rosso) nel Medioevo', in *Atti del 3º Congresso di studi coloniali* (1937), p. 367; Trimingham, op. cit., p. 45 n. 1. There seems to be a reference to this historic role as a place of exile in an inscription dated A.D. 1225, which describes the ruler of the islands as 'the refuge of the weak and disgraced; the shelter of strangers and exiles', Wiet, G., 'Roitelets de Dahlak' in *BIÉ*, t. 34 (1951–2), pp. 94–5.

[3] Yusuf Faḍl Ḥasan, loc. cit.

[4] The presence of such resident merchants in the kingdom is quite clear from the *Periplus*. Philostorgius refers to a Syrian colony near Aksum in the 4th century, quoted by Doresse, op. cit. i, p. 189. Cf. McCrindle, *The Christian Topography*, p. 56. According to Procopius, King Kalēb's governor of south Arabia, Abrham, was originally a slave of a Roman residing in Adulīs, *History of the Wars*, i. 20. 4.

[5] Conti Rossini, *Storia d'Etiopia*, pp. 213–14, 217; Contenson, H. de, 'Les fouilles à Axoum en 1957' in *AÉ*, iii (1959), pp. 32–4; id., 'Les principales étapes de l'Éthiopie antique', p. 22; id., 'Les fouilles à Axoum en 1958', *AÉ*, v (1963), pp. 13–14.

caliph 'Umar in A.D. 634.[1] In an important article Crowfoot has identified Baḍi with a site near the present port of Aqiq just to the north of Ras Kassar, which is the frontier between Eritrea and the Sudan.[2] This tradition of a Muslim exile at Baḍi during the Orthodox Caliphate may define the northern limits of the Aksumite kingdom at the time.

Similar traditions for the Umayyad and Abbasid caliphates refer only to the Dahlak islands. Thus the direct relevance of Islam as a political factor in the mainland districts of the kingdom was minimal in this early period. Ethiopic inscriptions which Conti Rossini dates to the seventh century indicate the presence of effective Christian power in the hot lowlands of the Barka basin.[3] The traditions collected by Munzinger of an ancient monastery (= agärä-nagran) in the region of Baqla in northern Eritrea probably belong to this period,[4] when the inhabitants were still predominantly Christian. Nevertheless, the loss of the maritime trade must have reduced the wealth and power of the Aksumite kings and gradually slackened the effective control of their provinces. This probably led to local revolts,[5]

[1] Conti Rossini, op. cit., p. 212.

[2] 'Some Red Sea Ports' in *GJ*, xxxvii (1911), pp. 542–7. Cf. also Crawford, O. G. S., *The Fung Kingdom of Sennar* (1951), pp. 104–7. Conti Rossini insists in equating Baḍi with Miṣiwwa, op. cit., pp. 212, 214, 273–4. The historical reasons for his identification are not apparent, and it seems to depend on a 19th-century tradition collected by Munzinger, cf. Al-'Umari, *Masalik el absar fi mamalik el amsar*, i (1927), tr. Gaudefroy-Demombynes, p. 19 n. 2. Ibn Haukal locates Baḍi on the African coast, at least four days' distance north of Dahlak and an equation with Miṣiwwa seems quite impossible, *Configuration de la terre*, tr. Wiet, G., i (1964), pp. 41–2.

[3] 'Documenti per l'archeologia eritrea nella bassa valle Barca', *RRAL*, ser. 5, vol. xii (1903), pp. 139–47.

[4] Quoted by Crawford, op. cit., pp. 104–5. The monastery is said to have been on the pilgrimage route to Suakin. Hagiographical traditions about 14th- and 15th-century pilgrims to Jerusalem do not refer to such important Christian sites north of the Bogos and Marya districts. It is also difficult to imagine a post-15th-century foundation for the monastery in this distant northern region.

[5] Three inscriptions by an Aksumite king allude to such troubled days. Two of them bear the name of the king Haṣanī Daniél, son of Däbrä-Färäm. One of these mentions an armed revolt of the 'people of Wälqayt' (already annexed by Ézana), who are said to have even marched against Aksum. The king and his troops suppressed the rising, which appears to have been widespread, Littmann, op. cit., Inscriptions 12, 13, and 14. Cerulli very cautiously dated these inscriptions between the 7th and 12th centuries, *Storia della letteratura etiopica*, p. 22. He does not give his reasons for this. But his views may have been influenced by the famous traditions of the pagan queen Gudīt, and the political decline attributed to her revolt dated in the 10th century, which nevertheless seems too late a date for the general historical context of the inscriptions of Haṣanī Daniél.

and weakened the defence of the northern frontiers with the pagan Béja who appear to have gradually pushed their way into northern and central Eritrea.[1]

Christian expansion in the regions of Amhara and Shäwa

As we have seen above, the Christian kingdom and the Aksumite Church had already been securely established in the heart of the Agäw country in the first quarter of the sixth century.[2] It was in this direction that the centre of gravity of the kingdom now began to shift. This development is quite apparent from an early Muslim tradition about the Aksumite king who was contemporary with the Prophet. His name is given as *El Asham*, son of *Abdjar*, and father of King *Arma*. *El-Asham*, the *Negashi*, had welcomed the companions of Muhammad whom the latter had sent to Aksum to take refuge from anti-Muslim persecutions in the Hijaz. When the news of the death of King El-Asham reached the Prophet in A.D. 630 he is said to have remembered him with affection and pronounced some prayers for him.[3] This has apparently created the tradition that the king was in fact a convert to the new religion,[4] and the tradition has in the end led to his being considered as a Muslim saint. In the sixteenth century, when Gragn's triumphant army was on its way from Tämbén to Agamé, the elated Muslim troops asked for their leader's permission to visit the tomb of this friend of the Prophet.[5] His name is here given as *Ashamat En-Nedjachi* (certainly a variant of Tabari's El-Asham) and the tomb seems to be near Wiqro where there is still a site remembered as such by the local people.[6] The significance of this is that we should have a tradition of the tomb of an early seventh-century king

[1] Conti Rossini, *Storia d'Etiopia*, pp. 267–76; Newbold, D., 'The Beja Tribes of the Red Sea Hinterland', in *Anglo-Egyptian Sudan from Within*, ed. and tr. Hamilton, J. A. de C., (1935), pp. 148–51; Crawford, op. cit., pp. 102, 104–8, 118–22. For the background of the Béja see Monneret de Villard, op. cit. pp. 24–60.

[2] See pp. 25–9.

[3] Conti Rossini, op. cit., pp. 210–11.

[4] Trimingham, op. cit., p. 46 n. 2.

[5] *Futuh al-Habasha*, tr. Basset, R. (1894), pp. 319–20.

[6] *Guida dell'Africa orientale italiana* (ed. 1938), p. 300. The name of the king has apparently undergone an onomatopoeic transformation into *Ahmad Negash*, but the reference is to the same person. Doresse has found many traditions of ancient royal tombs in the region of Gär'alta, *L'Empire du Prêtre-Jean*, i, p. 185. For the genealogy of King El-Asham by Muslim writers and for attempts to identify him with some of the names in the traditional lists of Aksumite kings, cf. Hartmann, M., 'Der Nagasi Asham und sein Sohn Arma', in *ZDMG*, xlix. (1895), pp. 299–300; Basset, op. cit., p. 419 n. 2.

(d. before the end of A.D. 630) of Aksum outside the ancient capital. Wiqro is about sixty-five miles south-east of Aksum, and the tradition of El-Asham's burial there is strongly indicative of a general southward movement of the centre of gravity of the Christian kingdom already in the seventh century. It is impossible here to follow this southward expansion of the kingdom and the Church in great detail. This must await a close investigation into the traditions of the churches and their congregations in the crucial area of southern Tigré, Lasta, and Angot. From about the first quarter of the ninth century, however, both the fragmentary Arabic references to the Ethiopian region and the traditions of the Church show the kingdom definitely established well beyond the central highlands of Angot which serve as a great water divide for the three major river systems of the central plateau of Ethiopia. Here rise the upper waters of the Täkäzé, the Bashīlo (which is a major tributary of the Blue Nile), and numerous other rivers flowing eastwards into the basin of the Awash. Strong traditional data show the Christian kings actively engaged in military campaigns of territorial expansion south of this central region in the ninth century. The traditions centre around a 'king of Aksum' remembered under the name of Digna-Jan:

> During his reign he (who) led 150 priests from Aksum to Amhara and assigned them [to teach?] there. As he came out of Tigré he camped at *Wäyna-Däga* (and had) with him 60 *tabots* . . . When he counted his troops there were found (among them) 180,150 dressed in coats of mail. Taking these he went to another country in Innarya, one month's journey away . . .[1]

Digna-Jan is noted for having ruled over a vast empire and he is elsewhere referred to as having travelled 'from horizon to horizon' in the course of a royal tour of his kingdom.[2] It seems possible to obtain a chronological framework for this vigorous movement of territorial expansion and evangelization from a comparative study

[1] 'Tarīkä-Nägäst', MS. Dīma, f. 43^{a}. D'Abbadie collected a shorter variant of this tradition in Bägémdir, Conti Rossini, 'Il libro delle leggende e tradizioni abissine dell'Ecciaghie Filpos' in *RRAL*, ser. v, vol. xxvi (1917), pp. 706–7. The local orientation of the recital is clear from the location of the camp at Wäyna-Däga in Bägémdir. No other places are mentioned between Tigré and Amhara, and this is no doubt due to the dominant post-Zagwé traditions of the Amhara Christians claiming direct descent from ancient Aksum. The specific mention of Innarya definitely shows that the tradition has been affected by events in the late medieval period and the exaggerations of the strength of the army are quite obvious. For all these, however, the essential value of the tradition as an indication of southern expansion remains strong.

[2] *Gädlä Yaréd*, ed. Conti Rossini, p. 23 (text).

of the available traditions. According to the *Life of Täklä-Haymanot* (*c.* 1215–1313) the advent of his ancestors to Amhara and Shäwa is connected with Digna-Jan's programme of evangelization of his southern provinces. The reference to the king in this tradition may be related to the settlement of the earliest of the saint's ancestors in Amhara eighteen generations before him.[1] This brings Digna-Jan to the first half of the ninth century.[2] It is also about the same time that local traditions refer to the foundation of the famous church of Däbrä Igzīabhér on the mountain-top overlooking Lake Hayq in the north-east. Two apparently independent traditions are preserved in *Gädlä Īyäsus-Mo'a* about the date of the foundation of this church. According to one of these traditions, the church was built by King Dilna'od and the Egyptian bishop Abunä Sälama II, who is said to have come to Ethiopia 618 years after the advent of Sälama I (Frémnaṭos), the first bishop sent to Ethiopia by the patriarch of Alexandria. The other tradition dates the event at 6362 Year of Creation. The two dates are remarkably close to each other, and both take the foundation of Däbrä Igzīabhér to the third quarter of the ninth century.[3] The chronicler of Ahmad Gragn also collected

[1] *The Life of Takla Haymanot*, ed. Budge, E. A. W., pp. 3–5 (text). Here the king is mentioned only with Yidla, the first ancestor of Täklä-Haymanot who is said to have settled in Shäwa ten generations before. In this hagiographical tradition, which is essentially of Shäwan origin, there is a clear tendency to emphasize the importance of the Shäwan branch of the family, and the association of Yidla with Digna-Jan may very well be an alteration of a more ancient tradition. Moreover in both the versions of the tradition about the king quoted above there is no mention of Shäwa at all.

[2] It is interesting to note that there is reference in the *Life* of Patriarch Yoséf (830–49) to an Ethiopian king at the time being engaged in a military expedition which kept him away from his court for some time. During the king's absence the queen and her courtiers are said to have dismissed the Egyptian bishop, Yohannis, who had already been in the country before Yoséf's accession to the episcopal seat of Alexandria, Sawirus, *History of the Patriarchs of Alexandria*, ed. and tr. in *PO*, x (1915), pp. 508–9. Cf. also Renaudot, E., *Historia Patriarcharum Alexandrinorum* (1717), pp. 273, 283.

[3] *Gädlä Īyäsus-Mo'a*, ed. and tr. Kur, S., in *CSCO*, vol. 259, Script. Aeth. t. 49 (1965), pp. 18–19. The advent of Sälama I is a reference to the establishment of the church in Ethiopia, which Ethiopic chronological tables sometimes place at 245 E.C.; cf. Gr baut, S., 'Table du comput', in *ROC*, i (1918–19), p. 325. Thus the advent of Sälama II was equivalent to A.D. 870/1. 6362 Year of the Creation is also equivalent to A.D. 869/70. Conti Rossini's copy of the *Gädl* probably omitted some words in the phrase '618 years after Sälama I' and he has adopted a much earlier date, *Storia d'Etiopia*, pp. 262–3. Little credence can be given to the actual names of either the king or the bishop. The prelate is called after the first bishop to Ethiopia in an obvious attempt to emphasize the expansion of the Church in his time.

a similar tradition that the church was built 720 years before 1531 when the Muslim army destroyed it. This does in fact make the church about half a century older than in the above tradition.[1] The ninth century was apparently a period of expansion for the Christian kingdom. According to Al-Yaqubi[2] (*fl.* 872), the Christian *habasha* had 'mighty cities' where the Arabs went 'for trading'. The Jacobite Christian king of the *habasha* ruled over many other kings who obeyed him and who also paid taxes to him. His capital city was *Ku'bar*, a site which is still unidentified but which was probably somewhere in southern Tigré or in Angot.[3] Christian traditions belonging to the same period of the ninth century also indicate that the capital of the kingdom had shifted in the direction of Lake Hayq.[4] It is quite clear from all these isolated notes that this period was marked by a continuous Christian expansion southwards.

One of the most characteristic aspects of the process of expansion was the establishment of military colonies in the newly conquered territories. It has been said above that the Agäw were the native inhabitants of the Ethiopian plateau north of the river Jäma.[5] The immigrants from south Arabia settled in the northern part of this region and lived among the Agäw population, who gradually adopted the language of the settlers. These linguistically semitized natives later constituted the dominant section of the peoples of Aksum. As the kingdom acquired additional territories, large groups of these people were apparently recruited and settled in distant frontier stations. Here they intermarried with the local people and formed yet another semitized zone in the interior of the Agäw country, which was gradually passing into the sphere of Aksumite political influence. It is apparent that all the Semitic linguistic groups south of the Tigré region had a similar origin. The Amhara tribal group is the most northerly of these communities and was probably the earliest to be established as such. Traditional material on the Ahmara is lacking and it is impossible here to give any specific dates for their origin. It

[1] *Futuh al-Habasha*, text ed. Basset, pp. 231–2. See also the translation of D'Abbadie and Paulitschke, *Futuh al-Habasha* (Paris, 1898), p. 266. Their translation is a better rendering here than Basset's, cf. Taddesse Tamrat, 'The Abbots of Däbrä Hayq 1248–1535', in *Journal of Ethiopian Studies*, viii, no. 1 (1970), note 3.

[2] *Historiae*, ed. Houtsma, i (1883), p. 219.

[3] Cf. Taddesse Tamrat, op. cit., note 7.

[4] Ibid., notes 5 and 6. This also seems to be confirmed by some remains of Christian settlements recently discovered near Kombolcha, only about 50 km. south of Lake Hayq, Gerster, G., *L'Art éthiopien* (1968), p. 25 (pls. 9 and 10).

[5] See p. 5 n. 4 above.

is most likely, however, that it belongs to the pre-Christian period of Aksumite history, and as we have seen above, the expansion of the kingdom in this direction was already in full swing during the intensive military activities of King Ézana. The earliest recorded tradition of Christian settlement in the region indicates that there was already a distinct Amhara population occupying the upper basin of the river Bashīlo. The tradition seems to belong to the first half of the ninth century, eighteen generations before the days of Saint Täklä-Haymanot.[1] These later Christian immigrations further enhanced the semitization of the area between the Bashīlo and the Jäma rivers. The story of Digna-Jan quoted above strongly implies that the expansion of the kingdom was undertaken as part of a definite programme of Christian settlement and evangelization. The kings built churches and established military colonies in their newly acquired provinces, and by the tenth century contemporary writers describe the kingdom as controlling a vast territory between the Dahlak islands and Zeila on the coast, and from the upper basins of the Ansaba-Barka rivers to the central Shäwan plateau in the interior.[2] In the region of the Ethiopian plateau itself this territory was much larger than in the Aksumite period. A new ethnic and linguistic group of people had also been added within the sphere of Christian military control. It is apparent that the Sīdama, who were probably the original inhabitants of the Shäwan plateau,[3] had already become tributary to the Christian kings by that time.

Pagan resurgence in the Shäwan region

The *History of the Patriarchs of Alexandria* makes a reference to a pagan queen of the *Bani al-Hamwiyah* who led her people against the Christians in the tenth century.[4] Conti Rossini has proposed the reading *al-Damutah* for the name of the people, and indicates that the queen was probably of Damoti (Sīdama) origin.[5] Her hostile activities are represented as a revolt of a vassal ruler and they had a

[1] *Gädlä Täklä-Haymanot*, ed. Budge, pp. 3–5 (text); ed. Conti Rossini, p. 102.

[2] Masudi, op. cit. iii, p. 34, Ibn Haukal, op. cit., pp. 16, 20, 22–3. Conti Rossini, *Storia d'Etiopia*, pp. 281–3. Ullendorff, E., *The Ethiopians* (ed. 1965), p. 60. Trimingham, op. cit., pp. 50–1.

[3] See p. 6 n. 1.

[4] Sawirus, op. cit., p. 171.

[5] *Storia d'Etiopia*, p. 286. There are other references to female rulers in the Sīdama region, cf. Bähaylä-Mīka'él, *Mäṣafä-Misṭīratä-Sämay Wämidr*, ed. in part and tr. Perruchon, J., in *PO*, i (1904), p. 25. Budge, *The Book of the Mysteries*

particularly religious undertone. The queen and her pagan followers destroyed churches and killed Christians. The Christian king himself probably lost his life in the conflict, and the queen appears not only to have restored the independence of her people from Christian rule, but she also seems to have been widely known as the most powerful ruler in the Ethiopian region for a long time:

> The country of the *habasha* has been ruled by a woman for many years now: she has killed the king of the *habasha* who was called *Hadani*. Until today she rules with complete independence on her own country and the frontier areas of the territory of the *Hadani*, in the southern part of [the country of] the *habasha*.[1]

There are specific indications of internal conflict and general decline in the first half of the tenth century which seem to account for the dramatic reversal of the fortunes of the Christian kingdom in the days of Ibn Haukal (*fl.* A.D. 943–77). It is about this time that we have the earliest recorded struggle for the succession of the Christian throne in which even the patriarchate of Alexandria seems to have actively participated. The story is related by the hagiographer of Patriarch Cosmas (933–42), and the episode appears to have practically rent the country in two contending factions.[2] The patriarch sent a new Egyptian bishop, Pėṭros, to Ethiopia. The anonymous king who welcomed him was apparently an old man and died soon after the bishop's arrival. The succession was contested by two of his sons, and Pėṭros gave his blessing to the younger brother. Two other Egyptian monks, Mīnas and Fīqiṭor, who were in the country at the time, disagreed with the bishop and joined the other prince. As part of the propaganda warfare that followed, they produced forged letters from the patriarch supporting the principle of primogeniture

of Heaven and Earth (complete ed. and tr., 1935), p. 31 (tr.). Cf. also Cerulli, Il sultanato dello Scioa nel secolo XIII', in *RSE*, i (1941), p. 22. Zorzi collected a tradition in 1523 about the province of Wäj, 'where the inhabitants would have none but a queen to govern them', Crawford, O. G. S., *Ethiopian Itineraries c. 1400–1524*, Hakluyt Society (1955), p. 161. This mention of the province of Wäj is particularly interesting in the context. According to the chronicler of Ahmad Gragn there lived in the vicinity of Wäj a tribe of formidable fighters called El-Maya. A small administrative unit in the district of Chäbo and Guragé still bears the name of Amäya, *Journal of the Ministry of Interior*, i, no. 2 (1961), p. 14.

[1] Ibn Haukal, op. cit., p. 56. The location of her centre of activities 'in the south of Ethiopia' according to Gaston Wiet's latest translation of Ibn Haukal's work is very interesting and goes to confirm Conti Rossini's proposed identification of the queen's origin.

[2] Sawirus, op. cit., pp. 118–20; cf. Renaudot, op. cit., pp. 339–41.

in the royal succession and declaring that Péṭros had come with false credentials. Mīnas claimed that he was himself properly ordained as bishop of Ethiopia. This weakened the other party, and the army rallied around the elder prince who was thus able to defeat his brother and cast him into exile. Péṭros was also banished from his seat. In his place Mīnas was declared metropolitan of Ethiopia. When the news reached the patriarch, he excommunicated Mīnas for his uncanonical assumption of the ecclesiastical power. Anxious to make amends for these irregularities, the new king arrested Mīnas on the arrival of the patriarch's letter and executed him. Then he ordered the return of Péṭros to his rightful chair. But it was soon found out that Péṭros had died in exile. It is apparent that the king asked for another bishop. The situation was clearly too embarrassing, and the patriarch refused to respond to his requests. Relations between the patriarchate and the royal court became very tense. Faced with such a deadlock, the king made an arbitrary decision to force a young (Egyptian) follower of the late metropolitan to fill the vacant seat in which he remained until the reign of Patriarch Fīlatéwos (979–1003).[1]

It is quite clear that the episode created much conflict and bad morale in the country. In Alexandrian circles the king was apparently held responsible for the death of Abunä Péṭros. The hagiographer of Fīlatéwos later accuses him for 'his falsifications and his fraud'.[2] No doubt, his political enemies at home also had recourse to the same argument. Public dissatisfaction within the Church and at the court probably received ample expression in the guise of continued loyalties to the patriarch of Alexandria. This weakened the power of the king, and from the available chronological data it even appears that the revolt of the queen of the *Hamwiyah* took place towards the end of his reign.[3] His own death in the conflict, and the military

[1] The story is given in the Ethiopic Synaxarium with a number of interesting alterations clearly intended to absolve the Egyptian Christians from any responsibility in the episode. Thus the two monks Mīnas and Fīqiṭor are said to be Syrian renegades who had already been dismissed from the famous monastery of St. Anthony in the eastern desert. Cosmas's refusal to ordain a new bishop in Peter's place is also denied, and blamed on his successors, *The Book of the Saints of the Ethiopian Church*, tr. Budge, iii (1928), pp. 666–8.

[2] Sawirus, op. cit., p. 171.

[3] As we have seen above, he was the contemporary of Patriarch Cosmas (933–42). Ibn Haukal, who wrote his book in about A.D. 977, speaks of the queen in the following terms: 'de nos jours elle [i.e. Ethiopia] est gouvernée par une reine *depuis une trentaine d'années* . . .', op. cit., p. 16. This brings her assumption of power to *c.* A.D. 945. It was probably an immediate successor of her adversary who wrote to King George of Nubia asking for his help in restoring relations with

reverses of the kingdom were taken as divine retribution for the sufferings of Abunä Péṭros. In such an atmosphere of public apathy the pagan resurgence in the southern provinces against Christian rule was a complete success. The struggle against the pagan revolt in the south and the discontinuation of spiritual links with Alexandria had greatly weakened the kingdom. The letter to King George of Nubia pathetically underlines the dangers for the very existence of the Church in Ethiopia at the time:

> . . . lest the Christian religion pass away and cease among us, for lo, six patriarchs have sat [on the Throne] and have not paid attention to our lands, but they [the lands] are abandoned without a shepherd and our bishops and our priests are dead, and the churches are ruined . . .[1]

Through the good offices of King George of Nubia, Patriarch Fīlatéwos accepted the entreaties of the Ethiopians and sent them a new bishop, Daniél. He was received with much joy and the hagiographer adds that 'God . . . put an end to the affairs of the woman who had risen up against them.' The establishment of normal relations with Alexandria no doubt restored public confidence among the Christians, who could probably withstand more effectively the anti-Christian activities of the queen of the *Hamwiyah*. But it does not appear that there was an immediate return of Christian control over her southern dominions. The only remnants of former Christian supremacy in these parts were a number of advance groups of Semitic-speaking military colonies. Effectively isolated from the kingdom in the north, these military settlements maintained their linguistic identity in a completely Sīdama environment and seem to provide an adequate explanation for the origin of the modern Haräri, Argobba, Guragé, and Gaffat.[2]

Trends of Muslim expansion in Ethiopia

For about a century and a half after the episode of the queen of the *Hamwiyah*, the effective political frontiers of the Christian kingdom were probably limited to the area north of the Jäma river. During the whole of this period relations with Egypt were close and regular. The chroniclers of the patriarchate of Alexandria took these contacts for granted and, unfortunately for us, they mentioned Ethiopian

Alexandria broken by 'the king who [was] before him', Sawirus, loc. cit. It seems that the letter was sent in *c.* A.D. 980.

[1] Ibid., pp. 171–2.

[2] Conti Rossini aptly described these groups as 'etniche e linguistiche sovravivinze delle antiche conquiste', *Storia d'Etiopia*, p. 282.

affairs only when conflicts arose or something unusual took place. In Ethiopia itself material for the study of the eleventh and twelfth centuries is highly limited. No doubt a close examination of local traditions in Angot, Lasta, and northern Amhara—the central parts of the kingdom at the time—will help fill the lacunae. However, despite the apparent weakness following the pagan reaction in the south, the general picture of the kingdom that emerges from the isolated references in the *History of the Patriarchs* is one of steady development and reconsolidation. Even the Coptic myth that the Ethiopian state was a strong champion of Egyptian Christendom finds its earliest expression in this period.[1] And, towards the beginning of the twelfth century, there are definite signs of the expansion of the Ethiopian Church. In the reign of Patriarch Gäbriél (1131–45) the request of the Ethiopians for more than the usual number of bishops provided a new source of conflict between them and the patriarchate.[2] It is also about this time that we find the Christians engaged, once again, in an active process of territorial expansion in the Shäwan region. A Muslim chronicle belonging to the region of eastern Shäwa preserves the tradition that early in A.D. 1128 the Amhara led an unsuccessful expedition in 'the land of Wärjih'.[3]

This is the first reference to the Wärjih, a pastoral people who had apparently lived in the vast semi-desert lowlands of the Awash valley east of the Shäwan plateau. The chronicler of King Amdä-Ṣiyon (1314–44) locates the Wärjih and Gäbäl nomads 'between the frontiers of Finṣäté and Biqulzär'.[4] Finṣäté is mentioned here for the first and last time and cannot be identified. Biqulzär was, however, east of the river Awash[5] and it was probably this region which was predominantly inhabited by the Wärjih and the Gäbäl in the reign of Amdä-Ṣiyon.[6] In the beginning of the twelfth century, when the

[1] See p. 49 n. 1.

[2] Renaudot, op. cit., pp. 510–13. Budge, *The Book of the Saints*, pp. 800–1.

[3] Cerulli, E., 'Il sultanato dello Scioa nel secolo XIII', in *RSE*, i (1941), p. 10 with n. 4, and p. 18. The actual wording in the chronicle is: 'E fu la fuga degli Amhara dalla terra di Wargih . . .'.

[4] Perruchon, *Histoire des guerres d'Amda-Siyon*, p. 284 (text). The Wärjih are specially mentioned (p. 282) as 'keepers of cattle' and camels.

[5] Cf. ibid., pp. 283, 432. The chronicler of Ahmad Gragn later placed it more than two days' journey east of the Awash, *Futuh al Habasha*, tr. Basset, p. 94.

[6] This seems to be quite clear from the Chronicle itself. Immediately after locating the Wärjih and Gäbäl between Finṣäté and Biqulzär, the author goes on to say that the land between the Awash and Zäbir was a Muslim area, op. cit., p. 284 (text). Zäbir was apparently a locality on the eastern edge of the plateau near Ifat, p. 292. Thus Amdä-Ṣiyon's chronicler seems to make a distinction

armed conflict with the Amhara took place, the Wärjih probably inhabited a more extensive area as far west as the foothills of the Shäwan plateau. It is not certain if they had already become Muslims at the time. There is, however, a tradition of the conversion to Islam of a still unidentified people called *Gbbah* towards the end of the year A.D. 1108,[1] and it is very clear that Islam was becoming an important political factor in the area.

We have seen above that Aksum had already lost to the Muslims the control of the maritime trade in the Red Sea by the middle of the eighth century A.D. The spread of Islam in the Ethiopian region must have already started by then. On the mainland, the process was most active where Christian power was felt least—that is, in the coastal settlements and among the pastoral peoples of the vast semi-desert between the Red Sea coast and the edge of the plateau.[2] Thus, from the start, Islam in Ethiopia was particularly associated with trade and nomadism. Muslim traders operated freely throughout the Christian kingdom, and in time they completely replaced the former Byzantine merchants. At first they were probably of foreign origin. Al-Yaqubi specially mentions Arab merchants,[3] and by the time he

between the more sedentary Muslims occupying the land from the west bank of the Awash to the north-eastern edge of the Shäwan plateau, and the completely nomadic peoples east of the river. In the long list of Muslim rulers who leagued and fought against Amdä-Ṣiyon are also mentioned the 'rulers of Zällan', and the 'rulers of Gäbäl', pp. 322–3. It is most likely that here the Wärjih are meant by the Zällan who, together with the Gäbäl, were located east of the Awash.

[1] Cerulli, op. cit., p. 10 and n. 3. The similarity of sound between *Gbbah* in Cerulli's Arabic text and Gäbäl in Amdä-Ṣiyon's chronicle is very tempting and suggests a possible identification. No serious topographical difficulties preclude the identification. If this is correct, the Wärjih nomads could have also been under a strong Muslim influence when they repulsed the Amhara expedition in their country in A.D. 1128, only twenty years after their neighbours, the Gäbäl, had formally adopted Islam. Another identification of *Gbbah*, with *Argobba*, has been suggested by Trimingham, *Islam in Ethiopia*, p. 62.

[2] Early references to the peoples of this lowland region are few and fragmentary. It appears, however, that the sharp difference between their nomadic life and that of the inhabitants of the plateau had taken shape already before the beginning of our era, cf. Strabo, *Geography*, 16. iv. 17. The author of the *Periplus* refers to them as Berbers in general, and, in the hinterland of the coast of the Gulf of Aden, he specially contrasts the political organization of the kingdom of Zoskales and their decentralized local democracy, Schoff, op. cit., pp. 25, 27. The inscription of Adulīs mentions two unidentifiable tribal names which seem to belong to this region: 'The tribes of *Rhausi* I next brought to submission: a Barbarous race spread over wide waterless plains in the interior of the frankincense country. (Advancing thence towards the sea) I encountered the *Solate*, whom I subdued, and left with instructions to guard the coast', McCrindle, op. cit., p. 63.

[3] *Historiae*, ed. Houtsma (1883), i, p. 219.

wrote his geographical treatise (*c.* A.D. 889) commercial relations between the Ethiopian region and the centre of Islam in Iraq were well established.[1] Similar relations with Yemen were particularly strong,[2] and probably most of the Arab traders came from there.[3] Their local partners were probably recruited from among the inhabitants of Dahlak and the coastal settlements. With these and a large group of caravan slaves they frequented the trade routes[4] and the numerous village markets[5] in the whole kingdom. Along these routes and in the market villages they established friendly relations with the local people and probably stationed their agents at regular intervals. The kings and their local officials encouraged these profitable commercial activities in the country, and the Muslim traders no doubt enjoyed official protection. It is apparent, however, that complete freedom of worship was not granted to the Muslims within the Christian provinces.

It seems that the problem became very acute with the conversion to Islam of an increasing number of local people in the important trading areas. This was particularly the case after the advent of the Fatimid caliphate in Egypt. Their meticulous organization and efficient system of religious propaganda[6] had brought the Fatimids to absolute power in Egypt in A.D. 969, and, for the first time since the Roman conquest of the Ptolemies, Egypt acquired a completely independent political status in the eastern Mediterranean. This marked the beginning of a new period and the centre of gravity of Islam in the Red Sea area shifted once and for all from the region of ancient Mesopotamia to the delta of the river Nile. It is a reflection

[1] *Livre des pays*, tr. Wiet, G. (1937), p. 4.

[2] Ibn Haukal, op. cit., pp. 22–3, 54. Masudi, op. cit., p. 35. Umarah, *Yaman, its Early Medieval History*, ed. and tr. Kay, H. C. (1892), pp. 8, 143.

[3] When the Dahlak islands were annexed in the early 8th century they were apparently part of the Governorate of Medina, Conti Rossini, *Storia d'Etiopia*, p. 213. Afterwards relations with the Hijaz and Yemen were regular, Basset, R., 'Les inscriptions de l'île de Dahlak', pp. 17–20. The rulers of Ifat and Adal later derived their origin from the Hijaz, Maqrizi, *Historia Regum Islamiticorum in Abyssinia*, ed. and tr. Rinck, F. T. (1790), p. 17. Cerulli, E., 'Documenti arabi per la storia dell'Etiopia', in *MRAL*, ser. 6, vol. lv (1931), p. 43.

[4] For the routes and major items of trade involved, see below, pp. 80–9.

[5] '. . . and they have mighty cities', Al-Yaqubi, *Historiae*, loc. cit. 'Les États (du Nedjachi) . . . renferment un grand nombre de villes', Masudi, *Prairies d'or*, iii (1841), p. 34.

[6] See Ivanow, W., 'The Organization of the Fatimid Propaganda', in the *Journal of the Bombay Branch of the R A.S.*, xv (1939), pp. 1–35. Canard, M., 'L'impérialisme des Fatimides et leur propagande', in *Annales de l'Institut d'Études orientales* (Algiers), vi (1942–7), pp. 156–93.

of this general phenomenon that Islam in Ethiopia grew particularly militant after the tenth century.

The whole region of the Near and the Middle East had acquired an unprecedented unity with the Arab conquest of Egypt and the eastern seaboard of the Mediterranean.[1] The economic warfare between the Byzantine and Persian empires had become a thing of the past. The gradual movement of the centre of the Muslim empire from the Hijaz to Damascus and then to Baghdad had also reduced the relative importance of the Red Sea as the thoroughfare of the eastern trade. It is even apparent that the economic and political decline of Aksum was occasioned not so much by the anti-Christian activities of the Muslims, as by the sudden change in the value of the Red Sea trade with the eastern Mediterranean, on which the Aksumite state was essentially based. In the second half of the tenth century the establishment of the independent Fatimid caliphate in Egypt completely reversed the situation, and the old struggle for the control of the eastern trade began to be played in an essentially similar fashion as on the eve of the rise of Islam. This greatly enhanced the re-emergence of the Red Sea as a major channel of commerce. It is ironical that, in the area with which this book is concerned, the end result of this vital development was not only the rapid expansion of Islam but also the steady revival of the Christian kingdom of Ethiopia.

Like the Ptolemies and the Romans before and the Mamlukes after them, the Fatimids took a keen interest in both the Arabian and African coasts of the Red Sea. Before their advent to power, Kolzum had become the chief Egyptian port to the Red Sea, and both pilgrims and the supplies of grain to the Holy Cities left for the Hijaz from there. With the increased volume of trade in the Red Sea, however, the Fatimids extended their frontiers further south and the port of Aydab developed under their auspices as a major entrepôt of the eastern trade.[2] Their political and religious envoys were very active in the Yemen and they finally succeeded in establishing the pro-Fatimid Sulaihi and Zura'i dynasties,[3] which successively dominated the political scene from about 1037 to Salah-al-Din's annexation of

[1] Lewis, B., 'The Fatimids and the Route to India', in *Revue de la Faculté des Sciences économiques, University of Istanbul*, xi (1949–50), pp. 50–4.

[2] Lewis, op. cit., p. 52. Hasan, *The Arabs and the Sudan*, pp. 68–9.

[3] Umarah, op. cit., pp. 15–34. Khazraji, *History of the Resuliyy Dynasty of Yemen*, ed. and tr. Redhouse, J. W., iii, no. 1 (tr.), pp. 10–18. See also *Encyclopaedia of Islam*, 1st edition, under 'Sulaihi'.

Yemen in 1173. Unlike Salah-al-Din, the Fatimids did not annex Yemen, but only encouraged the establishment of a strong pro-Fatimid state which would not only undermine the caliphate in Baghdad but also facilitate Egyptian commerce with the East. They supplemented this by organizing a special fleet to protect the regular flow of trade in the Red Sea.[1]

It is apparent that this gave a fresh impetus to the Muslim commercial activities that had been going on in the interior of the Ethiopian region. Just as in the Mamluke period some two centuries later, Fatimid protection was also extended to these inland traders. In this respect the spiritual dependence of the Christian kingdom of Ethiopia on the Patriarchate of Alexandria often created embarassing situations. The increasing number of Ethiopian converts to Islam, mainly along the trade routes and in the market towns, demanded complete freedom of worship in the Christian provinces. They pointed out that throughout the Muslim world, and in Egypt in particular, Christians were tolerated and even protected as *Dhimmis*. They claimed similar rights of public worship within the realms of the Ethiopian kingdom. It seems that these requests were met with the adamant refusal of the Christian kings and the tenacious opposition of the local clergy. Naturally, the Ethiopian Muslims approached Cairo through their commercial associates, and appealed to the Fatimids to put some pressure on the kingdom to grant them reciprocal rights of worship as were enjoyed by the Copts. Thus there began the historic role of Egypt as the champion of Islam in Ethiopia, a position first assumed by the Fatimid caliphate, and which has characterized Ethio-Egyptian relations throughout the centuries.

To carry out their responsibility to the Muslims in Ethiopia, the Fatimids hit hard on the most sensitive chord in Ethiopian Christendom. Not only did they press the patriarchs to send messages enjoining the Ethiopian kings to protect Muslim rights, but also interfered in the actual selection of the Egyptian candidate to be ordained as metropolitan of Ethiopia. An important incident related in the *History of the Patriarchs* indicates that the problem had assumed a serious character in the second half of the reign of Caliph Al-Mustansir (1035–94).[2] Badr al-Jamal, the Armenian, whom the

[1] Hasan, op. cit., p. 72.

[2] The story is told by the hagiographer(s) of patriarchs Christodulus (1046–77) and Cyril (1077–92), Sawirus, op. cit., vol. ii, pt. 3, pp. 316–17, 329–30, 347–51; Renaudot, op. cit., pp. 443–4, 453–4. Budge, *The Book of the Saints of the Ethiopian Church*, pp. 994–5.

caliph had appointed Amir al-Juyush in 1073 was the central figure in the incident which took place between this date and A.D. 1089.

Not long before 1077, the Egyptian bishop in Ethiopia, Fīqiṭor, died, and another Egyptian called Abdun presented himself at the Ethiopian court, pretending that he was sent by the patriarch to succeed him as Cyril, metropolitan of Ethiopia. It had been customary that, on the death of a metropolitan, the king should send an official delegation to Egypt asking for a replacement and the process usually took a long period of time. The sudden dispensation of this age-long convention, and the unexpected arrival of the pretender probably aroused suspicions in the Court and among the Ethiopian clergy over the claims of Abdun. An Ethiopian delegation was probably sent to Egypt to obtain a more tangible proof for Abdun's claims. Abdun also sent his own agents with the delegation and made secret representations to Badr al-Jamal through a man named Ali al-Kifti. He requested the Amir al-Juyush to command Patriarch Christodulus to confirm the episcopal seat on him. In return he promised to send a handsome annual tribute in gold, and to improve the conditions of the life of the Muslims in Ethiopia. This greatly impressed the Amir al-Juyush and he forced the patriarch to accede to the wishes of Abdun. Even the method used for his intended ordination was unorthodox:

> . . . there had been arranged the journey of Abba Mercurius, bishop of Wisim, to the lands of Abyssinia with a letter from the patriarch and one of his vestments to clothe the aforesaid Cyril, and to make him metropolitan, and the father, the patriarch, had wept when he was obliged [to do] this . . .[1]

Unfortunately for Abdun, just on the eve of the departure of this mission to confirm him, his arch-supporter at the Amir's Court, Ali al-Kifti, was disgraced for another intrigue in which he was also involved regarding Nubia,[2] and he was summarily executed. This brought the patriarch back to the Amir's favour and 'the affair of Cyril was cancelled'.

The self-styled metropolitan was the only loser in this drama.[3]

[1] Sawirus, op. cit., p. 317.

[2] Together with his protestations in favour of Abdun, Ali also accused the Egyptian bishop in Nubia of anti-Muslim acts. Enraged at this, Badr al-Jamal cast the patriarch into prison until another of his envoys returned from Nubia and reported the falsity of Ali's charge, ibid., pp. 316–17.

[3] Abdun remained in Ethiopia until the arrival of the rightful metropolitan, Sawīros. Then he fled to the Dahlak islands, where he was taken prisoner by the

Badr al-Jamal had no intentions of withdrawing the favourable conditions proposed by Abdun during his short misadventure. He imposed them on the next bishop, Sawīros, properly ordained and sent to Ethiopia by Patriarch Cyril (1077–92). Sawīros was a nephew of Fīqiṭor, the deceased metropolitan, and he had been brought up by him in Ethiopia. He knew the country very well and had probably established close friendly relations at the royal Court during his stay there with his uncle. He is also described as 'a learned man' and all these characteristics probably gave him much influence both in Ethiopia[1] and at the Patriarchal court in Cairo. For the purposes of Badr al-Jamal he was apparently thought to be the best candidate and was recommended to the patriarch for the ordination. On this occasion he is said to have made many promises to the Amir al-Juyush, '. . . that he would continue (to supply) him with presents from (Ethiopia) and would allow the kings to obey him'.

In October 1088 the bishop sent his brother, Rigal, to Egypt with a gift to the Amir al-Juyush. The Amir was not impressed by it and threw Rigal into prison. Then he angrily summoned the patriarch and the other bishops who were in Cairo at the time, and reproached them for what he called the bad faith of the metropolitan of Ethiopia. He accused him on three major charges: that he failed to raise the stipulated amount of tribute; that he did not build mosques for the Muslims in Ethiopia; and that he did little to protect the traders in that country where 'they have begun . . . to waylay the Muslim merchants and others than them'. The Amir demanded that the patriarch send a delegation of two bishops with an official letter ordering the Ethiopians to fulfil all the above requirements. Until the patriarch and his assembly of bishops agreed to do this he put them under house arrest. It is apparent that they courageously resisted his wishes for a long time. It was not until February 1089 that they agreed among themselves to dispatch the two bishops with a patriarchal letter. We are not told of the contents of the letter, but the Amir is said to have been pleased with it, and he had it sent to Ethiopia

local Muslim ruler, who confiscated all his possessions and sent him to Cairo. There he was condemned and executed at Badr al-Jamal's orders, probably in A.D. 1086, ibid., p. 329. Renaudot, op. cit., p. 453. I have here given preference to Renaudot's date of the execution. It is probable that there was a difference in the MSS. consulted by him and those used by the editors of the *History of the Patriarchs*, where the date is A.D. 1143/4, half a century after the death of Badr al-Jamal himself.

[1] This may have facilitated the reforms in the matrimonial customs of the people which he enthusiastically reported to the patriarch, ibid., pp. 329–30.

together with his own. The Amir's message was short and to the point: 'If thou dost not do thus and thus, I shall demolish the churches which [are] in the land of Egypt.' It seems, however, that the delegation came to nothing, and the Ethiopian king is said to have replied in similar vein to the Amir's threatening letter.[1]

The Egyptian bishop in Ethiopia held a difficult position. Technically he was a subject of the Muslim rulers of Egypt. Every act unfavourable to Muslim interests in his diocese with which he might be charged, closely affected the patriarch and the Christian community in general and his own relations in particular. There was, besides, an apparent misunderstanding in Cairo of the extremely limited powers of the metropolitan. In Ethiopia, the bishop was naturally expected to provide a strong leadership for the religious feelings of his congregation. Any sign of weakness or moderation would cost him not only his reputation among the influential clergy but even his episcopal seat.[2] When the problem involved Muslim interests in the country, his views would be received with apparent suspicion and would carry very little weight. This delicate situation in which their envoys to Ethiopia had to live was clearly understood by the patriarchs, who persistently disclaimed any responsibility for the political acts of an independent kingdom of which they were merely the spiritual heads. When Badr al-Jamal reproached him for the alleged insecurity of Muslim traders in Ethiopia, Patriarch Cyril meekly replied, 'O my lord, what have I to do with waylaying? Am I a watchman (Khafir)?'[3] In Ethiopia, too, it seems quite clear that the kings had given much cognizance to the sensitive position of the metropolitan, and had exempted him from direct public involvement in their strong anti-Muslim policies, particularly after 1270.[4] Even

[1] Ibid., p. 351. The Ethiopian king's reply is said to have been: 'If thou demolish a single stone of the churches, I shall carry to thee all the bricks and stones of Mecca, and I shall deliver all of them to thee, and if a single brick of it (Mecca) is missing, I shall send to thee its weight in gold.' Although there is no doubt that the terms of Badr al-Jamal were rejected at the Christian Court in Ethiopia, the tradition of the language of this reply seems to have been strongly affected by the apparent belief of the Copts that they had in the Ethiopian state a strong champion of their faith. The theme recurs throughout the medieval period.

[2] The temporary dismissal of Bishop Yohannis was apparently occasioned by a controversy on the institution of circumcision, Sawirus, op. cit., pp. 508–11. Renaudot, op. cit., pp. 273, 283–8. Later in the reign of Patriarch Mīka'él (1092–1102) Bishop Gīyorgīs was dismissed for apparently more serious charges of 'infamous affairs and . . . vile deeds (which) did not become his rank', Sawirus, op. cit., p. 394.

[3] Ibid., p. 349.

[4] This point emerges from the fact that neither the available chronicles nor the

for the difficulties of the expansion of Islam in Ethiopia, the metropolitan could fully declare his innocence and blame them on the religious fanaticism of the people. This seems to offer an explanation for the unlikely story reported in the *History of the Patriarchs* that Bishop Sawīros had built mosques for the Muslims in Ethiopia sometime before 1089. At the audience he granted the patriarch and his bishops in February 1089, Badr al-Jamal asked Rigal why his brother, Bishop Sawīros, did not build the four mosques he had agreed to erect in Ethiopia before his ordination. Rigal replied:

> 'O my lord, he built seven mosques in the places where it was possible to build [them], and . . . the Abyssinians demolished them and wished to kill him, and . . . when the news of this reached the king, he arrested the metropolitan and imprisoned him.'[1]

Egyptian protection of Muslim interests was only a myth, and did not constitute a crucial factor in the expansion of Islam in Ethiopia. Their own economic strength, arising from their almost complete monopoly of long-distance trade, gave the Ethiopian Muslims a growing influence in the Christian kingdom, and eventually led to the establishment of small Muslim principalities in the peripheral areas in the south.

Except in the islands of Dahlak, the growing political significance of Islam in the Ethiopian region was a post-tenth-century development. Masudi (*fl.* 946–56) clearly indicates this situation in his short description of the land of the *habasha*: 'The Muslim families who live there are tributary to the indigenous people.'[2] For over three centuries after the rise of Islam and the establishment of the extensive Muslim empire from the Atlantic to central Asia, this remained the political status of Islam in Ethiopia. As we have seen above, their commercial activities in the region constituted the *raison d'être* of these Muslim families. By the second half of the tenth century their important role as a link between the region and the outside world had already been recognized, and, no doubt through their agency,

hagiographical traditions about armed conflicts with the local Muslims make any reference to the part played by the Egyptian bishop. The important role of praying for the army when it set out on an expedition is assumed in these traditions by the local saints, cf. *Acta Sancti Mercuri*, ed. and tr. Conti Rossini, in *CSCO*, Script. Aeth., ser. altera, t. xxii, pp. 38–9 (text). *Gädlä Samu'él* (*Waldibba*), ed. and tr. Turaiev, B., in his *Monumenta Aethiopiae Hagiologica*, fasc. ii (1902), pp. 14–15. *Les Chroniques de Zar'a Ya'qob et de Ba'eda Maryam*, ed. and tr. Perruchon, pp. 90, 133–4.

[1] Sawirus, op. cit., p. 350.

[2] *Les Prairies d'or*, iii, p. 34.

the Ziyadite rulers of Yemen had contracted treaties of commerce and friendship with the Christian kingdom on the one hand[1] and with the pagan peoples in the south on the other.

Muslim penetration of the pagan south became a new and dominant factor in the political history of the region after this period. We have already referred to the withdrawal of effective Christian power from the Shäwan region following on the successful pagan revolt led by the queen of the *Bani al-Hamwiyah*. Ibn Haukal's invaluable information about Ethiopia at the time also indicates that the queen had established amicable relations with the Ziyadite ruler of Yemen: 'The queen of the *habasha* also sends him presents of good will, presents which are always offered to him. . . .'[2] Al-Yaqubi considered the Dahlak islands as the major outlet of trade of the Ethiopian region,[3] and only makes an incidental reference to the port of Zeila in his geographical treatise written two decades later.[4] It is apparent that in the days of Masudi and Ibn Haukal the importance of Zeila had considerably increased, and fresh lines of communication had been opened between the interior of southern Ethiopia and the Gulf of Aden. The new direction of contact was characterized by the extensive, hot, lowland plains between the Ethiopian plateau and the sea coast. It is certainly to this tract of land that Ibn Haukal refers as 'the wilderness and the deserts difficult to cross'.[5]

The indefatigable Muslim traders crossed these difficult roads and began the commercial exploitation of the rich natural resources of southern Ethiopia. We have no means of following in greater detail the activities of these traders and the early development of Islam in the region. The earliest Muslim tradition in eastern Shäwa is a record of the death of an apparently pagan ruler, Queen Badit, 'daughter of Maya' in A.D. 1063.[6] The prevalence of female rulers in the few

[1] Ibid., p. 35. The only ruler mentioned here by this author is the Christian *Nejashi*, who had trade agreements with Ibrahim b. Ziad, chief of Zabid: 'En vertu du traité d'amitié qui unit les deux pays . . .'. For the year A.H. 366 (= A.D. 977), Umarah also refers to the Christian king's relations with the ruler of Zabid: 'The kings of the Abyssinians, on the further side of the sea, sent him offerings of presents and sought his alliance'. *Yaman, its Early Medieval History*, p. 8 (tr.).

[2] *La Configuration de la terre*, tr. Wiet, G., i (1964), p. 23.

[3] *Historiae*, p. 219.

[4] *Livre des pays*, tr. Wiet, G., (1937), p. 159.

[5] Op. cit., p. 56. It is quite possible that he obtained his notes about the queen 'in the south of Abyssinia' through these new routes, and he seems to have had more information about her than he cared to relate: 'On raconte sur elle des choses curieuses', ibid., p. 16.

[6] Cerulli, E., 'Il sultanato dello Scioa', p. 10 n. 1. According to the same

available traditions about the region has already been referred to, and even the genealogy of this ruler seems to recall to mind the queen of the *Bani al-Hamwiyah* mentioned in the *History of the Patriarchs*. It is most likely that the mention of the 'daughter of Maya' in Cerulli's document refers to a period when the Muslim traders were attached to the Courts of the local pagan rulers and mainly engaged in commercial activities. In the main centres of these economic activities they probably gained, from among the local people, an increasing number of followers who gradually adopted their religion. It is clearly part of this development that they should have an early tradition of a major conversion to Islam in *the land of Gbbah* at the beginning of the twelfth century. Significantly this almost coincided with the renewed Christian attempt at southern expansion. Thus began the long struggle between the Christians and Muslims for the control of southern Ethiopia.

The Muslims entered the struggle at a disadvantage. The prestige of the Christian kingdom as the strongest power in the Ethiopian region since the Aksumite period was already established. Much of the area had been under its control in the ninth and early tenth centuries. In the whole of this period the Muslims had only been active as long-distance traders, with little or no political influence of their own, and often under the protection of the Christian kings and their local vassals. Even after the queen of the *Bani al-Hamwiyah* won back her independence from the Christians, the dominant section of the remnants of the former military colonies no doubt continued to look towards the Aksumite kingdom as a place of their distant origin. It is apparent that, at least in the region of eastern Shäwa, the descendants of these ancient Aksumite colonies provided the most important settled community in which Islam began to flourish.[1] Islam was a late-comer in the area, and even after the

chronicle the so-called Mahzumite dynasty is said to have ruled from the end of the ninth century until its final overthrow by the Wälasma ruler of Ifat, ibid., pp. 13, 35. The contemporary Arab writer, Masudi, clearly underlines, however, that before the middle of the tenth century, the Muslims were living in the region as clients of the local (pagan or Christian) rulers, op. cit. iii, p. 34.

[1] From an analysis of the names of the princes Cerulli has made an interesting conclusion that a Semitic Ethiopian language was spoken in the region of Ifat and eastern Shäwa, 'Il sultanato dello Scioa', pp. 32–4. Cf. also his *Studi etiopici*: i, *Harar*, p. 19. Although he also states that at least fifty different languages were spoken in the whole of the Ethiopian region, Al-'Umari nevertheless gives, in the case of Ifat, a number of still recognizable words, *Masalik*, pp. 8 n. 2; 9 n. 5; 10 n. 7; 11 n. 2; 21.

establishment of a number of Muslim principalities, it could never get rid of the stigma of being a second-rate power in the Ethiopian region.[1]

Moreover, the twelfth century, which is the period of the earliest traditions of active Muslim proselytization in southern Ethiopia, was also marked by the revival of the Christian kingdom in the north.

The Zagwé dynasty: a period of Christian revival

After the decline of Aksum, the Christian kingdom had centred around the region of southern Tigré and Angot.[2] Its population consisted mainly of the *Tigrä* and *Tigrīgna* speaking tribes in the north, the Christianized Agäw of Lasta and Wag, and the Amhara who inhabited the expanding zone in and south of Angot. At this stage of the history of the kingdom the main difference between these people was perhaps only linguistic. The northern people, who spoke *Tigrä* and *Tigrīgna*, constituted the dominant section of the population in the Sabean and Aksumite periods. It seems that during the expansion of the Aksumite kingdom into the Agäw plateau south of Tigré, *a narrow semitized corridor* had been created in the region of Angot. It consisted of the great watershed between the basins of the Täkäzé and the Awash, and was apparently used as a major passage to the region of Amhara. Immediately to the west of this corridor lived the Agäw people of the broken country of Wag and Lasta. It has already been suggested that Aksumite pressure of expansion on this area had started early, and King Kaléb's 'governor of Agäw' mentioned by Cosmas probably had his headquarters there. It is apparent that, despite the early progress of the Church among them, the compact and inaccessible nature of the area, which is almost totally enclosed by the rivers Ṣällärī and Täkäzé, had preserved the tribal and linguistic identity of the local people. This appears to have been the case even long after the spearhead of the Aksumite expansion had outflanked these people and almost encircled them with a semitized zone extending from southern Tigré through the highland districts of Angot, and stretching across the basin of the river Bashīlo, south of the upper Täkäzé. However, with the decline of Aksum and

[1] This status of the Muslims in the area was also recognized by the Mamlukes in Egypt, and according to Al-'Umari 'the [Mamluke] chancery was never in correspondence with the seven Muslim kings [in the country of the *habasha*] there was no protocol, therefore, [about them]', ibid., p. 33.

[2] Taddesse Tamrat, 'The Abbots of Däbrä Hayq', n. 7.

the establishment of the centre of the kingdom in the region of Angot, it is clear that the Christian Semitic pressure on Wag and Lasta became redoubled, and the local chiefs were completely integrated with the royal Christian court. After more than three hundred years of such a close association with the descendants of the ancient Aksumite kings, a new Christian dynasty emerged in the first half of the twelfth century and took control of the whole kingdom, deriving much of its political support from Lasta.

It has been known in traditional history as the Zagwé dynasty and it has been critically examined on many occasions, especially by Conti Rossini.[1] The circumstances of the advent to power of the Zagwé kings are very uncertain, and the traditions of the event that have survived are only brief and incomplete. An interesting version attributes the dynastic change to a marriage between a daughter of the last Aksumite king and one of his generals who came from Bugna in Lasta. The general rebelled against his father-in-law, killed him in battle, and usurped the throne.[2] This is apparently a non-official version,[3] and clearly underlines the continuity of the Ethiopian political tradition even in the emergence of the Zagwé dynasty. The rise of the Zagwé dynasty did not represent a break in the Aksumite tradition. For over three centuries the centre of the Christian kingdom was on the doorsteps of Wag and Lasta, and it was from here that it controlled its extensive sphere of influence in the ninth and early tenth centuries. The local traditions already referred to indicate that the earliest attempts to evangelize in the area may have started

[1] Perruchon, J., 'Notes pour l'histoire d'Éthiopie', in *RS*, i (1893), pp. 364–72; id., 'Le pays de Zague', in *RS*, v (1897), pp. 275–84. Conti Rossini, 'Appunti ed osservazioni sui re Zague e Takla Haymanot', in *RRAL*, ser. 5, vol. iv (1895), pp. 144–59; id., 'Lettera a J. Halévy sulla caduta degli Zague', in *RS*, x (1903), pp. 373–7; 'Lettera . . . sullo stato attuale della questione degli Zague', *RS*, xi (1903), pp. 325–30; *Storia d'Etiopia* (1928), pp. 303–21.

[2] Conti Rossini, 'Il libro delle leggende e tradizioni abissine dell'Ecciaghie Filpos', *RRAL*, ser. 5, vol. xxvi (1917), p. 707. *Storia d'Etiopia*, pp. 304–5; Doresse, J., *L'Empire du Prêtre-Jean*, ii (1957), pp. 50–1.

[3] Four of the Zagwé kings, Yimrha-Kristos, Lalībäla, Nä'akuto-Lä'ab, and Yitbaräk have hagiographies, two of which are still unpublished. None of these works mentions the above tradition of matrimonial connections. All of them were composed after the downfall of the Zagwé dynasty, of which the origin is simply attributed to the wrath of God on an excessively arrogant Aksumite king, 'Gädlä Yimrha-Kristos', MS., Lalībäla, Bétä-Maryam, ff. 40–2. Cf. also *Gädlä Yaréd*, ed. Conti Rossini, p. 23 (text). The tendency in these later official traditions is to show that the Zagwé kings were of a completely alien family who usurped power from the rightful princes of the House of Isra'el, 'Gädlä Yimrha-Kristos', f. 42[a]; *Gädlä Lalībäla*, ed. and tr. in part Perruchon (1892), p. 62.

in the sixth century.[1] Within this long period, the Church was securely established in Wag and Lasta, and it is apparent that by the eve of the rise of the Zagwé dynasty many of the local people had already taken active part in the religious, political, and military leadership of the kingdom. A close review of the few available historical notes on the period shows no signs of a sudden and dramatic advent to power of a completely new cadre of leadership in the country. It rather seems that the assumption of royal powers by the princes of Bugna was only the culmination of a natural political development within the Christian kingdom of which the central parts had long consisted of the crucial area of the headwaters of the rivers Täkäzé and Ṣällärī.

Conti Rossini used an incident preserved in the *History of Patriarch Yohannis* (1147–67) as part of his evidence for dating the rise of the Zagwé dynasty.[2] An Ethiopian king wrote to the patriarch and the Egyptian vizir, Ali ibn Sallar (d. 1153), asking for the replacement of the aged metropolitan, Abba Mīka'él. The vizir authorized the patriarch to send a new bishop. But the patriarch refused, on the grounds that it was not canonical to ordain a replacement for a living metropolitan, and he was imprisoned for it. The hagiographer also adds that the actual reason for the Ethiopian request was not that Mīka'él was too old for his office, but that he had refused to recognize the king who was a usurper. Conti Rossini took this as a reference to the first Zagwé king, and used it as confirming the date of the advent of the dynasty in about A.D. 1150.[3] But there is no

[1] See p. 26 n. 1

[2] Renaudot, op. cit. p. 525; Conti Rossini, 'Lettera a J. Halévy' (1903) p. 328; *Storia d'Etiopia*, p. 303.

[3] There are two conflicting traditions for the duration of the dynasty. The more common version is that it lasted for 333 years until the advent of Yikunno-'Amlak in 1270. The other version gives it only 133 years. Conti Rossini prefers the latter, essentially because it can easily be reconciled with the short list of Zagwé kings given in the traditions, cf. 'Il libro delle leggende', pp. 707–8. In two important land grants Lalībäla gives his genealogy as 'Son of Morara, son of Žan-Siyum, son of Asda', id. 'L'Evangelo d'oro di Dabra Libanos', *RRAL*, ser. 5, vol. x (1901), pp. 186, 189. Märara is elsewhere said to have been the first Zagwé king, *Gädlä Yaréd*, ed. Conti Rossini, p. 23 (text). The name of the general who married the daughter of the last Aksumite king and who founded the new dynasty is usually given as *Mära* Täklä-Haymanot. It is very likely that both this name and Märara refer to the same person. It is apparent that the curious system of succession to the throne has been the reason for the long list of Zagwé kings available in some traditions, cf. Conti Rossini, *Storia d'Etiopia*, pp. 305–6. It seems that the throne rarely passed from father to son, but either from brother to brother or from uncle to nephew, cf. *Gädlä Lalībäla*, ed. and tr. Perruchon,

evidence for a 'strong resistance . . . at first offered to the new dynasty by the clergy under Abunä Mīka'él'.[1] The metropolitan was probably sent to Ethiopia in the first years of the reign of Patriarch Mäqaryos (1102–31),[2] and had become very old by the middle of the century. He had also already been an object of a controversy before a replacement was asked for. In the reign of Patriarch Gäbriél (1131–45), the Ethiopian king asked Abba Mīka'él to ordain more than the prescribed number of seven bishops in Ethiopia. But the metropolitan declined to do this without patriarchal authorization from Cairo. The caliph apparently agreed. However, Patriarch Gäbriél explained to the caliph the implications of the Ethiopian Church having more than seven bishops. If the number reached ten, the Ethiopians would in future be able to appoint their own metropolitan, or even a patriarch, and would thus be completely independent of Egyptian influence. When he heard this the caliph reversed his decision and agreed with the patriarch in his refusal to let the Ethiopians have any more bishops.[3] Thus, both his old age and the earlier controversy surrounding his name were sufficient reason for the Ethiopian request to replace Abba Mīka'él. The incident certainly indicates that there was a succession struggle at the advent of the new king. But it had

pp. 32–40. *Gädlä Nä'akuto-Lä'ab*, ed. and tr. Conti Rossini, pp. 114–16, 147–8, 150. However, some lists also include the princes who did not occupy the throne. It seems possible now to provide a tentative genealogy of the princes with the help of additional notes from the unpublished 'Gädlä Yimrha-Kristos', ff. 2–4. In the following table the names of the crowned princes are in capitals. The numbers signify the order of succession:

(1) MÄRARA = ? Mäsobä-Wärq

(2) ṬÄNṬÄWIDIM — Girwa-Siyum — Žan-Siyum

Girwa-Siyum: (3) YIMRHA-KRISTOS

Žan-Siyum: (4) HARBÉ — (5) LALĪBÄLA

(4) HARBÉ: (6) NÄ'AKUTO-LÄ'AB

(5) LALĪBÄLA: (7) YITBARÄK

[1] Trimingham, *Islam in Ethiopia*, p. 56.

[2] Renaudot, loc. cit. About the end of the reign of Patriarch Mīka'él (1092–1102), Bishop Gīyorgīs had been sent to Ethiopia and had been deposed soon afterwards, cf. p. 49 n. 2, above. It is probable that Bishop Mīka'él was his immediate successor, ordained soon after the accession of Mäqaryos.

[3] Renaudot, op. cit., pp. 510–11. The story is altered in the Ethiopic translation, which was undertaken at the auspices of the Egyptian bishops. Here the role of the patriarch in the reversal of the caliph's decision is suppressed. On the contrary he is said to have been willing to grant the permission, were it not for the courtiers of the caliph who opposed such a measure, Budge, *The Book of the Saints of the Ethiopian Church*, pp. 800–1.

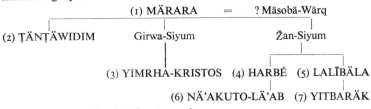

none of the drastic effects of the conflict between the two brothers who fought for their father's throne in the reign of Patriarch Cosmas.[1] The new king referred to may have been the first prince of Bugna to occupy the throne, but there is no sign of a dramatic episode at the time of his accession. Like all Ethiopian monarchs before and after him, he had a local base for power.[2] The region of Lasta, from which he derived much of his support, differed from the rest of the central parts of the kingdom in one important factor. The local people, although as much Christian and part of the Aksumite cultural tradition as the peoples of Tigré and Amhara, had apparently preserved their linguistic identity and used Agäwigna outside the church.[3] Essentially based on this linguistic difference, the Zagwé kings have been dismissed, in the dominant traditions of their political enemies, as an alien and impious group of adventurers. This has long obscured what is perhaps the richest and most artistic period of Ethiopian history since the conversion of Ézana. The advent of the Zagwé dynasty brought in fresh developments in the revival of the Christian kingdom for which there are noticeable indications at the turn of the twelfth century.

Relations with Egypt and the patriarchate were not affected by the Mīka'él incident, and there was a regular supply of Egyptian bishops to Ethiopia. Abba Mīka'él apparently remained in the country until his death, and must have had at least one successor before the end of the century.[4] An Ethiopian delegation sent with a letter and presents to Caliph Al-Adid (1160–71) was later received in 1173 by Salah-al-Din, who was greatly impressed by the presents.[5] The Arab historian

[1] Cf. p. 39 n. 3.

[2] This seems to be quite clear right from the Aksumite period. Many of the kings specifically mention what appears to be their regional or tribal origin in their inscriptions and coins, Littmann, *Deutsche Aksum-Expedition*, i, pp. 46–7; iv, Inscriptions 8, 9, 10, and 11; Kammerer, *Essai*, pp. 154–9.

[3] This is reflected even in the names of the princes, particularly Märara, Ṭänṭäwidim, and Lalībäla, Conti Rossini, 'Appunti ed osservazioni', p. 355. The following exclamation appears as having been pronounced by the people at the coronation of Yimrha-Kristos: '*Hawīsa, Hawīsa*, King of Ethiopia; *Hawīsa*, Yimrhanä-Kristos *Hawīsa*', 'Gädlä Yimrha-Kristos', f. 28^b. The word *huwash* appears in Conti Rossini's Kimant–French vocabulary and it means to anoint, *La Langue des Kemant en Abyssinie*, p. 209. Yimrha-Kristos's father is called Girwa-Siyum. In Conti Rossini's vocabulary again *girwa* means a virile man, ibid., p. 201.

[4] In A.D. 1199/1200 a delegation arrived in Cairo announcing the death of a metropolitan and asking for a new one, Abd al-Latif, *Relation de l'Égypte*, tr. Silvestre de Sacy (1810), p. 334. This cannot be a reference to Mīka'él's death, since he was already too old in *c.* 1150.

[5] Maqrizi, quoted in Conti Rossini, *Storia d'Etiopia*, p. 306.

is silent about the purpose of the delegation. But an interesting passage in the Life of the third Zagwé king probably refers to the same period:

> And . . . Yimrha sent a message to the king of Egypt saying: 'Send me the wooden door which is in your Great Hall so that it may serve me for [building] the House of God.' And he sent him much gold. When the king [of Egypt] saw the gold . . . he sent him the door [which was cut out of the tree of Lībanos].[1]

Yimrha inaugurated the Zagwé tradition of building rock-hewn churches, and his communication with the ruler of Egypt about building material probably indicates a fresh revival of the long and close cultural contacts between the two countries. There are further references to a number of foreign ecclesiastics who went to Ethiopia in Yimrha's reign and remained there after his death.[2] The number of Ethiopian pilgrims to the Holy Land also seems to have increased. In 1189, at his triumphant occupation of Jerusalem, Salah-al-Din is said to have given many sites to the Ethiopians there.[3] We still know very little about the cultural and religious impact of this two-way traffic on Ethiopia. But at no time does the Holy Land seem to have captured the imagination of the Ethiopians so much as in this period, which Conti Rossini so aptly characterizes as 'the dawn of a new period in Ethiopian literature'.[4] The beautiful churches of

[1] 'Gädlä Yimrha-Kristos', f. 39. It is apparent that the first European who saw a copy of this *Gädl* was Alvarez, who gives a brief but accurate description of it, *The Prester John of the Indies*, ed. Beckingham and Huntingford (1961), p. 204. Marianus Victor had also been given some excerpts of the *Gädl* by his informant Abba Täsfa-Ṣiyon (d. 1550) in Rome. In his list of Ethiopian kings he gives another version of the passage quoted above, cf. Perruchon, 'Notes pour l'histoire d'Éthiopie', *RS*, i (1893), pp. 368–9. Of all the known hagiographies of the Zagwé kings this *Gädl* is the most interesting for many of the historical traditions it preserves. Alvarez's testimony indicates its pre-16th-century composition, and internal evidence shows that it was written after 1270. The MS. I could consult in Lalībäla was however a recent (probably 19th-century) copy. King Yimrha was probably reigning at the end of the Fatimid caliphate and in the early years of the Ayyubids. Abu Salih, who refers to events in 1173/4 as having occurred in his own life time, reports that Ethiopia was ruled by kings who were also priests, *The Churches and Monasteries of Egypt*, pp. x, 286. In Ethiopian traditions this description only fits Yimrha, who was ordained a priest before his coronation and continued to celebrate mass after his accession, 'Gädlä Yimrha-Kristos', ff. 8–10, 30[b]; Alvarez, op. cit., p. 204.

[2] 'Gädlä Yimrha-Kristos', f. 35. Here they are called 'Romans'. Alvarez was told that one of the tombs beside the king's belonged to a 'patriarch of Alexandria', loc. cit. He also says that the local people told him that the rock churches of Lalībäla were built by Egyptian masons, op. cit., p. 227.

[3] Cerulli, *Etiopi in Palestina*, i (1943), pp. 33–7.

[4] *Storia d'Etiopia*, p. 306.

Lalībäla were in fact a deliberate attempt to reproduce the Holy City of Jerusalem in the mountains of Wag and Lasta.[1]

It is no doubt a reflection of the close and regular contacts with Egypt at the time that we should have a remarkable corroboration between the historical notes about King Lalībäla in his own land grants[2] and in the *History of the Patriarchs*.[3] His reign[4] marked the apex of the Zagwé dynasty. The Zagwé kings had their capital at a place called Adäfa, just outside the present site of the Lalībäla churches.[5] In Lalībäla's reign the metropolitan also lived at a site nearby, in a special 'palais episcopale' where the king often went to see him.[6] Thus Bugna had become the centre of the religious and political life of the kingdom. Many of Lalībäla's courtiers were drawn from the same district and held very high ecclesiastical and administrative positions. A brother of Queen Mäsqäl-Kibra, Hīrun, had

[1] This is represented in the hagiographical tradition that Christ was revealed to Lalībäla before he started building the churches. He then took him on a round trip of the churches of Jerusalem describing to him the significance of each and inspiring him to build similar sites in the kingdom, *Gädlä Lalībäla*, ed. and tr. Perruchon, p. 88. This is particularly true of the church of Golgota, where there is even a representation of the Holy Sepulchre, cf. Alvarez, op. cit., pp. 207–21.

[2] These have been published in an important article of Conti Rossini, 'L'Evangelo d'oro di Dabra Libanos', in *RRAL*, ser. 5, vol. x (1901), pp. 186–93.

[3] Perruchon, J., 'Notes pour l'histoire d'Éthiopie: extrait de la vie d'Abba Jean, 74ᵉ patriarche d'Alexandrie', ed. and tr. in *RS*, vi (1898), pp. 267–71, 365–72, and vii (1899), pp. 76–85. Cf. Renaudot, *Historia Patriarcharum Alexandrinorum* (1717), pp. 554–67.

[4] According to the king-lists he ruled for 40 years. It is impossible here to determine when the reign started, but he was certainly on the throne between 1205 and 1225, Perruchon, op. cit., pp. 79, 82, 84–5; Conti Rossini, op. cit., pp. 188, 191. The references to Lalībäla in the *History of the Patriarchs* belong to A.D. 1205 and 1210 and contain no mention of the rock churches. It is likely that they were not built as yet. Tradition has it that they took 24 years, cf. Alvarez, op. cit., p. 227; and Lalībäla was probably still alive as late as *c.* A.D. 1235.

[5] It is first mentioned in 1210 by the patriarchal envoys to Lalībäla, Perruchon, op. cit., pp. 84–5. Since it was not mentioned elsewhere, many ingenious attempts have been made to identify it, mainly by suggesting various readings for the Arabic name. Conti Rossini identified it with *Adwa* and supported his views with a quotation from Abu Salih, 'Note etiopiche', in *GSAI*, x (1897), p. 145 n. 5. Esteves Pereira rejected this with convincing arguments, but he suggested a curious identification with Yifat (in Shäwa), the reading of which he altered into *Adefat* or Ayfat, Perruchon, op. cit., pp. 86–7. The accuracy of the Egyptian envoy is now fully confirmed by the hagiographer of King Yimrha, 'They received him (with acclamation) from the district of Say (in Bugna) to the land of Adäfa and here he sat on the throne and ruled all (the people) according to the apostolic canons . . .', 'Gädlä Yimrha-Kristos', ff. 28^{b}–29^{a}. A local man casually pointed at a small site still bearing the name of Adäfa, near Mädagé Abbo among the western foothills of Mt. Ashätän overlooking Lalībäla on the north.

[6] Perruchon, op. cit., pp. 78–9.

been ordained a bishop by Metropolitan Mīka'él (1205–9) through the insistence of his royal sister. Soon afterwards the metropolitan left for Egypt, complaining that Hīrun had challenged his authority.[1] There is a constant mention of 'the great men of Bugna' in the land grants of the king. The abbot of the important monastery of Däbrä Lībanos of Shīmäzana, Yirdi'annä-Kristos, also came from Bugna and held that office between 1225 and 1268 until the eve of the fall of the dynasty.[2] Lalībäla had a large army,[3] and probably much of its leadership and the economic patronage deriving from it were also predominantly enjoyed by his Bugna courtiers. Zagwé power had been firmly established everywhere, and the dominance of Lasta in the political and religious life of the kingdom was complete. It is apparent that, towards the end of the eventful reign of Lalībäla, conflicts were beginning to flare up, and the Semitic-speaking peoples of Tigré and Amhara were organizing a strong political reaction. The characteristic weakness in the system of Zagwé succession to the throne greatly facilitated the anti-Lasta movement.

It is apparent that succession to the throne among the descendants of Märara, the founder of the Zagwé dynasty,[4] was determined by the same rules as those of inheritance of family property in Lasta. Two legal pronouncements attributed to King Yimrha by his hagiographer seem to offer a useful clue to the problem of succession among members of the royal family:

> [King Yimrha] decreed saying, 'If there are two or three brothers, born of the same father and mother, and if one becomes rich and the other poor, let the poor man share the property of his rich brother. For both are the fruits of the same womb.'[5]

It seems that the descendants of Märara considered the Christian throne on precisely the same terms. Each of the princes of Bugna apparently claimed rights of succession to the crown and, despite the

[1] Perruchon, op. cit., p. 79.

[2] Conti Rossini, op. cit., pp. 187, 190, 192, 193.

[3] The patriarchal envoys estimated it at 60,000 mounted soldiers without counting the numerous servants that followed them, Perruchon, op. cit., p. 83.

[4] Cf. p. 55 n. 3 above. His reign is said to have been very short, *Gädlä Yaréd*, p. 23 (text).

[5] 'Gädlä Yimrha-Kristos', f. 29^{b}. On another occasion the king was presented with the case of two brothers who had become deadly enemies over a land dispute. He called them to his presence and reconciled them by ruling as follows: 'Divide all your property into five parts. Let two parts go to the elder brother, and the rest to the younger. The residence of the (deceased) parents shall also belong to the younger', ibid., f. 26^{a}.

hagiographical traditions of divine intervention, the problem was probably decided every time by force of arms. The trouble had already started in the reign of the second Zagwé king, Ṭänṭäwidim. He had two younger brothers, Girwa-Siyum and Žan-Siyum, respectively, and he is presented as being worried about the prospect of being succeeded by Girwa's son, Yimrha:[1]

> [Yimrha] stayed with him [i.e. the king] for a week. When [Ṭänṭäwidim] saw him among his own sons he became jealous saying, 'He is going to reign, and my own sons will be his soldiers' . . . and he wanted to kill him . . . But his sorcerers told him 'send him to his mother so that he does not learn the secrets of your kingdom. Instead he shall grow with shepherd boys and herdsmen'. He was pleased with this advice and sent [Yimrha] to his father's house and he grew there.[2]

The struggle for the succession is a common theme in Zagwé royal traditions. During the reign of his brother, Lalībäla was an outlaw and wandered in self-exile for many years; and his half-sister almost poisoned him to death.[3] The events which led to his eventual advent to power are difficult to decipher. But since he came to the throne in the lifetime of his brother it was probably achieved by force of arms. The humble conditions with which King Harbé welcomed his triumphant brother '. . . on his feet . . . while his soldiers implored him to mount [the Royal Mule] . . .'[4] also lead to the same conclusion. This hagiographical tendency to alter historical traditions is even more problematic in the last years of the dynasty.

[1] In a curious passage Yimrha describes himself as follows: 'I am the son of Girwa Siyum; my bigger *father* is Ṭänṭäwidim and my younger *father*, Žan-Siyum' (f. 27ª). One may easily point out that a word is omitted in each case and that the italicized words stand for *brother of my father*. But since Lalībäla is also referred to as the *father* of Nä'akuto-Lä'ab, I have preferred to keep to the original, which probably indicates a clannish cohesion in the family, at least in times of peace, cf. *Gädlä Nä'akuto-Lä'ab*, p. 119 (text): Lalībäla is referred to as 'his father in the flesh and in the spirit'.

[2] 'Gädlä Yimrha-Kristos', f. 5.

[3] *Gädlä Lalibäla*, ed. Perruchon, p. 82. She is described as 'his sister, born of the same father'. This probably means that they had different mothers. Her attempt to kill him was undertaken in favour of their brother, King Harbé, who may have had the same mother as herself. Polygamy was common among the secular families of Christian Ethiopia despite the attempts of the metropolitans, Sawirus, *The History of the Patriarchs*, pp. 329–30. Among the legal reforms attributed to King Yimrha, a veritable priest-king himself, was his insistence on ruling the country according to the apostolic canons, 'Let every man live with one wife, and every woman with one husband', 'Gädlä Yimriha-Kristos', ff. 28ᵇ–29ª.

[4] *Gädlä Lalībäla*, pp. 108–9. Cf. also *Gädlä Nä'akuto-Lä'ab*, ed. Conti Rossini, p. 106.

The patriarchal envoys to his court in 1210 reported that Lalībäla had two sons: Yitbaräk[1] and Lä'ab.[2] The name of the second, Lä'ab, most probably stood for the much longer name of Nä'akuto-Lä'ab, which the Egyptians had obvious difficulty in remembering. Nä'akuto-Lä'ab was a nephew of King Lalībäla,[3] and was brought up at the royal court.[4] The story of his career, as given by his hagiographer(s), may be summarized as follows.[5] Lalībäla's queen, Mäsqäl-Kibra, requested her husband to abdicate in favour of the promising young prince. The king hesitated at first, but he eventually agreed to crown his nephew who began to rule the kingdom from a nearby capital of his own. Only eighteen months later, however, his soldiers mistreated a simple farmer by taking away his only cow for the royal tables of their young master. This displeased the saintly queen. She complained to Lalībäla, who summoned Nä'akuto-Lä'ab at once and took back the crown from him. The young prince meekly accepted the verdict and lived in absolute obedience until Lalībäla's death, when, once again, he ascended the throne and ruled for forty-seven years.

This is an unlikely story, and has undergone a deliberate process of transformation of which the major purpose seems to have been the exclusion of Lalībäla's own son, Yitbaräk, from the official record of succession. The envoys of Patriarch Yohannis to Adäfa in 1210 had no doubts of the precedence of Yitbaräk's position, and they listed his name with much accuracy, prior to that of his 'brother' Nä'akuto-Lä'ab, of whom they had only an imperfect memory. Nä'akuto-Lä'ab was probably the son of King Harbé,[6] who had been deposed by Lalībäla. The young prince was taken to court, where he grew up with Yitbaräk. Towards the end of Lalībäla's reign, the two princes were probably each given a governorate to administer. As

[1] That Lalībäla had a son is also mentioned in his *Gädl*, ed. Perruchon, pp. 51–2. But his name has been suppressed in both passages and only appears in what may be called unofficial king-lists, cf. Conti Rossini, 'Il libro delle leggende', p. 708.

[2] Perruchon, 'Extrait de la Vie d'Abba Jean, 74e patriarche d'Alexandrie', p. 85. The name is given here as *'Atyab* (*'Inab* or *'Itab*). The Arabic can also be read as Lä'ab.

[3] *Gädlä Nä'akuto-Lä'ab*, pp. 114, 129.

[4] Ibid., pp. 118–19, 125, 128.

[5] Ibid., pp. 126, 146–51.

[6] The tradition collected by Antoine d'Abbadie clearly states this, also giving the other name of the king, Gäbrä-Maryam, Conti Rossini, 'Il libro delle leggende', p. 708. His own hagiographer gives another name, Gäbrä-Mäsqäl, for the prince's father, op. cit., p. 115.

the son of a former king, Nä'akuto-Lä'ab was no doubt a rallying point for dissatisfied elements in the country and was deeply mistrusted, especially by Queen Mäsqäl-Kibra, who considered him a serious threat to the career of her own son.[1] Thus he was probably under close watch and was not allowed to move very far from the royal capital.[2] Yitbaräk on the other hand seems to have had a greater freedom of movement and was probably given, at one time, the command of a military contingent sent out to suppress a rebellious governor.[3] His name is also associated with Tigré where he may have had some responsibility.[4] It is most likely that on the death of Lalībäla there was an armed struggle for the succession between the two

[1] This emerges clearly from the contradictory roles she is said to have played in the career of Nä'akuto-Lä'ab (p. 62 n. 5). Her strong, practical influence in her husband's reign is quite evident in the land grants. One of the main reasons for which Bishop Mīka'él (1205–9) claimed he had to leave the country was the queen's interference with Church administration in favour of her brother, whom she had raised to a bishopric, Perruchon, op. cit., p. 79.

[2] His name has always been associated with a place called Qoqhinna, about three hours by mule east of Lalībäla, on the other side of Mount Ashätän. It is there that Lalībäla gave him leave to establish his official residence, *Gädlä Nä'akuto-Lä'ab*, pp. 147–8. It was also there that, dismissed from office at the insistence of the queen, he returned and continued to live, ibid., p. 150. At present there is a natural cave at the foot of Mt. Ashätän, on the eastern side, in which a pretty little church has been constructed in his name, ibid., p. 173.

[3] A tradition of local rebellion (no place-names are given) against which Lalībäla sent 'his son' is still preserved in *Gädlä Lalībäla*, p. 117. The name of the 'son of the king' is however suppressed. What seems to be the same incident is also mentioned in *Gädlä Nä'akuto-Lä'ab*, pp. 141–2, 146. The rebel here is however said to have been Ṣärä-Qimis of Gojjam, and Lalībäla sent Nä'akuto-Lä'ab against him. What makes this very dubious is the complete absence of Nä'akuto-Lä'ab's name in *Gädlä Lalībäla* both in this connection and in general. It is apparent that the author(s) of *Gädlä Lalībäla*, although forbidden to mention the name of Yitbaräk, were unwilling to substitute Nä'akuto-Lä'ab's and simply referred to 'the son of the king'.

[4] There is a curious composition entitled 'Gädlä Yitbaräk' of which I was able to consult a paper MS. at Lalībäla. Since its existence was unknown, the abbot, Mamhir Afä-Wärq, drew my attention to it and obtained the MS. for me from Mägabī Tägägn (see p. 26 n. 1). It is said to have been a copy of which the original is found in a monastery dedicated to Yitbaräk in Tigré at a place called Mäkanä Satwa. It is a collection of numerous anachronisms and contradictory traditions. It seems quite clear, however, that its general theme is Yitbaräk's dispossession of his rightful place in Lasta tradition. The book opens by stating that Lalībäla and Mäsqäl-Kibra forced him to go to Tigré and live in very poor circumstances, 'Gädlä Yitbaräk', paper MS., Mägabī Tägägn, pp. 1–3. At the time of my visit, there was much controversy about the book in the Lalībäla community, which did not give official recognition to the work. Yitbaräk's connection with Tigré is also referred to in the tradition of migrations of the Adkämä-Mälga of Säräwé: Yitbaräk was grandfather of Amotagär, first ancestor of the tribe, Conti Rossini, 'Studi su popolazioni dell'Etiopia', p. 82 (extract).

princes, in which Nä'akuto-Lä'ab was victorious at first and probably assumed the throne for a time. Soon afterwards, however, Yitbaräk seems to have taken over his father's throne. His own hagiographer seems to refer to this final defeat of Nä'akuto-Lä'ab: 'There was a man in the land of Ambagé. He went and entered the king's palace. He met the king and accused [Nä'akuto-Lä'ab] saying, "He took your kingdom before, and now he is hiding in a cave with your *tabot* of Ṣiyon" . . .'[1] Nä'akuto-Lä'ab's interregnum probably lasted for a short time, and in an early tradition of the period only Yitbaräk is referred to as 'the Zagwé king who is reigning in the place of Lalībäla'.[2]

Anti-Zagwé movements in Tigré and Amhara

The internal conflicts of the Zagwé princes greatly strengthened the political movements against them.[3] The earliest sign of anti-Zagwé feelings among the Semitic-speaking Christians of Tigré and Amhara is provided by the tradition about the first Arabic copy of the *Kibrä-Nägäst* in Ethiopia. We are told that the first Arabic copy of the book was translated from the Coptic in 1225, at the time of Lalībäla and Bishop Gīyorgīs[4] in Ethiopia. Nevertheless, an Ethiopic version could not be made right away because, as the scribe has it, 'It went out in the days of Zagua, and they did not translate it because this book says: "Those who reign, not being Isra'elites, are transgressors of the Law".'[5] Anti-Zagwé feelings were probably widespread in Tigré, where Lasta power was firmly established. For the same reason, too, the emergence of a strong anti-Zagwé leadership was practically impossible there, and the initiative seems to have passed to the region of Amhara.

The Amhara had long been the advance guard of Christian expansion in the south. We have already referred to an early Muslim tradition of the armed conflict between them and the Wärjih pastoralists in the Shäwan region, in A.D. 1128.[6] There are traditions of a slow

[1] *Gädlä Nä'akuto-Lä'ab*, p. 173. The reference is to the cave church of Qoqhinna.

[2] *Gädlä Īyäsus-Mo'a*, ed. and tr. Kur, S., p. 18 (tr.). That the reference is to Yitbaräk is clear from another passage which states that the saint settled at Hayq in Yitbaräk's reign, ibid., pp. 20, 26. Cf. also Conti Rossini, 'La caduta della dinastia Zague', pp. 282, 285, 287, 289.

[3] *Gädlä Nä'akuto-Lä'ab*, p. 109.

[4] Bishop Gīyorgīs is also mentioned in a land grant of Lalībäla's in the same year, 1225, Conti Rossini, 'L'Evangelo d'oro', pp. 189–91.

[5] Budge, E. A. W., *The Queen of Sheba and her Only Son Menyelek* (ed. 1932), p. 228.

[6] Cerulli, 'Il sultanato dello Scioa', p. 10 n. 4.

movement of isolated Christian families from Amhara to the region of the Shäwan plateau. A military expedition by a Zagwé monarch into the 'kingdom of Damot' is also referred to elsewhere.[1] It is apparent that by the first half of the thirteenth century, a large number of Christian families had already settled in the pagan-dominated

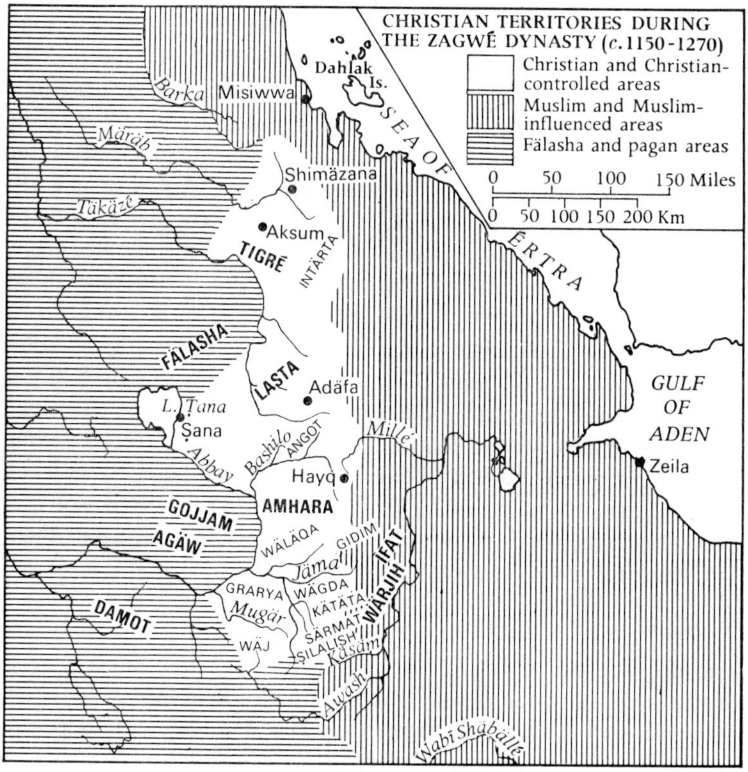

MAP 2.

area of the Shäwan plateau north of the Awash. The Muslim principalities established in the region only affected the eastern sections of the Sīdama area south of the Awash, and the hot, lowland basins of the western tributaries of the Awash in eastern Shäwa.[2] The Muslim kingdom of Īfat, which was the strongest among them, was itself only

[1] *Gädlä Yaréd*, pp. 22–6.

[2] This is quite evident, even from the place-names in the important document published by Prof. Cerulli, op. cit., pp. 5–42. Many of the identifiable place-names were still Muslim in Amdä-Ṣiyon's reign, ibid., pp. 25–32. And in that period they referred to the hot lowlands of the Shäwan plateau.

tucked into the north-eastern corner of the edge of the Shäwan plateau. This was no doubt due to the earlier establishment of Christian communities in the area. The Christian families in the Shäwan region were subjects of the Zagwé kingdom. In a tradition about the district of Tägulät in the thirteenth century, a salt trader is made to say: 'The king of Roha in Angot, . . . he is king over us in this period.'[1]

With the development of the commercial activities of the Muslims in the Shäwan region and the growing importance of the port of Zeila, the region of Amhara was of vital significance for the Christian kingdom and its Zagwé rulers. The major routes to and from Lasta passed through it, and it is apparent that very close contacts had been established between this province and the Gulf of Aden. In an early manuscript (fifteenth century) at the library of Hayq Isṭīfanos there is an interesting genealogy of a Jewish family which emigrated from Aden and settled in Amhara: 'In the days of the Zagwé kings there came out, from the country of Aden, a man, a Jew called Joseph, named after his father. He was exceedingly rich and wealthy. And he settled in Ilawz in the land of Amhara . . .'[2] This was probably a family of Jewish merchants, and it may not have been the only one. No doubt much of the economic and political benefits accruing from these growing contacts with the Gulf of Aden were shared by the local people, particularly the ruling families. There are many reasons to show that Yikunno-'Amlak and his supporters owed much of their success to this new situation.

Yikunno-'Amlak: founder of a new dynasty

The origins and early life of Yikunno-'Amlak still remain very obscure. On his father's side tradition makes him a descendant of Dilna'od who is said to have been the last Aksumite king deposed by the Zagwé.[3] His mother is nevertheless said to have been 'one of the slaves' of a rich Amhara chief in Sägärat.[4] This connection with a local chiefly family in Amhara is more significant in his career. He

[1] 'Gädlä Qäwisṭos' MS. Däbrä Lībanos, f. 57. A more uncertain tradition attributes a church on Dabra Fäntalé (eastern Shäwa) to a local chief who lived in the reign of Nä'akuto-Lä'ab, ibid., ff. 99–100.

[2] Taddesse Tamrat, 'The Abbots of Däbrä Hayq', pp. 112–13.

[3] *Gädlä Īyäsus-Mo'a*, p. 21 (tr.); Conti Rossini, 'La caduta della dinastia Zague', pp. 282, 287. The tradition that Dilna'od was the name of the last Aksumite king is by no means secure. Another version calls him Dignajan, *Gädlä Yaréd*, p. 23 (text).

[4] Conti Rossini, op. cit., pp. 283, 287; Sägärat is on the main road from Lake Hayq to Bägémdir.

grew there with the children of his master, and he is also said to have obtained some religious training with them. More important still another tradition reports that he was later imprisoned by King Yitbaräk in Mäloṭ from where he managed to escape.[1] He was probably involved in the struggle for succession between Yitbaräk and Nä'akuto-Lä'ab.[2] It is interesting that the most important part of his activities against the Zagwé are attributed to the period *after* his escape from Yitbaräk's prison. It is in this period that he is said to have made a religious pact with Īyäsus-Mo'a of Däbrä Hayq.[3] Yikunno-'Amlak seems to have organized an effective military revolt against King Yitbaräk within the crucial area of Amhara and the Shäwan plateau. We find him in communication with the Yemenite kingdom and the Mamlukes of Egypt immediately after his success over the Zagwé.[4] It is probable that this started much earlier. On the eve of the downfall of the Zagwé dynasty, Yikunno-'Amlak had apparently established a virtually independent kingdom of his own, comprising Amhara and the Christian communities of Shäwa.

Marianus Victor collected a pre-sixteenth-century tradition that, in his struggle against Yitbaräk, Yikunno-'Amlak obtained military assistance from Shäwa.[5] Conti Rossini has more recently published an interesting document which confirms the tradition: 'And when he went [for a battle] . . . with his warriors, the seven Gwidäm whose names were, Wägda Mäläzay, Dinbī Däbaray, Mugär Indäzabī, Wäj, Wäräb Inäkafé, Ṣilalish Inäkafé, [and] Mwal Awjajay . . .'[6]

[1] Ibid., pp. 284–5, 289.

[2] This is probably the origin of the tradition of an amicable settlement of the dynastic problem between Yikunno-'Amlak and Nä'akuto-Lä'ab according to some versions of the traditions about the advent of the new dynasty; cf. Bruce, *Travels to Discover the Source of the Nile*, i (1790), pp. 612–15. Among the Zagwa of the Eritrean region who have a tradition of migrating there from Lasta on the occasion of the fall of the Zagwé dynasty there is also another tradition which accuses Nä'akuto-Lä'ab of killing many of their ancestors and forcing the rest to migrate northwards, Conti Rossini, 'Studi su popolazioni dell'Etiopia', pp. 53–4, 72, 79 (extract).

[3] *Gädlä Īyäsus-Mo'a*, pp. 20–1 (tr.). Much later traditions have ascribed this religious role to Täklä-Haymanot of Shäwa. Conti Rossini has made a critical study of these traditions and has conclusively shown that Täklä-Haymanot does not seem to have played this role, 'Appunti ed osservazioni sui re Zague e Takla Haymanot' in *RRAL*, ser. 5, vol. iv (1895), pp. 444–68. A close study of the life and religious career of Täklä-Haymanot fully confirms this conclusion, see Ch. V.

[4] Mufazzal, *Histoire des sultans Mamlouks*, pp. 383–7; Maqrizi, *Histoire des sultans Mamlouks*, tr. Quatremère, vol. ii, pt. 2, p. 122 n. 151.

[5] Quoted in Perruchon, 'Notes pour l'histoire d'Éthiopie', in *RS*, i (1893), p. 368.

[6] 'La caduta della dinastia Zague', pp. 296–7. All the place-names appear in

With these and his Amhara troops Yikunno-'Amlak attacked the Zagwé king,[1] killed him, and declared himself King of Ethiopia. The title was probably only nominal for some time. Leading members of the Zagwé army and their followers appear to have left Lasta and moved northwards into Tigré.[2] There they joined forces with the Zagwé provincial officers and put up a hard resistance. In 1268, an interesting land grant to Däbrä Lībanos of Shīmäzana indicates that the Zagwé had crowned another king, Dilanda, and apparently organized themselves under a council of six military leaders.[3] Two years later, in 1270, another land grant to the same monastery is signed by 'King Yikwinat'[4] and all the various offices are held by a completely different group of people.

Yikunno-'Amlak founded a new Christian dynasty in the kingdom. Common resentment of Lasta domination probably brought him much support in Tigré, where the Amhara tradition of Tigré origin strengthened his position as against the Zagwé. The predominantly Agäw rulers of the Christian kingdom were deposed, and the throne was once again occupied by a Semitic-speaking monarch. Only in this sense was the advent of Yikunno-'Amlak a *restoration*.

the documents since the 14th century. Mugär Indabazé is mentioned in a slightly different form in 'Gädlä Samu'él (Wägäg)', MS. Däbrä Lībanos, f. 9[a]. There is also a reference to the 'chief of the seven Gwīdim' in 'Gädlä Märha-Kristos' MS. Däbrä Lībanos, pp. 28, 189. 'The people of Mwal' are mentioned in *Chroniques de Zar'a Ya'eqob*, ed. and tr. Perruchon, p. 83.

1 As has been already mentioned, the name of Yitbaräk had been systematically suppressed in the official hagiographical traditions. In the story of the struggle he is given an esoteric name and is simply called *Zä-Ilmäknun*, 'The Unknown, the hidden one'. In many cases his name Yitbaräk is also given; cf. Conti Rossini, 'La caduta della dinastia Zague', p. 299. In Lasta, however, the esoteric term has become a useful escape mechanism in denying that the king killed by Yikunno-'Amlak had anything to do with Lasta. Mägabī Tägägn vehemently stated that *Zä-Ilmäknun* was only a rebel in Wadla!

2 The Zagwa and Adkämä-Mälga in Eritrea have traditions of migration from Lasta as a result of an invasion from Shäwa, Conti Rossini, 'Studi su popolazioni dell'Etiopia', pp. 53–4, 60–1, 82 (extract).

3 Conti Rossini, 'L'Evangelo d'oro', p. 193. Together with the king's name there is a reference to 'the six strong men', which probably indicates a council of leading generals to conduct hostilities.

4 Ibid., p. 196. This curious form of the king's name also appears in another contemporary tradition, Cerulli, E., 'Il sultanato dello Scioa', pp. 13, 19.

CHAPTER III

Internal Conflict and Readjustment

(1285–1371)

MANY problems awaited the new dynasty founded by Yikunno-'Amlak. For more than ten years after the end of his reign, the most serious menace to the stability of the dynasty arose from the rivalries of his own sons and grandsons.[1] Yagba-Ṣiyon, who was probably his eldest son, seems to have already held a position of some authority before the death of his father.[2] Probably because of this, we do not have any traditions of succession problems on his accession to power. Nevertheless, there are clear indications of political unrest and internal conflict during the period of his reign (1285–94). In some of these conflicts the Ethiopian Church was also involved.

In 1290, some five years after his accession, Yagba-Ṣiyon wrote to the sultan of Egypt and to the patriarch of Alexandria requesting the appointment of a new Egyptian bishop. The letters[3] contain some interesting information about new developments which had taken place in the Ethiopian Church since the downfall of the Zagwé dynasty. Yagba-Ṣiyon complained to Patriarch John VII (1262–8; 1271–93) about the serious difficulties raised by the presence in Ethiopia of what he called 'Syrian metropolitans':

> These Syrian metropolitans who live in Ethiopia have provoked Our hate. Being uniquely attached to the patriarchate of Alexandria, We could not tolerate that these strangers exercise any longer the episcopal functions which they could enjoy until now only through the protection of Our father . . .[4]

[1] I have elsewhere examined the early traditions of these dynastic conflicts in my 'The Abbots of Däbrä Hayq 1248–1535', *Journal of Ethiopian Studies*, viii, no. 1, (1970), pp. 91–3.

[2] In a land grant given by Yikunno-'Amlak a certain Yagba-Ṣiyon is mentioned, immediately after the name of the king, as one of the officials of the royal court at the time of the grant, Conti Rossini, 'L'Evangelo d'oro di Dabra Libanos', in *RRAL*, ser. 5, vol. x (1901), p. 194. It seems likely that this Yagba-Ṣiyon was Yikunno-'Amlak's own son who succeeded him later.

[3] Quatremère, *Mémoires géographiques et historiques sur l'Égypte*, ii (1811), pp. 268–73.

[4] Ibid., p. 271.

No references to such Syrian prelates have yet come to light in the hagiographical and other clerical records of the Ethiopian Church itself. At the beginning of Yikunno-'Amlak's reign, in a land grant dated 1269/70, Abba Qérilos is mentioned as 'archbishop' of Ethiopia.[1] Three years later, probably because Qérilos had died in the meantime, Yikunno-'Amlak wrote to Sultan Baybars (1260–77) asking for a new bishop.[2] From the text of the letter it seems that Yikunno-'Amlak had put in an earlier request for the new bishop, and he had already been expecting his arrival in Ethiopia for some time. In his letter of 1273, Yikunno-'Amlak reminded the sultan that, although he had already received an envoy from the Mamluke governor of Kus, no bishop had come with this envoy as expected. Despite this second appeal, however, Yikunno-'Amlak did not succeed in obtaining a new bishop from Egypt. This may have induced him to look for a prelate from elsewhere.

Already in the lifetime of Patriarch Cyril III ibn Laqlaq (1235–43), there had arisen a quarrel among the Jacobites of the patriarchates of Alexandria and of Antioch. Before that time, it had been conventional for Antioch to appoint the Jacobite bishop for Jerusalem, whereas Alexandrian suzerainty on the Nubian and the Ethiopian Churches was never questioned by Antioch. However, Patriarch Cyril III seems to have used the growing military and political superiority of Egypt in appointing an Alexandrian bishop for the Jacobite church of Jerusalem. This angered the patriarch of Antioch, Ignatius II, who retaliated by appointing an Ethiopian pilgrim, Abba Tomas, as metropolitan of Ethiopia.[3] There is no evidence to show that Abba Tomas ever returned to his country to claim the episcopal seat. On the contrary, contemporary documents published by Cerulli seem to indicate that Patriarch Ignatius soon revoked his unusual appointment owing to strong pressure on him by the Dominicans in Palestine, who were anxious to please the Egyptian sultan.[4] Never-

[1] Conti Rossini, 'L'evangelo d'oro', p. 196. The title *Liqä-Papasat* which he bears here is rather unusual. But a bishop (= Papas) of the same name is also remembered elsewhere for the same period, *Gädlä Täklä-Haymanot*, ed. Conti Rossini, p. 104. 'Gädlä Zéna-Marqos', MS. Däbrä Lībanos, f. 7^{a}. 'Gädlä Qäwisṭos', MS. Däbrä Lībanos, ff. 44^{b}–48^{a}.

[2] Mufazzal ibn Abil-Fazal, *Histoire des sultans Mamlouks*, ed. and tr., Blochet, E., in *PO*, iv, pp. 353–87. Maqrizi, *Histoire des sultans Mamlouks*, tr. Quatremère ii, pt. 2, p. 122 n. 151.

[3] Renaudot, *Historia Patriarcharum Alexandrinorum*, p. 579. Neal, J. M., *History of the Patriarchate of Alexandria* (London, 1847), ii, p. 31. Cerulli, E., *Etiopi in Palestina*, i (1943), pp. 62–76.

[4] Ibid., pp. 66–8.

theless, Yagba-Ṣiyon's letters to Egypt[1] clearly indicate that the rivalry of the Alexandrian and Syrian Jacobites for the control of the Ethiopian Church had also reached Ethiopia, and by the time of the reigns of Yikunno-'Amlak and his son Yagba-Ṣiyon, the Ethiopians were apparently divided on the Syrian question.

In his letter of 1273/4, Yikunno-'Amlak says that a Mamluke delegation from Kus had come to his court 'about the monk who came to meet Us'.[2] It is not at all clear who this monk was or from where he had come to Ethiopia. But Yagba-Ṣiyon told Patriarch Yohannis in his letter of 1290 that his father, Yikunno-'Amlak, 'had no bishop of your choice in his court'.[3] This makes it most likely that Yikunno-'Amlak had accepted a prelate whom his son later called 'a Syrian metropolitan'. It is clear, however, that King Yikunno-'Amlak did not maintain 'the Syrians' in his court out of mere defiance of the Alexandrian patriarchate. He had repeatedly asked for a new Egyptian bishop who was never sent from Cairo. It is apparent from Yagba-Ṣiyon's letters that some clerics of Syrian origin had come to court with uncertain credentials and were accepted by Yikunno-'Amlak without the full consensus of the Ethiopian Church which had always been predominantly loyal to Alexandria. When doubts about the credentials were raised, Yikunno-'Amlak probably felt it unnecessary to refer the matter to Cairo, where his previous requests had been given only the slightest attention. Soon after his death, however, opposition to the 'Syrian' prelates had flared up once again, and the new king very wisely espoused the strong party still loyal to Alexandria. To offset the recurrence of similar uncertainties about the credentials of the new bishop, Yagba-Ṣiyon suggested to the sultan some precautionary measures:

> . . . I would like the new metropolitan to come to my kingdom accompanied by an ambassador of the sultan and my deputy. If the sultan, as I hope, accepts my request, his reply will calm the conflicts in Ethiopia and will bring peace both to the Muslims and the Christians . . .[4]

Thus, Yagba-Ṣiyon seems to have brought an end to the 'Syrian' interlude by a royal decree which prohibited the episcopal functions

[1] See p. 69, notes 3 and 4.

[2] Mufazzal, op. cit., p. 384.

[3] Quatremère, op. cit., p. 271. It also seems quite possible that, since the time of Patriarch Cyril III (1235–43), a Syrian, as well as an Egyptian, bishop was appointed for Ethiopia until 1290, cf. Hammerschmidt, E., 'L'Église Orthodoxe d'Éthiopie', in Gerster, G., *L'Art éthiopien* (1968), p. 43.

[4] Quatremère, op. cit., p. 269.

of the 'Syrian metropolitan' in Ethiopia.[1] But he did *not* succeed in obtaining a new Egyptian bishop. It is apparent that unrest among the clergy and their lay supporters continued to the end of his reign. This went on until the last struggle for power in which we find him engaged, with what appears to be another group of his own family. The incident is related in an interesting contemporary note in a manuscript (probably of the thirteenth century) of the library of Däbrä Hayq:

> I, Yagba-Ṣiyon, whose regnal name is Solomon, adorned this book of the Four Gospels and gave it to [the Church of St.] Stephen. After that, there came Yi'qäbännä and he wanted to take away my throne; but I defeated him and destroyed him with the power of Christ, my God.

This took place in A.D. 1293/4, and Yagba-Ṣiyon died soon afterwards.[2] But until the advent to power of Yagba-Ṣiyon's brother, Widim-Rä'ad, in 1299, the struggle for power among the descendants of Yikunno-'Amlak seems to have continued. This struggle for succession was so intense that the throne was occupied by five successive kings in the short period between the death of Yagba-Ṣiyon in 1294, and Widim-Rä'ad's accession to power in 1299. It was only from this last date onwards that the new 'Solomonic' dynasty regained its strength and internal stability.[3]

Consolidation of the dynasty in the north

The immediate result of these early conflicts was to weaken the power of the new dynasty within the Christian kingdom itself. At this stage of the history of the dynasty the most important parts of Christian Ethiopia consisted of Tigré, Lasta, and Amhara. As a result of Yikunno-'Amlak's successful revolt, Lasta had not only lost its primacy in the kingdom but also much of its leadership. This left Tigré and Amhara as the two outstanding parties in the Christian power structure. The claims by Yikunno-'Amlak and his Amhara troops of Tigré (Semitic) ancestry had been central in their movement against the Zagwé, and it is apparent that they got much support from the *Tigrīgna*-speaking population. In fact, it seems that a new cadre of local governors took over the leadership of Tigré immediately after Yikunno-'Amlak's accession to power.[4] The most

[1] Cf. p. 69 n. 4.
[2] Taddesse Tamrat, 'The Abbots of Däbrä Hayq', p. 92.
[3] Ibid., notes 27–31.
[4] Conti Rossini, 'L'evangelo d'oro', pp. 194, 196, 197–8, 199–200.

important among these new local leaders was the 'Governor of Intärta' who also held the titles of *Hasgwa* and *Aqabé-Ṣänṣän*. The latter title, 'Aqabé-Ṣänṣän', was apparently of ancient Aksumite origin, and gave a particular significance to the position of this official throughout Tigré.[1] Ingida-Igzī', who belonged to a local chiefly family,[2] held the office in the reign of Yikunno-'Amlak, and, like the king himself, he was also succeeded by his own son Täsfanä-Igzī'. It is apparent that in this initial period of the new dynasty, and especially at the time of the internal struggle of the sons and grandsons of Yikunno-'Amlak, the family of Ingida-Igzī' gathered a considerable influence in the area as a whole and held an almost independent power over its own province of Intärta in particular. In a land grant dated 1305, Täsfanä-Igzī' already refers to his province as 'my kingdom'.[3] Yagba-Ṣiyon and Widim-Rä'ad had little power to control the situation and were both apparently satisfied with a distant recognition by this family as King of Ethiopia. Only Amdä-Ṣiyon could muster enough strength to bring an end to this new development which threatened the unity of the Christian kingdom.

Before he turned his attention to Tigré, Amdä-Ṣiyon had accomplished his early campaigns against Hadya, Damot, and Gojjam, and his conquests in these regions[4] placed him in an excellent position to impose his will on his provincial governors. He commemorates his success in Tigré in a land grant to the island monastery of Däbrä Hayq: 'God delivered into my hands the ruler of Intärta with all his army, his followers, his relatives, and all his country as far as the Cathedral of Aksum.'[5]

The governor of Intärta at the time was Ya'ibīkä-Igzī', and his land grant of 1318/19 does not even mention the king. He apparently had a firm control of northern Tigré, and his following included both secular and clerical leaders in the area. The two influential abbots of Aksum and Däbrä Damo were among his prominent courtiers. There are also traditional indications that he had invited the governor of Tämbén to join him in his rebellion against Amdä-Ṣiyon.[6] He is

[1] During the formal coronation of Zär'a-Ya'iqob in Aksum, the governor of Tigré also held the title of Aqabé-Ṣänṣän (= the keeper of the fly whisks), Perruchon, J., *Les Chroniques de Zar'a Ya'eqob*, p. 50.

[2] He calls himself 'Son of Kul-Asgädé' in the land grant. This strongly suggests that the family already had a local importance before the dynastic change in 1270.

[3] Conti Rossini, op. cit., p. 199.

[4] See Ch. IV.

[5] Taddesse Tamrat, op. cit., n. 43.

[6] Wright, op. cit., Or. 695, ff. 38^{b}–40^{a}. Conti Rossini, 'Note di agiografia etiopica: Abīyä-Igzi', in *RSO*, xvii (1938), pp. 419–21.

said to have failed to enlist the support of this official, but it appears that his revolt was fairly well organized. Amdä-Ṣiyon's action against him and his followers was equally ruthless:

> . . . When Ya'ibīkä-Igzī' and Ingida-Igzī' rebelled, King Amdä-Ṣiyon decreed and deposed them, and destroyed these rebels. Moreover to eliminate the pride of their hearts and to efface their [traditional] honours, [the king] appointed over their country men who were not born from Adam and Eve who were called *Halästiyotat* . . .[1]

The multiple offices held by Ya'ibīkä-Igzī' and his predecessors were given to different individuals, and what appears to have been a military colony of troops from outside Tigré was stationed at Amba Sänayata, which was the centre of the rebellion. The king at first entrusted the office of the governor of Intärta to one of his own queens, Bilén-Saba, who was apparently herself of Tigré origin.[2] With her, a new group of subordinate officials was appointed for the various districts. The queen's administration of her province was probably indirect, and there is an early tradition of some local displeasure with her complete dependence on her local agents and advisers.[3] Probably because of this, one of the king's sons, Bahr-Sägäd, was soon given charge of a highly centralized administration in Tigré.[4] A new feature of this appointment in 1328 is the inclusion of the maritime provinces under the combined government of Amdä-Ṣiyon's son.

The term *Ma'ikälä-Bahr*, one of the titles held by this prince, probably referred to these maritime provinces, which apparently included the whole region between the Maräb and the Red Sea.[5] It has already been mentioned in the last chapter that the replacement

[1] *Liber Aksumae*, ed. and tr. Conti Rossini, pp. 30–1 (text). 'Halästiyotat' literally means 'bastards of mixed or low origins', and its use here certainly reflects the unpopularity of the military colony established by King Amdä-Ṣiyon.

[2] Conti Rossini, 'L'evangelo d'oro', pp. 204, 206. id., 'Racconti e canzoni bileni', in *Actes du 14ᵉ Congrès intern. des orient.*, Paris (1907), p. 335.

[3] Wright, op. cit., Or. 695, ff. 36–37[a].

[4] Conti Rossini, 'L'evangelo d'oro', p. 208.

[5] The title of *Ma'ikälä-Bahr* (lit. 'between the rivers or seas') was already used in the Zagwé period. Its application is very uncertain, and Conti Rossini has suggested that it could refer to either the region between the Täkkazé and the Red Sea or the Maräb, ibid, pp. 190, 194, 208. The limitation of the term 'Bahr' to mere rivers in such a pompous title is improbable, and *Ma'ikälä-Bahr* was apparently a title held by officials whose special duties concerned relations with the coastal areas and their immediate hinterland. It was probably the precursor of the title *Bahr-Nägash*, cf. Perruchon, J., *Histoire des guerres d'Amdä-Ṣiyon*, p. 293 (text); *Acta Sancti Mercuri*, ed. and tr. Conti Rossini, p. 26 (text).

of the Zagwé by the new Amhara dynasty had sparked off a series of population movements from the Lasta region to north-eastern Tigré, Akälä-Guzay, Hamasén, and Sära'é.[1] This had resulted in a struggle for power between the newcomers and the original inhabitants, and in the eventual transfer of political supremacy from the Christian Bäläw tribes to the Adkämä-Mälga who constituted a major part of the new Christian settlers in the area. The Bäläw tribes were of Béja origin, and before the end of the thirteenth century they dominated the region of the Eritrean plateau, including probably some of the districts south of the Märäb also. Their downfall at the hands of the Adkämä-Mälga created a new power vacuum in the area, and gave their former vassals a last chance to assert their independence before the Adkämä-Mälga consolidated their power. It is about this time that the traditions of the Christian tribes of Däqī-Mīnab indicate an intensive period of territorial expansion from their traditional centre of Gishnashim, north-west of Asmara.

They have a tradition that their ancestors originally came from Dämbya, north of Lake Ṭana.[2] However, a close examination of this tradition shows a rather recent formulation, and it appears that the Däqī-Mīnab were probably one of the original inhabitants of the Eritrean plateau, no doubt considerably affected by fresh population movements from the north and south.[3] Like all the other tribes around them, they were under the general political supremacy of the Bäläw.[4] Between the end of the thirteenth century, and in the first years of the fourteenth some branches were moving into what are today the districts of Garnashim, Dämbälas, and Akälä-Guzay, and already in 1328 two officials in Hamasén are mentioned among the influential local rulers.[5] The present tribal configuration of the rest of the Eritrean plateau was also taking shape about the same time. In the narrow lowland strip to the east, representatives of the Hazo-Teroa group of the Saho had already moved northwards into Samhar, and further inland on the plateau to form the Mänsa and

[1] See p. 68 n. 2.

[2] Kolmodin, *Traditions de Tsazzega et Hazzega*, Tr. 5, Tr. 7–Tr. 8. These traditions, like many others in north Ethiopia, are closely related to the legend of the queen of Sheba. Mīnab, the ancestor of the Däqī-Mīnab, is said to have been one of the companions of Menelik I on his way to Ethiopia from Jerusalem.

[3] Conti Rossini, 'Schizzo etnico e storico delle popolazioni eritree' in *L'Eritrea economica* (Novara, 1913), pp. 78–9. 'Studi su popolazioni dell'Etiopia' in *RSO* iii–vi (1910–1913), p. 2 (Extract).

[4] Kolmodin, op. cit., Tr. 6.

[5] Conti Rossini, 'L'evangelo d'oro', p. 209.

Marya aristocracies immediately to the north of the area occupied by the Bogos (or Bilén) people.[1] Except in the coastal strip, where the predominantly Saho population were under the increasing religious influence of Islam, all the sundry tribes in the plateau were Christians. The most important Muslim influence in the region came from the small sultanate of the Dahlak archipelago. Although the Christian inhabitants in the plateau maintained their old commercial relations with the Muslims, the Christian kingdom had long lost its direct control of the coast. The military colonies established on the way to the ancient port of Adulīs had already been disrupted by the northward movements of the Saho.[2] But this had only been a measure of the internal weakness of the Christian kingdom, and did not at all represent an organized attempt at Muslim expansion. The situation basically characterizes the relative position of Islam and Christianity in northern Ethiopia since the eighth century A.D. Although the presence of Islam in the Dahlak islands—by far the earliest and most important Muslim centre on the Eritrean seaboard—is well attested since the first century of the *Hijrah*, its influence as a base for the propagation of Islam into the interior remained minimal until the end of the period covered by this work. Only a section of the Saho nomads, wandering about in the lowland strip, could be affected in a religious sense; the inhabitants of the plateau were Christian, and even most of the people of the Samhar were either still Christian or pagan, as late as the fourteenth century. The political and economic importance of the Muslim settlements on the mainland and in the islands nearby had nevertheless been much more significant than their missionary value for Islam.

Just as in the southern provinces of Shäwa, Īfat, and Hadya, Amdä-Ṣiyon was deeply concerned about the dangers of the development of Muslim power on the Eritrean seaboard. He fully realized that the restoration of Christian supremacy in the Ethiopian region would only be complete if its impact was felt by the coastal Muslim settlements. His recent campaigns against the Muslims of Īfat and

[1] On his way to Jerusalem about 1337 Éwosṭatéwos is said to have visited first the Bogos, and then 'the two Marya', *Gädlä Éwosṭatéwos*, pp. 72–3. Despite this, however, Conti Rossini estimates that the formation of the Mänsa and Marya aristocracies was 'verso la seconda metà del secolo XIV', 'Tradizioni storiche dei Mensa' in *GSAI*, xiv, 1901, p. 43. Cf. also, id., 'Studi su popolazioni dell'Etiopia', p. 6 (extract).

[2] Conti Rossini, 'Al Ragali', in *Boll. Soc. Ital. d'esplor. geog. e comm.* (1904), fasc. II, p. 22. id. 'Studi su popolazioni dell'Etiopia', pp. 4–5.

eastern Shäwa were doubtless resented by their co-religionists in the north, who may have co-operated with the rebellious army in northern Tigré. This may have furnished Amdä-Ṣiyon with the immediate reasons for his expedition in the Eritrean region: 'I, King Amdä-Ṣiyon, went to the sea of Eritrea. When I reached there, I mounted on an elephant and entered the sea. I took up my arrow and spears, killed my enemies, and saved my people.'[1] There is also a reference to this successful expedition in the hagiographical traditions about the life of Éwosṭatéwos, whose monastic activities in Särа'é about the same time inaugurated a parallel revival of the Ethiopian Church in the Eritrean region.[2]

The major obstacles to a much bolder action against the coastal Muslims and the Saho nomads had always arisen from the internal weakness of the kingdom itself and, unlike the regions south of Amhara, they seem to have offered little resistance to the revival of Christian power over them. This was considerably promoted by the absence of a united front among the Muslim powers of the Red Sea area. Since the emergence of the Rasulid dynasty of Yemen, Egypt had lost direct control of its south Arabian province with the strategic port of Aden. Yemen was in fact becoming a strong rival of Mamluke Egypt in the control of the Red Sea trade.[3] Relations between the two states were very tense and the kings of Yemen showed no more than an attitude of formal respect to the superior force of Cairo. In the last two reigns of the Mamluke sultan Al-Nasir

[1] For the full text of this contemporary historical note, see my 'The Abbots of Däbrä Hayq', pp. 95–6. It is interesting to note that a similar use of an elephant was made by the king of Yemen in A.D. 1309 during a visit to the coast, on the opposite side of the Red Sea: 'The supreme Cortege proceeded to the Sea of 'Ehwa'd, the sea coast of Zebid . . . [the sultan] mounted an elephant when he entered Faza . . .', Al-Khazraji, *History of the Resuliyy Dynasty of Yemen*, ed. and tr. Redhouse, J. W., III, i, p. 288.

[2] *Gädlä Éwosṭatéwos*, p. 53. The passage has hitherto been completely neglected and was apparently thought of as a mere clerical eulogy of the king. But the essential basis of the tradition—i.e. Amdä-Ṣiyon's personal campaigns in Eritrea—finds an important confirmation in the contemporary historical reference quoted in the last footnote. The wording of the passage is however hagiographical in character: '(The king) travelled from sea to sea, from one end of the Eritrean sea to the other, fighting the infidels who are strong and who put their trust on astrological divinations; and he defeated the enemies of Christ and reduced his enemies with the power of God . . .' Éwosṭatéwos is also said to have met the king, ibid., pp. 52–4. This probably took place when the court was in northern Ethiopia. Éwosṭatéwos was in Armenia when the king died in 1344, and he is said to have been deeply upset by the news, ibid., p. 108.

[3] Wiet, G., 'Les marchands d'épices sous les sultans Mamlouks', in *CHÉ*, vii (1955), p. 88.

Muhammad b. Qalawun, there were very clear attempts at the reconquest of Yemen. On one of these occasions, in 1307, the king of Yemen 'prohibited the spice-merchants' until Egypt undertook to stop warlike preparations at the Nile river port of Kus, where ships were being built for the invasion of Yemen.[1] An uneasy peace was apparently concluded, and the spice trade continued to flow to the Egyptian dominions via Yemen. But the occasional arrival of large numbers of Egyptian troops for the annual pilgrimage to Mecca, which was still in Egyptian hands, brought fresh dangers of an ultimate confrontation between the two powers. The king of Yemen was at one time (in A.D. 1352) carried away to Cairo and detained there for fourteen months.[2]

The special concern of the Mamluke sultans of Egypt with the uninterrupted flow of the eastern trade also brought them into conflict with the unruly Arab and Béja tribes inhabiting the desert area between 'Aydab and the Nile river ports of Aswan and Kus. In A.D. 1316/17, these nomads attacked a Yemenite delegation and a number of merchants on their way to Cairo from 'Aydab. The sultan sent a punitive force against them, which had only a temporary success. Only three years later, in A.D. 1319/20, the Arabs and their Béja allies sacked 'Aydab itself and killed the Egyptian inspector stationed there. A stronger force was now sent, and 'Aydab was more effectively annexed. A Mamluke governor was stationed there with an impressive garrison to deal with any future recurrence of local revolt.[3] Further south, the island of Suakin was similarly dealt with,[4] and a distant but nevertheless dependent political relationship created between the rulers of the island and Egypt. In 1316/17 the island sultanate demonstrated its Mamluke loyalties by co-operating with the Egyptian army in pursuit of the tribesmen who had attacked 'Aydab.[5]

[1] Al-Khazraji, *History of the Resuliyy Dynasty of Yemen*, iii, pt. 1, pp. 285–6. Cf. Wiet, G., op. cit., p. 93. Sultan Al-Nasir of Egypt reigned on three occasions, 1293–4, 1298–1308, 1309–40. His reign was one of the most prosperous periods of Egyptian history, Wiet, G., *L'Égypte arabe 642–1517*, pp. 489–90; Hitti, P., *History of the Arabs* (ed. 1961) pp. 679–81.

[2] Al-Khazraji, op. cit., iii, pt. 2, pp. 27–9; 69–75; 100.

[3] Quatremère, *Mémoires*, ii, pp. 170–1. Cf. also Hasan, Yusuf Fadl, *The Arabs and the Sudan*, pp. 78–9.

[4] Ibid., pp. 84–5.

[5] The Mamluke army of 500 used a roundabout route on that occasion; starting from Kus they went to 'Aydab, thence to Suakin and then south-westwards. They crossed the Atbara, went a distance of three days' journey up-stream where they met the Halengo tribe which offered a weak resistance. From thence

The Dahlak islands were even less relevant than Suakin to the eastern trade, and the Mamluke sultans had nothing to fear from them. A mere diplomatic warning in 1265/6 had sufficed to stop anti-Egyptian piratical activities based in these islands.[1] This cautious attitude of the inhabitants of Dahlak towards the growing power of the Mamlukes in the Red Sea completely precluded Egyptian intervention, and helped them to preserve their complete independence from direct Egyptian overlordship. But it also weakened their position *vis-à-vis* a strong Christian power in the Ethiopian hinterland. While the ports of Baḍi, 'Aydab, and Suakin had always depended for their existence on trade with the interior of what is today the eastern Sudan and the Nile valley, the Dahlak islands had likewise succeeded ancient Adulīs on the Eritrean seaboard, and their *raison d'être* consisted of their commercial relations with the Ethiopian plateau.[2] But, unlike their northern counterparts, they did not serve as points of Arab penetration into the interior, nor did they lead to the development of Muslim communities of any political significance in northern Ethiopia. The Arab tribes who poured into the hinterlands of Baḍi, 'Aydab, and Suakin, had been lured by the mines of gold and emeralds for which the region had long been held in repute.[3] The hinterland of Dahlak did not offer such possibilities. The very rough physical characteristics of the edge of the plateau overlooking the narrow coastal strip opposite the Dahlak archipelago also kept the interior much more inaccessible than in the region north of Ras Kassar. But the most important reason for the considerable limitation of Muslim expansion in northern Ethiopia is to be sought in the strength of the Church, even when the central power of the kingdom had reached its lowest ebb. The region of northern Ethiopia centring round Aksum and the monastic establishments of the nine saints had long been the cradle of Ethiopian Christendom—since the mid fourth century, in fact—and its religious character long survived the political decline of the Christian kingdom. We have already seen how the Béja contributed to the decline of Aksum for whose political supremacy in the region of the Barka-Ansäba basin they had largely

they travelled back down the Atbara to the Nile, and thence to Cairo via Dongola and Kus, ibid., pp. 77–8.

[1] Al-Khowayter, Abdul Aziz, 'A Critical edition of an unknown source of the life of al-Malik al-Zahir Baibars', Ph.D. Thesis (London University, 1960), i, p. 285, ii, p. 498, Cf. also Hasan, op. cit. p. 75.

[2] Crowfoot, J. W., 'Some Red Sea Ports', in *GJ*, vol. xxxvii (1911), pp. 547–8.

[3] Quatremère, op. cit., p. 141. Hasan, op. cit., pp. 50–63.

substituted their own. In so doing, however, they were in time linguistically and even ethnically assimilated, so that by the end of the thirteenth century, the Bäläw princes of the Eritrean region were apparently Christian and spoke either Tigrä or Tigrīgna.[1] Indeed, during occasional periods of revival in the Christian kingdom they were even brought under its political overlordship, and by the middle of the thirteenth century the Bäläw governors of what are today the provinces of Särä'é and Hamasén seem to have been under the suzerainty of the Zagwé kings.[2] Despite the vicissitudes of the central power of the kingdom, therefore, the Christian character of northern Ethiopia was preserved throughout the centuries after the advent of Islam. As we have suggested above this development was further enhanced by the economic dependence of the islands of Miṣiwwa and Dahlak on their Christian hinterland, and their solitary political position in relation to other Muslim countries in the Red Sea area. Until they were finally annexed by the Ottomans in the second half of the sixteenth century, these islands remained in the backwaters of Muslim expansion, and their only importance to the Muslim world lay in serving as the outlet for the products of the Christian hinterland. Their value to the Christian kingdom also consisted in maintaining the long-distance commercial contact with the Muslim powers of Egypt and Arabia who firmly controlled the profitable trade of the Red Sea. In the final analysis, it was the need to share in this lucrative traffic between the Ethiopian interior and the Red Sea which provided Amdä-Ṣiyon with sufficient economic reasons to demonstrate his military prowess in the Eritrean region.

Trade and trade routes

It is significant that Amdä-Ṣiyon conducted this expedition immediately after his punitive campaigns against the rebellious governor of Intärta in northern Tigré. In these northern provinces as well as in the very rich areas south of Amhara, the king's military activities were essentially motivated by economic considerations. It is quite clear that his aim was to bring the network of trade routes in the whole Ethiopian region under his own control. From a close study of secular and hagiographical traditions, it is possible to determine the major routes which traversed the country in the fourteenth

[1] Conti Rossini, *Etiopia e genti d'Etiopia*, pp. 45, 126–9.

[2] The Bäläw rulers who were displaced later by the Adkämä-Mälga were subjects of the Christian kingdom, Conti Rossini, 'Studi su popolazioni dell'Etiopia' pp. 82–3. Cf. also Kolmodin, *Traditions de Tsazzega et Hazzega*, Tr. 6, 25, A. 29.

century. Since the emergence of the new dynasty, and particularly after the conquests of Amdä-Ṣiyon in the first two decades of the century, the heart of the Christian kingdom had consisted of the high ridge forming the watershed of the rivers Nile and Awash. On

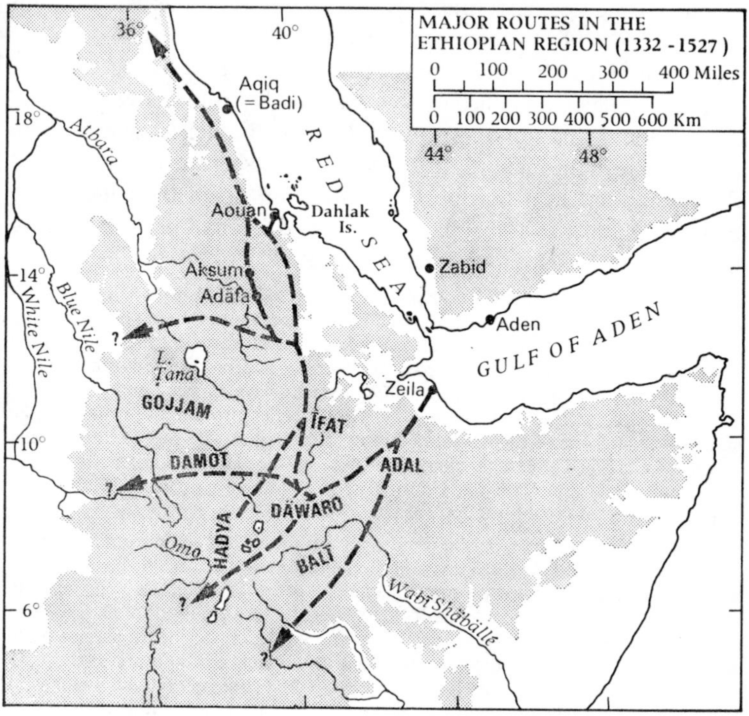

MAP 3.

this central crescent, stretching from the river Bashīlo in Amhara to the headwaters of Mugär and Awash in the Shäwan plateau, converged all the major routes coming from different directions.

From the northern provinces came two more or less parallel routes. The first of these ran from Lalībäla, the capital of the Zagwé dynasty, northwards across the difficult country of Lasta and Wag, across the river Ṣällärī, and apparently through the western parts of the Tigré districts of Tämbén and Gär'alta to the region of Aksum. From there it continued northwards across the river Märäb to Süra'é, Hamasén, Bogos, and Marya, whence, passing through the district of Bäqla, it merged with the Suakin–Nile caravan routes.[1]

[1] A combination of itineraries point to this route. Abba Aron travelled part of

This road appears to have been most popular during the Zagwé period, when the province of Lasta was the focus of political and commercial activities. But it traversed extremely difficult country and, already before the end of the Lasta dynasty, it was giving way to the second of the northern routes, which cut through the whole length of the kingdom from the region east of the upper course of the river Märäb in Hamasén and Bur, via eastern Tigré, the Doba country, Angot, Amhara, and further south to the Shäwan plateau.[1] At its northern end this route apparently had two branches: one of these joined up with the main route to Suakin somewhere around Asmara;[2] the other went in a north-easterly direction down the edge of the Eritrean plateau to a mainland port called 'Aouan probably facing the island of Miṣiwwa.[3]

it from Tämbén to Lalībala soon after A.D. 1341, *Gädlä Aron*, pp. 133–4. Yafqīrännä-Igzī' (in the beginning of the 14th century) and Samu'él after him, probably followed this route right from Aksum southwards on their way to the Lake Ṭana region. The northern part of this road was used by Éwosṭatéwos on his way to Egypt in about A.D. 1337, *Gädlä Éwosṭatéwos* pp. 62–3, 72–3, 78–9, 83; Conti Rossini, *Storia d'Etiopia*, p. 255. His disciples probably returned on the same route and one of them, Gäbrä-Īyäsus, travelled all the way to Infraz, east of Lake Ṭana, via Tigré, most likely also via Wag (his place of origin according to some traditions) and Lalībäla, Conti Rossini, 'Note di agiografia . . . Gäbrä-Īyäsus,' *RSO*, xvi (1938), pp. 441, 444.

1 Already in the Zagwé period there is a tradition of this route from Shäwa via Mänz, Amhara, and Angot. Here a branch left north-eastwards to Lalībäla, and another went directly northwards through Angot to E. Tigré, a road already frequented by the salt traders, 'Gädlä Qäwisṭos', ff. 54, 57. Fīlipos of Däbrä Asbo was banished to Tigré in 1341 along this route, of which the identity seems quite secure by the mention of the pass of Qorqwara, which also appears in the 1454 map *Egyptus Novelo* at precisely the same spot: 'the country of the nomads who were pagans and killed all men they encountered'—an unmistakable reference to the Doba people, *Gädlä Fīlipos*, pp. 219–20. Cf. also Crawford, op. cit., p. 14. Abba Aron also seems to have gone to Tigré via this road, described as 'the road of Angot', *Gädlä Aron*, p. 133. On his way back, he took the western route as mentioned in the last footnote. It is most likely that after the beginning of the Amhara dynasty the 'road of Angot' became increasingly important as the easiest and most direct route to the north. Amdä-Ṣiyon's troops, and those of his descendants, moving to Tigré and Eritrea and vice-versa, doubtless used it. It is to this route that Al-'Umari refers, *Masalik*, pp. 19–20. It is precisely this route, which ran, as it were, along the backbone of the kingdom, that is most carefully plotted in medieval maps of the Christian kingdom, and most frequently mentioned in the available itineraries. Cf. Crawford, op. cit., pp. 14, 21, 42–5.

2 This is represented by the Latin itinerary of the anonymous traveller who visited Ethiopia in the reign of King Dawīt (1380–1412), Jorga, N., 'Cenni sulle relazioni tra l'Abissinia e l'Europa cattolica nei secoli XIV–XV con un itinerario inedito del secolo XV' in *Centenario Michele Amari* (Palermo, 1910), pp. 146–7. Crawford, op. cit. pp. 28–39.

3 Ibn Said (1214–74) gives the best description of 'Aouan which was already Muslim in his time, Aboul Feda, *Géographie*, p. 212. Mufazzal also mentions it as

Another major route ran inland from the port of Zeila. This appears to have been the most important direction of Islamic penetration in the Ethiopian region, and already before the mid fourteenth century all the Muslim settlements were known in Egypt and Syria by the collective name of 'the Country of Zeila'.[1] The main road ran in a south-westerly direction, traversed the districts around the present sites of Harär and Dirédawa,[2] and continued eastwards, probably keeping on the northern side of the range of mountains which divide the basins of the Awash and the Shäbällé rivers.[3] As it approached the Awash crossing, it probably divided into two: one branch went in a south-westerly direction to Däwaro,[4] the other crossed the Awash, and then branched off once again into two main roads. One of these proceeded in a slightly north-easterly direction[5] across difficult

an Abyssinian port, north of the district of Sahart, and from which the main route to Amhara started, *Histoire des sultans Mamlouks*, p. 223. Amdä-Ṣiyon's expedition to the coast probably took this road. After the establishment of the monastery of Bīzän in A.D. 1388/9 the community kept its commercial relations with Miṣiwwa and Dahlak along this route, *Gädlä Fīlipos* (Bīzän), p. 106.

[1] Al-'Umari, op. cit. p. 4.

[2] A group of Muslim tombstones with Arabic inscriptions have been found at Chälänqo and Lasto, west of Harär, Azais, R. P., and Chambard, R., *Cinq Années de recherches archéologiques en Éthiopie*, pp. 125, 129. Two of the inscriptions of Lasto bear the dates A.D. 1267/8 and 1276, ibid., pp. 288–91, 308.

[3] This seems to be clear from the striking similarity between the geographical conditions of the itineraries of Amdä-Ṣiyon in his campaign against Adal in A.D. 1332 and those of Ahmad Gragn in his invasion of the Christian kingdom two centuries later, cf. especially Perruchon, J., *Histoire des guerres d'Amdä-Ṣiyon*, pp. 317, 432; Basset, R. (tr.), *Futuh al-Habasha*, pp. 84, 94. Both armies moved in the semi-desert regions on the north side of the Harär plateau.

[4] It was apparently along this branch of the eastern route on his return march from Adal, and immediately after his visit to Biqulzär, that Amdä-Ṣiyon led his punitive expeditions against the people of Däwaro and Sarka, who had been harassing his line of communications while he was in Adal, Perruchon, op. cit., pp. 432–8. Ahmad Gragn was also camping at Biqulzär, about two days east of the river Awash, when he explained to his generals '. . . the route to Däwaro is nearby and here is another route which will take us to the city of the Christian dog Wänag-Sägäd'. Basset, R., op. cit., p. 174.

[5] Säbrädīn apparently fled to Däwaro along this route in 1332, and the Christian army sent against him in Īfat probably travelled the same way to join Amdä-Ṣiyon east of the Awash, Perruchon, op. cit., pp. 290–1,302–3. Gragn's first raid on the kingdom west of the Awash was also conducted along this route and his army penetrated as far as Gindäbällo, Basset, op. cit., pp. 53–66. This is doubtless the route to Zeila reported in 1523 by 'Brother Antonio', Crawford, op. cit., pp. 173–5. Crawford identified this with a roundabout route from Zeila via Aussa to Gindäbällo, ibid., pp. 95–6, and fig. 20. This was based on his assumption that Genasere may have been in Aussa. But 'Djanasir' was a place in the Harär region, probably further east, Basset, op. cit., p. 146. The climatic descriptions in Zorzi's notes fit the area perfectly.

country in the eastern slopes of the Shäwan plateau to the Muslim principality of Īfat. The second branch probably passed near Mount Fäntalé, and climbed the plateau directly westwards.[1]

Other routes doubtless connected the Christian kingdom westwards with Damot,[2] and southwards with Guragé-land and with Hadya.[3] It is also apparent that some branches of the eastern route from Zeila proceeded in a south-westerly direction to eastern Däwaro, Balī, and further inland to Hadya and the lake region. It is most likely that these different roads branched off from the main route somewhere around the Harär–Dirédawa region and served as the lines of further penetration into the interior of south-eastern Ethiopia, where small and mutually independent Muslim settlements had already been flourishing in the first half of the fourteenth century.[4]

These were the life-lines of the Ethiopian region, and much of the

[1] This was apparently the road Amdä-Ṣiyon himself took in his 1332 campaigns when he is clearly said to have followed 'le chemin de droite', Perruchon, op. cit., p. 340. In the area between the edge of the plateau and Mount Fäntalé the community of Abba Qäwisṭos at Nibgé was consolidating its religious influence, and the same route was probably used in the local Christian–Muslim conflicts preserved in the hagiographical traditions, 'Gädlä Qäwisṭos', ff. 94–101[a]. Ahmad Gragn's forces used this route on their way to Badaqe on the eve of the battle of Shimbra-Kuré in 1529, Basset, op. cit., pp. 95–116. All these three branches of the eastern route to Zeila are vividly described by an Ethiopian chronicler in his report of the flight of the Christian troops after Gragn's first success against Dägälhan in Hubat, '. . . [there were some] who went on the route to Däwaro, [others] on the route to Fäṭägar, [others] on the route to Īfat and Gidim . . .', Conti Rossini, 'Storia di Libna Dingil re d'Etiopia', in *RRAL*, ser. 5, vol. iii (1894), p. 637.

[2] In Amdä-Ṣiyon's campaigns to Damot no itineraries are given. Among the provinces of the Kingdom in 1332 Damot, 'Arab (= Warab?), Indägäbṭan, Wage (= Wäj?), Mugär are enumerated, Perruchon, op. cit., p. 280. From the hagiographical traditions about the 14th century access to Damot also seems to have been via the region where the rivers Mugär, Awash, and Gudär have their headwaters. The military colonies in this region were most likely connected with the protection of this western route to the rich province of Damot.

[3] Alamale (= Aymellel) in northern Guragé-land is specially mentioned as one of the southern provinces of the kingdom in 1332, Perruchon, op. cit., p. 280. It may be that it was via this district that Amdä-Ṣiyon's campaigns against Hadya were conducted. See Ch. IV. In the beginning of the 16th century Alvarez witnessed royal troops passing to and from Hadya precisely in this direction, *The Prester John of the Indies*, pp. 427, 430, 434–6.

[4] See Ch. IV. Zeila was the port used by all, and this common dependence on the eastern route gave the users some measure of unity. According to Al-'Umari, Īfat, which controlled Zeila and the main route, enjoyed some kind of political supremacy over them, op. cit., pp. 5, 19. There are later references to direct routes from Hadya via Däwaro and Balī to the Harär region. Perruchon, *Chroniques de Zara Ya'eqob*, pp. 17–21, 58–60. The same routes were also used by the invading army of Ahmad Gragn, Basset, R., *Futuh al-Habasha* (tr.), pp. 132–70.

conflict between the Muslims and the Christians on the one hand, and the local princes and the royal court on the other, involved the control of the commercial traffic conducted along these major routes. Yikunno-'Amlak seems to have drawn much of his success in the dynastic struggle from his apparently very close contact with the Muslim merchant communities in Amhara and Shäwa.[1] His grandson, Amdä-Ṣiyon, translated this economic co-operation into strict political and military dominance and soon emerged as the richest and most powerful single ruler in the Ethiopian region.

Between his accession to power in 1314 and the Muslim wars in 1332 Amdä-Ṣiyon's energetic campaigns throughout the country had brought him full control of the different trade routes and the interior provinces which they served. His most important demand on the Muslim communities was to recognize his overlordship as 'the king of all the Muslim realms of Ethiopia'.[2] In economic terms this meant a complete freedom on his part to participate in, and to control, their lucrative commercial activities. It is clear that already before 1332 the king was not only levying tribute and taxes on his Muslim subjects but he had also organized a strong commercial concern of his own. One of his grievances against Säbrädīn of Īfat in 1332 was the latter's interference with the royal caravans operating along the eastern route: 'You took away the commodities belonging to me obtained in exchange for the large quantity of gold and silver I had entrusted to the merchants. And you imprisoned the traders who did business for me.'[3] Many of the Muslim traders 'did business' for him,[4] and their tributes to his treasury consisted of the items of trade they obtained from Egypt, Yemen, and Iraq[5].

Evidence for the exact nature of the items of trade is very hard to come by. But some general conclusions can be formed. An essential basis for the commercial activities of the Muslim traders in the Ethiopian region seems to have been the supply of domestic slaves

[1] See p. 126.

[2] Perruchon, op. cit., p. 304 (text).

[3] Ibid., pp. 298 (text), 344 (tr). Perruchon did not understand the passage very well. He could not see the obvious mistake made by the copyist in writing the word *Nädayan* for *Nägadyan* which makes all the difference between 'the poor' and 'merchants'. Even in the altered text, however, there is the word for 'sale' at the end of the sentence which is simply omitted by Perruchon in his translation.

[4] Ibid., pp. 304 (text), 348 (tr.). Here again Perruchon missed the point about trade contained in the passage to which Huntingford has recently done more justice, *The Glorious Victories of Amda-Siyon* (1965), p. 67.

[5] Al-'Umari, op. cit., p. 2.

to the Near and Middle East. Ethiopian slaves were highly priced in the Muslim world,[1] whither they were transported in considerable numbers through the principal ports of Dahlak[2] and Zeila. It appears that they were originally obtained from all of the non-Muslim districts, and cases of Sahart (= Tigré) and Amhara slaves are reported in Yemen.[3] With the revival of Christian political power, the number of Christian men and women thus taken for export into Arabia must have been drastically reduced. But even after 1270, isolated cases of Christians being carried away are available in many traditions.[4] It was mainly from among the pagan communities, however, that most of the slaves were obtained.

Hadya was an important centre of trade in the south. Ibn Said (1214–74) was the earliest Arab writer to mention the place as such, and he mentioned it in connection with the slave trade.[5] Here the slaves collected in the surrounding area were prepared for exportation. Many of them were rendered eunuchs at a neighbouring place called Washilu,[6] and brought to Hadya for medical treatment, after

[1] Aboul Feda, *Géographie*, p. 226. Al-'Umari, op. cit., pp. 30–1.

[2] It seems that this island port supplied particularly Yemen with Nubian and Ethiopian slaves. It is reported for the year A.D. 976 that an annual supply of 1,000 slaves, of whom half were Ethiopian and Nubian females, used to be sent to the Ziyadite rulers of Yemen, Umarah, *Yaman, its Early Medieval History*, ed. and tr. Kay, H. C., 1892, pp. 8, 143. The practice probably continued even after the fall of the Ziyadites when the 'Habesh slaves' exercised power in the coastal strip of Yemen for an almost unbroken period of over a century (A.H. 409–533). ibid., pp. 15–16, 81–93.

[3] Ibid., pp. 15, 104, 117. Faraj as-Sharti and Surur as-Amhari ruled one after the other as Wazirs of Zebid between A.D. 1133 and 1157. Another tribe represented as having come from the Ethiopian region is called *Jazali* and furnished the Banu Najah slave dynasty of Yemen, ibid., p. 96. In a short list of Ethiopian tribes Dimashqi also has 'the *Djazl* who are renowned for their beautiful physique', *Manuel de la cosmographie du Moyen Âge*, tr. Mehren, M. A. F., 1874, pp. 388–9. Dimashqi's *Djazl* may be the same as Umarah's *Jazali*, which is otherwise unidentifiable.

[4] Perruchon, op. cit., p. 314 (text). Some time before 1337, Abba Éwosṭatéwos is said to have quarrelled with his fellow countrymen of Sära'é, whom he blamed for 'the sale of Christians', *Gädlä Éwosṭatéwos*, p. 35. Occasional raids also seem to have affected the Ethiopian anchorites in Waldibba. *Gädlä Samuél*, p. 24. Wright, *Catalogue*, Or. 695, f. 51[a]. The security of the young community of Bīzän was overshadowed by the slave-lifting practices of the coastal Muslims in the lifetime of its first two abbots, *Il 'Gadla Filippos' e il 'Gadla Yohannes' di Bizan*, ed. Conti Rossini, pp. 106, 144. There are also later traditions of miracles about Christian slaves thus taken away, *Gli atti di Abuna Yonas*, ed. and tr. Conti Rossini, pp. 240–3, 245–7. It is most interesting, however, that all these incidents refer to frontier areas.

[5] Aboul Feda, op. cit., p. 229.

[6] Ibn Said does not name the place and only calls it 'a nearby village', loc. cit. The name is first given by Al-'Umari, op. cit., p. 16. It was probably south of

which they were sent to Zeila.[1] It is apparent that the region south of the organized states of Damot, Hadya, and Balī was a particularly rich field for continuous slave raids undertaken by the Muslim merchants and their local partners. Large-scale wars of conquest such as those of King Amdä-Ṣiyon also yielded great numbers of slaves.

Some hagiographical traditions tend to rule out Christian participation in the slave trade, which is considered to have been an exclusively Muslim affair. At one place a group of Muslims converted to the Church are made to say: 'We no longer sell slaves . . . (like the Muslims) . . . after being baptized in the name of Christ.'[2] This probably represented some monastic reservations about slavery in general.[3] But in fact many Christian families, including those of the local saints, had numerous slaves.[4] Gifts of slaves were even made to prominent monks.[5] The numerous captives taken during military campaigns were usually reduced to slavery. The terms used by Amdä Ṣiyon's chroniclers in describing his successes clearly indicate that slave-raiding was an important by-product of many of his campaigns: 'He went to the country of Hadya and killed [many of] the people of that land . . . and the rest he made captives with their king, great [men] and small, men and women, old and young, and transported them into his kingdom.'[6]

Of the destination of such captives of war Amdä-Ṣiyon is made to say elsewhere: 'I exiled them into another country.'[7] A large part of these was doubtless attached to the royal court itself and furnished new recruits for the king's army. Many of them ended in private families, and it is most likely that others passed into the hands of Muslim merchants engaged in the long-distance trade. In this period

Hadya but no specific identification is now possible. The best is still Arab Faqih's '*Washiloh*, in the frontiers of Ganz', an area which was to the south-west of Hadya in the 16th century, *Futuh al-Habasha*, tr. Basset, p. 201 and n. 5. Cf. also pp. 83 n. 2, 377–90.

[1] Al-'Umari, op. cit., pp. 16–17. Maqrizi, *Historia Regum Islamaticorum in Abyssinia*, pp. 14–15.

[2] 'Gädlä Zéna-Marqos', MS. Däbrä Ṣigé, f. 69ᵃ.

[3] Such reservations are apparent in some scattered references, Wright, *Catalogue*, Or. 719, f. 44ᵃ. *Gädlä Yafqirännä-Igzī'*, pp. 82–6 (text). *Gädlä Éwosṭatéwos*, p. 35.

[4] Abundant references show this. Together with his ownership of 300 beehives, the father of Abba Märha-Kristos (d. 1492) was noted for his numerous slaves, 'Gädlä Märha-Kristos', MS. Däbrä Lībanos, p. 82.

[5] *Gädlä Yafqirännä-Igzī'*, p. 82.

[6] Perruchon, op. cit., p. 287 (text); cf. also pp. 294, 434–8.

[7] Taddesse Tamrat, 'The Abbots of Däbrä Hayq', see pp. 95–6.

of great expansion of the kingdom, the need to ensure the full recognition of the growing power of Christian rule offered the king's troops invaluable opportunities for raids and counter-raids in the frontier areas, which kept the slave markets well supplied.

Ivory was another important item of trade. The valleys of the Täkäzé,[1] Barka, and Ansäba rivers, and other provinces of the kingdom,[2] were very rich in elephants and other wild animals. It is apparent that the kings undertook the systematic hunting of elephants, the tusks of which they entrusted to their commercial agents. A hagiographical tradition about the fourteenth century gives an interesting picture of the commercial exploits of the Christian kings:

> [The Muslim traders] did business in India, Egypt, and among the people of Greece with the money of the king. He gave them ivory, and excellent horses from Shäwa and red, pure gold from Enarya . . . and these Muslims . . . went to Egypt, Greece, and Rome and exchanged them for very rich damasks adorned with green and scarlet stones and with the leaves of red gold, which they brought to the king.[3]

The Ethiopian interior also seems to have supplied the coastal towns, probably on both sides of the Red Sea, with fresh fruits and cereals.[4] This was the general pattern of trade in the fourteenth century and it seems to have shown no appreciable change between the thirteenth and sixteenth centuries.

The royal court was the busiest centre of trade, and the kings benefited most from it. Of all his predecessors on the throne since 1270, Amdä-Ṣiyon's empire was by far the largest, and he was the first among them to reap economic fruits from the growing power of the kingdom. This dramatic change in the political and economic

[1] Wright, *Catalogue*, Or. 695, ff. 49^{b}–51^{a}. *Gädlä Samu'él* (Waldibba), p. 22.

[2] Al-'Umari, op. cit., p. 28. *Gädlä-Märqoréwos*, pp. 30–1 (text). Crawford, O. G. S., *Ethiopian Itineraries*, pp. 143, 145, 177.

[3] 'Gädlä Zéna-Marqos', MS. Däbrä Ṣigé, ff. 69^{b}–70^{a}. Cf. Al-'Umari, op. cit., p. 2. According to the latter, gold was obtained from Damot, p. 13. In the 12th century, Idrisi considered that gold was rare in Ethiopia and that silver and slaves constituted the most important exports of Zeila, op. cit., pp. 29–30. Cf. also Crawford, op. cit., pp. 149, 151 and n. 2. Alvarez, *The Prester John*, pp. 455–7. Basset, op. cit., pp. 70–1. *The Portuguese Expedition to Abyssynia in 1541*, tr. by Whiteway, R. S., Hakluyt Society, 2nd series, no. 10 (1902), pp. 234–9. For gold obtained from Innarya in the 17th century see Almeida. *Some Records*, tr. Beckingham and Huntingford, pp. 85, 149. Al-'Umari's mention of Narya and Ganj seems to suggest also that these areas were already in Amdä-Ṣiyon's hands, op. cit. pp. 23–4.

[4] Ibid., p. 26. Idrisi, op. cit., pp. 28–9. Andre Corsali, 'Letter to Duke Giuliano de Medici', in Ramusio, *Navigazioni et viaggi*, i (1563), ff. 183, 186.

status of the Christian kings was not lost to Amdä-Ṣiyon's chroniclers, who epitomized his reign with the following generous compliment: '. . . In his reign, gold and silver were as abundant as pieces of stone, and very rich dresses were as numerous in his court as the leaves of the trees and like the grass in the fields.'[1] Amdä-Ṣiyon used his fabulous wealth in building his huge army and in consolidating his power throughout the empire. His military exploits became widely known in the Muslim world, and the Mamluke chancery called him 'the glory of the Christian religion . . . the protector of the southern regions, the successor of the Apostles, of the learned doctors, and of the saints, the honour of the church of Syon, unique among Jacobite kings'.[2] Like Yagba-Ṣiyon before him, he had a Syrian secretary, who came from a well-known Christian family of Damascus,[3] and he kept in close touch with developments in the Near and Middle East. He raised public morale among his Christian subjects and ambitious young men rallied around his court in search of wealth and adventure. The most successful Muslim entrepreneurs offered their services to him, and the newly conquered pagan communities provided an inexhaustible source of manpower for his growing army.

The Christian army

Like many other institutions of his empire, the organization of Amdä-Ṣiyon's army was a direct replica of that of the kingdom of Aksum at the time of its greatest splendour. The description of the Aksumite army in one of Ezana's inscriptions makes it strikingly similar to that of the medieval empire. An essential common feature was the regional (or tribal) character of the military organization in both cases.[4] It seems clear that the Christian army under Amdä-Ṣiyon had two basic elements. First, there was an effective striking force closely attached to the royal Court, and this we may call the central army of

[1] Perruchon, op. cit., pp. 289 (text), 337 (tr.).

[2] Al-'Umari, op. cit., p. 33. Conti Rossini, 'Il "Libro di conoscimento" e le sue notizie sull'Etiopia', in *BSGI*, ser. 5, vol. vi (1917), p. 671.

[3] Al-'Umari, op. cit., p. 32.

[4] For the text of the inscription see *Deutsche Aksum-Expedition*, iv, p. 32. A French version is available in Kammerer, A., *Essai sur l'histoire antique d'Abyssinie*, pp. 95–7. Ezana's army consisted of contingents of Mahaza, Hara, Damawa Falha, Sera, Halén, Lakén, Sabarat. These names have not yet been identified, but they almost certainly stood for place-names or peoples. Halén, for example, was probably the place of origin or tribe of King Ezana himself. In his inscriptions and coins he styles himself as 'Ezana, the man of Halén . . .', ibid., pp. 89 n. 2; 90 n. 1; and 157–9.

the king. Secondly, in times of national or local crises, the monarch raised a huge local militia from the Christian provinces. These kept their local character and served in different contingents such as those from Tigré, Lasta (Bugna), Amhara, and Shäwa.[1] They were again subdivided into smaller units each commanded by its own local chieftain.[2] A substantial part of the Christian army during major expeditions consisted of these local units, but the control over them exercised by the monarch was often minimal. The tug-of-war between Court and country had been a constant factor in Ethiopian political and military history, and will be referred to below. It must be said here, however, that Amdä-Ṣiyon's reign opened up a new phase in the relations between the monarch and his vassals, and the balance of power decisively swung over in favour of the kings and basically remained so for over two hundred years. Amdä-Ṣiyon's best remedy for the centrifugal forces of his kingdom was the effective central army he had successfully built around his court.

The nucleus of this army consisted of a number of special contingents mainly organized in two different ways. First of all, there were a number of mutually independent regiments, each commanded by an officer directly responsible to the king himself. Every such regiment was given a symbolic name, and maintained an *esprit de corps* of its own. These picked warriors included the regiments of *Qästä-Nihb*, *Täkula*, and *Haräb-Gonda*.[3] They vied with one another[4] to fulfil the king's orders, and to please the monarch who 'raised us (from childhood) and fostered us to die (with him)'.[5] Their commanders were absolutely loyal to him, and some of them are specially mentioned as having been very intimate friends of the king.[6] Some were probably his relations. Among the prominent officers of the

[1] Perruchon, op. cit., pp. 293, 382–3, 399.

[2] Ibid., pp. 293 (text), 340 (tr.). We have here an example of such organization. The 'Mäkwanint' and 'Shums' cited in connection with the places quoted represent the local chieftaincies in the kingdom.

[3] Perruchon, op. cit., p. 382 (text). Qästä-Nihb literally means 'the sting of the bee'; Täkula means 'jackal'.

[4] Ibid., p. 290 (text). Of all the troops sent out together against Säbrädīn in Īfat, the regiment of Täkula distinguished itself by being the first to arrive in and attack Īfat despite the difficulty of the road.

[5] Ibid., pp. 410 (text).

[6] Simishähal commanded Qästä-Nihb, ibid., p. 382 (text), and he is mentioned with his colleague Inzä-Aygäb as 'most beloved' officers of the king who was greatly distressed when they were wounded at the Battle of Hagära, pp. 428–9. Inzä-Aygäb is almost certainly the same 'officer of the king's troops' whose name is a little differently given as Yanz-Aygäb, p. 289 (text).

army in 1332 for instance were Amdä-Ṣiyon's own son, Saf-Asägid, and also one of his brothers-in-law.[1] The rank and file of these regiments probably consisted of the best men recruited from different parts of the country, and professional soldiers of fortune who had joined the court in search of wealth and adventure.[2] These men had tied up their fortunes with that of the king and served him with complete devotion in various assignments. They formed the hard core of the fighting force in his expeditions against rebellious governors and in his wars of conquest in Muslim and pagan areas. He made use of them whenever swift and effective actions had to be taken. Sometimes, when emergency action was required, he sent his loyal officers on provincial assignments as local governors. Digna, the right-wing commander of the mounted regiment of Koräm in 1332, was at one time given such an assignment in Tigré, soon after the abortive revolt of the governor of Intärta.[3]

The other part of Amdä-Ṣiyon's central army seems to have been organized on a regional basis. Men of the same linguistic and tribal area were grouped together to form a separate contingent such as that of Koräm, Barya, Gojjam, Gondär, Damot, and Hadya.[4] A common feature among most of these troops was that they were recruited from frontier areas newly conquered by the king. It seems most likely that they were mainly drawn from the numerous prisoners of war. Some of these passed into private hands, others were exported through the slave markets, but a large proportion must have been recruited for the service of the royal Court. Of these some were adopted as mere domestic slaves in the huge Court, but the most promising young men were probably grouped together, trained, and organized into military units. Originally, their commanders may have also been of the same provenance, but they were probably men who had long proved themselves in the king's service and had won his confidence in the meantime. Each of these contingents was probably

[1] Ibid., pp. 400, 419 (text).

[2] Amdä-Ṣiyon was apparently very generously disposed towards his warriors. He occasionally gave them handsome presents and many of his followers possessed numerous male and female slaves, no doubt obtained from the large number of captives in his wars of conquest, ibid., pp. 289, 416 (text).

[3] Ibid., pp. 289, 382 (text). Conti Rossini, 'L'evangelo d'oro', pp. 206–7. Sämäy, who appears in the same list of officials as the new Ma'ikälä-Bahr, may have also been Amda-Ṣīyon's favourite commander of Qästä-Nihb referred to above. Even in the chronicle his name appears variously as Sumäy (-shähal), and Simiy (-shihal), Perruchon, op. cit., pp. 382, 428 (text).

[4] Ibid., pp. 293, 382–3, 399 (text).

large and divided into smaller units. Thus, in 1332, a section of the contingent of Damot went with the army sent against the Fälasha, while another participated in the Muslim wars in Adal.[1] These territorial contingents probably constituted the largest section of the central army and continuously received fresh reinforcements after every successful war of conquest. They also probably served as a training ground for the more prestigious regiments mentioned in the last paragraph, to which only the most tried soldiers were recruited. A brilliant young man, who may have started his career as a mere slave in the royal Court, could thus emerge as one of the king's most favoured officers of the court.[2]

Amdä-Ṣiyon's central army mainly consisted of these two types. Although no numerical estimates have survived, the army must have been very large, at any rate the largest and most effective single army in the whole Ethiopian region.[3] It was also relatively well armed. Both his chronicler and Al-'Umari give a strikingly similar account of the weapons used by the king's troops:

> their weapons of war are the bow with arrows resembling the *nussab*; swords, spears and lances. Some warriors fight with swords and with narrow and long shields. But their principal weapon is the spear which resembles a long lance. There are some [warriors] who fling darts which are [similar to] short arrows, with a long bow resembling a cross-bow . . .[4]

However, it appears that the superiority of the Christian army over

[1] Ibid., pp. 293, 383 (text).

[2] The immediate reason for Amdä-Ṣiyon's armed conflict with Haqädin was the latter's detention of 'one humble slave called Ti'iyintay', ibid., p. 283 (text). It may be that Ti'iyintay was for Amdä-Ṣiyon just what Mäharī-Kristos was for King Bä'idä-Maryam (1468–78). Originally a slave of the young prince, Mäharī-Kristos was cruelly tortured when his master was suspected of a plot against his father Zära'-Ya'iqob. When the prince eventually took the throne his former slave became one of the highest officials in the kingdom. Perruchon, *Chronique de Be'eda-Maryam*, pp. 107, 164, 180–1.

[3] Al-'Umari estimated the troops of Īfat and Hadya as 20,000 and 40,000, respectively, op. cit., pp. 6, 16. But he also stated that Amdä-Ṣiyon was much stronger than all of them, pp. 19, 24. The easy superiority of the Christian army can also be inferred from the fact that the king could send a large force for the suppression of local revolts in Fälasha country and Tigré on the eve of his more important Muslim wars in 1332, on which he himself set out with the rest of his troops, Perruchon, *Histoire des guerres d'Amde Sīyon*, pp. 289–90, 293–4 (text). Some of his predecessors were also noted for maintaining large armies; Lalībäla had 60,000 in *c.* 1210, Perruchon, 'Extrait de la vie d'Abba Jean', p. 83. Yikunno-'Amlak claimed to have had more than 100,000 troops, Mufazzal, op. cit., p. 384.

[4] Al-'Umari, op. cit., pp. 25–6. Cf. also Perruchon, *Histoire des guerres*, pp. 309, 313–14, 382–3 (text), 352, 355, 441–2 (tr.).

that of the Muslims in Amdä-Ṣiyon's reign was mainly numerical. In the passage quoted above, Al-'Umari added, 'they say that the arrows of the warriors of the Muslim borderlands are bigger'. This may not have been altogether a case of patriotism on the part of his Muslim informants.[1] Amdä-Ṣiyon's chronicler also indicates a marked difference in the kind of weapons used by the two adversaries. Thus, whereas 'swords, daggers, iron sticks (= *dimbus*), and *armah*' are invariably mentioned in connection with the Muslim troops,[2] the first two items only appear in special prestigious cases in the Christian army;[3] and the rest are never included in the list of Christian weapons in the hostilities of 1332.[4] Although the chronicler describes Amdä-Ṣiyon as having been armed with 'a sword', it is significant that throughout the narrative he only refers to the king's dexterity in the use of the shield, bow, arrows, and spears.[5] Amdä-Ṣiyon's army at this stage perhaps consisted only of mounted and foot soldiers, armed with arrows and spears, a description also given by the chronicler himself.[6]

It is apparent that, drawing heavily on the experiences of their brothers in the Near and Middle East, with whom they always kept in close contact, the Muslims of the Ethiopian region were better off in the variety of their arms. But this only gave them some advantage in cases of military engagements at very close range, which the Christians avoided,[7] and for which they more than made up by their superiority in numbers. Even in this difference of military weapons, however, Amdä-Ṣiyon had already made considerable strides in bridging the gap. As we have seen above, swords were already being

[1] He specifically mentions a certain Sheikh Abdallah Ez-Zeila'i and his companions as his informants, op. cit., pp. 2–5. Another Muslim merchant El-Hajj Farej el-Funi, and the Egyptian (Jacobite) Patriarch Benjamin (1327–39) also supplied him with some information, pp. 16–17, 27.

[2] Perruchon, op. cit., pp. 285, 394, 400 (text) 334, 449–50, 454 (tr.). He invariably renders 'armah' as 'lances'.

[3] Ibid., pp. 306, 309, 312, 313, 383 (text), 349, 353, 442 (tr.).

[4] They appear, however, in hagiographical descriptions of the Court where they only seem to have been employed for purposes of pompous display, *Gädlä Bäṣälotä-Mīka'él*, p. 27; *Gädlä Aron*, p. 140.

[5] Perruchon, op. cit., pp. 306, 307, 308, 401–3, 428 (text), 349, 350–1, 454–6, 474 (tr.).

[6] Ibid., p. 383 (text), 442 (tr.).

[7] The Christians seem to have been at a disadvantage when engagements were too close. The king was almost killed on one occasion. His Muslim assailant used a sword while the king only employed a spear with which he barely saved his life, ibid., pp. 307 (text), 350 (tr.).

used in his army to some extent. They were probably mostly obtained from abroad through Muslim traders themselves, and by the year 1332 King Amdä-Ṣiyon had created a separate group of warriors specially armed with swords.[1] Together with this group is mentioned another contingent of which the warriors are called 'carriers of shields'. Since every soldier armed with bows, arrows, and spears also carried a shield, the need for such a special group of 'carriers of shields' would seem rather superfluous. It is apparent, however, that here again Amdä-Ṣiyon was actively improving the effectiveness of his army. The clue to this seems to be found in his chronicler's complimentary description of the fighting skill of Adali warriors of whom he says at one place: 'There are some among them who shoot with arrows, and others protect them with shields.'[2] It is most likely that with the organization of the 'carriers of shields' Amdä-Ṣiyon had also started adopting similar tactics of warfare.

King Amdä-Ṣiyon was thus at the head of a large, well-organized, central army with which he effectively ruled his empire and undertook successful wars of conquest in the whole of the Ethiopian region. The pattern of the organization of the army was most favourable for the concentration of power in the person of the monarch. Amdä-Ṣiyon's army did not have a monolithic organization wherein the line of command ran from the king through successively subordinate officers down to the ordinary soldier. It was rather a group of mutually independent contingents commanded by numerous officers of equal rank, each responsible to the king himself. This made the king the sole master of his forces and the emergence of a warrior leader with sufficient influence in the army to challenge the king's position was quite impossible. Whenever one of the regional hereditary chiefs grew too powerful, the king used his central army to impose his will in the provinces. The constant state of mobilization throughout his reign, during which the kingdom was undergoing an active expansion in Muslim, pagan, and Fälasha areas, also gave an additional impetus to the consolidation of the personal power of the king.

Administration of the kingdom

Amdä-Ṣiyon's conquests covered a very wide area, and, as we shall see in a subsequent chapter, the administration of the new provinces

[1] Perruchon, op. cit, p. 383. The name of the commanding officer was Harb-'Asmi'a.

[2] Ibid., pp. 427 (text), 474 (tr.).

perfected itself only later under his fifteenth-century successors. But already in his own reign it had started to adopt the pattern of the feudal organization of the northern provinces. We have made a brief reference above to the general tendencies in these areas towards local autonomy. This was quite inherent in the administrative system long developed in the Christian kingdom. It seems that there had been two layers of local administrative officials. The first consisted of a series of hereditary chiefs whose position of authority was *originally* derived from the royal court. But, possessed of local power for many generations, they seem to have in time developed traditional rights of hereditary rule. Each of these local chiefs generally held the title of *Siyum*, which clearly indicates a royal appointment at least in its origin.[1]

These small chieftaincies were the basic units of the whole political and military structure of the medieval empire, and they served as a launching pad for the emergence of the leadership of Christian Ethiopia. A close study of the traditions of different royal dynasties often indicates their ultimate origin in these small local chieftaincies. A number of local traditions illustrate the characteristic pattern of this development. In many cases, a prospective leader started his career at the Court of a local chief, to whom he may have been a relative or just a follower. While in this humble position, he distinguished himself with bravery and other indications of leadership in the local feuds of his chief with other neighbouring districts. Thus he gradually acquired considerable influence, and became a focus of much interest among the followers of the chief. When the chief died he assumed power, by legitimate succession if he was a son, or otherwise by a simple act of usurpation of power, sometimes committed even in the lifetime of the chief. Once in the saddle of local power, the new ruler subsequently approached the royal Court with such demonstrations of loyalty that he was in time confirmed in the office, which he had already made his own by force of arms. He could even grow further in prestige, with the king's favour, acquire a prestigious title granted by the monarch, and be given charge of a larger political

[1] There are many references to such local officials with the title of 'Siyum', and 'Mäkonin' in many land grants, in Amdä-Ṣiyon's chronicles and in the lives of the saints of the period under review, Conti Rossini, 'L'evangelo d'oro,' pp. 208–10; Perruchon, *Histoire des guerres*, p. 293. *Gädlä Bäṣälotä-Mīka'él*, p. 24; *Gädlä Fīlipos* (Asbo), p. 220; *Gädlä Éwosṭatéwos*, pp. 38–41, 62, 72. The hereditary character of these offices is also implied, ibid., pp. 52–3; Wright, op. cit., Or. 695, ff. 38–40.

unit, including his own.[1] Under favourable circumstances such a resourceful local prince could easily grow into a serious rival of the monarch himself.[2]

A local ruler who acquired power in these ways fully excerised the king's authority in his own province. When the power of the kings was weak, there was little or no interference in his local administration by the royal Court. For all practical purposes, he maintained a virtually independent local Court modelled on that of the kings themselves. On his death he was normally succeeded by his own son who would get full royal confirmation as long as he continued to show the traditional signs of his loyalty to the king. These signs of loyalty consisted of two acts, both of cardinal importance: the collection and submission of the king's tributes accruing from the region,[3] and the readiness to contribute an adequate fighting force to the king's army during a national crisis or to send contingents against local rebellions in the name of the king when called upon to do so.[4]

This extremely local orientation of the structure of the Christian kingdom tended to make it a loose confederation of regional princedoms. It was particularly so at a time of a general decline in the power of the kings. This appears to have been the case in the final years of the Zagwé dynasty and Yikunno-'Amlak took full advantage of the situation. The first two decades of the new dynasty also saw local rulers trying to reassert themselves.

It is apparent that, to offset this chronic tendency towards local autonomy, the kings had instituted an altogether different layer of

[1] For examples of this vital development see Conti Rossini, 'Studi su popolazioni dell'Etiopia', pp. 82–4, 87–9, 90–2; Garrone, V., 'Gli Atcheme Melga', pp. 997–8.

[2] The case of the powerful rulers of Intärta before the reign of Amdä-Ṣiyon has been considered above. Basically, the emergence of Yikunno-'Amlak to power followed the same pattern. Most likely too, the beginnings of the Zagwé dynasty have to be looked at in the same light.

[3] Failure to bring him tributes was given as the reason of Amdä-Ṣiyon's campaigns against his vassals, Perruchon, op. cit., pp. 286, 298. In a hagiographical tradition, a local saint miraculously intervenes in favour of his congregation threatened with an imminent punitive campaign when they failed to pay tribute to the king, 'Gädlä Zéna-Marqos', f. 78b.

[4] Amdä-Ṣiyon used local forces to suppress local revolts, Perruchon, op. cit., p. 293. Hamasén troops returning from war in which they had served in the king's army visited a Tigré saint on the way, Wright, op. cit., Or. 695, f. 22b. The rulers of Sära'é and Bur are reported as being at the royal Court in Shäwa, *Gädlä Éwosṭatéwos*, pp. 38–41 (text). King Dawīt sent his governor of Tigré to suppress a local rebellion in Fälasha country, *Gädlä Yafqirännä-Igzī'*, ed. Wajnberg, pp. 56–8 (text). Conti Rossini, 'Appunti di storia e letteratura Falascia', in *RSO*, vii (1920), pp. 572, 577.

local officials appointed by them and put in charge of large political units. These officials were given a series of royal titles which signified the responsibilities of their position. The titles of *Aqabé-Ṣänṣän*,[1] *Ma'ikälä-Bahr*,[2] *Täwazat*,[3] *Hasgwa*,[4] and *Ṣähafä-Lam*,[5] apparently belonged to this second category of officials. These were the king's nominees and, as long as he mustered enough political and military strength, they were completely dependent on his power. He reshuffled them according to his wishes and his needs. Thus, between 1322 and 1328, the titles of *Ma'ikälä-Bahr* and *Hasgwa* were each held by at least two individuals.[6] Even at a time when his military power was considerable, however, this absolute discretion of the king to transfer his officials probably did not apply to the hereditary rulers of these areas. Except in cases of open rebellion, when a military show-down was unavoidable, it was always impolitic to interfere in their local affairs, and the kings seem to have left them in full possession of their traditional right of leadership.

The centrifugal forces in the kingdom arose mainly from this dual system of local administration; and it was precisely this system that Amdä-Ṣiyon began to apply in his newly acquired provinces. In a long list of local governors in 1332, his chronicler significantly uses the titles of *Nägasī* and *Mäsfin* for the various local officials in Gojjam, Shäwa, and Damot.[7] It is most likely that these titles refer to the descendants of the former rulers of these areas before their annexation by the Christian kingdom. With the gradual removal of the centre of the kingdom to the Shäwan plateau, the regions of

[1] This was an important title of royal officials. See p. 73 n. 1. It also seems to have been used in its shorter form *Aqanṣän*, cf. Taddesse Tamrat, 'The Abbots of Däbrä Hayq', n. 66.

[2] For this title see p. 74 n. 5.

[3] This title first appears in the reign of Amdä-Ṣiyon, Perruchon, op. cit., p. 293 (text). Conti Rossini, 'L'evangelo d'oro', pp. 208, 210. It seems that it referred to the local governors of one of the northern provinces, and since it was once held by the king's son it appears to have been of considerable importance.

[4] References to this title are found after A.D. 1225, Conti Rossini, op. cit., pp. 190–4, 199, 208. Wright, op. cit., Or. 695, f. 27[a], where an official bearing the title is seen apparently collecting the king's tribute in Tämbén. Cf. also Taddesse Tamrat, op. cit., n. 143.

[5] First mentioned in Lalībäla's reign with no regional connotations, Conti Rossini, op. cit., p. 190. Officials of the same title for Amhara appear also in the reign of Amdä-Ṣiyon, Perruchon, op. cit., p. 281.

[6] Conti Rossini, op. cit., pp. 204, 206, 208. Wright, loc. cit.

[7] Perruchon, op. cit., pp. 280–2 (text), 329–30 (tr.). Only the ruler of Gojjam is called *Nägasī* here. Cf. also *Gädlä-Yafqiränä-Igzī'*, pp. 16, 24. Elsewhere the rulers of pre-conquest Hadya and Damot are also referred to by the same title, Taddesse Tamrat, op. cit., pp. 95–6.

Amhara and Shäwa acquired a special status and became direct apanages of the royal court. In the outlying provinces, however, the traditional system of local administration fully obtained, and the king's intervention largely consisted in making sure that the hereditary succession of local power passed to favourable candidates. Al-'Umari's account of the king's control of the Muslim areas[1] also applied to the empire as a whole.

Conquest and Gult

The economic basis for the power of the Christian monarch lay in his traditional right to distribute fiefs in return for military or other services. The ideological background for this was ultimately derived from the theory that all land within his dominions belonged to the king. This constitutional theory was certainly antecedent to the 'Solomonic' dynasty, and it also appears in the traditions about earlier Ethiopian monarchs. The hagiographer of the Zagwé king Lalībäla compliments him for paying for the land on which he built his churches. He attributes this to the king's special sense of piety and saintliness and asks a rhetorical question to demonstrate the traditional power of the monarch in the distribution of land: 'Who would have forbidden the king if he had decided to take the land [without purchase]?'[2] In his famous conflict with the monastic leaders which we shall consider below, Amdä-Ṣiyon is also said to have demanded their absolute obedience to him because they lived 'on the land of the king'.[3] His son and successor Säyfä-Ara'd is also said to have made the claim that 'God gave [all the] land to me'.[4] A more practical example of this royal prerogative over land is furnished by the abundant records of land grants made by the kings and in their name to churches and individuals.

The vast tracts of land that had recently come into their possession by conquest provided Amdä-Ṣiyon and his successors with the real basis for their political and military power. In this they were merely following the precedents of earlier dynasties of the Christian kingdom. All the Christian provinces in the north were originally acquired by wars of conquest.[5] It is apparent that every such conquest was fol-

[1] Op. cit., p. 19.

[2] Perruchon, *La Vie de Lalībäla*, p. 123. Cf. also 'Gädlä Yimrhannä-Kristos', MS. Lalībäla (Béta-Maryam), f. 30[a].

[3] *Gädlä Aron*, p. 130.

[4] Ibid., p. 149. *Gädlä Fīlipos*, p. 242, 243.

[5] This seems to be very clear from the inscriptions of the early Aksumite kings, particularly that of Adulīs, first reported by Cosmas, McCrindle, *The Christian*

lowed by allotments of land being distributed in fief among the king's followers and heavy dues being imposed on the conquered people. With the passage of time, however, the conquerors and the conquered became religiously and ethnically assimilated and developed a single, albeit tribally diversified, Christian identity. It was precisely the same historical process that was being re-enacted in the recently acquired provinces under the new dynasty. The juridical effect of a fresh military conquest was to reduce all the conquered people and their entire belongings to the king's absolute power. He appropriated all the people and their land, and reserved every right to dispose of them according to his wishes. He executed all resistance fighters who fell into his hands, and reduced to slavery other captives of war. The conquering army then raided the country, burning and looting and taking away the cattle, horses, and other possessions of the local people. These acts of cruel repression were deliberately committed not only to replenish the ever-failing provisions of the huge Christian army, but also to force the people to surrender, and to give them a terrible example of the destructive force of the Christian army in case of further revolts.[1] At first such military conquests apparently did not lead to a large-scale occupation of the area by Christians. As soon as the people surrendered, they were offered peace terms and allowed to live under such members of their traditional chiefly families as were prepared to accept the Christian king as their overlord. These vassal princes were then required to appear at the royal Court and submit their occasional tributes in person,[2] and to protect the king's Christian subjects[3] within their jurisdiction. It appears that at first

Topography of Cosmas, an Egyptian monk (1897), pp. 57–66. Littmann, E. in *Deutsche Aksum-Expedition*, i, p. 42. Conti Rossini, 'Expéditions et possessions des Habashat en Arabie', in *JA*, ser. 11, vol. xviii (1921), pp. 5–36. Kammerer, A., *Essai sur l'histoire antique d'Abyssinie*, pp. 56–60.

[1] On the eve of the wars of 1332 Amdä-Ṣiyon reminded Säbrädīn of the destruction that befell Īfat and its dependencies when his predecessor Haqädīn provoked the Christian kingdom, Perruchon, op. cit. 282–4 (text), 332–3 (tr.). References to similar havoc committed by the Christian army are also abundant, ibid., pp. 287, 294, 425, 429–30, 434–8. See also Taddesse Tamrat, loc. cit.

[2] The highest expression of Säbrädīn's revolt in 1332 was his message to King Amdä-Ṣiyon saying: 'I shall not come to your palace, I shall not present myself in front of you . . .', Perruchon, op. cit., pp. 285, 334. The king of Hadya is also said to have revolted against Amdä-Ṣiyon when he listened to the advice of a Muslim cleric who told him: 'Do not go to the Court of the king of Ṣiyon, and do not give him any presents', ibid., pp. 287, 335.

[3] Amdä-Ṣiyon's quarrel with both Haqädīn I and Säbrädīn was partly because they interfered with the freedom of movement of his subjects, ibid., pp. 283, 289, 322, 344.

the tributes thus demanded were collectively raised by the people and passed over to the Christian court through their local rulers. Gradually, however, as the power of the kingdom consolidated, military colonies were established in the new areas and large-scale Christian settlements encouraged. The regions most affected by this new development in the period under review were particularly those in Shäwa, and in Damot.

By the end of the thirteenth century there were only small, isolated Christian settlements in the central Shäwan plateau. On the advent of the new dynasty, and particulary after the extensive conquests of Amdä-Ṣiyon, however, this vast territory became the very centre of the Christian kingdom. Besides its own abundant agricultural resources, Shäwa occupied a strategic position at the heart of the Ethiopian region, and served as a valuable gateway to the areas beyond the upper course of the Awash and the southern tributaries of the Blue Nile. The fertile districts of Wäj, Nar'it, Indägäbṭan, Wäräb, and Damot were soon made the objects of an intensive programme of Christian settlement.[1] The most important beneficiaries of this deliberate programme were no doubt the members of the king's army. It is apparent that Amdä-Ṣiyon and his immediate successors distributed allotments of land in these areas among their followers in return for specific services. It is not quite clear exactly how this was undertaken, nor is it possible here to determine in precise terms the relationship between the newcomers and the local people. But, from many of the available records of land grants made by these early kings, it seems possible to give a tentative reconstruction of the nature of these fiefs.

The technical term for these land grants is *Gult*, and it had specific political and economic implications. A church or an individual who received a piece of land as *Gult* by a royal decree enjoyed a number of rights in relation to the peasants living on the land. These mainly included rights to collect monthly and/or annual tributes from them. The tributes thus collected were not necessarily produced on the *Gult* land itself. They were only determined to meet the daily needs of the grantee and had to be collectively raised by the peasants. In a group of early land grants attributed to King Amdä-Ṣiyon, there

[1] It was also in these areas that the Egyptian bishop Abunä Ya'iqob (*c.* 1337–44) organized an active programme of evangelization. See Ch. V. A land grant made by Amdä-Ṣiyon to one of his courtiers indicates these regions as having been most affected by this programme of Christian settlement. See p. 102 n. 3 below.

are preserved some particulars about the general items of which these tributes consisted. They included specified amounts of home-made cloth, bushels of grain, honey, bars of salt, heads of cattle and sheep, and even simple implements such as axes and sickles.[1] The peasants were thus obliged to provide the owner of the *Gult* with the simplest of his needs, and their relationship with him was of the nature of an extended household. Although the land grants did as a rule make the minimum specifications of the amount and types of tributes, it appears that the demands of the grantee on the peasants and their families were in fact arbitrary and largely depended on the kind of relationships that developed between them. The tributes due from the peasants could be exacted in kind, or in personal services, or in both.[2] It seems that particularly in areas recently annexed the exactions on the local people were invariably heavy, and entirely depended on the discretion of the individual concerned.

The owner of a *Gult*, who was termed a *Balä-Gult*, was basically different from a landlord in that he had originally no rights on the land itself, but only on the peasants living and working on it. The ownership of the land remained in the hands of the local people, who passed it on to their descendants according to their own local customary laws. It seems that the *Gult* system was essentially a rationalization in peacetime of the emergency measures taken during military expeditions. When an army was sent out on a campaign, it collected its provisions from the country through which it happened to march.[3] It is apparent that, to avoid conflicts among the regiments on such occasions, a number of homesteads were evenly distributed among the different sections of the army who obtained their provisions from

[1] Wright, op. cit., Or. 481, ff. 124, 208[a].

[2] The only bases for these conclusions are the particulars given in the available land grants attributed to the medieval kings. A useful guide for the system of land tenure and taxation in Ethiopia was published by a senior public servant who made use of existing Government archival material and local traditions. Although it deals only with the period since the end of the last century, the book also provides an excellent introduction even for earlier centuries, Gäbrä-Wäld Ingida-Wärq, *Land and Taxation in Ethiopia* (Amharic), Addis Ababa, 1956. See pp. 15, 17–19 about *Gult* in particular. Cf. also Conti Rossini, 'I Loggo e la legge dei Loggo Sarda', in *GSAI*, xvii (1904), pp. 31–3. Examples of more recent military colonizations, which are no doubt based on medieval parallels, can also be observed in the 19th-century expansion of Christian Ethiopia, Cerulli, E., *Etiopia occidentale*, i (1933), pp. 133–4, 233–8.

[3] In 1332 Amdä-Ṣiyon's troops suffered a number of casualties while thus collecting provisions in the hostile region of Adal, Perruchon, op. cit., pp. 430–1 (text), 476 (tr.).

the people as long as they remained in the area. At the time of such expeditions this only affected the people living on the main roads or within easy reach of the military camps. When an effective and a more permanent occupation was intended, however, the same arrangement was simply extended far and wide, and the occupied land was divided into a number of *Gults* each assigned for the maintenance of an officer and his dependants.

The *Gult* system was much more than an economic arrangement. It occupied an important place in the administration and the defence of the whole empire. A *Balä-Gult* was also the local representative of the king, and he exercised much authority within his territory. He was responsible for the maintenance of law and order there; he led the local commandos, organized to hunt down local criminals, and he was also responsible for the local prisoners.[1] Together with his superiors in the region, he also raised and commanded local contingents in times of hostilities with external forces. He was helped by the traditional hierarchy of the local people in the execution of these responsibilities. In the absence of the *Balä-Gult* at the royal Court, or elsewhere, his representative acted for him in keeping peace. Every part of the kingdom was thus divided into numerous *Gults*, which were also administrative units at the head of which were placed a hierarchy of the king's political and military officials. This organization served a double purpose. On the one hand, it provided an excellent means of maintaining a large territorial army, and on the other, it considerably simplified the task of governing the expanding empire by dividing it into small, easily manageable units.

Gults were originally given to a person in return for specific services to the monarch. The services were generally military,[2] but numerous retainers of the royal Court could also obtain pieces of land as *Gults* for sundry reasons.[3] The tenure of the *Gult* was at first strictly per-

[1] The monks exiled to the provinces by Amdä-Ṣiyon and Säyfä-Ar'ad seem to have been in the custody of such officials, *Gädlä Bäṣälotä-Mīka'él*, pp. 23–4, 30; *Gädlä Fīlippos*, pp. 214, 220; *Gädlä Anoréwos*, pp. 89–90. *Gädlä Aron*, pp. 138–40, 145.

[2] It is interesting that Al-'Umari uses the same term for Amdä-Ṣiyon's troops as is employed in Mamluke Egypt to denote the soldiers who were given fiefs in return for military services, op. cit., p. 25 n. 1. In his description of the Muslim army of Īfat, however, he maintained that no such land grants were given to the soldiers, pp. 13–14. The editor's note (p. 13 n. 6) contradicting this is based on the assumption that this last description was that of the Christian army. It is apparent, however, that the author meant to underline the difference in the organization of the Christian and Muslim armies in Ethiopia.

[3] An interesting land grant to a resourceful courtier from Hadya made by

sonal, and did not entail hereditary rights. Even during the lifetime of the *Balä-Gult*, his tenure only lasted as long as he properly executed the responsibilities for which he was given the land. This insecurity of tenure was very convenient for the maintenance of effective control by the royal Court over the activities of the provincial officers. *Gults* were a medieval substitute for salaries and provided the king with a ready means of rewarding his loyal servants. It is apparent, however, that with the pacification of the newly conquered areas, and with the consolidation of the empire, the *Gults* gradually assumed a hereditary character so that they could be inherited together with the responsibilities attached to them. In fact it seems that the land holdings known as *Rist*, or hereditary estates, in the more ancient parts of the Christian kingdom, were also in origin *Gults*,[1] and their transformation into *Rist* was only a measure of the degree of religious and ethnic equilibrium long created in these areas since the Aksumite period. The mainstay of the *Gult* system was the difference between the conquerors and the conquered. At the initial period of the expansion of the kingdom, the general picture that emerges is one of two layers, of which the bottom layer consisted of the local subject people. Over and above them came the conquerors with their numerous allotments of *Gults* which entitled them to use the local people as no more than domestic servants. Gradually, however, with an increased social contact and intermarriage between the two classes, the difference between them became less and *Gults* were transformed into hereditary holdings. Wherever this development was impeded by deep religious and ethnic prejudices, the *Gult* system maintained its original character, and the power of the Christian kingdom always remained alien and only skin-deep.

The royal Court

The most important centre for this transformation was the royal Court itself. Being at the pinnacle of the military and administrative organization, the royal Court was a perfect model of the whole

Amdä-Ṣiyon towards the end of his reign is preserved in Or. 821, MS. (B.M.), ff. 106^{b}–107^{a}; MS. Bruce 88 Bodl., ff. 33^{b}–34^{a}. The Hadya courtier was surprised at the great expense incurred by the king in purchasing mules, and suggested they could be bred in a series of royal stables in the country. The king was delighted and said to him 'Choose any *Gults*; and he chose Mätämat in Fäṭägar, Ilqidar in Inari't, Sär in Dinbī, Dīwan and Ebortīn in Wäräb, Hawayat Amba, and 'Algot in Amhara', where royal stables were successfully established.

[1] Cf. Conti Rossini, 'I Loggo e la legge dei Loggo Sarda', pp. 33–5.

empire. Its internal structure saw its fullest development in the first half of the fifteenth century, and a detailed study of its characteristic organization and its place in the administration of the kingdom will have to be deferred to subsequent pages.[1] It suffices here to sketch a broad outline of its basic elements for the purposes of this chapter. It seems possible to consider the Christian Court during the period under review as consisting of two major sections:

(*a*) a large number of civil, clerical, and military functionaries permanently attached to the Court, and
(*b*) a floating population occasionally coming to Court for sundry reasons.

According to an early tradition, King Amdä-Ṣiyon is said to have formally organized in his Court fifteen 'houses' each of which had its own special responsibility.[2] At the head of each 'house' were appointed a chief and an assistant chief who were directly answerable to the king for carrying out the specific responsibilities assigned to their house. It is interesting to note that the duties assigned to them also reflect the king's increasing wealth, and his particular concern with military activities. At least seven of these 'houses' were placed in charge of his special treasures of gold and vestments of honour;[3] and three of them looked after his defensive armour, his various other weapons of war, and the fittings of the horses of the right and of the left.[4] The establishment of these 'houses', with their special duties seems to provide an interesting clue to the organization of the whole court. It is apparent that the rest of the numerous retainers of the king, and his family, were also similarly organized in separate

[1] See Ch. VIII.

[2] The tradition is preserved in 'Tarīkä-Näghäst', MS. Bruce 88 Bodl., f. 32^{b}. This MS. is described in Dillmann, *Catalogus Codicum Manuscriptorum Bibliothecae Bodleianae Oxoniensis, pars vii. Codices aethiopici* (Oxford, 1848), No. 29. Cf. also Wright, op. cit., Or. 821, ff. 103^{b}–104.

[3] Many of the words used for the sundry objects kept by these 'houses' are archaic and their specific meanings are difficult to decipher. But from the recognizable names in the list it seems quite possible to determine the nature of the responsibilities of each house. The seven 'houses' referred to above included Gimja-Bét, Mijlé-Bét, Märäba-Bét, Wärq-Bét, Bä'alä-Ṣirh Bizt-Bét, Qäsiy-Bét, and Mätälat-Bét. It seems that it is to these 'treasure houses' that the king's chronicler also makes a reference when he says of Amdä-Ṣiyon 'He took out of his treasure houses [much] gold and silver and vestments of honour . . . and conferred them upon his soldiers', Perruchon, *Histoire des guerres*, p. 289 (text) and cf. also p. 337 (tr.).

[4] These included Harb-Bét, Dir'i-Bét, and Ṭiqaqin Dir'i-Bét.

groups, according to their respective functions. Outside this inner circle of courtiers, whose special duties were mainly to look after the personal needs of the royal family, there came the political and military officials of the king with their numerous followers, consisting of the royal guards and the various contingents of the army. Each of these officials and their followers were also accompanied by their own families and other dependants. In a short description of the court during the hostilities of 1332 in Adal, reference is made to 'the wives, children, and the male and female slaves' of the troops as having constituted a substantial part of the Court.[1] It no doubt maintained a similar pattern in relatively more peaceful times. The size of the Court fluctuated with the seasons. In the dry season, when local officials and vassal rulers normally brought their tributes, the Court received huge reinforcements from the provinces. Another occasion when it was at its greatest was on the eve of major military expeditions, when provincial governors joined the Court with their regional forces.[2] During the rainy season, however, many of the king's court officials and their followers went to their home districts or to their official stations and the Court was reduced to its smallest size.

The Court itself appears to have been continuously moving from one province to another. It seems that it was to this aspect of the court that Al-'Umari made a reference when he wrote: 'They say that this king and the soldiers of his army have tents which they carry with them during their marches and during their mobilization.'[3] The statement did not refer only to the movements of the army during military expeditions. Traditions of many sites of the Christian Court also provide an ample confirmation for its mobile character in peaceful times as well.[4] Thus, it was not only that the king's subjects came to his residence, but also that his Court actually changed its location at regular intervals. This two-way traffic between Court and country played a great role in establishing Christian power in the new areas. The appearance of the Court in a region was a dramatic representation of the presence of the Christian kingdom. During the first years of conquest and expansion in any new region, it brought with it utter destruction and havoc to all the local people. Once Christian overlordship was accepted, however, members of the local ruling families

[1] Perruchon, J., op. cit., p. 415 (text). Cf. also pp. 416 (text), 465–6 (tr.).

[2] Ibid., pp. 293 (text), 339–40 (tr.). Many of the governors of the northern provinces of the kingdom are here mentioned as having been at the court on the eve of Amdä-Ṣiyon's campaigns to Adal.

[3] Op. cit., p. 25.

[4] See p. 274 n. 3.

were gradually drawn into the Court and into the feudal system of the Christian administration. At first they were probably kept at Court as mere hostages for the good behaviour of their relatives and their subjects. After a period of readjustment at Court, they were brought forward as favourite candidates for the leadership of their people. A typical example of this pattern of development was the relationship between the Wälasma ruling house of the Muslim state of Īfat and the Christian Court.[1] The chronicler's description of the first conquest of Hadya also points to the same conclusion:

> [Amdä-Ṣiyon] did a great massacre of the people of this country, killing or massacring some at the point of the sword, and carrying away others into captivity with their king, big and small, men and women, old and young, whom he transported into his kingdom.[2]

We are not told here or elsewhere what happened to Amano, the king of Hadya, after his capture and detention at Court. But the power which the Christian kingdom had in his country remained quite secure after that, and it seems possible to suppose that Amdä-Ṣiyon and his immediate successors pursued an exactly similar policy towards him and his family as with the Muslim Wälasma princes in Īfat. The same case no doubt applied to the leaders of other communities recently brought under the suzerainty of the kingdom. The historic role of the Court was to serve as a training ground for loyal district officers and provincial governors.

Amdä-Ṣiyon was the most important architect of this dynamic system of Christian expansion, and it is ironical that his name should be an object of hostile monastic propaganda in the hagiographical traditions of the Ethiopian Church. Yet, even this was an essential by-product of the intensive development which the Church was undergoing, particularly in the period of his reign. The traditions of his violent conflicts with the monastic leaders are only an indication of the growing importance of monasticism in the organization of the Ethiopian Church.

[1] On his victory in Īfat in 1332 Amdä-Ṣiyon appointed as 'King of all the Muslim districts' Säbrädīn's brother, Jämaldīn, who was apparently in prison before the war. Perruchon, op. cit., pp. 301 (text), 346 (tr.). When later he proved to be unco-operative another brother, Näsrädīn, was appointed instead, ibid., pp. 323–4, 432–4 (text), 362, 478–9 (tr.). King Säyfä-Ar'ad (1334–71) also kept Säbrädīn's son Ali and his family at his court and appointed them in turns as vassal rulers of Īfat, Maqrizi, *Historia*, pp. 18–21.

[2] Perruchon, op. cit., pp. 335 (tr.), 287 (text). Cf. also Taddesse Tamrat, op. cit., pp. 95–6.

Revival of monasticism in Ethiopia

Despite its early introduction in the sixth century with the advent of the Nine Saints,[1] monasticism could assume a dominant position in the Ethiopian Church only seven centuries later. Ethiopian monastic traditions before the last quarter of the thirteenth century revolve around Egyptian and 'Roman' founders, and they are, as a whole, extremely defective and fragmentary. This is quite clear from the spiritual genealogies given for the two dominant monastic 'houses' of the Ethiopian Church, namely those of Täklä-Haymanot of Shäwa (d. 1313), and Éwosṭatéwos of Sära'é (d. 1352).[2] The emergence of militant national leaders in Ethiopian monasticism was a post-thirteenth-century development, and the Church seems to have been dominated until then by the secular clergy. This was particularly so in the regions of Amhara and Shäwa, where the new-born monasteries seem to have made a strong bid for influence as champions of better moral standards in the administration of the Church, and in the daily lives of the Christians, including the monarchs themselves. The opposite sides taken by the secular clergy and the monks in the subsequent conflicts were determined by their respective positions in relation to the royal Court.

The hierarchy of the Coptic Church consisted of eight orders.[3] Only five of these are represented in the traditions of the Ethiopian Church.[4] The highest of these five orders, namely that of the

[1] For the Nine Saints, see p. 23–5.

[2] Both these 'houses' derive their origin from the Nine Saints. But Täklä-Haymanot and Éwosṭatéwos are placed *only* eight and thirteen generations after St. Anthony (d. 356), respectively, Conti Rossini, *Il 'Gadla Filipos ed il Gadla Yohannis di Dabra Bizan'*, in *MRAL*, ser. 5, vol. viii (1901), p. 156. How very defective monastic traditions before the 13th century are, can better be illustrated in the genealogical tables for Abīyä-Igzī' who lived in the first half of the 14th century. Whereas as many as 8 generations are given between him and the wars of Gragn (1527–43), only 9 separate him from St. Anthony, Conti Rossini, 'Note di agiografia etiopica: 'Abiye-Egzi', in *RSO*, xvii (1938), pp. 416–17.

[3] Ibn Saba (Yuhanna ibn Zakariya), *La Perle précieuse traitant des sciences ecclésiastiques*, ed. and tr. Perier, J., in *PO*, xvi (1922), pp. 661–4. Wansleb, J. M., *Histoire de l'Église d'Alexandrie* (1677), pp. 33–8.

[4] The orders which are not represented in the Ethiopian church are those of the patriarch, sub-deacons, and 'agnostes' (or readers). There are some differences between Ibn Saba, who wrote in the end of the 13th century, and Wansleb (17th century) in the number of orders. Whereas the former referred to metropolitans and bishops as being of the same grade, the latter took them as different. In another passage where he compares the orders of the Church with the 'seven celestial orders', Ibn Saba reduced the number to seven by arguing that patriarchs, metropolitans, and bishops were in fact of the same grade, op. cit., pp. 660–1. At the end of Wansleb's lists is a church functionary he calls 'Sacristain'

metropolitan, was always conferred on an Egyptian monk who was chosen by the patriarch in Cairo and sent to Ethiopia.[1] Next came the order of the Epīsqopos, to which Ethiopians also could be raised.[2] Below these ecclesiastics came the priests, archdeacons,[3] and deacons. These last three orders made up the backbone of the church, and they consisted of both the secular and monastic clergy.

The monastic clergy

The differences between these two elements of the Ethiopian Church was fundamental. The most distinctive aspect of the monastic clergy was that they entered into special oaths of celibate life, and their activities were limited to their monasteries. Very little is known about the organization and discipline of the monasteries before the middle of the thirteenth century. It is, however, considered that the Lives of St. Paul the Hermit and St. Anthony, and the Rules of St. Pacomius were translated from the Greek into Ge'ez already in the Aksumite period.[4] There is no doubt that this monastic literature provided the earliest guide-lines, and the monasteries were probably organized according to a simple application of the Rules of St. Pacomius, with whom the Nine Saints are traditionally connected. At the moment, an examination of the traditions about the establishment of new com-

or 'Keiim'. He defines his duties as being limited to guarding and taking care of the precincts of the church in general, op. cit., p. 38.

[1] Instances of Egyptian resistance to the ordination of Ethiopians to this order are available in the Lives of the patriarchs, Budge, E. A. W., *The Book of the Saints of the Ethiopian Church*, iii, pp. 798–801; Renaudot, *Historia Patriarcharum Alexandrinorum*, pp. 273, 283. See also p. 70, notes 3–4.

[2] Three Ethiopian ecclesiastics are mentioned as having held this title in the reign of Lalībäla, Conti Rossini, 'L'evangelo d'oro', pp. 187, 190. In the same reign an Egyptian bishop is said to have consecrated an Ethiopian *Évêque* at the king's request, Renaudot, op. cit., pp. 554–67; Perruchon, 'Extrait de la vie d'Abba Jean', in *RS* (1900), p. 79. This is curious because according to the customs of the Coptic Church a metropolitan or a bishop cannot ordain 'un évêque', Ibn Saba, op. cit., p. 746. It seems that the term 'Epīsqopos' was used in Ethiopia as equivalent to 'hagumenos', which was the inferior title next to that of the bishop, ibid., p. 665; Khs-Burmester, O. H. E., 'The Canons of Cyril III ibn Laklak', in *Le Muséon*, pp. 110–11.

[3] The position of the archdeacon was very important in the Coptic Church, Ibn Saba, op. cit., 665–6; Wansleb, op. cit., pp. 36–7. It also appears to have been of special importance in Ethiopia and the title is given in early lists of influential officials on very solemn occasions, Conti Rossini, 'L'evangelo d'oro', pp. 187, 190.

[4] Cerulli, E., *Storia della letteratura etiopica* (1956), pp. 25–9. The Ethiopic version of the Rules of St. Pacomius was translated by Basset in his collection *Les Apocryphes éthiopiennes*, 10 vols. (1895–1915).

munities since the middle of the thirteenth century is the only way of attempting to reconstruct the development of monastic institutions in Ethiopia. At the beginning of this period references to monastic communities are limited to some of the ancient establishments of the Nine Saints,[1] and other sites incidentally mentioned as monastic retreats in the region north of Amhara.[2] A much more complete picture of the rapid development of monasticism emerges only after the middle of the thirteenth century. The trends of this development are represented by the traditions of the 'houses' of Täklä-Haymanot and Éwosṭatéwos.

For all the differences which subsequently developed between these two groups,[3] their early traditions represent the same phenomenon of monastic revival in the Ethiopian Church. In its early stages the movement was characterized by its simplicity and proverbial sense of independence, both of which found their fullest expression in the background of the political and military revival of the Christian kingdom in the whole of the Ethiopian region. While the growth of the Täklä-Haymanot group of monasteries followed on the most decisive directions of the expansion of the kingdom, the increasingly militant attitude of the Christian tribes of Särа'é and Hamasén towards their Muslim and pagan neighbours, was also reflected in the intensive monastic activities of the 'house' of Éwosṭatéwos. Nowhere was this parallel religious and political development of Ethiopia brought into more direct confrontation than in the regions of Amhara and Shäwa, which had become the centre of the political and military activities of the Christian kings. It was also in these parts of the kingdom that the militant leaders of the new monastic

[1] As the origin of the most dominant monastic group in the 15th century Däbrä Damo is represented best in these traditions, *Gädlä Arägawī*, ed. Guidi, I., in *MRAL* (1896) ser. v, vol. ii, pt. 1, Memorie, pp. 54–96; *Gädlä Īyäsus-Mo'a* ed. and tr. Kur, S., pp. 9–13 (text); Conti Rossini, '*Il Gadla Takla Haymanot*', in *MRAL* (1896), ser. v, vol. ii, pt. 1, Memorie, pp. 107–8; Budge, *The Life of Takla Haymanot*, pp. 72–3 (text); *Gädlä Bäṣälotä-Mīka'él*, ed. and tr. Conti Rossini, p. 19 (text). The monastery of Abba Gärīma at Mädara is also referred to, 'Gädlä Gärīma', Or. 702, MS. B.M., ff. 128b–138; 'Gädlä Qäwisṭos', MS. Däbrä Lībanos, ff. 17–24. Since Pänṭäléwon and Afṣé also have their *Gädls*, compiled probably in the 15th century, it may be surmised that the communities they had established were still intact at the same time. Däbrä Lībanos of Shīmäzana which belongs to about the same period as the Nine Saints was apparently the most important community towards the end of the Zagwé period, Conti Rossini, 'L'evangelo d'oro', pp. 177–93.

[2] Cf. Budge, *The Life of Takla Haymanot*, pp. 73–4 (text); *Gädlä Bäṣälotä-Mīka'él*, p. 19.

[3] See Ch. VI.

movement came into open conflict with King Amdä-Ṣiyon and his successor Säyfä-Ar'ad.

The earliest traditions of monasticism in this region at our disposal go back only to the middle of the thirteenth century, when Īyäsus-Mo'a settled at the island church of St. Stephen in Lake Hayq. In about 1248 he left his monastery of Däbrä Damo and started his own school of Hayq where many students from Amhara and Shäwa joined him.[1] He conferred the monastic habit on many of them, and some subsequently left Hayq to establish their own communities. Täklä-Haymanot left for his native land of Shäwa, and others appear to have dispersed in the province of Amhara.[2] Within a short time after his coming to Hayq, Īyäsus-Mo'a firmly established the position of monasticism which was to be the effective vehicle for the expansion of the Church.

This vital development was greatly enhanced by the simplicity of the process of establishing a monastic community. Īyäsus-Mo'a himself settled at a very well-established centre of Christian population where his special role as a teacher was appreciated, and he was not faced with the initial problem of starting a new community from scratch. His disciples who left him to live on their own were not as fortunate. A monastic community normally started by being an isolated place of private retreat for its founder.[3] Alone, or accompanied by a few followers, the founder of the community pursued a strict life of extreme ascetism, in almost complete seclusion. Inaccessible hillsides, forest or semi-desert areas, were most popular as the sites of a young community. At times they were apparently very far away from where even churches could be found.[4] Contact with neighbouring settlements was kept to a minimum at first, and when some of the inmates of such a secluded community ventured out to gather food supplies the task usually fell on the junior members.[5]

[1] Taddesse Tamrat, 'The Abbots of Däbrä Hayq'. pp. 88–9.

[2] See Ch. V.

[3] Conti Rossini, *Il 'Gadla Takla Haymanot'*, p. 109; Budge, *The Life of Takla Haymanot*, p. 79 (text); *Gädlä Bäsälotä-Mika'él*, p. 14; *Gädlä Yafqirännä-Egzi*, pp. 26, 36, 38, 40; *Gädlä Samu'él (Waldibba)*, p. 9; *Gädlä Tadéwos*, ed. and tr. de Santis, R., in *Annali Lateranensi*, vi (1942), pp. 34–5.

[4] The nearest church where Abba Samu'él of Waldibba could receive Holy Communion was at a distance of three days' journey, *Gädlä Samu'él*, p. 23. A similar story is told of Abba Tadéwos of Bärṭarwa and his followers, who travelled all the way to Aksum from Tämbén until they finally built their own church, *Gädlä Tadéwos*, loc. cit.

[5] Ibid., pp. 33–4.

The leader of the community remained inside, and his followers made use of their meagre contacts with the surrounding people to spread the news of his monastic renown.[1] The reaction of the local people to the earliest signs of the existence of such a community largely depended on their religious loyalties. In predominantly Christian areas the news was generally welcome, and the young community received fresh reinforcements.[2] In frontier areas the reaction was one of hostility and acts of outright persecution were attempted until local Christian officials came to the aid of the monks.[3] Gradually, as the monastic prestige of the leader became established among the neighbouring people, more people joined him, and the economic and religious organization of the community began to take shape.

At first the small community lived a very simple life by gathering wild fruits for their daily needs,[4] and by hiring their services to the nearest farming villages at harvest time.[5] When the community got bigger, it looked around for a suitable site, built a small church, and a number of little huts for their abode:

And they built a small shelter, they placed the *tabot* of St. Mary [in it] and celebrated mass there. And they planted some 'Dagussa' and 'Nihigo' for the purposes of the church . . . And [Tadéwos] sent [a disciple] one day to clear a piece of [more] land [for cultivation] . . .[6]

The religious influence of the group soon spread among the neighbouring villages with whom more frequent contacts were established. The people came to pray and to ask for the prayers of the monks, and they brought various gifts with them.[7] The monastic exploits and

[1] In a chronologically untenable reference to the visit paid by Täklä-Haymanot to Bäṣälotä-Mīka'él on his way to Hayq, he meets one of the latter's disciples who tells him of the monastic exploits of his master, Budge, op. cit., pp. 60–1; cf. Conti Rossini, 'L'agiografia etiopica e gli atti del santo Yafqirännä-Igzī, in *ARIV*, Sc., lett. ed arti (1936–7), vol. 96, pt. 2, p. 408.

[2] Conti Rossini, *Il 'Gadla Takla Haymanot'*, pp. 115, 138; *Gädlä Fīlipos*, pp. 187–8; *Gädlä Anoréwos*, p. 68; *Gädlä Éwosṭatéwos*, p. 29.

[3] *Gädlä Yafqirännä-Igzī*, pp. 24–6, 50–8; 'Gädlä Zäyohannis' MS. Kibran, ff. 19–20; *Gädlä Anoréwos*, pp. 78–9. In some cases the traditions attribute the protection of the young communities to God's miraculous intervention, Budge, op cit., pp. 79– 81; *Gädlä Samu'él*, p. 18.

[4] Conti Rossini, *Il 'Gadla Takla Haymanot'*, pp. 112, 115; *Gädlä Samu'él*, p. 31.

[5] *Gädlä Tadéwos*, pp. 33, 48; cf. *Gädlä Abäkäräzun*, p. 13 (text).

[6] *Gädlä Tadéwos*, p. 35; cf. also Budge, op. cit., p. 219; Conti Rossini, op. cit., pp. 112, 115; id., *Il 'Gadla Filippos' ed il 'Gadla Yohanis' di Bizan*, p. 96.

[7] *Gädlä Yafqirännä-Igzī*, pp. 58, 62, 64, 66; *Gädlä Fīlipos* (Asbo), pp. 221–2. Éwosṭatéwos is said to have prohibited his followers from accepting gifts from unworthy people or from non-believers. He enjoined them to live on the fruits of their own labour, *Gädlä Éwosṭatewos*, pp. 32–3. His descendant Fīlipos of Däbra Bīzän also confirmed this, Conti Rossini, op. cit., p. 96.

sanctity of the founder became widely accepted, and stories of astounding miracles were built around his name while he was still alive.[1] Canonization in Ethiopia was a simple act of public recognition of the saintly pursuits of a monk, who soon emerged as a patron saint of the area in which he conducted his monastic labours.[2]

Firmly established in such a small locality, the prestige of the saint later spread further afield and similar recognitions were given to him by neighbouring districts, who asked for his prayers and spiritual protection. He soon became a rallying point for the sick, who came to him in search of miraculous cures, and the poor, who saw an economic and social security in the growing influence of the community. Thus, between the middle of the thirteenth century, when Īyäsus-Mo'a had opened his monastic school at the island of Lake Hayq, and the reign of Amdä-Ṣiyon (1314–44), many such communities had been established in Amhara and Shäwa. The most notable among these were the community of Däbrä Asbo in Shäwa, founded by Täklä-Haymanot in *c.* 1284,[3] and Däbrä Gol in southern Amhara, which was originally a private retreat of 'Anoréwos the priest' and later developed into an important community under his remarkable disciple Bäṣälotä-Mīka'él.[4] At this stage of their development an essential feature of these communities was their complete independence from the kings and their local representatives. They enjoyed this position of economic freedom in striking contrast with the secular clergy, who had always been dependent on the royal Court and on the politico-military structure of the kingdom.

The secular clergy

The secular clergy consisted of the married priests, the deacons, and the other functionaries of the church. Before the development of monastic communities, they alone provided for the routine religious needs of the Christian communities. It seems that the priestly families constituted a special class of society, with special rights of succession

[1] A study of the miracles offers a useful means of understanding the life and beliefs of the people in the medieval period. They are of special interest since they deal with the day-to-day economic and social problems of the region with which the memory of the saint is associated.

[2] *Gädlä Tadéwos*, p. 43.

[3] See Ch. V. Other communities had also been established in Shäwa besides Däbrä Asbo, 'Gädlä Zéna-Marqos', ff. 14–15; 'Gädlä Qäwisṭos', ff. 101^{b}–102^{a}.

[4] See Ch. V. Here also there are references to yet other communities, *Gädlä Bäṣälotä-Mīka'él*, pp. 8–10.

to the clerical profession. Despite the tendency of Ethiopian hagiographers to connect this hereditary system with the much-diffused legend of the Queen of Sheba,[1] its origin may have only been an ancient custom of the Coptic Church concerning the secular priesthood, later confirmed by the Canons of Patriarch Cyril III (1235–43) in 1238.[2] The purpose of such a stratification of a congregation may only have been administrative in origin. In medieval Ethiopia, however, it appears that it had resulted in the creation of a different caste of people in whom the rights of priestly function were exclusively invested. References to 'the parentage of priests', as a separate, elevated class, are available in the hagiographical traditions about the origins of some local saints.[3] It also appears that members of this priestly class enjoyed distinctive marks of respect in their relations with the local people:

> [Young Bäṣälotä-Mīka'él] trod over the chains of the king's mule while passing by, and [the keepers] caught him and took him to their chief. And their chief saw the tunic [slung] on the shoulders of the child and said to them: 'Leave him alone because he is *of the parentage of priests*, and do not beat him.'[4]

In the stratified society of the period the priestly class came next only to the class of local rulers. The two classes, whose relationship is aptly described in the traditions of Minīlik I and his high priest Azaryas, were always very close and complementary. The secular clergy lived in society, and only looked after the routine services of their local churches. The programmes of religious training which they underwent at the beginning of their career[5] were probably short and only

[1] This relates to the tradition of the Jewish origin of the Ethiopian kingdom, and the priestly class derived its origin from Azaryas, son of Zadok, King Solomon's high priest, who accompanied Minīlik I to Aksum, Budge, *The Queen of Sheba and Her Only Son Menyelik* (1932), pp. 61–3. Cf. also *The Life of Takla Haymanot*, i, p. 5.

[2] Khs-Burmester, 'The Canons of Cyril III ibn Laklak', pp. 132–5. In a congregation of a church precedence is here given to sons of priests (*a*) over sons of deacons, (*b*) over sons of priests of other churches, and (*c*) over sons of laymen.

[3] *Gädlä Bäṣälotä-Mīka'él*, p. 5. The distant origin of this marked respect and considerable sanctity surrounding the priestly function may in fact be found in the pre-Christian and Kushitic religious practices of the ancient Ethiopians, cf. Conti Rossini, *Storia d'Etiopia*, pp. 78–9, 81.

[4] *Gädlä Bäṣälotä-Mīka'él*, p. 9; in the text the word 'priest' is used in place of the phrase italicized, so that '. . . because he is a priest' would be a more literal translation. But since he was still a small child the above rendering is probably preferable for the context.

[5] These were provided by a local priest who taught his own children and probably also some of his relatives, Budge, *The Life of Takla Haymanot*, p. 20

limited to reciting some prayers, singing the hymns, and reading some selections from the Bible. This only enabled them to practise and preserve the liturgical traditions of the church. Probably, very few among them went beyond these limits. But this was not an important part of their difference from the monastic clergy, of whom the majority were probably in the same position. The basic difference between them arose in that the secular clergy lived in, and completely depended on, society, of which they constituted an integral part. This complete dependence on society denied them the economic and spiritual freedom, which enabled the monks to be fully engaged in religious pursuits, and to pose as champions of a more rigorous observance of the rules of the church.

Reform movements in the Church

A youthful monastic militancy swept through the second generation of the descendants of Īyäsus-Mo'a in Amhara. It seems that their first aim was to bring about basic reforms within the church itself. Bäṣälotä-Mīka'él,[1] who apparently led the movement, first accused the Egyptian bishop Abunä Yohannis of practising simony:

> Bäṣälotä-Mīka'él went to the priests of the royal court and asked them to take him in to the king. And they told the king [about it] and took him in. He said [to the king]: '. . . the Apostles excommunicated those who received money in return for either baptism or ecclesiastical ordinations. But this bishop contravenes their order; he ordains and receives money' . . .[2]

The Egyptian bishops in Ethiopia were very well provided for, and it is curious that Abunä Yohannis should be accused of simony. In

(text); 'Gädlä Qäwīsṭos', f. 44^{a}; *Gädlä Bäṣälotä-Mīka'él*, p. 6; or by a cleric attached to a local church, *Gädlä Anoréwos*, p. 68; *Gädlä Fīlipos*, p. 175; *Gädlä Samu'él*, p. 1; or where they were available, by monastic communities, *Gädlä Éwosṭatéwos*, pp. 7–8.

[1] About the life of this monastic leader see Chap. V.

[2] *Gädlä Bäṣälotä-Mīka'él* pp. 22–3. Bäṣälotä-Mīka'él is reputed in these traditions to have been a very learned man, ibid., pp. 19–20. The quotation here of the Canons of the Apostles is interesting because it seems to show an intensive literary development in Ethiopia. Amdä-Ṣiyon's chronicler, who must have written his work between 1332 and 1344, also quotes the Canons of the Apostles, Perruchon, *Histoire des guerres*, pp. 310, 312 (text), 352, 354 (tr.). This monastic movement of reform may have been a result of increasing contact with Arabic Christian literature in Egypt. It is remarkable how the above quotation is an almost verbatim repetition of a similar accusation made in Egypt against Patriarch Shenuti, Sawirus, *History of the Patriarchs of Alexandria*, ii, pt. 2, p. 233. See also pp. 136, 150. At the Council of 1238 held in Cairo Patriarch Cyril III had also condemned simony in his Canons, Khs-Burmester, op. cit., pp. 105–6. Cf. Conti Rossini, 'Il "Senodos" etiopico' in *RRAL* (1924), p. 44.

the reign of Lalībäla, the metropolitan, Abunä Mīka'él, is said to have had numerous servants and a fief of forty 'villages' for his maintenance.[1] It is most likely that with the expansion of the kingdom and the gradual increase of the wealth of the monarchs, the metropolitan's possessions also became more substantial. It is possible, however, that in the days of Bäṣälotä-Mīka'él, which was a period of active expansion of the Church, the monks may have been presented with some difficulties at the episcopal residence in their increasing demand for the ordination of more priests and deacons. That this was in fact a serious problem at the time is suggested in another passage where a young monk is said to have assumed the functions of a priest of his own accord, without being ordained.[2] However, the king was not apparently impressed by the accusation against the bishop, and he is said to have exiled Bäṣälotä-Mīka'él to Tigré instead.[3]

Bäṣälotä-Mīka'él returned to Amhara two years later, and started a series of reforms in the monastic practices in Amhara. Monasticism was only a recent development in Amhara and Shäwa, and this lack of experience was seriously showing in the organizational difficulties of the recently established communities. One of the most serious problems was the difficulty of effectively separating the living quarters of the male and female members of a monastic community. The traditions of monasticism in Tigré indicate that convents usually grew beside important monasteries,[4] and by the thirteenth century there were very well-established convents.[5] In Amhara and Shäwa, however, the custom had apparently developed for both monks and nuns to live together.[6] Bäṣälotä-Mīka'él fiercely attacked this custom, and he is said to have obtained a royal decree against it.[7] Abba Anoréwos, a senior disciple of Täklä-Haymanot, and a great admirer of Bäṣälotä-Mīka'él, is also said to have effected similar reforms at

[1] Perruchon, 'Extrait de la vie d'Abba Jean', pp. 79–80.

[2] *Gädlä Bäṣälotä-Mīka'él*, p. 41.

[3] Ibid., pp. 23–4.

[4] *Gädlä Arägawī*, ed. Guidi, p. 64.

[5] Lalībäla and his queen, Mäsqäl-Kibra, are said to have made a number of land grants to such convents in the region of Shīmäzana, Conti Rossini, 'L'evangelo d'oro', pp. 186–9. In the tradition about the life of Lalībäla himself, his wife is said to have waited for him in a convent, where men had no access, until his return from his alleged visit to Jerusalem.

[6] Conti Rossini, *Il 'Gadla Takla-Haymanot'*, pp. 115–16, *Gädlä Bäṣälotä-Mīka'él*, pp. 36, 40–1.

[7] Ibid., p. 36.

Däbrä Asbo in the lifetime of his master, for which he became extremely unpopular among his colleagues.[1]

Bäṣälotä-Mīka'él next came into open conflict with King Amdä-Ṣiyon, whom he denounced for his non-Christian matrimonial habits:

> God has ordered us, Christians, not to marry two wives nor buy [lit.] concubines, nor sleep with the wives of others. But you have broken all [these] orders of God. And worse of all, you married the wife of your father; and you did not desist from keeping numerous other women [of pagan origin] . . .[2]

The matrimonial habits of Ethiopians had already been called in question before. In the reign of Patriarch Cyril (1077–92) the metropolitan, Sawīros, reported that he had succeeded in persuading the king's courtiers to live each with only one wife. The king himself had also agreed to drop many of his concubines, and to keep only two wives.[3] What is most significant in the fourteenth century is that the movement for reform was no longer initiated from Cairo, and this indicates the tremendous development which the Ethiopian Church had undergone at the time. Abba Éwosṭatéwos of Särа'é is also reported in the same period to have demanded similar reforms from the local rulers.[4] But the movements of the Ethiopian monks were no more successful than those of Bishop Sawīros in the eleventh century. Bäṣälotä-Mīka'él was beaten and disgraced at court, and

[1] *Gädlä Anoréwos*, pp. 71–2. Anoréwos is said to have been 'Oeconome' of the community in Täklä-Haymanot's lifetime, and was apparently tipped for the succession. He failed to get the succession and left for Tigré immediately after the death of his master. Ibid., p. 75. His reforms may have played a part in this. He met Bäṣälotä-Mīka'él in Tigré, and probably stayed with him until his death. Later, after 1337, Anoréwos returned to Shäwa and seems to have played a leading role in Abunä Ya'iqob's reorganization of the monasteries there. See Ch. V.

[2] *Gädlä Bäṣälotä-Mīka'él*, p. 29. That the king did in fact have more than one wife and many concubines is also confirmed elsewhere, *Histoire des guerres d'Amde Sīyon*, pp. 326, 387–9. Conti Rossini, 'L'evangelo d'oro', p. 202. But Amdä-Ṣiyon denied that he had married his father's wife. He declared that Widim-Rä'ad (1299–1314) was not his father. The sceptical monks retorted that he was only creating excuses based on the rumours that he was the issue of an illicit affair between Widim-Rä'ad's queen and Qidm-Asägid, his brother, *Gädlä Bäṣälotä-Mīka'él*, loc. cit.

[3] Sawirus, *History of the Patriarch of Alexandria*, ii, pt. 3, p. 339. Characteristically, the Ethiopic version reports that the bishop's efforts were an unqualified success, and the king also dropped all but one of his wives, Budge, *The Book of the Saints*, p. 995. It is stated elsewhere that one of the Zagwé kings was an ordained priest and that he decreed a strict monogamy in his kingdom, 'Gädlä Yimriha-Kristos', MS. Lalībäla, ff. 28^b–29^a.

[4] *Gädlä Éwosṭatéwos*, p. 35.

exiled once again, apparently back to Tigré, where he died at Gilo-Mäkäda.[1]

The question was reopened once again on the advent of Abunä Ya'iqob, the new Egyptian bishop, *c.* 1337 after the death of Bäṣälotä-Mīka'él. Ya'iqob added a new dimension to the movement. His predecessor, Yohannis, had been unpopular among the new monastic leaders of the country by maintaining the traditional close contact with the royal Court and the secular clergy. Ya'iqob now reversed this policy, and established excellent relations not only with the spiritual heirs of Bäṣälotä-Mīka'él, but also with the growing community of Däbrä Asbo in Shäwa. His first attempt was to organize a successful programme of evangelization in the pagan and Muslim provinces of the kingdom.[2] He probably tried to persuade the king in private to reform his matrimonial habits. When these quiet protestations failed he openly sided with the monks, and excommunicated the king.[3] Amdä-Ṣiyon threatened to expel the bishop, flogged his monastic allies, and dispersed them into exile.[4] It was probably this conflict with the Church which led to the rumours that Amdä-Ṣiyon was converted to Islam. Al-'Umari has recorded this rumour in his contemporary work on Ethiopia: 'It has been reported to us that the king ruling [Ethiopia] at present has been secretly converted to Islam, and that he continues to practise Christianity only to preserve his crown.'[5] An Ethiopic hagiographical tradition also accuses him of being indifferent to the conversion of Muslims to the Church. He is once said to have dismissed some of the converts [from Islam] of Bäṣälotä-Mīka'él with the following words: 'Go, and live according to the rules of your forefathers.'[6]

When Amdä-Ṣiyon died, Bishop Ya'iqob is said to have made an agreement with the new king that he would recall all the exiles and keep only one wife.[7] But the new king, Säyfä-'Ar'ad, soon went back on his word. Although he seems to have recalled the exiled monastic leaders, Säyfä-'Ar'ad formally married three wives just like his father and predecessor, Amdä-Ṣiyon. The bishop and his monastic followers protested once again, but it was all in vain. King Säyfä-'Ar'ad

[1] *Gädlä Bäṣälotä-Mīka'él*, pp. 29–30, 47–51.
[2] See Ch. V.
[3] *Gädlä Aron*, pp. 129–30.
[4] *Gädlä Fīlipos*, pp. 206–15. *Gädlä Aron*, pp. 131–2.
[5] Op. cit., p. 32, and n. 1.
[6] *Gädlä Bäṣälotä-Mīka'él*, p. 31 (text).
[7] *Gädlä Fīlipos*, p. 224; *Gädlä Aron*, p. 85.

deported Bishop Ya'iqob back to Egypt, and sent out all the recalcitrant monks to the southern part of the kingdom in exile.[1] The difficulties which thus befell these militant leaders apparently created divisions in the monastic movement. Many of the monks are accused of having accepted land and money from the king, to live with him on his own terms.[2] Others are said to have refused to give even a temporary shelter to the king's opponents.[3] Quite a new period had now started for the monasteries, and the will of the king had been triumphant over their ephemeral puritanical movements. To a very large extent, the first major Ethiopian attempt to reform the spiritual life of the Church had thus become a failure.

[1] Ibid., pp. 141–9, *Gädlä Fīlipos*, pp. 226, 233–6. *Gädlä Anoréwos*, pp. 89–90. For the full story of these exiles and their contribution to the expansion of the Church, see Ch. V.

[2] *Gädlä Bäṣälotä-Mīka'él*, pp. 45–6.

[3] Fīlipos was turned away from the gates of Däbrä Asbo (his own monastery) and Mäkanä Ṣäräbt because of his quarrel with the king, *Gädlä Fīlipos*, p. 241.

CHAPTER IV

Territorial Expansion
(1270–1430)

THE Christian kingdom at the time of Yikunno-'Amlak's accession in 1270 apparently extended to the region of Shīmäzana and the Märäb river, in the north;[1] the Täkäzé river, southern Bägémdir, and the upper basins of the eastern tributaries of the Blue Nile, in the west; the edge of the plateau from northern Ethiopia down to the Shäwan region, in the east; and the northern part of the Shäwan plateau, in the south.

A large section of the army which Yikunno-'Amlak led against the last Zagwé king came from the Shäwan region.[2] It is most likely that in the Shäwan districts which contributed these troops a number of Christian families had already been living for many generations. In hagiographical traditions about the thirteenth century, it is reported that small and isolated Christian communities were to be found unevenly scattered in the pagan dominated districts of Ṣilalish,[3] and Mugär[4] on the Shäwan plateau. Wägda, at the edge of the plateau

[1] Däbrä-Lībanos of Shīmäzana has a tradition of land grants by Yikunno-'Amlak, Conti Rossini, 'L'evangelo d'oro', pp. 194–5, 196. The Adkämä-Mälga, who have traditions of migrating from Lasta as a result of a Shäwan invasion, settled in Sära'é, and the incident was probably related to the fall of the Zagwé, Conti Rossini, 'Studi su popolazioni d'Etiopia', p. 82 (extract). Garrone, V., 'Gli Atcheme-Melga', pp. 997–9.

[2] Marianus, V., extract quoted by Perruchon, 'Notes pour l'histoire d'Éthiopie', in *RS*, i (1893), p. 368. Conti Rossini, 'La caduta della dinastia Zague', pp. 295–6. The Shäwan districts mentioned as having contributed these troops are *Wägda, Dinbī, Mugär, Wäj, Wäräb, Ṣilalish,* and *Mwal,* collectively referred to as the seven *Gwidim.* See also p. 67 n. 6.

[3] Täklä-Haymanot's ancestor, Yidla, is believed to have settled here ten generations before the saint, Conti Rossini, *Il 'Gadla Takla Haymanot'*, pp. 102–3. Budge, *The Life of Takla Haymanot*, pp. 5–6 (text). 'Gädlä Zéna-Marqos', f. 1[a]. Its location had been uncertain ever since Conti Rossini placed it, for unknown reasons, in Shäwa, 'towards the Nile', op. cit., p. 125 n. 4. But it is an ancient name for Itīsa, which is still a popular centre of pilgrimage as the birth-place of Täklä-Haymanot, cf. Täklä-Ṣadiq Mäkurya, *History of Ethiopia* (Amharic), ii, p. 20.

[4] This still survives in the name of the river Mugär flowing into the Nile, *west* of Däbrä Lībanos. Anoréwos (d. 1374), a disciple of Täklä-Haymanot, was born

overlooking Tägulät and Morät, is on the way to both Mugär and Ṣilalish from Amhara, and traditions of the Däbrä Lībanos cycle indicate that it was a Christian area by the middle of the thirteenth century.[1]

Christian immigrants had long been moving from Tigré, in the north, to the region of Amhara, and further south to Shäwa. It appears that this process was in full swing by the ninth century.[2] This slow population movement cannot be fully documented, but from the available traditions about the genealogy of Täklä-Haymanot[3] it seems possible to infer the gradual Christian settlement in Amhara and Shäwa.[4] The essential value of these traditions only lies in showing that, for many generations before the period covered by this study, a chain of Christian settlements had been forming from the northernmost fringes of Amhara to the south-eastern corner of the Shäwan plateau. However, these early population movements brought only a handful of Christian families to the pagan south, and only served as a pointer to the direction of the eventual expansion of the Christian kingdom. And, despite the clerical bias of these traditions which give a missionary origin to the migrations,[5] more than eight generations passed before any appreciable evangelization was carried out. When this was at last started, it was inextricably connected with the rise of the new dynasty in the Christian kingdom.

Both Christian and Muslim traditions indicate that the whole of the Shäwan region was dominated by a strong pagan kingdom—the

in this region, *Gädlä Anoréwos*, p. 67 (text). Fīlipos (d. *c.* 1349), second successor of Täklä-Haymanot as abbot, was also born at a place called Zim, a day's journey *west* of the monastery, *Gädlä Fīlipos*, pp. 175, 187 (text).

[1] 'Gädlä Qäwisṭos', MS. Däbrä Lībanos, ff. 2, 4, 68; 'Gädlä Zéna-Marqos', ff. 3[b], 12[a].

[2] See pp. 35–7, 156–7.

[3] This genealogy is given in both versions of the Life of the saint, and in some other related hagiographies, Conti Rossini, *Il 'Gadla Takla Haymanot'*, p. 102. Budge, *The Life of Takla-Haymanot*, pp. 3–5 (text). 'Gädlä Qäwisṭos', ff. 19–23. 'Gädlä Zéna-Marqos' ff. 13–18.

[4] The ancestors of Täklä-Haymanot are said to have moved to Shäwa in three different stages: Hizbä-Barik, a Tigré cleric, first settled in Dawint (Amhara), 18 generations before. His grandson, Asqä-Léwī, is said to have moved further south and 'baptized the people of Wäläqa, Amhara, Märhabīté, and Mänzih'. One of his descendants, Yidla, ten generations before Täklä-Haymanot, migrated still further south to Ṣilalish in Shäwa.

[5] According to some versions of the traditions of Digna-Jan, king of Aksum, the ancestors of Täklä-Haymanot are said to have been sent to Amhara and Shäwa with numerous other priests to evangelize the region, Budge, op. cit., pp. 3–5 (text).

kingdom of Damot[1]—before the last quarter of the thirteenth century. According to Christian tradition, Motälamī, a legendary monarch of Damot, invaded the Shäwan region as far north as the Jäma river, and almost completely annihilated the small Christian communities in the area. He is said to have conducted these invasions on two occasions: some time before the birth of Täklä-Haymanot,[2] and when the saint was a fully grown young man of twenty-five.[3] If the chronology of the life of Täklä-Haymanot (*c.* 1215–1313), transmitted by the hagiographical traditions, is correct,[4] the invasions of Motälamī must have taken place in the first half of the thirteenth century. This tallies very well with the period of the revival of the Christian kingdom in the north, and with the local traditions of renewed Christian attempts at southern expansion. About two centuries after the queen of the *Bani al-Hamwiyah* had successfully got rid of Christian overlordship in the Shäwan region,[5] the Christians of Amhara are reported as having been in military conflicts with their south-eastern neighbours—the *Wärjih* pastoralists—in the second quarter of the twelfth century.[6] Probably, similar moves were also

[1] Until the Muslim invasions of the sixteenth century, Damot referred to the region immediately south of the Blue Nile, and west of the sources of the Awash river. Its limits are indefinable, but it may have extended as far west as the Didéssa, and as far south as the region of Innarya. To the east, it probably bordered on Hadya, and Conti Rossini thinks that the region of Wälamo may have also been included in it, cf. *Futuh al-Habasha*, tr. Basset, p. 54 n. 2. Conti Rossini, 'Postille al "Futuh al-Habasha"', in *Le Muséon*, vol. lix (1946), pp. 180–1.

[2] Conti Rossini, *Il 'Gadla Takla Haymanot'*, p. 102, Budge, op. cit., pp. 8–15 (text). 'Gädlä Qäwisṭos', ff. 5–7.

[3] Conti Rossini, op. cit., pp. 105–7. Cf. also Budge, op. cit., pp. 45–53. According to the Waldibban version edited by Conti Rossini, Täklä-Haymanot was himself taken prisoner to Damot on this second invasion, and there, he preached until he succeeded in converting Motälamī. In the much-paraphrased text published and translated by Budge, however, Täklä-Haymanot apparently made the trip of his own accord to preach the Gospel. In both versions, however, Motälamī's power was strongly felt in the whole region of Shäwa.

[4] The saint is said to have died in the 14th year of the reign of Widim-Rä'ad (1299–1314), Basset, R., *Études sur l'histoire d'Éthiopie*, p. 99 (tr.). This also fits other comparative chronological notes. Thus, Fīlipos, who succeeded the saint as abbot of Däbrä Asbo, only three months after his death, had occupied the chair for 28 years, when he was exiled to Tigré by Amdä-Ṣiyon in 1341, *Gädlä Fīlipos*, pp. 192, 246 (text). Täklä-Haymanot is said to have been 55 years old when Yikunno-'Amlak acceded to the throne in 1270, Basset, op. cit., pp. 98–9 (tr.). He lived for just over 99 years, Budge, op. cit., p. 96 (text).

[5] See pp. 38–41. We have seen there the persistent traditions about strong female rulers in the Shäwan region. It is interesting to note in this connection that the genealogy given for the legendary king of Damot, Motälamī, only refers to his mother: 'Motälamī, whose mother's name was Esländané', Budge, op. cit., p. 21 (tr.).

[6] Cerulli, E., 'Il sultanato dello Scioa', p. 10, and note 4.

directed towards the northern districts of the Shäwan plateau, where a new wave of Christian settlements were apparently established. The tradition of the military expedition of a Zagwé king into Damot may belong to this period.[1] Christian pressure in the area probably increased over the years, and the traditions of Motälamī's invasions may only represent a strong pagan reaction against this process of expansion.

The story of Yikunno-'Amlak's revolt against the Zagwé indicates —as mentioned above—that he procured substantial military support from Shäwa. In the tradition, the troops who served under him on that occasion are referred to as 'his warriors', and this most likely means that all the seven districts, from which they were recruited,[2] had already become tributary to him. No doubt his success against the Zagwé and his assumption of the Christian throne also enhanced his power in Shäwa. For the period after the overthrow of the Zagwé, both Christian and Muslim traditions are unanimous in showing that Yikunno-'Amlak conducted a strong offensive against the pagan 'kingdom of Damot' which gave the Christian kingdom, once and for all (until the end of our period), a dominant position in the Shäwan plateau. According to one version Yikunno-'Amlak 'appointed [Motälamī] king of Innarya . . . and gave him the land beyond the Gibé river'.[3] This only means that Christian military success in the Shäwan plateau forced the withdrawal of the centre of Damoti resistance further south, and as we shall soon see, it was not until the reign of King Amdä-Ṣiyon that pagan Damot was effectively reduced to a vassal state. But the most valuable account of the conquests of Yikunno-'Amlak in the Shäwan region, which was once under Damoti overlordship, is given by the Arab historian Ibn Khaldun (1332–1406):

To the west of the countries of the king of the *habasha* is situated the city of *Damout*. A great king ruled there in former times, and he had a large empire. To the north of the same [countries] was found another king belonging to the same race [of the *habasha*], and called Hack ed-Din ibn Muhammad ibn Ali ibn Oulasma. He lived in the city of Oufat. . . . Since

[1] *Gädlä Yaréd*, ed. Conti Rossini, pp. 22–6.

[2] See p. 119 n. 2.

[3] Guidi, I., 'Strofe e brevi testi amarici', in *MSOS*, x (1907), pp. 180, 182. The tradition is here given as part of a compilation of historical notes made in the middle of the nineteenth century. Just as in the dynastic struggle between Yikunno-'Amlak and the Zagwé, Täklä-Haymanot is said to have intervened to effect amicable relations with Motälamī also.

his ancestor Oulasma had recognized the authority of the king of Damout, the *Hati* was offended by it, and he took away his kingdom from him.[1]

Wälasma, also called 'Umar, was the first historical ruler of the Muslim principality of Īfat,[2] and just like Yikunno-'Amlak, he flourished in the last quarter of the thirteenth century. The last part of Ibn Khaldun's passage is clearly a reference to that period. At that stage of the history of the region, therefore, the principal contenders for what appears to be the control of the Shäwan plateau were the Christian kingdom and the king of Damot, and the outcome of the conflict was a Christian success. Local Christian traditions also report that already at the time of Yikunno-'Amlak, the Shäwan plateau north of the Awash river was under Christian administration.[3] To a very large extent this is confirmed by Ibn Khaldun's story quoted above, and written only about a century after the events took place.[4] Maqrizi also refers to this early predominance of Christian power in the Shäwan region already by the second half of the thirteenth century. According to his informants, who were Muslims themselves, even 'Umar Wälasma owed much of his power to the Christian king. He speaks of the reign of this founder of the ruling house of Īfat and Adal in the following terms: 'This man administered for a long time with great power the government of Awfat and the country subject to it *which he had received from the Hati* . . .'[5]

[1] *Histoire des Berbères*, tr. de Slane, new edition, Casanova, P. (1927), ii, p. 108. Cerulli, E., 'L'Etiopia medievale in alcuni brani di scrittori arabi', in *RSE*, iii (1943), p. 284. Trimingham, J. S., *Islam in Ethiopia* (ed. 1965), p. 59.

[2] Maqrizi, *Historia Regum Islamaticorum in Abyssinia*, tr. Rinck, F. T. (1790), pp. 17–18. Cerulli, E., 'Documenti arabi per la storia dell'Etiopia', in *MRAL*, ser. 6, vol. iv (1931), pp. 42–3. Id., 'Il sultanato dello Scioa', pp. 15–17.

[3] 'Gädlä Qäwisṭos', ff. 1–5. 'Gädlä Zéna-Marqos,' ff. 2–3. According to these traditions the districts of Wägda and Kätäta, Mugär, Ṣilalish, Fäṭägar, and even Däwaro were ruled by Christian chiefs. The pagan king of Damot, always referred to by the legendary name of Motälamī, was the most dominant power south of the Awash. In their details, these traditions are hagiographical in character and cannot be accepted literally. Their reference to Däwaro at that early period is particularly dubious. North of the Awash, however, they seem to have been based on early historical recollections.

[4] The effect of Ibn Khaldun's invaluable reference to this early confrontation between the Christian kingdom and the kingdom of Damot is considerably obscured by his attempt to round off a long history in a relatively short passage. Thus immediately after his reference to the period when the *Wälasma* was tributary to Damot he jumps to the long-drawn armed conflicts between the Christian kingdom and the descendants of 'Umar Wälasma. Cf. the translations of the passage quoted in Cerulli, E., 'L'Etiopia medievale', p. 284. Trimingham, op. cit., p. 59. The Arab historian simply passes over the crucial developments transmitted in the document published by Cerulli in his 'Il sultanato dello Scioa', and in the chronicles of Amdä-Ṣiyon.

[5] Op. cit., p. 17.

According to Masudi, the Muslims in the Ethiopian region were still living as clients of the native inhabitants in the middle of the tenth century.[1] Ibn Khaldun's description of the ruler of Īfat as an autonomous vassal chief, tributary to the king of Damot, provides another stage of development in the political status of Islam in the area. By the second half of the thirteenth century, a chain of Muslim commercial settlements and principalities had already been established along the major routes from Zeila to the interior of the Ethiopian plateau.[2] The most important among these were the principalities of Īfat and eastern Shäwa.

Both Maqrizi and the chronicle of the Wälasma dynasty give a Quraysh or Hashimite origin for 'Umar Wälasma.[3] According to Maqrizi, the ancestors of 'Umar Wälasma first settled in *Jabara* (or *Jabarta*) a region which he says belonged to Zeila; they gradually moved further inland and occupied Īfat also.[4] But Maqrizi gives us no information on the rulers before 'Umar Wälasma; nor does the chronicle of the Wälasma dynasty, despite the long genealogy it gives for 'Umar, who in fact assumes the characteristics of a legendary figure.[5]

The traditions of the 'sultanate of Shäwa' take its origin back to the end of the ninth century, ascribing it to a ruling house of Arab origin,

[1] *Les Prairies d'or*, iii, p. 34.

[2] Apart from the royal chronicles of the Christian kingdom our knowledge of the seven Muslim 'states' in the region mainly comes from Al-'Umari's work, later almost completely reproduced by Maqrizi with some additions. Recent investigation has brought to light the short chronicle of the Wälasma dynasty of Īfat and Adal, of which the translation was first published by Paulitschke and later by Cerulli with many useful notes and additions. A still more recent find has been the chronicle of the so-called 'Sultanate of Shäwa' edited and translated also by Cerulli. On the other six 'states' mentioned by Al-'Umari and Maqrizi—Däwaro, Balī, Hadya, Aräbabni, Sharkha, and Dara—we still have no additional material. All of these places, except Aräbabni, are later mentioned as outlying provinces of the kingdom in the royal chronicles.

[3] Maqrizi, op. cit., p. 17. Cerulli, 'Documenti arabi per la storia d'Etiopia', p. 43. It is interesting to note that Al-'Umari, Ibn Said, and Ibn Khaldun do not mention the Arab origin. According to Ibn Said (1214–74), 'The population of Īfat is very much mixed', Aboul Feda, *Géographie*, tr. Reinaud, M., ii (1848), p. 229. For Ibn Khaldun the Wälasma family belonged simply 'to the same race [of the *Habasha*] . . . and it derived its origin from a family which embraced Islam at a time which we cannot specify', op. cit., p. 108.

[4] Maqrizi, loc. cit. Ibn Said says that Īfat was also called *Djabara*, Aboul Feda, loc. cit. For the general connotation which the term *Jabarti* later acquired, see Bruce, *Travels to Discover the Source of the Nile* (1790), ii, pp. 8–9. Trimingham, op. cit., p. 150 notes 1 and 2.

[5] He is said to have lived for 120 years, and to have ruled for 80. He had 300 sons and 360 daughters, Cerulli, 'Documenti arabi', p. 43.

this time from the family of the Mahzumi Khalid b. Al-Walid.[1] Its annals before the middle of the thirteenth century consist only of an incomplete record of successive reigns. After 1234 its history describes continuous internal conflicts among the different branches of the ruling house, until 'Umar Wälasma gives it the *coup de grâce* in 1285 by finally annexing it to his own kingdom of Īfat.

The motive behind the actions of the Wälasma was clearly to consolidate the conflicting interests of the Muslims into a strong political power in the area. Before this attempt at a united Muslim political front, the nature of the penetration of Islam was still essentially commercial and the small 'sultanates' were conterminous with the trading interests of each. The internal conflicts among the different family groups in the thirteenth century do not represent a period of decline of Muslim political power, which was still in its early stages. This was only inherent in their competitive trading concerns in the interior. The policies of the Wälasma were directed at this essential weakness of Islam as a political force in the Ethiopian region. Looked at in another way, 'Umar Wälasma was doing in the Muslim communities exactly what Yikunno-'Amlak had just accomplished in the Christian kingdom, and it is more than a coincidence that the military and political activities of both were in full swing during precisely the same period of time. Īfat was evidently responding to the revival of the Christian kingdom and its growing involvement

[1] Cerulli, 'Il sultanato dello Scioa', pp. 15–16. The meaning of Shäwa as applied to this Muslim principality is very uncertain. In Christian documents the name applied to the whole plateau south of the Wänchīt-Addabay gorge and extending as far as the Awash river. There is nothing tangible to show that the Muslim 'sultanate of Shäwa' ever included any of the districts in the highland area west of the edge of the plateau. All the identifiable place-names in Cerulli's document were still Muslim in Amdä-Ṣiyon's reign, ibid., pp. 25–32. And in that period they clearly referred to the hot lowland areas east of the Shäwan plateau where the 'sultanate of Shäwa' must also be sought. For Al-'Umari 'Shäwa' was one of the 'mother cities' of Īfat together with *Biqulzär*, *Sime*, and *Adal*, op. cit., pp. 8–9. By the time he wrote (1342–9) it cannot have referred to the Shäwan plateau, which was securely in the hands of Amdä-Ṣiyon and Säyfä-Ara'd. Among the different contingents that joined Gragn at *Biqulzär*, his chronicler mentions a group recruited from a Muslim tribe called *Shoa* together with those of *Hargaya*, and *Gidayah*, *Futuh al Habasha*, tr. Basset, p. 173. In the Ethiopian chronicles *Hargaya* and *Gidayah* are mentioned in reference to Muslim districts east of Awash and Däwaro, cf. Perruchon, *Histoire des guerres d'Amde-Siyon*, pp. 283, 318, 321. *Les Chroniques de Zar'a Ya'eqob*, p. 166. Guidi, I., 'Le canzoni ge'ez-Amarina', p. 63. Probably the Muslim tribe of Shäwa also referred to the same region. More interesting still, a district of *Scioa* is mentioned among the other Adali districts of *Sim*, *Nagab*, *Gidaya*, and *Dakar* in a document regarding the sixteenth century, Cerulli, 'Documenti arabi', p. 57, and n. 6.

in the south.[1] As it happened, however, this Muslim bid for political supremacy in the Shäwan region came rather too late in time, and the initiative was soon lost in favour of the Christians.

In the early part of his reign, Yikunno-'Amlak was friendly, not only with the local Muslims, but also with the rulers of Yemen and Egypt. A letter he wrote to Sultan Baybars (1260–77) of Egypt, asking for a new bishop, reached Cairo in 1273/4 accompanied by a covering letter from the then ruler of Yemen, Al-Malik al-Muzeffar (1250–95), through whom the message had been sent. After the usual humble protestations Yikunno-'Amlak declared his friendly sentiments to all Muslims: 'All the Muslims who come to Our Kingdom, we protect them, and we permit them to travel in our realms as they wish.'[2] The letter also suggests that there was an earlier exchange of messengers in which the Mamluke governor of Kus had sent an envoy to Amhara where he was taken ill at the time of writing. Yikunno-'Amlak apologizes, in addition, for not having sent 'the ambassadors' back to Egypt as soon as he would have liked, because he was engaged in a campaign elsewhere.[3] Finally Yikunno-'Amlak informs the Egyptian ruler that his large army included a hundred thousand Muslim cavaliers, and a still greater number of Christians. This number is almost certainly an exaggeration, but the essential part of the message—that his troops included some Muslims—is not hard to accept.[4]

In the later part of his reign, however, Yikunno-'Amlak was

[1] A chronological study of some of the events that took place in the two communities suggest this. For instance: Yikunno-'Amlak became king in 1270. Marriage relations between the reigning sultan of Shäwa and a daughter of the Wälasma were contracted in 1271. The Wälasma's first visit (probably hostile) to eastern Shäwa happened in 1277. His son burnt what appears to be the capital of the Mahzumite sultanate in the same year. The deposed Mahzumite ruler took refuge in Yikunno-'Amlak's court in 1278/9; cf. Cerulli, op. cit., pp. 11–14.

[2] Mufazzal, op. cit., pp. 384–5. Maqrizi, *Histoire des sultans Mamlouks de l'Égypte*, tr. Quatremère, i, pt. 1 (1840), p. 122 n. 151. Abdul Aziz al-Khowayter, 'A Critical Edition of an Unknown Source of the Life of al-Malik al-Zahir Baibars', Ph.D. Thesis (London University, 1960), ii, pp. 315–16.

[3] Blochet thinks this may be a reference to envoys previously sent by Baybars to Ethiopia, cf. Mufazzal, op. cit., p. 384 n. 3. It was in Baybars's time that Egypt took a more decisive action against Nubia, and the sultan took a special interest in ensuring the safety of the Dahlak–Suakin–Aydab–Kus route. Yikunno-'Amlak's contacts with the governor of Kus and with Baybars must be seen against this background. Cf. Al-Khowayter, op. cit. i, pp. 283–5; ii, pp. 498, 580.

[4] In an Ethiopian MS. at the British Museum there is a representation of Yikunno-'Amlak seated on his royal dais and surrounded by Muslim ambassadors and servants. The inscription reads: 'Muslims and slaves', Wright, *Catalogue*, Or. 503, ff. 75^{b}–76.

definitely taking offensive actions against the Muslims. This was partly a result of the failure of his mission to Cairo, which was largely due to the apparent lack of full co-operation on the part of the ruler of Yemen. Yikunno-'Amlak had sent his envoys, charged with the letter to Baybars, via Yemen. He expected that the ruler of Yemen would send them on to Cairo as soon as possible, and also facilitate their return with the new bishop by the same route. Yikunno-'Amlak promised to send the presents to the sultan of Egypt, usual on such occasions, upon the arrival of the bishop in Ethiopia, through the good offices of the ruler of Yemen. The latter, however, detained the envoys at his court, alleging that he would have to ask for the authorization of the sultan before sending them to Cairo. He then sent the king's letter to Baybars together with his own request for permission to send the envoys also to his court. This is clear from Baybars's reply to Yikunno-'Amlak:

> Regarding the request for a bishop, submitted to Us in the letter, no one has come to Our Court to discuss the matter with Us on behalf of the king; so that We do not know at all what you expect from Us. As for the letter of Sultan Al-Malik al-Muzeffar, it has reached Us, explaining that the latter has received a letter and an envoy from the king of Ethiopia whom he has kept with him until he receives a reply [from Us] to his letter.[1]

It is not known if this reply ever reached Yikunno-'Amlak. We only find it sent back to Cairo in 1290 enclosed in another letter from his son and successor, Yagba-Ṣiyon (1285–94). From this second letter it is clear that Yikunno-'Amlak did not succeed in obtaining the bishop he asked for.[2]

Yikunno-'Amlak resented the serious limitation imposed upon him by the fact that he was dependent on the goodwill of neighbouring Muslim states, even for the religious needs of his kingdom. This feeling contributed to his growing anti-Muslim activities and probably led to armed conflicts also.[3] His son's letter referred to these hostilities from which he was clearly anxious to dissociate himself: 'My father . . . was an enemy of the Muslims . . . But as for me, I am not like my father at all in this respect; but I protect the Muslims in all the realms of my kingdom.'[4]

Yikunno-'Amlak's policies were directed towards creating a united

[1] Mufazzal, op. cit., p. 386. Maqrizi, *Histoire des sultans Mamlouks*, loc. cit.

[2] See pp. 70–2.

[3] Conti Rossini, 'Marco Polo e l'Etiopia', in *ARIV*, vol. 99, pt. 2 (1940), pp. 1024–8.

[4] Quatremère, *Mémoires géographiques et historiques*, ii (1811), p. 268.

kingdom, militarily and politically dominant throughout the whole Ethiopian region. This would give him the necessary control of the lucrative trade of the Muslims in the interior and eventually ensure their complete dependence on his kingdom. This would, in turn, make his bargaining power *vis-à-vis* the sultans of Egypt much more effective. In the Shäwan region his policy took the form of an active political intervention in the local rivalries of the Muslim princes. In one such conflict Dil-Marrah, the Mahzumite sultan of Shäwa, who was also the son-in-law of the Wälasma, escaped from his enemies and took refuge at the court of Yikunno-'Amlak in December/January 1278/9. He apparently remained there until his return in April/May 1280. Probably enraged by this unpatriotic act of his son-in-law, Wälasma sent his son Ali to join forces with Dil-Marrah's local rival, Dil-Gamis, and to fight against another attack of Dil-Marrah from the Christian Court. At the beginning, the league failed in both these missions: Abdallah succeeded in taking power for a short time, and Dil-Marrah was able to return to Abut in Shäwa. Dil-Marrah was probably accompanied by a few Christian troops on his way back and was able to resist Īfati hostilities for three years. By then, however, the Wälasma himself had come to Shäwa once more, and had assumed full powers in the region. He led what appears to have been punitive expeditions against many areas, in one of which Dil-Marrah was captured and executed in May 1283.[1]

The ruler of Īfat now began consolidating his power against Shäwa. in July/August 1285 he captured all the contending Mahzumite princes and massacred them to a man. In their place he nominated a certain Mhz (?) and returned to Īfat feeling assured that, with the removal of the traditional rulers, the last vestiges of Shäwan resistance to his power were destroyed once and for all. He was soon disappointed in this. No sooner did he return home than Mhz himself led a rebellion in an attempt to regain Shäwan independence. The Wälasma invaded Shäwa once more, and furiously pillaged the country and its allies of Gidaya and Haddimorra. It appears that this determined move on the part of Īfat to control all the Muslim regions brought about much local resistance, and it was necessary for the Wälasma to send campaigns against each. Mora, Adal, Hobat, Zatanbar were each attacked and occupied. The predominance of Īfat in the Muslim regions was now taking shape.[2]

[1] Cerulli, E., op. cit., pp. 12–13 and pp. 16–17.

[2] As will be seen below, Al-'Umari reports, in the first half of the fourteenth

After the return of Dil-Marrah to Shäwa from his court, it is not clear what Yikunno-'Amlak's role was in these local conflicts. It is, however, unlikely that he could have been indifferent to these events in Shäwa. The fact that the Muslim chronicle of Shäwa found it necessary to record his death strongly implies that the king had always maintained a close contact with developments in the south.[1]

Yagba-Ṣiyon began his reign on friendly terms with the Muslims.[2] As mentioned above, he confirmed this to the sultan of Egypt and requested him to hold a similar attitude towards his Christian subjects: '. . . I protect the Muslims in all the realms of my kingdom; and I wish that the Sultan . . . does the same to the Christians of his realms, so that durable friendship would reign between the two of us, and so that this would be cemented by mutual embassies.'[3] Yagba-Ṣiyon had a Christian (Egyptian?) secretary, called Daud ben Azz, who wrote his letters for him in Arabic and had the title of '*Wazir* of the king'.[4] He was thus in close touch with developments in the Near East. Very little internal (Ethiopic) material for this reign is as yet available, and the king's name is only barely mentioned in the lists of kings. However from his letters to the sultan, to the patriarch of Alexandria, John VII (1262–8; 1271–93), and to the Ethiopian community in Jerusalem,[5] he emerges as one determined to maintain friendly relations with the Muslims both at home and abroad. His envoys to Cairo were led by an Ethiopian Muslim called Yusuf Abderrahman, who died in Cairo. On his death another member of the delegation whom the Arab chronicler calls 'an Abyssinian'[6] assumed the position of ambassador and submitted to the sultan both the letters and the presents[7] sent by Yagba-Ṣiyon.

century, this predominance of Īfat among the Muslims in the Ethiopian region as a whole, and in the corridor between Zeila and Shäwa in particular. It is very likely that the emergence of Īfat as a strong power started with these early actions of the Wälasma against his neighbouring Muslim principalities; cf. Al-'Umari, op. cit., p. 5.

[1] Cerulli, op. cit., pp. 13, 19.

[2] His father died in 1285. His letter reached Cairo in 1290, five years after his accession to power, and it may have been sent from Ethiopia even earlier.

[3] Quatremère, op. cit., p. 268.

[4] Ibid., pp. 270–1.

[5] This is the first time we have an official royal message to the community. This in itself indicates that the king was able to command considerable goodwill among the Muslims, who were his major channel of communication.

[6] This probably means a Christian Abyssinian. That Yusuf was also Ethiopian is suggested by a cousin of his who sent a note to Cairo about Yusuf's death from Aydab where he had just disembarked on his way back to Ethiopia from Mecca. Cf. Quatremère, loc. cit.

[7] These consisted of a eunuch and 'une pique dorée servant en guise de lampe', ibid., pp. 268, 270–1.

This policy of co-operation with the Muslims was not, however, a renunciation of Yikunno-'Amlak's intentions of making the Christian kingdom the strongest single power in the area. In fact, as we have seen from his letter to Qalawun, Yagba-Ṣiyon was giving a new dimension to the growing power of his kingdom by posing as the protector of his fellow Christians in Egypt. That he could do this with sufficient confidence, only less than five years after his accession to power, shows how much the prestige of the kingdom had been enhanced in the momentous reign of his father. This special concern for the Christians of Egypt, which Yagba-Ṣiyon initiated, would henceforth be invoked time and again by his descendants in their relations with both Egypt and their Muslim subjects and neighbours at home.

It is possible, however, to detect a great deal of internal weakness in Yagba-Ṣiyon's unreserved declaration of friendly sentiments towards the Muslims in his letters to Cairo. The policy of strong Christian offensive against Damot and the Muslims in the Shäwan region was seriously interrupted by the internal conflicts following the death of Yikunno-'Amlak. These dynastic problems only came to an end with the accession to power of Widim-Rä'ad (1299–1314)[1] which introduced a new period of protracted hostility between the Christians and the Muslims.

It is apparent that this started with a determined Muslim offensive against the Christian districts on the eastern borders of the Shäwan plateau. A certain Sheikh Muhammad, also called Abu-Abdallah, is reported to have gathered a huge following in 1299 in an attempt to lead a *jihad* against the Christian kingdom.[2] Widim-Rä'ad intervened, we are told, by intriguing through his agents in the sheikh's camp, and managed to persuade many of the soldiers to forsake the cause of the sheikh. Faced with these mass desertions, Abu-Abdallah had to conclude an honourable peace with the Christian king:

> . . . the lord of Amhara sent a delegation to Sheikh Abu-Abdallah, and he conceded to him many districts on the frontiers of the land of the *habasha*; [these districts] would constitute a territory in which [the sheikh] and his companions could settle on the formal condition that they would demand nothing more from the prince of the Amhara who also undertook to

[1] Taddesse Tamrat, 'The Abbots of Däbrä Hayq', pp. 91–3.

[2] Mufazzal, *Histoire des sultans Mamlouks*, ed. and tr. Blochet, in *PO*, xx (1929), pp. 56–8. Cerulli, 'L'Etiopia medievale in alcuni brani di scrittori Arabi', in *RSE*, iii (1943), pp. 281–4.

provide them with all their needs until they are completely satisfied; and they would recognize his sovereignty.[1]

We are not told exactly where the camp of the sheikh was. The only definite thing that can be said from the text about the centre of the Muslim movement is that it was *east* of the Blue Nile. The Christian king sent his envoys to Sheikh Abu-Abdallah 'from the direction of the Nile'.[2] It appears that the incident represented a further stage in the consolidation of the power of Īfat. We have already seen that the Wälasma had unified the Muslims of eastern Shäwa under his own leadership in about 1280. Encouraged by the internal difficulties of the descendants of Yikunno-'Amlak, they were now making a bid for the control of the Shäwan plateau also. Nevertheless, although the story had a Muslim origin, Sheikh Abu-Abdallah's adventure shows the essential weakness of Islam as a political force. Abu-Abdallah's followers displayed very little unity of purpose, and the Christian king had great influence in the rank and file of the Muslim community. The incident also indicates, however, Widim-Rä'ad's internal problems which did not permit him to take a more decisive action against the new Muslim challenge. Both Widim-Rä'ad and Sheikh Abu-Abdallah concluded their agreement of 1299 from a position of relative weakness. It is most likely that, in the military engagements that must have followed the disclosure of Abu-Abdallah's plans, the two parties reached a stalemate which could only be decided by the conclusion of an agreement. This is indeed what is implied in Mufazzal's own passage: '. . . They sent their envoys from the direction of the Nile to establish the terms of a peace settlement; and this situation lasted for six months.'[3] We have no further information on Widim-Rä'ad's relations with the Muslims after this incident. It seems, however, that in the following fifteen years of his reign, he had considerably improved his position, and that his control of the

[1] Mufazzal, op. cit., p. 58.

[2] The name of the sheikh may also give an additional clue to the area of the conflict. In the district of *Käsäm*, on the eastern edge of the Shäwan plateau, there is still a locality known as *Abdälla*. The church of St. George there is called Abdälla Giyorgis. This is most probably the area where Widim-Rä'ad allowed the sheikh and his followers to settle. It fits the historical topography of the period very well. In the hostilities of 1332 a certain Abdallah was killed in Adal. The Christian chronicler refers to him as 'their ruler whom they revere like a bishop', Perruchon, *Histoire des guerres*, p. 422. This took place only three decades after the attempted *jihad*, and in the reign of Widim-Rä'ad's son and immediate successor. Al-'Umari also had an informant in Cairo whom he calls, 'le pieux Cheikh "Abd Allah ez-Zeila'i"', op. cit., p. 3.

[3] Mufazzal, loc. cit.

Shäwan plateau had become secure. This is quite clear from the relative ease of military superiority which Amdä-Ṣiyon enjoyed from the very beginning of his remarkable reign.

King Amdä-Ṣiyon (1314–1344)

Amdä-Ṣiyon inherited the military and political problems of the turbulent reigns of his immediate predecessors. These included the final consolidation of the powers of the new dynasty in all the Christian provinces; programmes of expansion into the Agäw districts in the north-west, the kingdom of Gojjam in the west, and Damot in the south-west; and the more important struggle with the Muslims in the east and south-east.

A state of uneasy peace with the Muslims seems to have existed at the time of Amdä-Ṣiyon's accession to power. One of the most important reasons for Christian–Muslim conflicts was the need for the kingdom to ensure a free and unmolested passage of its nationals or agents to the Red Sea and beyond. This had already created the difficulties between Yikunno-'Amlak and the ruler of Yemen. The same consideration motivated the attempt to create a spirit of co-operation based on mutual respect between the Muslims and the Christian kingdom in the reign of Yagba-Ṣiyon. The Muslims had always enjoyed an almost complete monopoly of long-distance trade in the whole region. Sometimes they acted as the agents of the Christian kings, sometimes as independent traders. In either case Muslim rulers were masters of the areas through which the main trade routes passed. This technical dependence of the Christians on the service and goodwill of the Muslims was easily liable to be used for political purposes, especially in times of hostile relations. This appears to be the immediate reason which sparked off the first major military encounter between Amdä-Ṣiyon and the ruler of Īfat.

Amdä-Ṣiyon complained that Haqädīn, the ruler of Īfat, had arrested a certain subject of his called Ti'iyintay, who had probably been proceeding on a mission to the coast.[1] He answered this offence with an all-out attack against Īfat, and the Muslim regions in the south. Taken by itself the Ti'iyintay incident was a minor one. The king himself describes Haqädīn's Christian captive as 'one of his least servants'. But it touched a sensitive chord in Christian–Muslim relations in the area, and precipitated a series of military encounters

[1] Perruchon, op. cit., p. 352 (tr.).

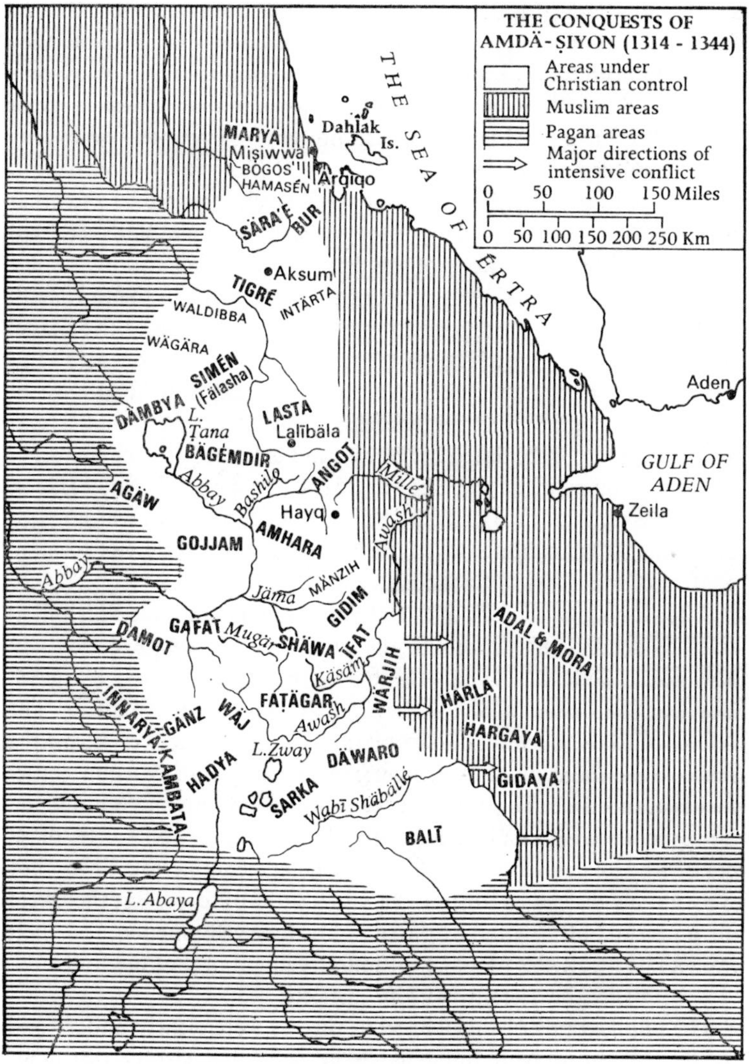

MAP 4.

which changed the balance of power in the Horn of Africa in favour of the Christians, for more than two centuries.

At this time Amdä-Ṣiyon was at Shagura, a place in the immediate neighbourhood of Īfat, probably to the north-west.[1] He marched

[1] Ibid., p. 332 n. 1, and p. 339 (tr.). Cf. also *Gädlä Abäkäräzun*, ed. and tr.

south and attacked Īfat, which seems to have been quite unprepared for the encounter. The Christian army scored an easy success; they pillaged the country and sacked the town of Īfat itself. Amdä-Ṣiyon's description of this town gives an impression that it was a great centre of trade and Muslim political power: '. . . And then came my troops and destroyed the great [city] called Īfat. And I took from it a large quantity of gold, silver, and precious clothes. As for the other metallic objects I took from there, they were as innumerable as pieces of stone . . .'[1] The implications of this description are remarkably similar to those of Ibn-Said's description of the same town in the thirteenth century, which confirms its position of great importance as the citadel of Islam in the region: 'The palace of the king is built on a hill . . . The town is at a great distance from the sea; it is located west of Zeila . . . Its inhabitants profess Islam . . .'[2] It was here that 'Umar Wälasma had consolidated his power and extended it over the other Muslim principalities from Shäwa to Hubat, near present-day Harär, in the last years of the thirteenth century. Its destruction was a major blow against Islam and opened the way for a more effective Christian control of the districts to the east and south-east.

After his signal victory over Īfat Amdä-Ṣiyon continued his offensives by sending his troops to the other Muslim establishments in Kwilgorä, Gidayä, Kubät (Ḥubat?), Fädisé, Qädisé, Hargayä, Biqulzär, and eastern Shäwa beyond the edge of the plateau. The reference to the burning of 'strong forts' in these places confirms the respectable stage of development reached by these Muslim settlements at this time. These early advances of Amdä-Ṣiyon do not seem, however, to have resulted immediately in a direct control of these conquered places. Like most other engagements at the time, they were largely occasions for plunder and a show of force. But they were an unmistakable pointer to later political developments, and their immediate result was to make the military might of the kingdom more closely felt by the distant Muslim districts.

The implications of this Christian success were clearly understood by the Muslims, who immediately organized a strong resistance which at first seemed to reverse the situation. They rallied around Haqädīn's son, called Däradir.[3] The new leader furiously attacked

Conti Rossini, pp. 25–6 (text). *Sägura* is here mentioned as being near Diror in Īfat and Zéga. The saint was travelling to Tigré from the south.

[1] Perruchon, op. cit., p. 283 (text). [2] Aboul Feda, op. cit., p. 229.

[3] Perruchon, op. cit., p. 284 (text). Haqädīn himself seems to have lost his life in one of the earliest engagements.

the south-eastern districts of the kingdom with what appears to have been a large army consisting of Wärjih pastoralists of eastern Shäwa and of the regions east of the Awash.[1] Amdä-Ṣiyon himself bemoans his own defeat which followed in no flattering terms to himself:

The people called Wärjih and Gäbäl, who are experts in killing and war, came to fight me from the confines of Finṣäté to the frontiers of Biqulzär. From the river of Hawash to Zäbir [there were] also Muslims. And the land of the Christians was destroyed, and the land of Ziga and Mänzih. All these leagued against me and surrounded me.[2]

It is not clear for how long this military superiority of the Muslims lasted. The Christian chronicle which is the only source for these hostilities, reports that Amdä-Ṣiyon soon resumed his victorious position and later developments confirm it. Däradir himself was captured and killed. This probably resulted in the immediate disbanding of the largely tribal Muslim forces. The morale of the resistance was seriously damaged and it appears that for most of the period before the advent of Säbrädīn, Amdä-Ṣiyon's adversary in 1332, Īfat was ruled alternately by a series of usurpers and military adventurers.[3] This state of affairs may have been promoted by the increasingly more direct intervention of Amdä-Ṣiyon.

One of the earliest campaigns of Amdä-Ṣiyon was conducted against Damot and Hadya. It took place in A.D. 1316/17 and the king commemorates his success in a contemporary note in an early Ethiopic manuscript at the library of the island monastery of Hayq:

. . . [In A.D. 1316/17] I went to war trusting the prayers of [St.] Stephen and my Father Kristos-Täsfanä . . . [And] God gave me all the people of Damot into my hands: its king, its princes, its rulers, and its people, men and women without number, whom I exiled into another area. And after that God gave me all the people of Hadya, men and women without number, whom I exiled into another area . . .[4]

[1] About the earliest conflict between the Christian Amhara and the Wärjih see Cerulli, 'Il sultanato dello Scioa', p. 10 with n. 4.

[2] Perruchon, op. cit., p. 284 (text).

[3] The chronicle of the Wälasma dynasty has eight short reigns between Haqädīn and Säbrädīn, only two of which belonged to the grandsons of Umar Wälasma. The origin of the rest is not given. Maqrizi does not even mention these eight intervening reigns, most probably because of the unstable political conditions into which Īfat had fallen at the time. It also seems to be the reason why he assumed too early a date for Säbrädin's accession to power; he also makes him die at a very advanced age, Maqrizi, op. cit., pp. 17–18. Cerulli, 'Documenti arabi per la storia dell'Etiopia', pp. 43–4.

[4] This text has already been published in my 'The Abbots of Däbrä Hayq', p. 96.

These early victories had given the king a great source of wealth and manpower in the rich interior south and south-west of the river Awash. At first the king's control of these areas seems to have been minimal and limited to levying occasional tributes from the local rulers. This appears to be the case with Hadya in particular. Al-'Umari mentions Hadya as one of the 'seven Muslim states' in the Ethiopian region, placing it west of Balī.[1] It is not clear from his work when exactly Muslim influence became predominant in Hadya. The Christian report of Amdä-Ṣiyon's successful campaign in Hadya about 1316/17 does not at all imply that the king was fighting against Muslim troops. Al-'Umari's 'Muslim state of Hadya' may have been in fact a pagan kingdom in which a growing number of Muslim merchants had been settling; they had probably also converted some of the local people. But it does not seem that in Amdä-Ṣiyon's time the rulers of the country were as yet Muslims.[2] It is quite clear, however, that the influence of the Muslims in the area was very strong, and they used it to undermine the consolidation of Christian power there. Just before 1332, Amdä-Ṣiyon led another expedition against the kingdom of Hadya to offset such hostile activities.

According to his chronicler, the ruler of Hadya, called Amano, refused to come to the king's court and submit the usual tributes. He was encouraged in this by a Muslim 'false prophet'. Amdä-Ṣiyon's response to this was very swift. He led his army into Hadya, pillaged the country, and took many prisoners including Amano. The Muslim preacher himself fled to Īfat.[3] Amdä-Ṣiyon seems to have made a thorough job of his reconquest of Hadya which soon became an important source of manpower for the Christian army, of which contingents from Hadya would henceforth form a considerable part.[4]

With Hadya and the regions immediately to the north and west under his control, Amdä-Ṣiyon was now within measurable distance of achieving his initial programme of controlling the inland trade of

[1] Op. cit., pp. 15–17.

[2] Hadya is first mentioned by Ibn Said (1214–74), Aboul Feda, op. cit., p. 229. Although he specifically describes Īfat as Muslim in the same passage, his reference to Hadya has no political or religious connotations. On the slave trade see pp. 85–8. Cerulli's article in which he discusses all the available historical and traditional material on Hadya is still the best on the subject, 'Note su alcune popolazioni Sidama dell'Abissinia meridionale', in *RSO*, x (1925), pp. 599–610.

[3] Perruchon, op. cit., pp. 286–7 (text).

[4] Ibid., p. 293. Already in 1332 a contingent called Hadya was sent as part of the Christian troops to suppress a Fälasha revolt in Wägära.

the Muslims. The reconquest of Hadya in particular dealt a hard blow to the slave trade for which it had long been the major source of supply. It was largely on this trade that Muslim activities in the area were based, and the effect was felt, not only by the local traders of Hadya and their immediate neighbours, but by all the chain of Muslim settlements as far as the Red Sea coast. Moreover, Christian power and influence was fast growing in the newly conquered regions, and it looked as if it would soon extend further afield. The future of Islam *per se* was threatened as it had never been threatened before.

The response of the Muslims to this new challenge was equally striking. Until now the different settlements had been operating largely independently of one another, and the attempt of Īfat to create a united Muslim front had been only partially successful in its immediate neighbourhood, and even that had already been seriously damaged by the early successes of Amdä-Ṣiyon against Haqädīn and Däradir. Now, however, the time was ripe for a united action against the Christian intruder. Amdä-Ṣiyon's dauntless campaigns in areas hitherto unknown to Christian troops further shook their sense of security, and made the need for a league even stronger.

Once again, Īfat took the lead in the ensuing hostilities. Säbrädīn was the ruler of Īfat at the time, and he seems to have been at the centre of the new movement for which he was perfectly suited as the son of the great 'Umar Wälasma. Although evidence is lacking to determine the intellectual or doctrinal content of this movement, there are references in the chronicles to religious leaders helping in its organization. One of these is the 'false prophet' of the Christian chronicler, who fled to Īfat on the Christian conquest of Hadya. He appears to have continued his hostile propaganda in Īfat also, where he is represented as one of the advisers of Säbrädin:

> The false prophet fled to the land of Īfat and lived there propagating his false teaching . . . And when Säbrädīn asked him for counsel he told him saying: 'The kingdom of the Christians has now come to an end; and it has been given to us, for you will reign on *Siyon.*[1] Go, ascend [the mountains], and fight the king of the Christians; you will defeat him, and rule him together with his peoples . . .'[2]

There is also another religious leader referred to in the chronicles, this time in the Adal-Mora region: '. . . [it was] a man called Salīh whose title was *Qazī*, [a title] resembling that of an Archbishop, whom

[1] For the implications of the use of this Biblical term see pp. 249–50.
[2] Perruchon, op. cit., pp. 287–8 (text).

kings and rulers revere, and whom they fear like God; [it was this man] who gathered the Muslim troops, kings, and rulers [against Amdä-Ṣiyon] . . .'[1] The Muslim league against Amdä-Ṣiyon had therefore assumed the characteristics of a *jihad*. Its purpose was very ambitious, and not limited merely to regaining the provinces recently lost by the Muslims. It aimed at a complete take-over of all the Christian provinces, in order to remove the Christian threat once and for all. It appears that the political and military moves of Säbrädīn and his allies were extremely well planned.

Säbrädīn declared hostilities in the first months of 1332.[2] Together with the news of the Muslim risings in the east, Amdä-Ṣiyon also received reports of rebellions in the northern provinces of his kingdom.[3] It is not impossible that Säbrädīn deliberately chose the timing so that Amdä-Ṣiyon's huge army could be diverted elsewhere. This in fact suited the grandiose intentions of the ruler of Īfat.

According to the chronicler, one of the earliest steps taken by him was to nominate his own Muslim governors for all the provinces of the Christian kingdom.[4] He accordingly divided his army into three: The first part was to march due north to the province of Angot, the second due north-west to Amhara, and the rest led by himself was to march on Shäwa, where Amdä-Ṣiyon was camping.[5] Apparently, the king was warned of these plans and made a swift move to frustrate them. He sent a large force to attack Säbrädīn and his army at

[1] Ibid., p. 318 (text). Elsewhere, there are passing references to Säbrädīn's religious programmes after his victories, pp. 328–9 (tr.); and the plans of the 'king of Adal', are also mentioned, p. 363.

[2] Ibid., p. 279 (text). It is here said that hostilities started in 516 Year of Grace, in the 18th year of Amdä-Ṣiyon's reign. According to a contemporary historical note which has come to light only recently, Amdä-Ṣiyon succeeded Widim-Rä'ad on the throne in 498 Year of Grace, Taddesse Tamrat, 'The Abbots of Däbrä Hayq', n. 39. This shows the chronicler's accuracy in considering 516 Year of Grace the king's 18th regnal year. The two dates are equivalent to A.D. 1313/4 and 1331/2. For the rules of how to convert these dates see, Grébaut, S., 'Table de comput et de chronologie', in *ROC*, i (1918/19), pp. 324–6. Mauro da Leonessa, P., *Cronologia e calendario etiopico* (Tivoli, 1934), pp. 100–3. Id., 'Un trattato sul calendario redatto al tempo di re Amda-Syon I', in *RSE*, iii (1943), pp. 302 ff. Huntingford's dating of Amdä-Ṣiyon's wars in 1329 does not appear to be justified, see his *The Glorious Victories of 'Āmda-Seyon, King of Ethiopia* (Oxford, 1965), p. 53 n. 2.

[3] Perruchon, op. cit., p. 339–40.

[4] Ibid., pp. 280–1 (text), 328–30 (tr.).

[5] Ibid., pp. 288 (text), 336 and n. 1 (tr.). Shäwa here doubtless refers to the central Shäwan plateau where Amdä-Ṣiyon was camping. '. . . and to *ascend* to the country of Shäwa', left out in Perruchon's translation, clearly indicates the direction of the hostilities.

their headquarters in Īfat, before they could move to their several assignments. The mission had the intended result. The Muslim army was defeated, Īfat sacked once again, and Säbrädīn narrowly escaped, probably to Däwaro in the south-east.[1]

Amdä-Ṣiyon sent some contingents of his army to the rebellious provinces in the north, and himself marched to Däwaro[2] to follow up the success of his troops in Īfat. He had more than one reason to march in this direction. Despite the religious and political overtones of the Muslim movement led by Säbrädīn, the immediate reason for the hostilities in 1332 was exactly similar to the Ti'iyintay incident at the time of Haqädīn. Säbrädīn's interference in the free movement of the king's commercial agents still held an important place in Amdä-Ṣiyon's multiple grievances against the ruler of Īfat.[3] Amdä-Ṣiyon's preoccupation with the safety and freedom of the trade routes was quite central to these conflicts, and was a prime factor in determining the direction in which the campaigns had to be conducted.[4]

It will be remembered that soon after his victory over Haqädīn Amdä-Ṣiyon had sent troops to other Muslim districts such as Kwilgorä, Gidayä, Kubät, Fädisé, Qädisé, Hargayä, and Biqulzär. Most of these areas were originally conquered and annexed by the Wälasma at the end of the thirteenth century and, having conquered Īfat, Amdä-Ṣiyon was also indirectly the master of these districts. It is hard to determine in precise terms the actual nature of the political relationship between the Christian kingdom on the one hand, and Īfat and its satellites on the other. Nevertheless, it seems clear from the chronicles that occasional tributes were collected through the

[1] Ibid., pp. 338–9 (tr.).

[2] This is the first time we have a reference to Däwaro. Neither the chronicle of the 'sultanate of Shäwa', nor that of the 'house' of Wälasma mentions it. Al-'Umari later makes it one of the 'Muslim states' in the region, op. cit., pp. 14–15. It occupied the western section of the Harär plateau, throughout our period, Perruchon, *Chroniques de Zar'a Ya'eqob*, pp. 15 n. 7, 133 n. 1. *Futuh al-Habasha*, tr. Basset, pp. 16 n. 2, 30, 55. A small administrative district in central Harär still bears the name of Däwaro, *Journal of the Ministry of Interior*, Addis Ababa, ii, no. 3 (1964), p. 6. It is probable that most of the inhabitants in the area were of Sīdama origin, Cerulli, E., *Studi etiopici*, I: *La lingua e la storia di Harar*, pp. 6–14.

[3] Perruchon, op. cit., pp. 298, 344.

[4] Huntingford has recently proposed a different route for these campaigns, *The Glorious Victories*, pp. 36–8. I have indicated my objections to his proposed route in a short review of the book in the *Journal of African history*, vii (1966), pp. 512–13. Many of the place-names and tribal groups referred to in the chronicle are also mentioned in other documents in connection with the area of the Harär plateau, east of the Awash and Däwaro.

ruler of Īfat, and that the freedom of movement of both Christians and Muslims in these areas was ensured.

Amdä-Ṣiyon's growing control of the interior and his military prestige in the whole Ethiopian region had also obtained for him the respect and willing co-operation of the rulers of the communities where Īfat did not have direct political influence, such as in Däwaro and Sarka.[1] This was important for the security and prosperity of trade in the area, and was promoted by the Muslim traders who had considerable influence at the king's court and in those communities. All these areas lay along the main routes to Zeila which had long been the chief outlet of trade for the region. As long as the safety of these routes to his Christian and Muslim agents was ensured, Amdä-Ṣiyon appears to have been satisfied with distant but friendly relations with these provinces. With the organization of Säbrädīn's resistance, however, all these Muslim areas were persuaded to unite in an attempt to abolish the growing Christian control of their old commercial and political activities in the interior.[2] Their success in this disastrous plan could have reversed the political situation back to its original position at the end of the thirteenth century, and could have made the Christian kingdom entirely dependent on the Muslim principalities for its commercial needs and its external communications in general. It was to solve these important problems that Amdä-Ṣiyon personally led his army to Däwaro, Mora, and Adal.

He fortified his mundane reasons for these campaigns with sufficient religious motives and could thus more effectively inspire his troops with a crusading spirit. 'You fought for my sake in the past,' he told them, 'and now fight for Christ.' He doubtless had the full support of the leading churchmen of his kingdom in this. He specially received a message from a local saint, Amanu'él, which message the king quoted in his speech to his troops: 'Behold, the kingdom of the Muslims has come to an end. In former times, you used to fight for

[1] Amdä-Ṣiyon's chronicler later accuses 'the ruler of Sarka' of having co-operated with the Muslims of Däwaro against the Christian army. The king led a punitive expedition against *Sarka* immediately after passing through Däwaro, Perruchon, op. cit., pp. 436–7. According to Al-'Umari, *Sharkha* was a small Muslim state bordering on Hadya, op. cit., p. 17. Just like Amdä-Ṣiyon's army Gragn's troops also raided *Charkha* after having passed through Däwaro, *Futuh al Habasha*, tr. Basset, pp. 190–3. It seems therefore that it was to the north-east of Hadya, and on the western borders of Däwaro. There is still a small administrative unit called *Shirka* in eastern Arussī, *Journal of the Ministry of Interior*, i, no. 12 (1962), p. 15.

[2] Perruchon, op. cit., pp. 340–1, 358–63, 478–82.

the sake of your transitory kingdom, and for the sake of gold, silver, and precious clothes. But today, rise and fight for the sake of Christ . . .'[1]

The campaigns of 1332 were long and difficult. They were conducted in regions completely hostile and apparently unknown to the Christian troops. The heat and the scarcity of water in the semi-desert regions, where the fighting largely took place,[2] were intolerable to the highland troops, and the whole campaign was overshadowed with constant threats of mass desertions which were only averted by the king's determination, and by the possible dangers that awaited such recalcitrant soldiers on the long way home.[3] Despite these difficulties, the campaigns were a brilliant success. Säbrädīn surrendered, and was imprisoned together with his friend and ally, Haydära, king of Däwaro, and his own brother Jämaldīn was appointed 'king of all the Muslims'.[4] The other members of the league in Mora and Adal, further to the east, were similarly attacked and defeated one by one.[5]

It appears that this superiority of the Christian army lay in its characteristic organization, consisting of numerous contingents recruited from the different provinces of the kingdom, each with its own commander and under the united leadership of the king himself at the top. That the campaigns took place in distant, very hostile regions was also an important cohesive factor in 1332. The Muslim troops, on the other hand, largely consisted of elusive nomadic tribes of the area, who were only suited to making occasional surprise attacks and immediately retreating into the bush after causing considerable damage in the Christian camp.[6] These tactics, although they may have

[1] Ibid., p. 312 (text).

[2] Although most of the place-names mentioned in the chronicle cannot be precisely identified as yet, it seems clear that the campaigns followed more or less the same line as the Addis–Jibuti railway along the northern slopes and foothills of the Harär plateau. What is very interesting to note here in this connection is that, from the description of the terrain through which they led their armies, both Amdä-Ṣiyon and Ahmad Gragn seem to have used the same routes, see pp. 83–4. It is impossible here to determine how far east Amdä-Ṣiyon led his troops, and it is not clear where Bruce got the report that Amdä-Ṣiyon had actually entered Zeila. The chronicle, of which Bruce's chapter on Amdä-Ṣiyon is a free translation, has 'the king of Zél'a' as one of the members of the Muslim league against the Christian king. It is quite possible that Bruce got his idea of Amdä-Ṣiyon's occupation of Zeila from this note. Cf. Perruchon, op. cit., p. 318 (text); Bruce, op. cit., ii, p. 45.

[3] Perruchon, op. cit., pp. 347–8, 351–5, 465–9.

[4] Ibid., pp. 343–7.

[5] Ibid., pp. 346–7, 349–51, 354–63, 455, 470–4, 477–8.

[6] Ibid., pp. 349, 356, 358.

caused high casualties among the Christians, were not suited to pursuing the campaigns with the necessary tenacity and single-minded continuity which characterized Amdä-Ṣiyon's leadership. This weakness was further aggravated by the lack of essential unity in the Muslim league. This, indeed, seems to have been the key to Amdä-Ṣiyon's success in those areas at a considerable distance from the centre of his kingdom. The political superiority of the kingdom, which was now an accomplished fact after these campaigns, also drew its strength very largely from this basic disunity among the Muslims.

The political control of Īfat in the districts originally conquered by the Wälasma—Mora, Adal, Gidayä—was only minimal. What seems to have resulted from these early conquests was, at best a loose confederation of the old trading settlements, with the ruler of Īfat at its head, largely because of his military prestige and his strategic position at the heart of the trade routes from Zeila to Angot, Amhara, and Shäwa. And much of this early political influence was already lost to Īfat with the growing importance of the Christian kingdom. South of this east–west corridor from Zeila to Īfat, which was apparently limited in the south by the northern slopes of the Harär plateau, there throve another chain of Muslim commercial states along the routes from Zeila to the south-east, namely Däwaro, Sharkha, Balī,[1] Dara,[2] Arababni,[3] and Hadya.

The commercial nature of all these states, and their vulnerable positions *vis-à-vis* a strong power controlling the rich interior, made complete unity among them an impossible ideal. Faced with the considerable army of Amdä-Ṣiyon, the initial warlike preparations inspired by religious and economic motives virtually flickered out of existence. The league was already seriously weakened at the begin-

[1] Unlike Däwaro and Sharkha, Balī is not mentioned in the long list of Muslim areas who fought against the Christian army in 1332. But the songs about Amdä-Ṣiyon refer to it as one of his conquests, Guidi, I., 'Le canzoni', pp. 62–3. It is not clear when the Christian conquest was first undertaken, but by the time Al-'Umari wrote it was one of the vassal Muslim kingdoms, very rich in its resources, op. cit., p. 18. Maqrizi, op. cit., p. 15. The Wabī Shäbällé separated it from Däwaro in the north, and Adal in the north-east, *Futuh al-Habasha*, tr., p. 68 n. 3; its original inhabitants were probably Sīdama, of the eastern group, Cerulli, *Studi etiopici*, II (1938), pp. 1–2, 31–2.

[2] See p. 188 n. 3.

[3] Arababni is not mentioned as such in Christian or Muslim documents other than Al-'Umari's work. It has therefore been impossible to suggest any specific identification. It is clear, however, that Al-'Umari placed it between Däwaro and Hadya, south of the Awash, in the region of what is today Arussī province, op. cit., p. 15 with n. 1.

ning of the war when Amdä-Ṣiyon first attacked Īfat, as it appears, before the numerous 'kingdoms' and 'principalities'[1] could send their share of the army to Säbrädīn. This does not seem to have been due to the king's strategic moves any more than to the deliberate delay on the part of Säbrädīn's allies. Even after the hostilities were in full swing, divisions of interest seriously affected the efficacy of the Muslim strategy.[2]

These fraternal divisions seem to have furnished Amdä-Ṣiyon with sufficient allies among the Muslims themselves. This is clearly brought out throughout the struggle, and provides a more logical reason for his success in these distant regions. It will be remembered that one of the major immediate reasons for the conflicts of 1332 was the seizure of the king's commercial agents, and their detention, by Säbrädīn. These merchants were most probably Muslim themselves, and the incident was a clear case of jealousy by the more distant Muslims of the large profits such royal agents were doubtless making, protected as they were by the political and military power of the king. It is unlikely that these Muslim commercial interests, strongly organized around the Christian court, were immediately disbanded on the declaration of war between the two religious communities. These traders, like many of their Christian counterparts, were no religious crusaders and would, at most, only try to make the best of the two worlds.[3] Rival members of the ruling families among them also seem to have offered themselves for nomination as new governors of the districts conquered from their brothers.[4] Such rivalry among local princes for the royal favour was not unique in the Ethiopian polity, and it was the mainstay of the medieval empire as a whole. What is new, in the case of Īfat and the Muslim provinces, is that the principle was also being more boldly extended to them despite their former political and economic importance and the religious difference with the Christian kings. The dependent status of the Muslim provinces became an accomplished fact after the conquests of 1332, and by the

[1] The chronicler gives a long list of 16 'kings', and 2,712 'princes' who fought Amdä-Ṣiyon after the defeat of Īfat, Perruchon, op. cit., pp. 359–62.

[2] Ibid., pp. 381–2.

[3] There seems to have been a strong Muslim pressure group in the Christian court anxious to see hostilities discontinued and peace resumed. The earliest such instance is when the queen was made to intercede for Säbrädīn on the occasion of his surrender. Amdä-Ṣiyon persistently refused to accept such half-measures; many requests were submitted to him during the course of the campaigns to return to his kingdom. Cf. ibid., pp. 342–3, 347–8, 471–3.

[4] Ibid., pp. 422–6.

time Al-'Umari was writing, this relationship between the kingdom and the Muslim states was definitely established:

> Although all the sovereigns of these [Muslim] kingdoms transmit their power on the basis of heredity, none among them has effective authority without being invested by the king of the Amhara. When one of these [Muslim] kings dies, and if he has any male issues, all of them go to the king of the Amhara and they employ all possible means to gain his favours; because it is he who chooses the one on whom he confers power . . ., because it is he who has supreme authority over them, and in front of him, they are only his lieutenants.[1]

This policy of 'divide and rule' was specially directed to the family of Säbrädīn, and was in the end responsible for the militant members of the family moving their headquarters from Īfat further to the east, and continuing the struggle throughout the period.

Amdä-Ṣiyon's conquests of 1332 did not bring about a permanent settlement to the Muslim question. It has already been mentioned that, soon after Säbrädīn's defeat, Amdä-Ṣiyon appointed his brother Jämaldīn in his place. Jämaldīn was himself in prison before he was elevated to this office.[2] This probably means that there had already been a reaction in the Wälasma family to the growing Christian dominance since Däradir's defeat, and the king may have consequently held some of the princes in custody, either as hostages or virtual prisoners. Like many individuals under similar circumstances, these princes reconciled themselves (at least temporarily) with their positions, and could later be used as rival nominees of the king for the leadership of their people, especially in times of hostilities. This may have been the case with Jämaldīn as it would soon be with the son and grandsons of Säbrädīn. However, although he accepted the office of his brother, Jämaldīn did not intend to be a passive agent for the king's expansionist policies. At first, he requested him to

[1] Op. cit., p. 19. Al-'Umari (1301–49) wrote in the years between 1342 and 1349. But much of the material for his book seems to have been collected in 1329–37, when he assisted his father, who was head of the chancery in Cairo. He mentions Patriarch Benjamin (1327–39) as one of his informants on Ethiopia (p. 27). Much of his work is therefore contemporary with Amdä-Ṣiyon, and the relationships which he gives between the two communities were characteristic of that reign and the years immediately following it. By the time Maqrizi wrote (1435/6) however, the situation was different, although he simply copies Al-'Umari in enumerating the seven 'Muslim states'. As is clear from his own story of the subsequent wars, Īfat was no longer the centre of Muslim resistance, and the other Muslim 'states' of Balī, Däwaro, and Hadya were integral parts of the kingdom.

[2] Perruchon, op. cit., p. 479.

relinquish his intentions of continuing the war further east to Adal. When Amdä-Ṣiyon rejected this idea, Jämaldīn began secret arrangements with 'the king of Adal' and his allies to take concerted action against the Christian army, and attack them on two flanks. The plan failed because of disagreement among the allies.[1] But it seems that Jämaldīn continued his hostile intentions, and Amdä-Ṣiyon found it necessary to imprison him once again, and appoint another brother in his place on his way back from Adal. The immediate reason for his dismissal was his failure to bring to the king's court all those Christians living in the realm of Īfat who had been converted (or reconverted?) to Islam during the war. He alleged that 'the son of his brother' prevented him from doing so. This presumably means Säbrädīn's son, and implies that although Amdä-Ṣiyon may have appointed his own governors over Īfat, the legitimate ruler was still Säbrädīn's son. This in fact seems to be the case since, according to both Maqrizi and the chronicler of the 'house' of Wälasma, Säbrädīn was succeeded by his son Ali, who was the contemporary of Säyfä-Ar'ad, son and successor of Amdä-Ṣiyon.[2]

Amdä-Ṣiyon's successors (1344–1430)

Säyfä-Ar'ad (1344–71)[3] continued his father's military policies towards the Muslims. It appears that his was a policy of maximum intervention in the local affairs of Īfat, undertaken with the view of incorporating it completely into the system of his medieval empire. He went further in this than even his father, and his direct attempts at assimilating the ruling house of the Wälasma created a split in the family, the more militant group moving further east, and eventually emerging as the undisputed champions of Islam in the region.

Ali, the son of Säbrädīn was, according to Maqrizi, 'the first to revolt from the customary allegiance to the Haṭi'.[4] Since Maqrizi does not refer to the war of 1332 this appears to mean that, after Amdä-Ṣiyon's military display of power, the ruler of Īfat and his

[1] Ibid., pp. 362–3, 441.

[2] Ibid., p. 479. Maqrizi, op. cit., p. 18. Cerulli, 'Documenti arabi', p. 44. It is significant that the chronicler of Amdä-Ṣiyon does not say what happened to 'the son of his brother' when Jämaldīn was cast into prison. This may very well represent the position of strength which the son of Säbrädīn enjoyed at the time, *vis-à-vis* the wishes of the conqueror.

[3] Bruce reports that Säyfä-Ar'ad had accompanied his father on the 1332 campaigns, op. cit. ii, p. 60. He probably misread the name of another son of the king, Saf-Asägid, who did take part in the Adal wars, Perruchon, op. cit., p. 400.

[4] Op. cit., p. 18.

followers showed no more resistance to the demands and political domination of the Christian kingdom, until after the death of the conqueror himself in 1344. This was sound policy, since the damage done to the economic life of the Muslim regions in the long and desperate campaigns of 1332, and the military prestige of Amdä-Ṣiyon himself, could not have been favourable to another series of hostilities. Ali, therefore, seems to have given a breathing space to his people before summoning them to help him restore their independence. The accession to power of a new king was probably thought to have created the necessary conditions for a new rising. But Säyfä-Ar'ad took stern action against such a move, and popular feeling in Īfat was not favourable to Ali's rebellion since, according to Maqrizi, 'they not only disagreed with his action but rebelled against it'.

This popular complacency towards Christian rule in these Muslim regions, a thing which is lamented by both Al-'Umari and Maqrizi,[1] was of course merely the result of the considerable loss they had already suffered in the earlier hostilities. It was also a result of the difference in the relative position of the two communities. For the Christians, led by their warrior kings, it was a period of conquest and expansion when they were always on the offensive. Possessed of a huge army and a mobile destructive power, they had much less to lose in the conflict than their Muslim counterparts, in whose territory the campaigns were conducted, with all their disruptive effect on the trade routes and on the marginal agricultural economy of these areas. The location of Īfat itself, which was its greatest asset in the thirteenth century, as the spearhead of Muslim expansion in this direction, was now becoming a liability, since physical contiguity with the centres of the Christian power offered much scope for direct political and military intervention by the Christian royal court. The over-all result of these unfavourable circumstances doubtless fell heavily on the influential merchant class, which probably helps to explain their apparent reluctance to engage in further hostilities.

This strengthened Säyfä-Ar'ad's position. He imprisoned Ali, the son of Säbrädīn, together with all his sons, except for Ahmad with whom the king was on very good terms. Ahmad was appointed governor of Īfat in his father's place. Eight years later his father, Ali, was set free and reinstated.[2] He was apparently released together

[1] Al-'Umari, op. cit., p. 2; Maqrizi, loc. cit.

[2] Maqrizi, op. cit., p. 18. Maqrizi says elsewhere (p. 27) that Ali was in prison for 30 years and died there in the reign of Sä'adädīn. This would mean that he was

with his other sons, and he nominated them to positions under himself. He excluded Ahmad from these nominations, and the king's personal intervention was required for him to be given a district to rule. Ahmad was alienated from his family for his friendship with the Christian king. When he died, his children were looked upon as outcasts by the Wälasma family, and they were excluded from local-government posts.

A bitter struggle for power started between Ahmad's children on the one hand, and their grandfather, Ali, and his sons on the other. Among Ahmad's sons were Haqädīn II, and Sä'adädīn. The latter was actually born at the Christian royal court,[1] and probably Haqädīn also accompanied his father during his sojourn there. But despite their father's apparent friendship with King Säyfä-Ar'ad, both Haqädīn and Sä'adädīn grew up to be the strongest champions of Islam in the Ethiopian region. Their father Ahmad represented a major success in the king's deliberate policy of dividing the Wälasma family. But it is ironical that the deadliest enemies of the Christian kingdom should have come from his branch of the family.

Haqädīn, the elder of Ahmad's two famous sons, was in fact the founder of the kingdom of Adal as we know it in its protracted struggle with the Christian kingdom from the last quarter of the fourteenth century right to the end of our period. Maltreated by his grandfather and his uncle, Mola Asfaḥ, Haqädīn started his career as an outlaw. He apparently had a great deal of Islamic learning, and, unlike his father, he was completely reluctant to use the goodwill of the Christian king in regaining his rights as the son of Ahmad. He took the opposite course, gathered a large following around him, and rebelled against his grandfather and his uncle, both of whom he forced to identify themselves with the much-hated Christian kingdom. Accusing them of being the puppets and vassal chiefs of the Christian king, Haqädīn assumed the sole leadership of militant Islam in the region. No doubt the religious leaders of the Muslim communities approved of his action, and probably encouraged many to join him. Thus, surrounded by numerous followers, Haqädīn declared war on his grandfather and his uncle. They asked Säyfä-Ar'ad for Christian

imprisoned more than once. The chronicle of the Wälasma dynasty also gives him a long reign of 40 years which is, however, followed by that of Ahmad, who is given only two years. But we know from Maqrizi that Ahmad died before his father, and the succession was not as neatly legitimate as the official Wälasma chronicler has it. Cf. Cerulli, 'Documenti arabi', pp. 44 n. 5 and 45 n. 1.

[1] Maqrizi, op. cit., p. 19.

assistance against the rebel Muslim prince. In a series of military engagements, Haqädīn was victorious against the combined force of his relatives and the Christian army. His greatest enemy and uncle, Mola Asfah, was killed in action, and the breach in the family feud grew even wider. Haqädīn triumphantly entered Īfat where his grandfather resided. He was magnanimous to the old man, and confirmed him as titular ruler of the old city. However, he established his own capital at another site, in 'the land of Sawa', according to Maqrizi, 'where he built the town of Wahal'.[1]

It is very uncertain what Maqrizi meant by 'Sawa' in this context. Almost certainly, however, the name cannot be a reference to any of the districts of the Shäwan plateau, which was definitely a Christian province at the time. Most likely, it was in the region south-east of Īfat, and east of the edge of the plateau, just like the former 'sultanate of Shäwa'.[2] Haqädin's change of his capital was the most drastic action taken by the Muslims since active struggle with the Christians started, and the establishment of a new centre of Muslim resistance marked a new chapter in the relations between the two communities. Haqädīn inaugurated a new, and uncompromising spirit of Muslim leadership in the area, which was no longer satisfied with a mere local autonomy. The prime motive of his new move was to be completely independent of the Christian kingdom. For this he needed to acquire much of the mobility and warlike character of the Christian kings themselves, and his emergence to power was a clear case of self-adaptation to the Christian challenge.

According to Maqrizi, Haqädīn began his reign in about A.D. 1363–4.[3] His advent to power was preceded as we have seen, by a series of armed conflicts, which seriously disturbed the process of

[1] Op. cit., p. 21.

[2] See p. 125 n. 1 above. It is interesting that Maqrizi locates Sä'adädīn's centre of military activities at twelve days' journey from Balī, op. cit., p. 25. This is most likely a reference to the Harär region, and probably *Wahal* was also in the same general direction as Dakar and Harär, cf. Cerulli, 'Documenti arabi', pp. 42 n. 1, 50 n. 1. *Futuh al-Habasha*, tr., pp. 24, 67.

[3] Ibid., p. 22: '. . . he fell in the year A.H. 776, the tenth year of his reign.' His reign was probably considered as having started on his successful take-over of Īfat, although his grandfather was still alive, until after his own death, see p. 146 n. 2. above. According to the Wälasma chronicle, 'Haqädīn . . . initiated the movement of the holy war along the path of the Lord for a period of ten years'. This description tallies with Maqrizi's reports about him. But the chronicler gives his dates as A.D. 1376–86, Cerulli, 'Documenti arabi', p. 45 notes 2, 3, and 4. These dates are too late by about twelve years since, according to Maqrizi, Haqädīn was already active in the reign of Säyfä-Ar'ad (1344–71).

quiet assimilation that formed the cornerstone of Säyfä-Ar'ad's Muslim policy. It seems reasonable to suppose that it was also about this time that Säyfä-Ar'ad is reported to have taken desperate repressive measures against his Muslim subjects. The new upsurge of hostilities damaged the business and security of the merchants to such an extent that they appealed for help to the sultan of Egypt. In Egypt itself, Muslim popular feeling had flared up against the Copts, and relations between the two communities were extremely tense.[1] This probably induced the sultan and his court to treat with special urgency the petition of the Muslims in Ethiopia. Patriarch Marqos (1348–63) was summoned at once, and ordered to send a delegation asking the king of Ethiopia to stop his hostile actions against the Muslims:

> At that time ruled a king called Säyfä-Ar'ad . . . He killed many of the Muslims who rebelled against him. There were also some whom he expelled from his country. These went to the king of Egypt and appealed to him. They told him: 'The king of Ethiopia destroyed the Muslims: Some of them he killed, and some he made Christians'. When the king of Egypt heard this he was greatly concerned for his religion and forced the patriarch to send prominent persons . . . [to] the king of Ethiopia . . . about the remaining Muslims in his kingdom.[2]

It is not clear what exactly were the results of the embassy, but the delegation, which consisted of the Coptic archbishop of Jerusalem and the bishop of Ahnas, was not allowed to leave the country. Säyfä-Ar'ad doubtless realized that the patriarch was only induced to send such a delegation by forceful means, and probably distrusted it as a result. Armed hostilities continued with Haqädīn until he was killed in action in A.D. 1373–4, in the reign of Niwayä-Maryam (1371–80), the son and immediate successor of Säyfä-Ar'ad.[3]

[1] Quatremère, *Mémoires géographiques et historiques*, ii, pp. 250–7.

[2] Budge, E. A. W., *The Book of the Saints of the Ethiopian Church* (1928), pp. 177–9. Cf. Basset, *Études*, n. 93.

[3] Maqrizi, op. cit., p. 22. Here Maqrizi calls the Christian king in whose reign Haqädin lost his life, Dawīt. But this is an obvious error, since he himself says that the Muslim prince fought until the death of Säyfä-Ar'ad 'who was succeeded by his son Dawīt'. This no doubt refers to the *immediate* successor of Säyfä-Ar'ad who was also his son, but his name was Niwayä-Maryam which Maqrizi took for Dawīt (1380–1412), probably because of the more widely known exploits of the latter. Professor Cerulli bases his defence of the dates of the Wälasma chronicle on this error of the Arab historian. Consequently he alters many dates given by Maqrizi and partly confirmed by Ethiopian sources—namely, that Haqädīn began his reign in the days of Säyfä-Ar'ad; that he was killed in the reign of his *immediate* successor; that Sä'adädīn, who succeeded him, died on the occasion of the Christian invasion of Zeila in the reign of Dawīt, in A.D. 1402–3. He alters

The power of resistance of the Muslim kingdom of Īfat had already been exhausted by the second half of the fourteenth century. A hundred years of continuous warfare with the much stronger Christian kingdom had sapped its economic and military strength, and it had been reduced to the position of a provincial governorate. As such it was no longer of much use as a platform for organizing and leading a political and religious warfare against the Christians. Haqädīn and his militant followers understood this, and they displayed a remarkable sense of realism in moving their centre of hostile activities away from the expanding Christian empire.[1] Thus on the one hand, Haqädīn's transfer of the centre of Islam in Ethiopia from Īfat to *Wahal*, probably located much further to the south-east, represented a major success in the expansionist policies of the Christian kings since the days of Yikunno-'Amlak. But it also brought new dangers to the kingdom. Īfat had always been within a short distance from the highland Christian provinces, and it was more vulnerable to swift punitive expeditions sent out against it. But the kingdom of Adal which sprung up in its place, after the eventful career of Haqädīn II (A.D. 1363/4–1373/4), was very remote, and it had at its command an

all these to establish the validity of the Wälasma dates, of which the reliability is also questioned sometimes by himself, Cerulli, 'Documenti arabi', p. 45 notes 2, 3, and 4: and p. 46 notes 1, 2, and 3. Cf. also *Gädlä-Märqoréwos*, ed. Conti Rossini, p. 38 (text). Basset, *Études*, notes 90, 93.

[1] This transfer of the political centre also represents, it seems, the vast displacement of peoples which always accompanied the expansion of the kingdom in every direction. In the Adal region, the hot lowland plains were largely inhabited, it appears, by the eastern Kushitic group of people represented today by the Soho, Afar, Somali, and Galla. An interesting theory on the origin of these people has recently been proposed, Lewis, H. S., 'The Origins of the Galla and Somali', in *JAH*, vii (1966), pp. 27–46. Most likely, the pastoral tribes to which references are made in the chronicles belong to this stock of people. It seems possible to detect, after 1270, a general eastward movement of a section of these people. The relative positions of the *Harla* in the fourteenth and sixteenth centuries seems to illustrate the general phenomenon. Ibn Said (1214–74) mentions the *Karla* as an important people in the Ethiopian region, Aboul Feda, *Géographie*, pp. 225–6. Mufazzal (wrote before 1358) makes them one of the subject peoples of the Christians, *Histoire des sultans Mamlouks*, p. 386. Amdä-Ṣiyon's chronicler describes their hostile action against the king's army in the region between Biqulzär and Däwaro, *Histoire des guerres*, ed. Perruchon, p. 435. In the time of Gragn, however, their habitat seems to have been east of Harär, *Futuh al-Habasha*, tr. Basset, pp. 149–50, 170–1. Azais and Chambard collected some vivid traditions about the early importance of the *Harla* in the Harär region, *Cinq Années de recherches archéologiques en Éthiopie* (1931), pp. 33, 35–6, 132–3, 139. Conti Rossini, 'Postille al Futuh al-Habasha', pp. 181–2. Still today, there is a small village called Harla, just outside Dirédawa on the road to Harär. A number of Arabic inscriptions are reported to have been found in and around this village.

extremely mobile and elusive force, considerably more destructive than what Īfat could ever have at its disposal. It also held a strategic position on the major eastern route to Zeila. The region of Harär, where the new Muslim centre seems to have been established, was the focal point for all the trade routes from the eastern provinces of the Christian kingdom—namely, Īfat, Fäṭägar, Däwaro, and Balī.[1] Islam was the dominant religion in all these eastern provinces. This gave the successors of Haqädīn II additional power and influence within the boundaries of the Christian empire itself. The political loyalties of the inhabitants were seriously divided, and often changed sides with every shift in the balance of power between the Christians and the Muslims.[2] The new Muslim kingdom of Adal fully exploited these favourable circumstances, and began to harass the long frontier lines of the Christian kingdom from the outskirts of Īfat in the north, to the left bank of the Wabī Shäbällé in the south.

Haqädin II was succeeded by his brother Sä'adädīn,[3] who continued the aggressive policy of his predecessor. Both Christian and Muslim sources are unanimous in reporting his military successes against the Christian army in the early part of his reign. An Ethiopic hagiographical tradition relates that 'a rebel called *Sä'alädīn* . . . son of *Haqälädīn*, in the country of Adal . . . fought against King Dawīt whose army he easily destroyed.'[4] Ahmad al-Qalqashandi (d. 1418), the Egyptian encyclopedist, also describes Sä'adädīn as the most successful Muslim prince in his resistance against the Christian kingdom, which nevertheless maintained its position as the strongest power in the Ethiopian region:

The Haṭi, king of Ethiopia, after the year eight hundred,[5] led his Christian [troops] in the greater part of these [Muslim] provinces which he devastated and of which the inhabitants he killed, burning their holy books, and forcing most of them to be converted to the Christian religion. Of the Muslim kings [in Ethiopia] only the following remain intact: Ibn Mismar whose country is just opposite the island of Dahlak and who obeys the

[1] For these routes see pp. 83–4.

[2] Instances of this unstable situation in the frontier districts are abundant throughout our period, Perruchon, op. cit., pp. 433–4, 478–9. *Les Chroniques de Zar'a Ya'eqob et de Ba'eda-Maryam*, pp. 16–21, 58–60, 45–6, 157–8. Conti Rossini, 'La storia di Libna Dingil', pp. 623, 628.

[3] Ibn Khaldun, *Histoire des Berbères*, p. 108. Maqrizi, op. cit., p. 22. Cerulli, 'Documenti arabi', p. 46.

[4] *Gädlä Märqoréwos*, ed. Conti Rossini, p. 38 (text). The Christian scribe has slightly altered the names of the princes, and has considered *Sä'adädīn* as the son of *Haqädīn*, presumably because he was his immediate successor.

[5] A.H. 800 = A.D. 1397–8. The *Haṭi* at the time was King Dawīt (1380–1412).

Haṭi to whom he pays a fixed tribute; and Sultan Sa'd-ed-Din, king of Zeila and its dependencies, who resists and refuses to obey the Haṭi; there are some continuous wars between them, and most of the time, it is Sultan Sa'd-ed-Din who remains victorious.[1]

The successes of Sä'adädīn after this Egyptian report were only short-lived. The Christian kingdom had taken up the challenge brought about by the emergence of the new state in Adal, and had considerably strengthened the military colonies stationed in the eastern provinces. The locations of King Dawīt's favourite camping sites are particularly expressive of his special preoccupations with the Muslim threat from Adal. One of these sites was at a place called *Ṭobya*, in north-western Īfat, where the king apparently settled for a long period of time.[2] *Ṭobya* lay in the most important pass which led to the highland Christian districts of Mänz and Gishé, and further north into Amhara. The so-called Īfat route from Zeila passed through it, and it was precisely this road which Ahmad Gragn later followed on his way to Amhara. Gragn actually camped at *Ṭobya* for a time.[3] The other site where Dawīt established his court was at *Ṭilq* in Fäṭä-gar, and it also looked towards the eastern frontiers. The Christian court was apparently maintained here for many years: Zär'a-Ya'iqob (1434–68), and his grandson Iskindir (1478–94) were born at Ṭilq, and Bä'idä-Maryam (1468–78) also spent much of his childhood there.[4] King Dawīt had also stationed numerous troops in Balī,[5] Däwaro,[6] and Hadya[7] who fought against the Muslims with a varying degree of success. The elusive character of Sä'adädīn's army presented

[1] Quoted in Gaudefroy-Demombyne's translation of Al-'Umari, *Masalik*, p. 37 n. 1.

[2] *Les Chroniques de Zar'a Ya'eqob et de Ba'eda Maryam*, ed. and tr. Perruchon, J. p. 152. Dawīt apparently lived here for a fairly long period of time. The chronicler seems to suggest this when he says: 'Previously our King Dawīt had lived in this land, and had planted many trees in it.' Perruchon's translation, and his proposed punctuation are imperfect.

[3] A renegade Christian governor of Īfat defected and joined Gragn at *Ṭobya*, *Futuh al-Habasha*, p. 272, cf. also pp. 56–65.

[4] *Les Chroniques de Zar'a Ya'eqob*, pp. 67, 91–2, 155.

[5] Maqrizi, op. cit., p. 24.

[6] Ibid., p. 35. Zär'a-Ya'iqob's chronicler complains that the military colonists settled here—apparently before the king's reign—and called *Žan-Haṣäna*, had become insubordinate, and often took refuge in the Muslim kingdom of Adal whenever measures of discipline were taken against them, *Les Chroniques*, pp. 45–6. Other colonists were organized, and settled there.

[7] Sä'adädīn also fought against 'Amano, the Haṭi's emir in *Hadya*', Maqrizi, op. cit., p. 23. This is a reference to the hereditary king of Hadya. He was definitely Muslim himself in the reign of Zär'a-Ya'iqob who married his daughter, *Les Chroniques*, pp. 16, 59.

the settled Christian military colonists with serious technical problems. Sä'adädīn only launched a series of raids which had little or no motive of actual empire-building, such as characterized the early struggle between Amdä-Ṣiyon and Säbrädīn. His raiding parties descended upon the frontier districts by surprise and, when successful, they did considerable material damage on the local people.[1] The Muslim troops never followed up their occasional victories with a more settled military occupation. By the time the local Christian troops were reorganized for another round of hostilities, the Muslim army would disappear from the area, taking away its spoils usually consisting of many head of cattle and numerous slaves. It was this characteristically nomadic aspect of the Muslim army that distinguished it from that of the Christians, and gave a special sense of urgency to the Adal question. King Dawīt himself led his army into Adal on more than one occasion.[2] In the final encounter Sä'adädīn was pursued by the king's troops as far as Zeila, where he was captured and killed in 1402/3.[3] Ethiopic clerical traditions also make a reference to this victory as one achieved through the special favour of God.[4]

This is the first Christian invasion of Zeila on record in our period. It is indicative of the persistence of the struggle with Sä'adädīn and of the degree of the resultant weakness of the Muslim forces. With Sä'adädīn's death, Muslim power in the Ethiopian region reached its lowest ebb, and remained so for a long time. But the ephemeral success of King Dawīt's army in Adal did not lead to a permanent settlement. Dawīt's immediate successors—Téwodros (Oct. 1412–June 1413) and Yishaq (1413–30)—persistently continued their father's aggressive policy towards Adal, and probably both of them lost their lives there.[5] When Sä'adädīn was killed, his sons had been exiled in Arabia and Christian superiority was assured in Adal which was

[1] Maqrizi, op. cit., pp. 23–5.

[2] A land grant attributed to him refers to at least two such campaigns he personally led to Adal, Wright, *Catalogue*, Or. 481, f. 154[a].

[3] Maqrizi, op. cit., pp. 26–7. For the date see also p. 149 n. 3.

[4] *Gädlä Samu'él*, ed. and tr. Turaiev, B. (1902), pp. 14–15 (text). *Gädlä Märqoréwos*, ed. and tr. Conti Rossini, pp. 40–1 (text).

[5] Ethiopic hagiographical material indicates that the body of Téwodros was brought from beyond the river Awash for burial in Amhara, extract published and translated in Sapeto, G., *Viaggio e missione cattolica fra i Mensa* (Rome, 1857), pp. 437–8. Maqrizi reports that Yishaq was killed in action, op. cit., p. 39. There seems to be no reason to contradict the story. In the royal chronicles and other traditions for the period, one can detect a deliberate attempt to suppress the violent ends of Ethiopian kings at the hands of their enemies.

occupied for a time: '. . . the strength of the Muslims was abated. For the Haṭi and the Amhara having acquired this country settled in it, and from the ravaged mosques they made churches. The Muslims they harassed for the space of twenty years . . .'[1] On the return to Adal of Sä'adädīn's sons,[2] the struggle started once again, and Muslim raids and counter-raids followed one another in a monotonous regularity, right down to the end of our period. Of the Christian kings at the time, Yishaq was most successful in his Adal policy. He had reorganized his army and the administration of his kingdom with the help of Egyptian advisers.[3] It is apparent that he particularly made use of these new developments in his characteristic attempt to solve the Adal question once and for all.[4] Maqrizi seems to refer to this desperate policy when he describes a Christian attack against Adal 'with the object of rooting out utterly all the Muslims living in Abyssinia'.[5]

But Adal could never be an integral part of the medieval empire of Christian Ethiopia. This was unwittingly prevented by Amdä-Ṣiyon in 1332, when he appointed a descendant of the Wälasma as 'King of all the Muslims'.[6] His own intention was to centralize Muslim affairs in Ethiopia under one person, with whom he could deal more effectively, and a friendly member of the 'house' of Wälasma was, of course, most suited for the post. But this tremendously helped the process of the final emergence of the Sä'adädīn branch of the Wälasma family as a champion of Islam in the whole of the Ethiopian region. Haqädīn II and his successors had been successful in establishing complete independence from the Christian kingdom. Yet as the descendants of Wälasma the price they paid for this was very

[1] Maqrizi, op. cit., p. 27.

[2] Maqrizi does not specifically state how long they had remained in Arabia. But he says that the Christian superiority lasted for twenty years after Sä'adädīn's death in A.H. 805. He is also very consistent, for the next date he gives is A.H. 825, when Säbrädīn died a natural death apparently after one year of armed struggle with the Christians settled in Adal, ibid., pp. 28–30.

[3] Maqrizi, op. cit., pp. 6–8. Ethiopic traditions also seem to confirm Maqrizi's report about this, and a royal panegyrist refers to Yishaq as follows: 'Your wisdom is that of Egypt and your strength is that of India', Guidi, 'Le canzoni', pp. 54–5. It is also interesting to note that Maqrizi's account of the king's pompous appearance on solemn occasions is remarkably similar to the story reported by Pietro, the Neapolitan in 1432, *Le Voyage d'outremer de Bertrandon de la Brocquière*, ed. Schefer, Ch. (Paris, 1892), p. 147.

[4] Maqrizi, op. cit., pp. 8, 31.

[5] Op. cit., p. 33. Yishaq pursued a similar policy towards the Fälasha, see Ch. V., pp. 200–1.

[6] Perruchon, *Histoire des guerres*, p. 301.

high: by relinquishing Īfat as their traditional centre, they gave up all their advance positions, and their more direct political influence, in the interior. Īfat, the whole of Shäwa, Däwaro, Hadya, and Balī were now under the direct control of the Christian kingdom. The almost regular frontier conflicts and political intrigues, in which Adal was always involved, were no longer relevant to the Christian control of these very rich areas as long as the Christian kingdom maintained its military supremacy.

For a period of just over a century and a half after the establishment of the new dynasty in 1270, the Christian kingdom underwent an intensive process of expansion throughout the Ethiopian region. In the south, with the early conquest of Damot and Hadya—the strongest political units beyond the Awash—the presence of the kingdom was strongly felt in the predominantly Sīdama country of the basins of the Gibé, Gojéb, and Omo rivers.[1] In the north-west, the Fälasha country was gradually brought under Christian control, and King Yishaq (1413–30) probably sent his troops into the country of the so-called *Shanqilla* west of Agäw-Midir in Gojjam.[2] These military conquests throughout the Ethiopian region opened up a vast field for the expansion of the Church, and it is to this important question that we must now turn in the next chapter.

[1] The southern frontiers of the kingdom are more difficult to determine in precise terms. It is possible, however, to detect in the chronicles an increasing amount of knowledge about the Sīdama region over the centuries. Most likely this represents a closer contact, probably also a more direct military control of the area. Amdä-Ṣiyon's panegyrist only sang of the king's exploits in Damot, Gänz, Hadya, and Balī in this direction, Guidi, 'Le canzoni', pp. 50 et seq. In the case of King Yishaq, a century later, numerous recognizable tribes of the Gibé-Gojéb-Omo basin are listed, ibid., pp. 56–7. Zär'a-Ya'iqob married a Hadya princess, and his chronicler can enumerate many tribal groups in Hadya, Perruchon, *Les Chroniques*, pp. 16–18. At one time, this king is believed to have established his court on the hill of Jibat which is part of the high ridge dividing the high-waters of the Gibé and Gudru rivers, Annequin, G., Notes on 'Jibat and Adadi Maryam, in *AE*, vi (1965), pp. 13–16. Zär'a-Ya'iqob still has an important place in the traditional recollections of the people of this area, Haberland, E., 'The Influence of the Christian Ethiopian Empire on Southern Ethiopia', in *Journal of Semitic Studies*, ix, (1964), pp. 235–8. It is most likely that the chain of Sīdama aristocracies in the whole of this area were originally formed under the stimulus of the Christian expansion, Conti Rossini, 'Sui linguaggi dei Naa e dei Ghimira nell'Etiopia meridionale', in *RRAL*, ser. 6, vol. i (1925), pp. 612, 616, 633–6. Id., 'Il popolo dei Magi nell'Etiopia meridionale e il suo linguaggio', in *Atti del 3⁰ Congresso di studi coloniali*, vi (1937), pp. 108–18. Id., *Etiopia e genti d'Etiopia* (1937), pp. 369–71.

[2] Cf. Guidi, op. cit. p. 55.

CHAPTER V

Evangelization

(1248–1430)

THE evangelization of the Ethiopian region followed very closely the expansion of the Christian state. The fourteenth century, which was marked by the maximum expansion of the kingdom, was also the period when the Ethiopian Church exerted its pressures most on the non-Christian peoples in the area. The Shäwan plateau, which had increasingly come to be the most important theatre for the military activities of the Christian army, also assumed a key position as the centre for propagating Christian teaching among the conquered peoples.

It is apparent that the presence of isolated Christian families in Shäwa preceded the establishment of effective Christian political control of the area. These early Christian immigrants in Shäwa apparently lived in a pagan country, under pagan chiefs. Despite the tendency in the hagiographical traditions to give them a long clerical background they were probably mostly lay Christians who were anxious to maintain peaceful co-existence with their pagan neighbours. They kept contact among themselves and with their distant kinsmen in Amhara and Tigré. Their long-distance contacts probably gave them an advantage over their locally orientated neighbours, and many of these families appear to have lived a relatively comfortable life with numerous slaves and substantial farms.[1] Some of these communities probably built small churches in their respective areas. These churches were staffed by a handful of clerics, who provided the most primary religious needs of the Christian families. The long distance from the court of the Egyptian bishops, and from the centres of Christian learning in Tigré must have always kept the number of the clergy to a bare minimum. Some rudimentary teaching may have been given by very few local priests to their own children, who would almost invariably succeed them in their clerical posts, and to some other

[1] Such traditions of material wealth are told about the families of many of the early Church leaders, and they may not have been completely unfounded, cf. Budge, *The Life of Takla Haymanot*, pp. 28–30 (text). *Gädlä Anoréwos*, p. 67 (text).

children entrusted to them.[1] These meagre educational facilities may have been strengthened from time to time by the arrival of clerical reinforcement from the north.[2] Some of the more adventurous members of these early Christian communities may have also travelled all the way to Tigré in order to obtain a clerical education. On their return home they, no doubt, established their own schools among their relatives, whose children they helped to educate.[3] But such educational enthusiasm does not seem to have been a general characteristic of the Christians in the south and, before the advent of the new dynasty, the picture of the Church that emerges from a study of these early traditions is one of precarious existence. These early Christian settlers were no religious crusaders, and it would seem that in general they participated in the ordinary life of their pagan neighbours. Even the hagiographer(s) of Täklä-Haymanot inadvertently point to this conclusion in the story of his wild youth: 'He learnt riding horses, hunting wild animals and using arrows and other implements . . . And his arrow never missed, and was always smeared with blood.'[4] They had reached a *modus vivendi* with their environment and were generally reluctant to disturb their amicable relations with their neighbours. The same conclusion emerges from the attitude of cautious opposition assumed by the older generation of Christian settlers against the more militant anti-pagan activities of the younger men in the traditions concerning the last quarter of the thirteenth century. We have one such tradition in the story of the early life of Fīlipos of Däbrä Asbo. His father is represented as punishing him for his hostile actions against a local witch-doctor, and he thus explained his position: 'I punished you so that the people of this country may not kill you, and confiscate our belongings.'[5] This cautious attitude seems to have characterized the life of the Christian settlers in the south for many generations.

[1] Budge, op. cit., p. 20. *Gädlä Fīlipos*, p. 175. 'Gädlä Qäwisṭos', MS. Däbrä Lībanos, f. 44[a].

[2] *Gädlä Anoréwos*, p. 68. Anoréwos is here said to have been instructed by one Harankīs who seems to have entered his parents' service.

[3] 'Gädlä Qäwisṭos' ff. 17–24. Here is given the tradition about the life of Hiywät-Binä-Bäṣiyon, great-grandfather of Täklä-Haymanot. He is said to have travelled to Aksum and Däbrä Gärīma where he was educated. On his return he opened a school in Shäwa. This tradition is almost certainly an attempt to increase the importance of the saint's family. But the essential part of the story, that some of the distant Christian settlers used the educational facilities of Tigré, is not inconceivable as a general pattern.

[4] Budge, op. cit., p. 24 (text).

[5] *Gädlä Fīlipos*, pp. 182–3.

The province of Amhara was exposed to Christian influences much longer, and the Christians were clearly dominant by the beginning of the thirteenth century. Even there, however, the politically dominant position of the Christian Amhara does not seem to have been accompanied by a similar development of Christian learning and a Christian zeal for evangelization. As among the Christians of Shäwa, there were only small secular churches serving the daily needs of the local congregation. The growing political importance of the Christian Amhara may have increasingly drawn to the Church many of the non-Christian groups in the area. But even clerical traditions are lacking about any Christian centres of learning and monastic activities in the area until the middle of the thirteenth century. The cultural centre of the Ethiopian Church still remained in Tigré, particularly in the centres of the monastic activities of the Nine Saints established over seven centuries before. The story of monasticism in Amhara and Shäwa, and systematic evangelization of the newly conquered areas only starts with Īyäsus-Mo'a of the island monastery of Däbrä Hayq.

Īyäsus-Mo'a

Īyäsus-Mo'a (d. 1292)[1] was born at Dahna[2] of a Christian family. Very little is said about his early life in his native land. He may have received some primary religious education in his home district as his hagiographer reports, no doubt with much exaggeration.[3] But the turning-point in his religious career only occurred when he decided to travel to Tigré in about 1241, and to join the famous monastery of Däbrä Damo of which the abbot at the time was Abba Yohannī.[4] Īyäsus-Mo'a was a young man of about thirty when he joined the monastery, and he was given arduous assignments by the abbot:

[1] For the chronology of the life of Īyäsus-Mo'a see Taddesse Tamrat, 'The Abbots of Däbrä Hayq', n. 20.

[2] The hagiographer of Īyäsus-Mo'a locates this place in Bägémdir, *Gädlä Īyäsus-Mo'a*, ed. and tr. Kur, S., in *CSCO*, vol. 259, Script Aeth., tomes 49, 50 (1965), p. 5 (tr.). Amdä-Ṣiyon's chronicler speaks of a 'governor of Dahna' together with the 'governor of Wag', Perruchon, op. cit., p. 293 (text). Cf. also p. 29 n. 1 above.

[3] *Gädlä Īyäsus-Mo'a*, p. 7 (tr.).

[4] Very little is known about him. There is a short hagiographical notice about his early life, ibid., pp. 16–17. A still more uncertain tradition about him is that he is said to have been the 7th abbot of Däbrä Damo after Arägawī, one of the Nine Saints of the sixth century, *Gädlä Arägawī*, ed. Guidi, I., pp. 85–6. This is chronologically impossible, and it may be that by the time the *Gädl* was written many of his predecessors were forgotten.

Four Leaders of Däbrä Hayq

From a fourteenth-century MS. of the Four Gospels which belonged to *Aqabé Sä'at* Kristos-Täsfanä, abbot of Däbrä-Hayq in A.D. 1316/17

'[Yohannī] ordered him . . . to travel much [on the business of the monastery] . . . and he thus travelled for a long time and by the will of God he returned to his master Abba Yohannī . . . and delivered to him the things for which he was sent . . .'[1] Apart from thus 'fulfilling the orders of his master' he devoted much of his time to learning and solitary contemplation. The most important art he acquired here was that of writing: he learnt how to write and lived on his own (in a cell) on the precipice and wrote the Four Gospels there.[2] His sojourn in Däbrä Damo lasted about seven years after which he travelled south and settled on the island of Lake Hayq. His advent to Lake Hayq was a turning-point for the history of monasticism in Ethiopia, and for the story of evangelization with which we are specifically concerned here.

It does not seem that Īyäsus-Mo'a's final choice of Lake Hayq as a place of settlement was motivated by a need for a solitary retreat, as some traditions have it. His own *Gädl* transmits the tradition that a church dedicated to St. Stephen had already been built by an Aksumite king and an Egyptian bishop of his time four centuries before.[3] For a long time before the advent of Īyäsus-Mo'a the lake-side region seems to have continued to be one of the centres of Christian population in what is now the rich district of Tähulädäré. Besides Däbrä Igzīabhér and the island church, there were apparently other churches in the neighbourhood. Īyäsus-Mo'a himself stayed in a church dedicated to Saints Peter and Paul, apparently on the western shore of the lake, for six months before being admitted to the island.[4] On the island itself lived Christian men and women clustered around the secular church of St. Stephen. Having a long tradition of royal foundation, the island church may have been associated with the local Christian chiefs, and even with the power groups in Amhara claiming descent from the ancient royal house of Aksum. Däbrä Damo itself, where Īyäsus-Mo'a obtained his monastic instruction in Tigré, had always cherished its ancient associations with the Aksumite kings for which it was apparently neglected by the

[1] *Gädlä Īyäsus-Mo'a*, pp. 10–11 (text). The translation (p. 9 with n. 1) does not take full account of the practical aspect of Īyäsus-Mo'a's travels. It was usual in the monasteries for young novices to be given such business assignments on behalf of the community, cf. *Gädlä Fīlipos* (Bīzän), ed. Conti Rossini, pp. 97–8.

[2] *Gädlä Arägawī*, p. 86.

[3] *Gädlä Īyäsus-Mo'a*, pp. 18–19 (text). See also Taddesse Tamrat, op. cit., notes 1, 3, 5–7, and 9.

[4] *Gädlä Īyäsus-Mo'a*, p. 22 (text).

Zagwé kings.[1] It appears that Īyäsus-Mo'a also found in Hayq a viable Christian community with respectable connections which offered tremendous possibilities for further development. Like many of the churches in Amhara and Shäwa at the time, Hayq Isṭīfanos was insufficiently supplied with priests and deacons, and probably had no adequate schools of its own. This last need was now amply provided for by Īyäsus-Mo'a on his advent to Hayq in about 1248. He thus opened new opportunities of learning for the Christians of Amhara and Shäwa, and many appear to have taken full advantage of this. Many young men from among the local Christians and from areas further afield seem to have joined the monastic school which he founded. When they graduated from there, they are believed to have left Hayq and established their own monastic centres in different areas.[2] Among the pupils of Īyäsus-Mo'a, Täklä-Haymanot of Shäwa has later assumed particular significance in the monastic traditions of the Ethiopian Church.

Täklä-Haymanot

Täklä-Haymanot was born about 1215 at Ṣilalish[3] in Zoräré, in what is today the district of Bulga. As we have seen above, tradition derives his origin from an ancient clerical family who had settled in Shäwa for over ten generations.[4] His own father is presented as having been a priest who served in the church of Ṣilalish. He is also said to have given Täklä-Haymanot his first religious instruction and to have even taken him to the court of the Egyptian bishop, Qérilos, for ordination as a deacon while still a young boy.[5] This is quite possible in the light of our attempt above at a reconstruction of the small Christian communities of Shäwa, based on their early traditions. There also seems to be an additional factor that may help in understanding the background of Täklä-Haymanot's later activities. We have already alluded to the persistent traditions that strong anti-

[1] Cf. *Gädlä Arägawī*, pp. 71–3. Many of the land grants to Däbrä Lībanos of Shimäzana in the Zagwé period make no mention of either Aksum or Däbrä Damo. But, no sooner was the new dynasty established by Yikunno-'Amlak, than both these communities begin to assume particular importance, cf. Conti Rossini, 'L'Evangelo d'oro di Dabra Libanos', pp. 194–201.

[2] For the traditions about Īyäsus-Mo'a's early students who later founded their own monastic communities see Taddesse Tamrat, op. cit., notes 12–15.

[3] For the date see p. 121 n. 4.

[4] See p. 120 n. 4.

[5] Budge, op. cit., pp. 20–1. Cf. also Conti Rossini, *Il 'Gadla Takla Haymanot'*, p. 128 n. 5. 'Gädlä Qäwisṭos', ff. 44^{b}–51^{a}.

Christian manœuvres were undertaken by the pagans in Shäwa between the last years of the twelfth and the first quarter of the thirteenth centuries. In Täklä-Haymanot's *Gädl*, and in related hagiographies of the Däbrä Lībanos cycle these pagan activities are said to have been led by the legendary Motälamī, king of Damot.[1] The immediate effect of this reaction on the Christian communities in Shäwa appears to have been disastrous. Churches were burnt down, and Christian homesteads destroyed.[2] This must have created a great strain on the still modest position of the Church at the time, and must have further weakened the religious life of the Christians. It is this picture of general decline of the Shäwan Church that seems to offer a reasonable background for the religious career of Täklä-Haymanot which finally resulted in the regeneration of the Church in the south.

The Waldibban version of his *Gädl* explicitly states that he had already been ordained a priest, and had officiated as such in Shäwa, long before he joined Īyäsus-Mo'a in Hayq.[3] But it is difficult to give much credence to these later hagiographical assertions of which the motive is clearly to show the importance of Täklä-Haymanot, and to minimize his dependence on his monastic associations with Hayq and Tigré. But it is apparent that he joined Īyäsus-Mo'a when he was already well over thirty years of age.[4]

[1] See pp. 121–3.

[2] Budge, op. cit., pp. 8–9. 'Gädlä Qäwisṭos', ff. 4–5. It is probable that the traditional founder of the Ziqwala community, Gäbrä-Mänfäs-Qiddus, belongs to this early period. A hagiography, which is still unpublished, is available about his life and activities in Ethiopia. The date of its composition is very uncertain, Wright, W., *Catalogue*, Or. 711. Conti Rossini once thought that it may have originally been written in the reign of King Dawīt, 'Appunti ed osservazioni sui re Zague', in *RRAL*, iv (1895), p. 444. Gäbrä-Mänfäs-Qiddus is believed to have been an Egyptian who came out to Ethiopia in the reign of Lalībäla, Wright, op. cit., Or. 711, ff. 2^b, 63^b–64^a, 78–9. Evangelicalactivities are attributed to him in the region of Ziqwala and immediately south of it in 'the land of Käbd', ibid., ff. 18–21. All these are very uncertain, and the saint is not mentioned at all in traditions of Däbrä Lībanos, which became the dominant monastic group in the area after the 14th century. Probably, Gäbrä-Mänfäs-Qiddus only represents the the beginnings of Christian Zagwé pressure on Shäwa, soon repulsed by local pagan reaction, which may also explain the uncertainties of the traditions about him. It is interesting to note that a place-name, *Lalībäla*, is reported by Gragn's chronicler, not far from Ziqwala, *Futuh al-Habasha*, tr. Basset, p. 112.

[3] Conti Rossini, *Il 'Gadla Takla Haymanot'*, p. 104; the same point is also made in the Däbrä Lībanos version which describes (in even greater detail) his alleged missionary activities even before joining Īyäsus Mo'a. Budge, op. cit., pp. 25–59 (text).

[4] Īyäsus-Mo'a himself came to Hayq in about 1248, and it seems that Täklä-Haymanot joined him when he was already well established on the island and well known in the area.

Täklä-Haymanot's advent to Hayq is of great significance for the important role that his community of Däbrä Asbo would soon play in the expansion of the Church, particularly after his death in the fourteenth century. But, despite later traditions that grew around his name, his own arrival at the monastic community of Īyäsus-Mo'a did not create a sensation, and his life on the island is not even mentioned in the contemporary notes of Däbrä Hayq. These notes are not a complete record of every aspect of the island community, and this negative evidence does not at all invalidate the historicity of Täklä-Haymanot's sojourn there. What it does is to underline his rather modest position in those early days, and to offer a basis for a historical reconstruction of the gradual development of his religious career.

Very little is known about his life in Hayq,[1] but he no doubt made use of his stay with the widely travelled Īyäsus-Mo'a to improve his knowledge of the Scriptures, Church history, and monastic traditions. Contacts between Tigré and Hayq were probably frequent, and Täklä-Haymanot may have collected further information about the ancient centres of Ethiopian Christendom and the monastic communities long established by the Nine Saints. This appears to have increased his curiosity, and he decided to have a more personal experience of these places. After nine years in Däbrä Hayq, therefore, Täklä-Haymanot left for Tigré.[2]

At this stage he apparently concentrated on his own personal

[1] I am adopting here his itinerary according to the Waldibban version of his *Gädl*, Conti Rossini, op. cit., p. 107. The Däbrä Lībanos version, due to what appears to be a much later addition, relates that he stayed for 12 years with Bäṣälotä-Mīka'él of Däbrä Gol before going to Hayq, Budge, op. cit., pp. 60–9 (text). But according to his own *Gädl*, Bäṣälotä-Mīka'él lived much later and was still a young boy at the time of Widim-Rä'ad in whose reign Täklä-Haymanot died at a very advanced age, *Gädlä Bäṣälotä-Mīka'él*, pp. 8–9. *Gädlä Īyäsus-Mo'a*, which is a much later work than the Däbrä Lībanos version of *Gädlä Täklä-Haymanot*, also refers to Bäṣälotä-Mīka'él as the senior of Täklä-Haymanot. The passage, which is strongly polemical, also contains other anachronisms, *Gädlä Īyäsus-Mo'a*, pp. 28–31 (tr.). For these anachronisms see Taddesse Tamrat, op. cit., n. 15.

[2] Conti Rossini, op. cit., p. 107; Budge, op. cit., p. 72 (text). An interesting passage in *Gädlä Īyäsus-Mo'a* indicates that Täklä-Haymanot left for Tigré after Yikunno-'Amlak had already overthrown the Zagwé dynasty. This is stated in the message Täklä-Haymanot is said to have taken from Īyäsus-Mo'a to his former master Abba Yohannī, Abbot of Däbrä Damo: '[Yikunno-'Amlak] prevented me from coming to you myself . . .', p. 37 (text). The passage is significant in showing that Täklä-Haymanot was still in the early stages of his monastic career in 1270, and that the role which he is said to have played in bringing Yikunno-'Amlak to power is only legendary.

salvation, and does not seem to have been contemplating evangelical activities in his native land of Shäwa. More than anything else, his departure from Hayq was motivated by a desire to make a pilgrimage to the holy places of Tigré, and even further to Jerusalem.[1] Täklä-Haymanot doubtless visited Aksum and the other monastic centres of the Ethiopian Church; but it was at Däbrä Damo, Īyäsus-Mo'a's old monastic school, that he finally settled. Īyäsus-Mo'a's spiritual father, Yohannī, was still alive and welcomed him to his fold. Here again we know very little about his activities in this community. Täklä-Haymanot was now a middle-aged man with many years of monastic labours behind him. His origin in distant Shäwa, from where he had long banished himself in the name of Christ, must have further enhanced his reputation among his fellow monks. This may have attracted many close friends and younger followers to him. This personal following may have substantially increased over the years, and it may be in this period that Ar'ayänä-Ṣäggahu, Mädhanīnä-Egzī, and Bärtälomḗwos joined him.[2]

All the available traditions of the Church are unanimous in attributing a great monastic influence to Täklä-Haymanot while he was still in Tigré, and they even make him personally responsible for the establishment of many communities.[3] It is more probable, however, that such communities only developed later after his own return to Shäwa. It is important to appreciate, nevertheless, that the development of monasticism in Ethiopia was extremely personal in character, and a monastic leader with sufficient hagiographical and religious reputation could always draw many disciples. Monastic loyalties always transcended regional considerations. It was within this framework that Täklä-Haymanot could gather a number of followers around him in Tigré, where some of them remained. Each of them appears to have established his own community on Täklä-Haymanot's return to his native land of Shäwa. The period in which he stayed in Tigré saw a tremendous revolution in the history of monasticism in Ethiopia in general. In the long period between the sixth and the mid thirteenth centuries, Ethiopian monasticism had always revolved around the old establishments founded by the Nine Saints.

[1] *Gädlä Arägawī*, pp. 85–6. Täklä-Haymanot does not seem to have succeeded in going to Jerusalem, despite the apocryphal traditions to the contrary.

[2] Wright, *Catalogue*, Or. 769, f. 4: Budge, op. cit., pp. 74, 77 (text). Basset, R., *Études*, pp. 10–11, 99–100.

[3] Conti Rossini, op. cit., pp. 107–8. Budge, op. cit., p. 73 (text). Cf. also *Gädlä Arägawī*, p. 86.

Together with the secular churches which enjoyed royal or local princely patronage, they alone provided the cultural leadership which kept Ethiopian Christendom alive. Apart from some individuals who may have abandoned their homes to wander freely in isolated woods and desert regions, no independent monastic communities seem to have been established before the middle of the thirteenth century. This age-old convention was now seriously compromised. We have already seen how Īyäsus-Mo'a started his own community in distant Lake Hayq about 1248. In the north, Abba Dani'él of Däbrä Maryam in Gär'alta, the spiritual father of Éwosṭatéwos, was similarly developing his own community.[1] It is this picture of an intensive monastic development at the time which explains the religious career of Täklä-Haymanot both in Tigré and back in Shäwa.

Täklä-Haymanot returned to Däbrä Hayq before he finally went back to Shäwa. His encounter with Īyäsus-Mo'a on this second occasion is shrouded with uncertainties in the traditions, and has become one of the most controversial points in Ethiopian ecclesiastical history. The controversy basically revolves around the mutual claims of seniority later advanced by Däbrä Hayq and Däbrä Lībanos for their respective founders. As such it is of a relatively recent origin, and concerns the rules of investiture of monastic habits in the Ethiopian Church.

Four elements constituted the essential parts of the Ethiopian monastic habit. These were the *qämīs*,[2] *qinat*,[3] *qob*,[4] and the *askéma*,[5] which were formally acquired by the novice at different

[1] *Gädlä Éwosṭatéwos*, ed. Turaiev, B. (St. Petersburg, 1905), pp. 7–8. *Gädlä Fīlipos* (Bīzän), table facing p. 156. Conti Rossini, 'L'evangelo d'oro di Dabra Libanos', in *RRAL* (1901), p. 179. A parallel revival of Ethiopic literature is also seen in this period and is closely related with these monastic developments. The Ethiopian Church was just beginning to share in the renaissance of Christian Arabic literature in Egypt, Conti Rossini, 'Il "senodos" etiopico', in *RRAL* (1941), pp. 42–3. Cerulli, E., *Storia della letteratura etiopica* (1956), pp. 31–7, 67–70.

[2] A long (cotton or leather) cloak worn by the monks. It is usually white in colour, but some monasteries prescribe yellow cloaks, cf. Alvarez, *The Prester John of the Indies*, p. 70.

[3] The leather belt worn over the cloak. Guidi's definition is '. . . a blessed cord which a monk carries on his neck . . .', *Vocabolario amarico–italiano* (Rome, 1901), col. 283.

[4] The head-piece of a monk.

[5] Guidi defines it most adequately: 'A kind of scapular made up of two parts, one part resting on the breast and the other on the back, and each ending with a large leather cross, with ten other crosses, altogether twelve crosses . . . It is worn by monks who have completed the third profession . . .', op. cit., cols. 445–6. Kīdanä-Wäld Kiflé's definition is not very different, *Mäṣhfä-Säwasiw Wägis*,

stages of his career. On the first occasion, the novice was given the *qämīs* and the *qinat*. Then, after a further period of re-examination and preparations he was invested with the *qob*. The last and highest stage, that of the *askéma*, was only open to the most saintly and the most tried members of the community.[1] It appears, however, that these specific rules of *gradual investiture* were of a relatively recent date.

Most of the hagiographical traditions available for our period do not mention these different stages of investiture, and they seem to indicate that the monastic habit was conferred upon the novice *on only one occasion*: 'Abba Tomas . . . took the holy *askéma* of the angels, and the *qab* and the *qinat*, and invested the monastic habit [upon Täklä-Ṣiyon].'[2] In many of these traditions, however, even the terms used to describe the four vestments are inconsistent, and only the more generic term of 'monastic habit' is usually given.[3] This inconsistency of language in the description of such essential elements of Ethiopian monastic life clearly indicates the relatively recent date of the institution of the rules of gradual investment. The controversy in the traditions we have about Īyäsus-Mo'a and Täklä-Haymanot is also very largely a result of this uncertainty of language. The following passage can best illustrate this point:

> There came Īyäsus-Mo'a and said to Abba Yohannī, 'Father, confer upon me the *askéma* of the monks', and he conferred it upon him. And Īyäsus-Mo'a stayed [at Däbrä Damo] for a long time . . . He then went and entered a place called Hayq . . . without receiving the *askéma* and the *qob* . . .[4]

The same contradiction is repeated in the Life of Īyäsus-Mo'a himself.[5] The two versions of the Life of Täklä-Haymanot deny that

p. 245. Almeida defines it in a slightly different manner, *Historia de Ethiopia a alta*, bk. ii, ch. 18.

[1] Almeida describes the ceremony, and the special prayers for the occasion, loc. cit.

[2] 'Gädlä Täklä-Ṣiyon', B.M. Add. MS. 16257, f. 6[a]. The saint probably lived in the 15th century. The *qämīs* is missing in the list here and in many other such passages. Even in Almeida's time the *qämīs*, *qinat*, and *qob* were granted at the same time. Only the *askéma* required a special occasion, loc. cit.

[3] *Gädlä Yafqirännä-Igzī* p. 16. *Gädlä Fīlipos* (DA), p. 190. *Gädlä Aron*, p. 126, *Gädlä Bäṣälotä-Mīka'él* p. 14. *Gädlä Anoréwos*, p. 69. *Gädlä Samu'él* (Waldibba), p. 2.

[4] *Gädlä Arägawī*, pp. 85–6.

[5] *Gädlä Iyäsus-Mo'a*, p. 21. Here again Yohannī is said at one place to have already given him 'the *askéma* and the *qob* of the angels'; then Īyäsus-Mo'a is said to have left Yohannī 'without receiving the *askéma*', p. 37. This indicates an imperfect and direct borrowing by Īyäsus-Mo'a's hagiographer (late 15th century) from *Gädlä Arägawī*.

Īyäsus-Mo'a had received the *askéma* and the *qob* from Yohannī. These symbols of monastic excellence, we are told, were only conferred upon him by his own former disciple Täklä-Haymanot on his return from Däbrä Damo.[1] This is also partly accepted by Īyäsus-Mo'a's hagiographer, who however contests that Īyäsus-Mo'a had already been invested with the *qob* and that it was *only the askéma* which was later given to him by Täklä-Haymanot at his own request.[2] There is, however, no satisfactory reason to believe that Täklä-Haymanot conferred even the *askéma* on his former master. Īyäsus-Mo'a's profession as a monk was already complete even before Täklä-Haymanot's first arrival from Shäwa in Däbrä Hayq. Before Täklä-Haymanot's departure to Tigré, many, including himself, had already received the monastic habit from Īyäsus-Mo'a. This is accepted by all the traditions. Only the *Gädlä Arägawī* partially contradicts this, when it reports that Täklä-Haymanot arrived at Däbrä Damo in Tigré 'dressed like a soldier'. This is however contradicted by its own assertion that he had previously stayed with Īyäsus-Mo'a, who had already been conferring the monastic habit on his disciples.[3] It is most unlikely that Täklä-Haymanot could have left for Däbrä Damo without first receiving the monastic habit from Īyäsus-Mo'a. This Däbrä Damo tradition seems to be the original source of all the controversy, and was apparently invented by an over-zealous scribe of the monastery to stress the historical fact that both Īyäsus-Mo'a and Täklä-Haymanot derived their monastic origin from the 'house' of Abunä Arägawī. The story was then anxiously adopted by the spiritual descendants of Täklä-Haymanot because it brought them one step nearer to Däbrä Damo. The *Gädlä-Īyäsus-Mo'a* itself was only composed much later, and thus partially accepted the tradition. Nevertheless, no satisfactory evidence seems to be available to show that Täklä-Haymanot did in fact confer any of the monastic habits on Īyäsus-Mo'a. Based on an earlier but confused source in the hagiographical records of Däbrä Damo, this tradition was only too readily adopted by the 'house' of Täklä-Haymanot in an attempt to give a secure basis for the growing dominance of Däbrä Lībanos of Shäwa in the fifteenth century. This vital process of the transformation of hagiographical traditions is more than confirmed by a similar attempt elsewhere to show the seniority of Fīlipos of Däbrä Asbo over his

[1] Conti Rossini, op. cit., p. 108. Budge, op. cit., pp. 71, 76–7.

[2] For the whole story see, *Gädlä Īyäsus-Mo'a*, pp. 38–40 (text).

[3] *Gädlä Arägawī*, p. 85.

contemporary Aron of Däbrä Darét.[1] It is also quite apparent that this controversy about Īyäsus-Mo'a and Täklä-Haymanot was further complicated by applying to the thirteenth century the rules of gradual investiture which apparently developed in Ethiopian monasticism only later.[2]

Täklä-Haymanot's second stay at Däbrä Hayq was not long, and he soon moved further south to Shäwa. This is a major landmark in the history of organized mission work of the Ethiopian Church, and it is significant that according to the traditions it was in fact Īyäsus-Mo'a who persuaded Täklä-Haymanot to return to his native land. Equipped with much learning and with a great monastic reputation Täklä-Haymanot returned to Shäwa as an emissary of the Church which was at the time undergoing an important period of revival in Tigré and in Amhara.[3] His own special role was to transmit this spirit of revival to the Christian communities of Shäwa, and, for the first time in the history of the Church there, to establish a permanent centre of Christian learning and monasticism through which the Church would soon make its influence felt on the pagan people of Shäwa, Damot, and Gojjam. Many of the evangelical achievements in Shäwa and Damot attributed to him personally seem, however, to be apocryphal, and were almost completely the work of his disciples in the eventful years of the fourteenth century.

At first, Täklä-Haymanot probably went to his own native district of Ṣilalish.[4] His return after a long absence in the holy places of Tigré

[1] Wright, *Catalogue*, Or. 797 f. 107^b^. Aron is here said to have received his *qämīs* and *qinat* from his accepted master Bäṣälotä-Mīka'él, and his *qob* and *askéma* from Fīlipos; cf. also Or. 769, MS. B.M, ff. 54^b^–55^a^. But since we have the *Gädl* of each of these monks we can check the alterations in this case.

[2] No chronological study of the development of these rules is possible here, mainly because, as has been said above, the hagiographical traditions available do not seem to have been affected by these rules in general. The question is only raised in cases of important rivalries among the major monastic groups. But it seems most likely that in the 15th century, when these controversies were raised about Īyäsus-Mo'a and Täklä-Haymanot, the rules of gradual investiture as described by Almeida were taking shape.

[3] Cf. Conti Rossini, op. cit., p. 108. The Däbrä Lībanos version is not clear about the role of Īyäsus-Mo'a in asking Täklä-Haymanot to go to Shäwa, and characteristically attributes it to Abba Yohannī of Däbrä Damo, Budge, op. cit., p. 76 (text).

[4] It is unlikely that Täklä-Haymanot followed the itineraries given in both versions of his *Gädl*, Conti Rossini, op. cit., pp. 108–9. Budge, op. cit., pp. 78–9 (text). This was a route frequented in the 15th century when the *Gädl* was first completed, probably in the reign of Yishaq, Conti Rossini, op. cit., p. 123. Precisely in this reign Abba Gīyorgīs of Sägla seems to have used this route on his way to Däbrä Lībanos, 'Gädlä Abba Gīyorgīs', MS. Hayq, f. 27^b^. The

and Lake Hayq must have created a great sensation, particularly among his own relatives. For Täklä-Haymanot himself, the relative position of weakness of the Church of Shäwa may have greatly impressed him, and it seems that he soon took it as a personal challenge. This was also a period when the prestige of the Christian Amhara was keenly felt in Shäwa, particularly since the establishment of the Amhara dynasty by Yikunno-'Amlak in 1270. These new developments opened tremendous possibilities for evangelical work, and Täklä-Haymanot set out preaching in the surrounding area of the Shäwan plateau.

His early preaching probably involved some travelling, but it does not seem that he himself moved out of the central area between Ṣilalish and Grarya, where he finally settled.[1] Before he established his monastic community at Däbrä Asbo, he probably moved from place to place in Shäwa for some time. In many of these districts, which were still dominated by pagan worship, his activities may have brought him into conflict with many of the inhabitants of Kätäta and Grarya. The memory of these conflicts must have then furnished the scribes of Däbrä Lībanos with the basis for their fabulous tales of Täklä Haymanot's miraculous activities, culminating in the conversion of Motälamī. But Täklä-Haymanot himself seems to have been specially preoccupied with the spiritual stagnation of Shäwan Christendom, and he particularly addressed himself to his fellow Christians.

The intellectual content of his teaching has been given little attention by his hagiographers, and we have as yet no way of studying this in detail. But one can imagine that, fresh from his long and edifying monastic experience in Tigré and Hayq, Täklä-Haymanot found

Däbrä Lībanos version takes Täklä-Haymanot further west to Däbrä Dada in Amara Saynt, although this was apparently established only after his death, Budge, op. cit., pp. 77–8. It is most likely that he himself followed a route much more to the east: Hayq–Mänz–Tägulät–Kätäta–Ṣilalish, where there was an almost unbroken chain of Christian settlements. There is also a tradition that this route was used in the 13th century. 'Gädlä Qäwisṭos', ff. 54, 57.

[1] Both versions of his *Gädl* tell us of his evangelical exploits beyond these areas, especially in Damot, Conti Rossini, op. cit., pp. 105–7. Budge, op. cit., pp. 43–59 (text). But they both attribute this to the period before his travels to Hayq and Tigré. This is almost impossible in the cultural milieu of Shäwan Christendom at the time. The saint must have also been in his sixties when he returned from Hayq. This may have been the reason for his hagiographers to transfer his mission work to his more youthful days. His movements were limited to the Shäwan plateau after his return from Hayq, Conti Rossini, op. cit., pp. 108–22. Budge, op. cit., pp. 79–87 (text).

Christian life in Shäwa much more complacent towards its pagan environment. His early teachings were therefore probably aimed at removing this state of indifference in the religious life of the Christian communities. He exhorted his audience to be much more rigorous in their observance of the prescriptions of the Church, and he set an example for them by establishing a completely different community of his own with its own rules and regulations. In the wider Christian context this was not especially original of Täklä-Haymanot. But it greatly impressed his fellow Shäwans, who had had no direct experience of monastic life before. Täklä-Haymanot offered a spiritual challenge to the Christians, a new religion to their pagan neighbours, and a new life and monastic career to the younger members of the Christian families who soon began joining him. Some of these early followers of Täklä-Haymanot may have been his own younger relatives, and the group was probably mobile at first.[1] His influence had spread considerably even before he finally decided to settle at Däbrä Asbo.

Däbrä Asbo, later called Däbrä Lībanos

According to his hagiographer(s), Täklä-Haymanot obtained the site of his monastery with the help of a local chief recently converted by him. This was done in the face of serious opposition by the pagan inhabitants of Grarya.[2] The main significance of the tradition is that the site was in a pagan area. Its general location and the physical characteristics of the surrounding region indicate that Täklä-Haymanot had a definite reason for his choice of the place. Däbrä Asbo was directly north-west of his native district of Ṣilalish. Apart from his evident desire to establish his community outside his home district, it appears that Täklä-Haymanot also considered the future possibilities of his mission in choosing an area towards the west. Ṣilalish was itself a frontier area on the eastern edge of the plateau overlooking the river basin of the Awash and the vast desert lowlands beyond. The whole of this area had long been exposed to a very slow process of Muslim expansion, and by the thirteenth century the broken country immediately to the east and north-east of Ṣilalish,

[1] Mentioned as his relatives are Zéna-Marqos and Qäwisṭos, Budge, op. cit., p. 81 (text); 'Gädlä Zéna-Marqos', f. 18; 'Gädlä Qäwisṭos', ff. 4–5. There is however a general tendency in the later hagiographers to relate most of the 14th-century church leaders, 'Gädlä Zéna-Marqos', ff. 1ª–3. 'Gädlä Samu'él' (Wägäg), f. 7.

[2] Conti Rossini, op. cit., pp. 109–10. Budge, op. cit., pp. 80–5 (text).

between the slopes of the plateau and the left bank of the Awash, was apparently the home of the so-called 'Mahzumite sultanate of Shäwa'. It was also precisely in this period of the return of Täklä-Haymanot to Shäwa that the Wälasma rulers of Īfat had incorporated this internally divided Muslim community under their direct control.[1] Conditions were not suitable for an immediate establishment of an effective monastic community in this direction. Ever since Christian families began migrating south of the headwaters of the Jäma river, their settlement had always been in the central Shäwan plateau, which forms a great watershed between the basins of the Blue Nile and the river Awash. We have seen that there were already Christian communities in the Mugär area further west before Täklä-Haymanot's settlement in Grarya.[2] Although still dominated by pagan worship, Täklä-Haymanot's new abode was not at all unknown to Christians before. The site of Däbrä Asbo is also strikingly similar to that of Ṣilalish. Like its eastern counterpart, it is on the edge of the plateau, overlooking a wide panorama as far as the mountains of Gojjam beyond the river Nile to the west, and to the north, the mountains of Amhara across the eastern tributaries of the Abbay. The country immediately below is intersected by the numerous tributaries of the river Jäma. To the south-west is the district consisting of the river basin of the Mugär from which it also derived its name. Further still in the same direction, was the region of the headwaters of the river Awash and the river basin of Gudär, beyond which lay medieval Damot. Located in this area, Däbrä Asbo was very well placed for its future offensives against the pagans of the region. It was clearly chosen to serve a double purpose: tucked into a cliff difficult of access, it could pass unnoticed by the hostile pagan neighbourhood; and being within easy reach of the plateau, the small community could gradually spread its influence on the local people.

It was however as a solitary retreat that it must have first impressed Täklä-Haymanot. This was specially so because of the long preparation required to undertake active evangelical work. For this Täklä-Haymanot needed to gather around him a sufficient number of disciples and instruct them properly for the purpose. In the cultural

[1] See pp. 124–6. Neither version of Täklä-Haymanot's *Gädl*, both composed at a time of unquestioned Christian predominance, gives any attention to the Muslim factor in his life. This was one of the reasons that led Almeida to date him between the 7th and the 8th centuries, op. cit., book ii, ch. 18.

[2] Cf. pp. 119–20. Conti Rossini curiously locates Mugär 'a nord di Jama', op. cit., p. 134 n. 5.

milieu of the Church in Shäwa at the time, it is unlikely that he could have received much help from the local clergy. It may therefore be that on his return to Shäwa he was accompanied by some of the individuals who had joined him in Tigré and Hayq.[1] Helped by such younger companions, Täklä-Haymanot began to train the young men who joined him during his round trip of some of the Christian communities. The process must have started before his settlement at Däbrä Asbo. But while his small group was still mobile and completely dependent on the sedentary communities, he must have found it difficult to ensure the necessary degree of discipline and sense of urgency among his new followers. This increased the need for a secluded area not only for the pursuit of strictly monastic ways of life, but also for instituting a permanent programme of religious training.

A monastic community was specially relevant to the circumstances in Shäwa. As we have briefly seen above, the position of the Church there was very weak, and the frontiers between Christian and pagan ways of life were probably difficult to demonstrate. In such a society any attempts to create better standards from within were bound to fail. The creation of a completely separate community acting, as it were, as a miniature Christian society, had better chances of success, both for the personal salvation of its individual members, and as the training ground of eventual religious leaders for the local people. This was indeed the dual purpose which Täklä-Haymanot and his early companions intended for their new community of Däbrä Asbo.

At first the monastery of Däbrä Asbo only consisted of a small cave divided into two to make room for a church, and also for the living quarters of Täklä-Haymanot and his disciples: 'He kept the *tabot* [consecrated] in the name of St. Mary in half the cave, which he partitioned with a curtain of straw. He lived with his fifteen

[1] The growth of Däbrä Asbo founded by him in his sixties cannot be fully explained without the help of his early companions in the north. The role of such non-Shäwans is of course played down by the subsequent growth of a strong local group vying for the leadership of the community. There are tantalizing indications of a struggle for the succession on the death of Täklä-Haymanot: after the short reign of Élsa'i, whose origin is not given, there is a miraculous selection of the Shäwan Fīlipos to the chair, Conti Rossini, op. cit., p. 122. Budge, op. cit., pp. 95–6 (text). Anoréwos also seems to have been a candidate, *Gädlä Anoréwos*, p. 75. He left for Tigré on the appointment of the next abbot. He may not have been the only one to do so, and the foundation of Däbrä Dada in Amara Saynt may also represent a similar exodus, cf. Budge, op. cit., pp. 77–8 (text). The community of Bärtäloméwos in Janamora in north Angot may also be of a similar origin, cf. 'Lidätä-Abäw', Or. 769, MS. B.M., f. 4.

disciples in the remaining half . . .'[1] Hemmed in by the densely wooded slopes of the plateau, the young community lived on the wild fruits of the forest. They began to have some contact with the local people, who could not understand their strange ways of monastic life.[2] Täklä-Haymanot and his disciples probably used these early contacts for teaching the new religion to the local people. This could have obtained for them their first converts. There are many traditions of such conversions which are said to have provoked the opposition of the pagan religious leaders.[3] Täklä-Haymanot's reputation also followed him to Däbrä Asbo, and when the news of his settlements in Grarya spread among the Christians many came to join him: 'When they heard his fame, the men who lived in distant areas came to Abunä Täklä-Haymanot, they took the yoke of monasticism from his hands, and they stayed with the holy Abunä.'[4] The sudden growth of the community at first presented some economic and organizational problems. Täklä-Haymanot's disciples began clearing the forests and cultivating the land; and a simple monastic organization soon began to take shape.[5]

Täklä-Haymanot lived for about 29 years after he established Däbrä Asbo.[6] The last three decades of his life were most fruitful years during which he created an effective centre of Christian propaganda in Shäwa. Almost all the future leaders of the Church there, and in the newly conquered areas further south and in Gojjam, derived their origin from Täklä-Haymanot's new community of Däbrä Asbo. He revived the religious consciousness of his fellow Christians, and raised the relative degree of Christian learning among them. Once he had started the process, many of his early disciples seem to have followed his example in establishing their own communities, even before his death.[7] By the time he died, the position

[1] Conti Rossini, op. cit., p. 115. Budge, op. cit., p. 80 (text).

[2] There are some caricatures in the hagiographies about the people's idea of the novelty of monastic life. A group of shepherd boys who showed Fīlipos the way to Däbrä Asbo also warned him: 'We heard our fathers say, "those monks, they eat human beings"', *Gädlä Fīlipos*, p. 188 (text). Cf. also Budge, op. cit., p. 81 (text). *Gädlä Anoréwos*, p. 77 (text).

[3] Budge, op. cit., p. 85 (text). 'Gädlä Täkästä-Birhan', MS. Dīma, ff. 2–3[a].

[4] Conti Rossini, op. cit., p. 138. Budge, op. cit., pp. 84–7 (text). *Gädlä Fīlipos* (D. A), p. 188 (text). *Gädlä Anoréwos*, p. 68 (text).

[5] Conti Rossini, op. cit., p. 115. Budge, loc. cit. *Gädlä Anoréwos*, p. 70.

[6] Budge, op. cit., p. 96 (text). Since he is believed to have died in 1313 Däbrä Asbo was probably established in about A.D. 1284. This fits in perfectly with the chronology given in *Gädlä Fīlipos*, p. 246 (text).

[7] 'Gädlä Zéna-Marqos', ff. 14–17. 'Gädlä Qäwisṭos', f. 69.

of the Church in the districts of Kätäta and Grarya, and in the whole of the Shäwan plateau, was very secure, and it was ready to take some advantage of the expansionist policies of King Amdä-Ṣiyon (1314–44).

Amdä-Ṣiyon succeeded Widim-Rä'ad only one year after the death of Täklä-Haymanot. His predecessor's realm had already included the central Shäwan plateau, where the religious activities of the saint had been conducted, and it was from this area that the new king led his successful campaigns against the Muslims to the east and south-east. Already before the campaigns of 1332, he had also reduced Damot and Hadya to vassal states. These military conquests did not, however, mean an immediate Christianization of the inhabitants. But they tremendously boosted Christian morale and prestige, and contacts between the Christian communities and the new subject areas became open and more frequent. The numerous captives of war were reduced to slavery; some were distributed among the conquering troops, and others were probably sold to the Christian settlers in the north. The contingents, frequently raised from the conquered areas, always took part in the campaigns of the king, side by side with his Christian troops. As such, they were increasingly exposed to Christian influence in a religious sense also. All these offered invaluable opportunities for the expansion of the Church. But the fourteenth century was not the only occasion for the Ethiopian Church to be provided with such opportunities of which she often failed to take full advantage. It is very clear that the Church was not yet sufficiently well organized for such a great task.

We have already made a distinction between the secular and monastic clergy in the Ethiopian Church. Before monastic institutions were developed in Amhara and Shäwa, any semblance of Christian teaching was done by the secular clergy, whose meagre religious training only suited them for routine services. Their essential function was merely to serve the religious needs of the troops or colonists. The conversion of the conquered peoples was always left for time to solve. As long as the military dominance of the Christians lasted, the inhabitants of the conquered areas were slowly and imperfectly absorbed into the new religious framework. This seems to be the general pattern in which the Ethiopian Church always secured its members in the new areas, and the influence of Christianity lay only in its position as the religion of the dominant political group. It is not at all clear what, if anything, the Egyptian bishops did to change this state of affairs before the fourteenth century. From the condition of the Church in Amhara and Shäwa in the thirteenth century, it is apparent that they did little or nothing more than ordaining priests and deacons to maintain the precarious existence of the secular clergy in the distant corners of their extensive diocese. Abunä Ya'iqob, the second metropolitan in the long reign of Amdä-Ṣiyon, however, presents an altogether different picture.

Bishop Ya'iqob and his programmes of evangelization

His name is first mentioned in a contemporary note of 1339/40 at the library of the island monastery of Hayq, and he apparently came to Ethiopia in 1337.[1] From the traditions we have about him, he emerges as a man with a more than average gift for organization. He was also fully committed not only to ensuring a more rigorous application of the rules of the Church, in the daily life of the Christians, but also to evangelizing the non-Christian provinces of the kingdom. At the time of his advent to Ethiopia, Amdä-Ṣiyon was at the zenith of his power, and Ya'iqob intended to use this opportunity in the service of the Church, and drew up plans for systematic missionary work in the region. His attempts were made much simpler by the work already done by Īyäsus-Mo'a and Täklä-Haymanot in the provinces of Amhara and Shäwa.

At the community of Däbrä Asbo, there was apparently a struggle for succession on the death of Täklä-Haymanot. His immediate successor, Élsa'i, ruled for a short period of time, and Fīlipos took over on his death only three months later. This has made the name of Fīlipos most renowned in the traditions of Däbrä Lībanos, only second to that of Täklä-Haymanot himself. In his long tenure of office of twenty-eight years Däbrä Asbo emerged, from a relatively obscure private centre of monastic life, into one of great significance in the history of the Church as a whole. After the apparent struggle for succession, which probably induced some of the early members to leave Däbrä Asbo, the community went on growing, and new accommodation had to be built for the fresh arrivals.[2]

However, it was the advent of Abunä Ya'iqob that dramatically changed the importance of the community. The Egyptian bishop saw that the success of his intended evangelical programme would depend on the co-operation of the local clergy. His problems were very clear,

[1] Taddesse Tamrat, 'The Abbots of Däbrä Hayq', notes 56 and 57.
[2] *Gädlä Fīlipos*, p. 193.

and the following words put in his mouth by the hagiographers also relate the solitary position of his predecessors: 'I have been thinking for a long time to establish the law of God. But I am alone in this big country with no one to help me in teaching the people who are numerous.'[1] To free himself from this position of helplessness, Ya'iqob set about reorganizing the clergy on his side. This involved a major decision. As an integral part of the royal court, the Egyptian bishops had always been surrounded by the secular clergy. Ya'iqob had to break this historic connection, and bring his chair back to its natural monastic ambience. This radical move alienated him from the court.[2] Its effect on the position of the future Egyptian bishops in Ethiopia was probably short-lived, and his immediate successors seem to have opted for a happier compromise. But it left an indelible mark on the organization of the Ethiopian Church.

Ya'iqob's re-organization of the monastic groups in Shäwa and Amhara is variously told in the traditions of the Church, and it is only natural that the spirit of rivalry among these communities should be reflected in the stories.[3] His immediate plan was to establish permanent centres of Christian teaching in the new pagan areas conquered by Amdä-Ṣiyon. The province of Shäwa was most affected by the king's latest military successes, and it was also in this direction that the Egyptian bishop felt the need for immediate action. He divided the area among Täklä-Haymanot's disciples, whom he urged to preach the Word of God in their various districts:

> [The Holy Spirit] . . . inspired him to appoint preachers to strengthen the rules of the Holy Church and keep [God's flock] in the teachings of Christ.

[1] Ibid., p. 194.

[2] See pp. 117–8.

[3] The story is told in the Däbrä Lībanos cycle of hagiographies and in *Gädlä Aron*, pp. 126–7 (text). According to the latter, Bäṣälotä-Mīka'él was made 'Head of the 12 Shepherds of Ethiopia'. In his own *Gädl*, however, he was already dead before Ya'iqob's arrival in Ethiopia, *Gädlä Bäṣälotä-Mīka'él* p. 53 (text). The position of Fīlipos is exaggerated by apocryphal stories that he was even invited to become a bishop for Shäwa, *Gädlä Fīlipos*, pp. 194–8. Cf. also ibid., p. 204, Budge, op. cit., p. 84 (text). The geographical delimitations of the sphere of influence of Däbrä Asbo are essentially based on Ya'iqob's reorganization; but in their present form they show the cumulative effect of the post-15th-century history of the monastery, 'Lidätä-Abäw', Or. 769, MS. B.M., ff. 10–12. A more readable copy is available at Däbrä Lībanos, and the Patriarchal Library at Däbrä Ṣigé also has the tradition in 'Rules for the Administration of Däbrä Lībanos', pp. 121–3, 139–40. A comparative study of these successive editions of the same tradition is most helpful in the identification of historical place-names.

Each of them was to keep to his assigned area without trespassing in that of his neighbour according to the instructions of the Apostles.[1]

The disciples among whom Ya'iqob made this arrangement are said to have been twelve in number, including Fīlipos. Among these we have the *Gädls* of only three of them, and a complete review of the traditional activities of all cannot be made at the moment. It is however very clear from the geographical setting that the bishop intended to cover all the corners of the province of Shäwa and that he sent his emissaries in different directions from the central plateau:

(*a*) to the east, in the direction of the Muslim frontiers, the following were assigned:

Yohannis for Kil'at,[2] Qäwisṭos for Mähagil,[3] Tadéwos for Ṣilalish,[4] and Matyas for Fäṭägar;[5]

(*b*) to the north-west, beyond the western edge of the Shäwan plateau, were assigned:

Anoréwos 'the junior' for Morät and Wägda,[6] and Märqoréwos for Märhabīté;[7]

(*c*) to the extensive new areas in the south and south-west were sent:

Anoréwos 'the elder' for Wäräb and Ṣigaj,[8] Adhanī for Damot,[9] Iyosyas for Wäj[10] and, Yosef for Inar'it.[11]

[1] *Gädlä Fīlipos*, p. 193.

[2] *Gädlä Fīlipos*, p. 197. The place is often mentioned together with Särmat, with which it apparently had common frontiers, Perruchon, *Histoire des guerres d'Amda-Siyon*, pp. 280, 329.

[3] *Gädlä Fīlipos*, loc. cit. Cf. also Wright, *Catalogue*, Or. 769, f. 12^a. In his own *Gädl*, Särmat was also his district, 'Gädlä Qäwisṭos', ff. 68^b–69^a, 105^b–106. Särmat seems to be an ancient name for what is today the central part of Bulga, cf. Or., 769, f. 7^b, Pereira, F. M. E., *Chronica de Susenyos*, p. 18–20 (text). A river of this name is also mentioned in the region, 'Gädlä Qäwisṭos', f. 83.

[4] *Gädlä Fīlipos*, loc. cit. Or., 769, ff. 10^b–11^a. For the location of Ṣilalish see p. 119 n. 3.

[5] *Gädlä Fīlipos*, loc. cit. Or., 769, f. 11^a. This area was immediately south of Ṣilalish on the plateau, 'Gädlä Qäwisṭos', ff. 4–5. It included what are today the districts of Minjar, Shänkora, and Ada, cf. *Futuh al Habasha*, tr. Basset, pp. 96–116. 'Rules for the Administration of Däbrä Lībanos', MS. Däbrä Ṣigé, p. 123.

[6] *Gädlä Fīlipos*, loc. cit. Or., 769, f. 10^b. Wägda is still the name of the edge of the plateau overlooking the precipitous districts of Tägulät to the north, and Morät to the south. Morät borders on Insaro to the south, and the river Addabay to the west. Anoréwos was a disciple of Zéna-Marqos and his appellation 'the junior' is derived from this, 'Gädlä Zéna-Marqos', ff. 19–20^a.

[7] *Gädlä Fīlipos*, loc. cit. Or., 769, f. 11^b. Märhabīté is still the name of the district between the rivers Wänchīt and Addabay before they join to form the Jäma in Düra.

[*Notes 8–11 opposite.*]

These were all disciples of Täklä-Haymanot, and the whole region south of the Jäma river[1] was thus left for them to evangelize. In the fourteenth century, when there were no other monastic groups in the region Ya'iqob had no other alternative, and Shäwa remained an inexhaustible sphere of influence for the 'house' of Täklä-Haymanot. But despite later traditions of Däbrä Lībanos, it was not with Däbrä Asbo alone that the Egyptian bishop began to work. As we have seen above,[2] one of the first things he did on his arrival in Ethiopia was to create amicable relations with the monastery of Däbrä Gol, and we have traditions of a similar organization of the disciples of Bäṣälotä-Mīka'él in Amhara.[3]

Bäṣälotä-Mīka'él was also a follower of Īyäsus-Mo'a, but of the second generation. Some disciples of Īyäsus-Mo'a, other than

[8] *Gädlä Fīlipos*, loc. cit. Or. 769, f. 10. *Gädlä Anoréwos*, p. 76. Wäräb and Ṣigaja (= Ṣigaga) were in the district of Indägibṭan, ibid., p. 93. 'Gädlä Zéna-Marqos', f. 44[a]. Indägibṭan was in the Gudär river basin, south-west of Gindä-Bärät, cf. *Chronica de Susenyos*, pp. 32, etc. (text).

[9] *Gädlä Fīlipos*, loc. cit. Or. 769, f. 11[b]. For the location of medieval Damot see p. 121 n. 1. There are traditions of early Christian expansion into Damot, *Gädlä Yaréd*, ed. Conti Rossini, pp. 22–6. For the first conquest of Damot by Amdä-Ṣiyon's army, see p. 135.

[10] *Gädlä Fīlipos*, loc. cit. Or. 769, f. 12[a]. Wäj appears to have been the area immediately to the south of the headwaters of the Awash, and west of its upper course, including the northern part of Gurageland, *Futuh al-Habasha*, tr. Basset, pp. 215, 234, 242. *Chronica de Susenyos*, p. 36.

[11] *Gädlä Fīlipos*, loc. cit. Or. 769, f. 12[b]. Inar'it and Inarya seem interchangeable. The upper course of the great Gibé is still called *Gibé Inarta*. A kingdom of Inarya apparently existed immediately to the north of what would later be the famous kingdom of Käfa. Inarya is the area where Motälamī, the legendary king of Damot, is said to have withdrawn on being conquered by Yikunno-'Amlak, Guidi, 'Strofe e brevi testi amarici', in *MSOS*, x (1907), p. 182. Cf. also *Chronica de Susenyos*, pp. 156, 191–7. Almeida, *Some Records*, pp. 11, 18–19. Most likely the origin of the later kingdom of Käfa should be sought in medieval Inarya.

[1] The 12th unit in Ya'iqob's delimitation is said to have been Dimbī, assigned to one Gäbrä-Kristos. In more recent editions of the story, the place is called 'Dämbya, also called Amara Tabor', Or. 769, f. 11. The accompanying notes seem to favour an identification north of the Jäma or in Bägémdir. But this is very unlikely for the 14th century; cf. Ya'iqob's organization in *Gädlä Fīlipos*, pp. 197–8. A more satisfactory identification must be sought in southern Shäwa, in Gurageland, for instance, where Gäbrä-Kristos is said to have had some parishes. A land grant by Amdä-Ṣiyon (1314–44) mentions *Dinbī* together with Wäräb and Inar'it, and seems to confirm a southern identification, Wright, *Catalogue*, Or. 821, ff. 106[b]–107[a]

[2] Cf. p. 117.

[3] *Gädlä Aron*, pp. 126–7. The organizational characteristics—'12 Shepherds of Ethiopia, 72 disciples'—are suspect. But an attempt at the revival of the Christian movement in Amhara also fits very well the traditions we have about Ya'iqob. For the chronological problems see p. 175 n. 3.

Täklä-Haymanot, also seem to have withdrawn from Hayq and founded small monastic communities in Amhara. The most important among these was the community of Däbrä Gol. It was still a private hermitage when its founder Anoréwos, 'the priest', was joined by Bäṣälotä-Mīka'él, probably in the second half of the reign of Widim-Rä'ad (1296–1314).[1] After having received the monastic habit from Anoréwos, Bäṣälotä-Mīka'él travelled to Tigré and stayed at Däbrä Damo for some time. Like Īyäsus-Mo'a and Täklä-Haymanot before him, he appears to have made extensive use of this ancient centre of Christian learning in Ethiopia: 'He stayed here reading the books of the Old and New Testaments, and pondering over their meanings.'[2] He visited many other communities in Tigré, and on his return to Amhara he made Däbrä Gol an important monastic centre. Much of the story of his life concerns his famous conflicts with Abunä Yohannis and King Amdä-Ṣiyon.[3] But when Ya'iqob came to Ethiopia, Bäṣälotä-Mīka'él had already died in exile, and Aron was left as the most senior of his disciples. It was with Aron and Fīlipos of Däbrä Asbo that the Egyptian bishop now began to work, in an attempt to unite the spiritual descendants of Īyäsus-Mo'a in a common struggle against non-Christian elements both within and outside the Ethiopian Church. He saw in these leaders the only hope, not only for the expansion of the Church, but also for the regeneration of strictly Christian ways of life within the Church itself. His leadership in this was completely followed throughout his short term of office. We have seen above how they co-operated with him in staging a frantic attack on the king for his non-Christian matrimonial habits. They also took up their evangelical assignments with a similar youthful enthusiasm.

From the purely hagiographical records at our disposal, it is very

[1] *Gädlä Bäṣälotä-Mīka'él* (text). p. 14. There is also a mention of other communities in the area, pp. 8–10. Bäṣälotä-Mīka'él tried to join one of these while still very young. His mother appealed to Widim-Rä'ad, who was her relative, and the king returned him to his parents by force. That Anoréwos may have been a disciple of Īyäsus-Mo'a is implied in later traditions connecting Bäṣälotä-Mīka'él with Hayq, *Gädlä Īyäsus-Mo'a*, pp. 28–31 (tr.). The curious appellation 'Anoréwos the Priest' does in fact suggest that he was a retired secular priest who may have visited Hayq, obtained his monastic habit, and retreated to Däbrä Gol.

[2] *Gädlä Bäṣälotä-Mīka'él*, p. 19. Curious revelations are attributed to him, pp. 20–1. These have striking similarities with the apocryphal work of the still little-known author Bähaylä-Mīka'él, *Mäṣhafä Misṭīrä-Sämay Wä-midr*, ed. in part and tr. by Perruchon, J., in *PO*, i, pp. 1–97. Budge, *The Book of the Mysteries of Heaven and Earth*. The connection becomes even more intriguing since the author at times calls himself Bäṣälotä-Mīka'él also, Perruchon, op. cit., p. x n. 7.

[3] See pp. 114–17.

difficult to give an adequate reconstruction of the pre-Christian beliefs of the regions in which Täklä-Haymanot and his followers began to work. What one gathers is a general picture of animistic practices and nature worship: 'At that time the people of that district [Zim, west of Däbrä Lībanos] worshipped the rocks, trees, or rivers. They did not know God except very few [among them]. They lived by eating, drinking, and committing adultery all their lives.'[1] The religious leaders of these pagan communities assume a character analogous to that of witch doctors. They had a very strong power over their people and some curious rituals are associated with them in the hagiographies:

> Täklä-Haymanot came to a hill called Bīlat. This was the headquarters of the sorcerers and here they sacrificed the blood of cows and goats [to the devils] . . . There lived their king and the witch-doctors, the diviners, and all the men of magic worshipped him. They stayed in his palace at the foot of the hill . . . waiting for his words. If he has good words for them it presages good luck; if he makes bad pronouncements evil befalls them. Because of this they have made him king over themselves.[2]

This pagan priesthood offered the greatest resistance to the work of the disciples of Täklä-Haymanot in the south. Their countries were only recently opened to Christian influence in a religious sense, and they naturally staged a long and desperate struggle against the establishment of churches and monasteries among their peoples. After the military successes of Amdä-Ṣiyon the local chiefs had long accepted the fact of Christian political dominance, and were reconciled to the idea of Christian expansion. Their religious leaders nevertheless continued their hostile policies on their own. The systematic programme of mission work inaugurated by Abunä Ya'iqob specially provoked such organized hostilities.

[1] *Gädlä Fīlipos*, p. 175. Other references to similar practices are abundant, cf. Conti Rossini, *Il 'Gadla Takla-Haymanot'*, p. 104. Budge, *The Life of Takla Haymanot*, p. 30 (text). 'Gädlä Zéna-Marqos', ff. 11^b–12^a, 13^a. 'Gädlä Samu'él' (Wägäg), ff. 81^b, 116^b. For a review of the pre-Christian (Kushitic) religious practices see pp. 233–5.

[2] Budge, op. cit., pp. 40–1 (text). Cf. also *Gädlä Fīlipos*, pp. 179–81. *Gädlä Anoréwos*, pp. 76–8, 80–1, 94–7. 'Gädlä Qäwisṭos', ff. 71^a, 83–4. There are also references to some kind of fire cult, Conti Rossini, op. cit., p. 106. Budge, op. cit., p. 52 (text), 'Gädlä Qäwisṭos', f. 71^a. The worship of the serpent-god which often appears in the early traditions of the peoples of the Aksumite kingdom also finds a place in some of these traditions about Amhara, Shäwa, Damot, and Gojjam in the 14th century, Budge, op. cit., pp. 77, 79. Conti Rossini, op. cit., pp. 107, 109–10. *Gädlä Anoréwos*, pp. 94–5. 'Gädlä Zäyohannis', MS. Kibran, ff. 19–20.

It was an ancient custom of the Christian kings to send some of the clergy to their frontier military colonies. These were secular priests, and their primary function was to meet the religious needs of the Christian troops themselves. With the development of monastic institutions, however, and with Ya'iqob's reorganization of the disciples of Täklä-Haymanot in particular, a new and powerful element was added to the process of Christian expansion. A prominent monastic leader, with special evangelical responsibilities, began to accompany the Christian troops stationed in an area.[1] He was in charge of the secular priests and co-ordinated their work according to the evangelical needs of his province. He established a monastic community of his own, where he trained more of his followers for the religious leadership, and which he used as a centre for his activities in general. From this centre he travelled widely in the area, preaching, baptizing new converts, and building churches at convenient places. Ya'iqob's programme of missionary work had the approval of King Amdä-Ṣiyon, who naturally placed his royal authority behind it.[2] Besides his frontier troops, the local chiefs were also under some obligation to ensure the security of the king's religious emissaries. This background of royal protection clearly accounts for the sudden development of evangelical activities in the new areas, and for the traditions of early association between the preachers and some of the local chiefly families.[3] A clear picture of this regional missionary organization emerges from the traditions we have about the life of Anoréwos of Wäräb.

We have seen above that Anoréwos was assigned to teach in the district of Wäräb.[4] His first preoccupation on his arrival in the region was to look for a suitable place for establishing his monastic centre. This seems to have taken some time during which he moved from

[1] Christian troops were stationed in the area where Anoréwos was operating. On one occasion he was accused of undermining the frontier defence of the kingdom by accepting some of the soldiers as novices, *Gädlä Anoréwos*, pp. 89–90 (text). This refers to the reign of Säyfä-Ar'ad (1344–71), and it is most likely that the practice also existed before him.

[2] *Gädlä Fīlipos*, p. 197 (text); 'Gädlä Qäwisṭos', ff. 105^{b}–106^{a}.

[3] In the hagiographies the monks could only enlist the help of the local chiefs through their spectacular miracles, Budge, op. cit., pp. 45–53 (text). Conti Rossini, op. cit., p. 106. *Gädlä Anoréwos*, pp. 78–81, 94–6. 'Gädlä-Qäwisṭos', ff. 94–101^{a}.

[4] See p. 176 n. 8. It is interesting that his assignment was to the immediate southwest of his native district of Mugär, *Gädlä Anoréwos*, p. 67. 'Gädlä Samu'él (of Wägäg)', f. 9^{a}. This also seems to be the case with Qäwisṭos, Zéna-Marqos, Anoréwos 'the junior', and probably also of the other preachers.

place to place, preaching and baptizing some of the local people for whom he also built churches:

and he began teaching [the people] . . . saying 'It is better to believe in God than in mortal human beings'. He told them much about Truth from the Scriptures. He gave them penance and baptized them in the name of the Holy Trinity. He also provided them with *tabots* and built churches for them in their country . . .[1]

Anoréwos continued his search for a convenient place to establish his monastery. It is characteristic of these hagiographical traditions that he finally obtained the site with the help of a local man.[2] Bäragban (later called Zäkaryas) is said to have been the chief of the district of Ṣigaga. Having heard about the religious activities of Anoréwos in the nearby districts, Bäragban invited the saint to come to his district and establish his monastic centre. Anoréwos accepted the invitation, but on his arrival there he was met by an organized resistance of the local religious leaders. Bäragban took the Christian side, and the issue was decided by force:

Bäragban took his arrow and went to the woods. He found there three [men of magic] sitting at the foot of an oak tree. He shot at one of them who fell and died; the second fled away, and he captured the third, tied up his hands backwards, and took him to Abunä Anoréwos. When [Anoréwos] saw him he wondered and said, 'After all a man of magic is a human being!' And at that time [the chief] took a knife and slew [his captive] at the feet of [Anoréwos]. After some time [the saint] built a small church on the site.[3]

This gruesome story is a distant echo of the bitterness of the struggle which confronted the Ethiopian Church in its early attempts to extend its influence in this direction. The bitterness of the conflict seems to have been further promoted by the insistence of the preachers on building their churches on the sacred places of the pagan clergy.[4] It was also on such a site that Bäragban helped Anoréwos to establish his monastery of Däbrä Ṣigaga.[5]

[1] *Gädlä Anoréwos*, p. 77.

[2] Ibid., pp. 78–81. Similar traditions of early associations with local chiefs are abundant, Conti Rossini, op. cit., pp. 104–7, 109–10. Budge, op. cit., pp. 43–58 (text). 'Gädlä Qäwisṭos', ff. 77–81, 83–4, 94–101. 'Gädlä Zéna-Marqos', ff. 15^{b}–17.

[3] *Gädlä Anoréwos*, p. 79.

[4] The theme is repeated in various traditions, Conti Rossini, op. cit., p. 104. Budge, op. cit., pp. 37, 40, 78. 'Gädlä Qäwistos', loc. cit. 'Gädlä Zéna-Marqos', loc. cit.

[5] *Gädlä Anoréwos*, p. 80.

The community of Däbrä Ṣigaga grew fast, and many new disciples joined Anoréwos, including some of his own relatives from the north.[1] From here Anoréwos continued his preaching in the surrounding area. He also seems to have assigned evangelical duties to some of his own disciples:

> He called one of his disciples, whose name was Dawīt, a respectable man and a great master of the scriptures, and said to him: 'Come, my son. Go to the country of Adamat at a place called Bäzīrgoy. Take some priests and deacons with you, and prepare the Holy Communion until I come.'[2]

The evangelical activities of Anoréwos seems to have extended far beyond Indägäbṭan, and the traditions attribute to him much pioneering work in Inar'it to the south-west and Damot to the west.[3] But since we have no other hagiographical records for this region, this tradition of the descendants of Anoréwos cannot be controlled. Nevertheless, it seems quite clear that before the end of the third quarter of the fourteenth century, Ya'iqob's evangelical programmes had borne fruit and the presence of the Church was already felt in the outlying provinces of the kingdom in this direction.

Similar work was being done on the Muslim frontier beyond the eastern edge of the Shäwan plateau.[4] We have seen above that there already were Christian communities in the region of Ṣilalish in the Zagwé period, and the immediate result of the advent of the new dynasty had been the consolidation of Christian power in Amhara and Shäwa. On the religious side, a similar development of Christian influence was soon promoted by the activities of Täklä-Haymanot in the central Shäwan plateau. By the time Täklä-Haymanot started his teaching, the region beyond the eastern slopes of the plateau was undergoing a tremendous political upheaval, culminating in the final ascendancy of Īfat over all the other Muslim communities. This,

[1] *Gädlä Anoréwos*, p. 81. Four sons of his sister (in Wäläqa) and a son of his brother (in Mugär) are specially mentioned. The latter is called Gäbrä-Nazrawī, and is remembered as a prominent monastic leader. It seems quite possible to identify him with his namesake commemorated on *Tahsas* 5, *Synaxaire*, in *PO*, xv, pp. 603–10. Here also he is made a monastic descendant of Anoréwos but of the second generation. The tradition (ibid., p. 607) associating him with an evangelical effort in Hadya makes the identification quite secure.

[2] *Gädlä Anoréwos*, p. 94.

[3] Ibid., pp. 85, 89.

[4] In Ya'iqob's time the parish divisions in this direction seem to have been, from north to south, Kil'at (Yohannis), Särmat and Mähagil (Qäwisṭos), Ṣilalish (Tadéwos) and Fäṭägar (Matyas). Of these, I have only 'Gädlä Qäwisṭos' at my disposal pertaining to this period.

however, did not affect the Christians on the plateau and on its eastern edge. Here, Täklä-Haymanot was preaching among his fellow Christians and their pagan neighbours, moving from one community to another. It was probably on one of these occasions that Qäwisṭos came under his influence.[1]

In *Gädlä Täklä-Haymanot*, Qäwisṭos is mentioned only in a list which has the generic title of 'disciples of Täklä-Haymanot', and there are no clear references to him as a resident member of the community of Däbrä Asbo.[2] According to his own *Gädl*, he received his monastic habit from Täklä-Haymanot during the latter's visit to the church of Nibgé Maryam recently built by Qäwisṭos in Ṣilalish.[3] Here also there is no mention of him staying at the new monastery of Grarya. This seems to indicate that Qäwisṭos came under the influence of Täklä-Haymanot before the establishment of Däbrä Asbo. After these early associations with his master, he seems to have returned to his native district of Ṣilalish, and eventually established his own community at Nibgé.[4]

In the region of the eastern slopes of the plateau, Īfat was still the dominant political power, and the community of Nibgé could only have a strictly local significance for about two decades. In the meantime, however, it became an increasingly important religious centre among the local Christians, and Qäwisṭos consolidated his reputation as a monastic leader and as the disciple of Täklä-Haymanot. Nibgé reflected in the east the spirit of Christian revival propagated by Täklä-Haymanot at Däbrä Asbo, with which Qäwisṭos probably kept a close contact. This was probably increasingly felt, not only by the Christians, but also by their Muslim and pagan neighbours. Although Christian and Muslim communities had long been living side by side in these frontier districts, they do not seem to have completely rid the area of its ancient pagan ways of life. The evangelical activities of Qäwisṭos outside his Christian group probably started among these marginal communities. The traditions about his early

[1] Qäwisṭos is said to have been a cousin of the saint, only six months younger, 'Gädlä Qäwisṭos', ff. 44^{b}–48^{a}, 52^{a}. But he is also said to have been killed in the reign of Amdä-Ṣiyon for his part in the monastic attack *c.* 1341 on the king's unorthodox matrimonial habits, ibid., ff. 106–9. This is chronologically impossible, and he must have been a much younger disciple of Täklä-Haymanot.

[2] Budge, op. cit., pp. 88–9 (text).

[3] 'Gädlä Qäwisṭos', ff. 101^{b}–102^{a}.

[4] The traditions of his earlier visits to Tigré and Jerusalem, and his alleged preaching in Särmat before his monastic professions, are almost certainly apocryphal; cf. ibid., ff. 60–68^{a}.

contacts with these people present them as given to magico-pagan practices of a very hybrid character, but strikingly similar to those which Täklä-Haymanot and his disciples confronted in the west and south-west:

He found the inhabitants of the country worshipping the devils at the foot of a *kobäl* [?] tree. They were sitting there eating, drinking and amusing themselves in the fashion of the Muslims. They fanned the fire with their hands and held hot flames in their mouths and chanted saying 'O people of Gälan and Yäy, see what your god Qorké [can] do! . . . And they brought for [Qorké a daily present of] two fat cows, five sheep, five goats, and twenty-one baskets of white [wheat?] bread. All these were eaten by the functionaries of the gods . . .[1]

It was only after Amdä-Ṣiyon's initial successes over Haqädin I and Däradir,[2] however, that the community of Nibgé seems to have taken further advances towards the east. The military prestige of the Christian kingdom impressed the frontier peoples. There is a clear indication that among these Christian and Muslim frontiersmen very close ethnic, linguistic, and probably even family connections existed;[3] and their religious associations often depended on the political fortunes of the day. A tradition about the conversion of a local chief in the area amply illustrates the point:

[His convert told Qäwisṭos:] 'I was (originally) a Christian living in the country of Fäṭägar. A Muslim chief took me away while still ten years old (together with my mother) . . . The son of another chief married her . . . and gave me his sister to wife from whom I had this son . . . He also appointed me chief of this district and my mother . . . used to teach me in secret the rules of the Christians. I have always been a Christian at heart while observing Islam in public.'[4]

The essential message of this story is that the growing political power of Amdä-Ṣiyon was being reflected in the intensive evangelical activities of the descendants of Täklä-Haymanot long stationed in the region. The influence of the Church developed, and more

[1] 'Gädlä Qäwisṭos', f. 71^{a}. The passage is about a people living near a place called 'Mt. Yäy'. From the comparative topography given in the Life itself, f. 75^{a}, Mt. Yäy seems to be somewhere east of Kätäta and therefore to the immediate north-east of Nibgé. The indirect mention of Muslims is interesting, and indicates superficial Islamic influences on the practices of the people who were otherwise unmistakably pagan.

[2] Cf. pp. 132–5.

[3] Cf. Cerulli, E., 'Il sultanato dello Scioa', pp. 32–4.

[4] 'Gädlä Qäwisṭos', f. 77.

churches were being built.[1] The rulers of the kingdom of Īfat deeply resented this expansion of the Church, and it provided them with additional grievances against the growing power of Amdä-Ṣiyon. Säbrädīn's inimical attitude to these religious activities played a considerable part in the hostilities of 1332. On the eve of the war, Amdä-Ṣiyon accused the ruler of Īfat of taking strong repressive measures against the Christians in the area: 'He sent to him, saying, "This thing that I hear about you, is it true or not? Did you burn the church of God and kill many Christians? Did you take away the rest of the Christians and convert them into your religion?" '[2] This mention of churches and Christian communities doubtless refers to the region of the eastern slopes of the Shäwan plateau, and constitutes an important confirmation of the hagiographical traditions of the church. The religious content of the struggle of 1332 was furnished by the attempts of Īfat, and indeed of all the Muslims in the region, to stop this tide of active expansion of the Ethiopian Church. During the war, many of the Christians in the frontier area were converted (or reconverted?) to Islam, and after the war Amdä-Ṣiyon decreed strong measures against them. On his way back from Adal, he ordered Jämaldīn, his new governor of Īfat, to deliver to the Christian Court all such 'apostates':

> The king of the unbelievers . . . brought to king Amdä-Ṣiyon the renegades who were found there, and who included priests, deacons, and soldiers of his [i.e. Amdä-Ṣiyon's] army. Amdä-Ṣiyon . . . had them flogged each thirty times and he had them branded on the breast and on the back with a mark of the perpetual slavery into which they were thenceforth reduced . . .[3]

Those who were thus punished constituted only part of the elusive frontiersmen who had characteristically changed sides during the hostilities; and Jämaldīn's failure to deliver still more of them to the king's judgement cost him both his freedom and his new appointment as ruler of Īfat.[4]

[1] Ibid., f. 81; more Christian clerics are said to have come from Fäṭägar, Zim, and from Wägda to help Qäwisṭos in his work for a time. Cf. the tradition collected by Azais and Chambard at Fäntalé, *Cinq Années de recherches archéologiques en Éthiopie* (1931), p. 145: 'At Fantale, a priest . . . told us that there was a church and an Abyssinian town on the site of Lake Metahara, and that the first successors of Täklä-Haymanot belonged to this church . . .'

[2] Perruchon, J., *Histoire des guerres d'Amda-Seyon*, pp. 282, 299 (text), 331–2, 344 (tr.).

[3] Ibid., pp. 433–4 (text), 478–9 (tr.).

[4] Ibid., pp. 434, 479. Jämaldīn was arrested and his brother Nasrädīn appointed in his place.

After 1332, the Christians enjoyed a greater freedom of action in the area. On the advent of Abunä Ya'iqob, Qäwisṭos was confirmed as head of the Churches of Särmat and Mähagil, and his other colleagues, Yohannis, Tadéwos, and Matyas were also assigned for Kil'at, Ṣilalish, and Fäṭägar respectively.[1] Besides greatly enhancing the prestige of these preachers as monastic leaders this act of the Egyptian bishop seems to have intensified their work. The traditions indicate the extension of the influence of the Church even across the Awash;

> And the chief of Fäntalé [recently converted by Qäwisṭos] crossed the river Awash, fought with the rulers of the Muslims and defeated them . . . He destroyed their place of worship and built a church in the name of St. George . . . and many of the Muslims believed.[2]

The region was no longer a forbidden ground for Christian religious activities, and the disciples of Täklä-Haymanot were free to spread the Christian teaching, particularly through the local chiefs. Essentially, however, the loyalties of these frontier people to the Church were political, and the Church could not flourish beyond the last fringes of the plateau. Apart from the strong militancy of Islam, the semi-desert conditions of the area were also unfavourable for this development.

We have already examined the traditions of the religious conflict between Amdä-Ṣiyon and his successor Säyfä-Ara'd on the one hand, and Abunä Ya'iqob and his monastic allies on the other.[3] The exile inflicted upon the Ethiopian Church leaders by these kings on that occasion marked an important stage of the evangelization of the Ethiopian region. This followed two general patterns:

(*a*) the banished monks tried to convert the local people of their temporary abodes of exile; and

(*b*) some of the younger monks went further away from their place of exile and settled in new areas altogether.

The monks were temporarily exiled in two general directions. In the first period of the conflict, in the lifetime of Amdä-Ṣiyon, all the

[1] See p. 176 notes 2–5 above.

[2] 'Gädlä Qäwisṭos', f. 101ª. The chief is said to have been a brother of a powerful woman who offered great resistance to Qäwisṭos's work in the area. She had a great influence among the local people between the rivers Särmat and Awash. Ibid., ff. 83–4, 94–101. It is interesting to compare the position of this woman with Cerulli's comments on female rulers in the area, 'Il sultanato dello Scioa', pp. 21–2. For the tradition of a church built in that area see p. 185 n. 1.

[3] See pp. 116–18.

traditions we have (with only one exception) indicate that the exiled monks were sent northwards to Amhara and Tigré.[1] Amdä-Ṣiyon banished the leading disciples of Täklä-Haymanot northwards out of Shäwa,[2] and those of Bäṣälotä-Mīka'él north of Amhara.[3] Those exiled to Tigré, where some churches are attributed to Aron,[4] are not relevant to our story of evangelization. In the regions of Amhara and Bägémdir, however, these places of refuge served not only as centres of spreading Christianity among the local people, but also as a launching-pad for further evangelical work in Gojjam and in the Lake Ṭana region.

Anoréwos of Wäräb spent his first three years of exile in the district of Wäläqa where he is said to have preached among the local people: 'He converted many of the people of Wäläqa into the worship of God.'[5] He was not the earliest preacher in the district where his own sister was already married to a local Christian before his exile.[6] Apart from early traditions involving an ancestor of Täklä-Haymanot,[7] another prominent monastic leader called 'Zä'amanu'él of Wäläqa' is also mentioned elsewhere in connection with the region in an earlier context of the fourteenth century.[8] But it seems that many parts of the district were still pagan and both Anoréwos and Fīlipos appear to have helped in its evangelization.[9]

[1] The exception referred to is the alleged exile of Bäṣälotä-Mīka'él (d. before 1337) by Amdä-Ṣiyon to Dära and Lake Zway, *Gädlä Bäṣälotä-Mīka'él*, pp. 30–4 (text). The conflict with the kings was conducted on two different occasions. On the first occasion, before 1337, Bäṣälotä-Mīka'él led the clergy against Amdä-Ṣiyon. He was exiled to Tigré on two occasions and he finally died there. The conflict started again on the advent of Bishop Ya'iqob. Amdä-Ṣiyon again exiled the monks to Tigré in 1341. They were recalled on his death in 1344. Soon afterwards, however, they quarrelled with his successor, Säyfä-Ar'ad. It was probably on this occasion that the monks began to be exiled to the south, and Bäṣälotä-Mīka'él's alleged participation in this later event may have only been based on the experiences of his monastic descendants led by Aron.

[2] Probably both Anoréwos and Fīlipos were first exiled together to Wäläqa, *Gädlä Anoréwos*, pp. 84–5. *Gädlä Fīlipos*, p. 242. Fīlipos was later sent further north to Tigré, ibid., pp. 214–15.

[3] Aron and many of his followers left Däbra Gol and went northwards to Angot and Tigré, then back to Wag and Lasta, and to Däbrä Qäṭin across the upper Täkäzé, *Gädlä Aron*, pp. 133–6.

[4] Ibid., p. 133.

[5] *Gädlä Anoréwos*, pp. 84–5.

[6] Ibid., p. 81.

[7] See p. 120 n. 4.

[8] *Gädlä Bäṣälotä-Mīka'él*, pp. 43, 45–6. Amdä-Ṣiyon mentions 'a monk called Amanu'él' as having sent his blessing and encouragement to the expedition of 1332, Perruchon, op. cit., p. 311 (text); it seems quite possible to identify Amdä-Ṣiyon's 'Amanu'él' with Zä'amanu'él of Wäläqa, a district in Amhara.

[9] Cf. *Gädlä Fīlipos*, pp. 242, 246 (text).

In the second period of the conflict, in the reign of Säyfä-Ar'ad, the monks' places of exile were in the south or south-east, in the newly conquered areas beyond the river Awash. Here the most important place seems to be a locality called Dära. It is mentioned in the hagiographies of the descendants of both Täklä-Haymanot and Bäṣälotä-Mīka'él, and it appears that all these monastic leaders were first sent there at the same time.[1] But only Aron and his followers stayed there for a period of about seven years.[2] It is also in *Gädlä Aron* that we possess an interesting description of the area: 'The soldiers [of the king] brought them to the land of Zängo . . . in the neighbourhood of Astran, near *Dära* and Bosato, facing Lama. Gwatr was also near them, and Zway was visible from far. And there ruled the *Gärad* of Balī.'[3] The inhabitants of the area were apparently Muslims and are remembered in these traditions as having been very hostile to the exiles: '. . . those who lived there were Muslims and they did not know Christ. They were murderers, and the king sent [his enemies] to them so that they might take his revenge for him.'[4] Aron and his followers were forced to stay here for seven long years, and although they suffered many casualties, they eventually made their peace with the local people. They cleared a piece of land and transformed it into a garden on the fruits of which they managed to live.[5] They preached

[1] *Gädlä Fīlipos*, pp. 231, 240. *Gädlä Anoréwos*, pp. 87–8. *Gädlä Aron*, pp. 145–50. *Gädlä Bäṣälotä-Mīka'él*, pp. 30–1.

[2] *Gädlä Aron*, p. 149. Fīlipos and Anoréwos were both transferred to an island in Lake Zway after a period of three months, *Gädlä Fīlipos*, loc. cit. *Gädlä Anoréwos*, loc. cit.

[3] *Gädlä Aron*, p. 145. Some of these places are perfectly identifiable. Al-'Umari has a Muslim state called Dara bordering on Balī, op. cit., pp. 1, 18–19. The general direction given for it is also similar in *Gädlä Fīlipos*, which places it, however, in Däwaro, p. 240. It is also said elsewhere that it was inhabited by Muslims, *Gädlä Bäṣälotä-Mīka'él*, pp. 30–1. Gragn's chronicler has 'Darah' on the frontiers between Däwaro and Balī, *Futuh al-Habasha*, tr. p. 387. The identification of Dära with a district east of Lake Ṭana is misleading, Almeida, *Some Records of Ethiopia*, p. 233. Gwatr is also mentioned elsewhere as being near Däwaro, 'Gädlä Esṭīfanos', ff. 82, 86. *Gädlä Abäkäräzun*, p. 26. It is probably the same district as Djaoutir, a frontier district of Christian Däwaro, *Futuh-al Habasha*, tr., p. 134 n. 3. The area where the monks were exiled was also a week's journey east of the Awash, *Gädlä Aron*, p. 150. The additional mention of Zway and the *Gärad* of Balī suggests that the place was between Däwaro and Balī. It is precisely here that a modern Ethiopian religious scholar located the place of Aron's exile, Aläqa Lämma, *Mäṣhafä-Tizita*, ed. Mängistu Lämma (Addis Ababa, 1967), pp. 36–7.

[4] *Gädlä Bäṣälotä-Mīka'él*, p. 30. Cf. also *Gädlä Fīlipos*, p. 231. *Gädlä Anoréwos*, p. 88.

[5] *Gädlä Aron*, pp. 148–9.

among their neighbours, and it appears that they left some churches behind them at the end of their exile: '. . . they prayed in the churches they built in Dära and Zängo, and left some monks and priests there.'[1]

Fīlipos and Anoréwos were transferred to Lake Zway. They were taken to one of the islands, and the hagiographical traditions about this exile provide the earliest description of the lake and the people who lived there in the fourteenth century: 'The lake was famous for its great depth and width, and no one can enter it without *Wäbäl* [?]. They took them into an island inhabited by pagans who did not have any religion and who ate the flesh of both properly slain and dead animals.'[2] The monks are believed to have converted some of these peoples, and it seems probable that the island monastery of Lake Zway had its origin in this early mission work.[3] According to these traditions the monks were soon transferred from the lake region to what appears to be the area further south and south-west of Lake Zway, where they are also said to have preached.[4] By the middle of the fourteenth century, therefore, the Ethiopian Church had already begun to make direct contacts with what is today a predominantly *Sīdama* country.

Early missionary work around Lake Ṭana

It has been stated above that the communities established in Amhara during these exiles also served as a stepping-stone for further mission work in Gojjam and in the Lake Ṭana area. This was made possible by Amdä-Ṣiyon's successful military activities in the area

[1] Ibid., p. 150. Cf. also *Gädlä Bäṣälotä-Mīka'él*, loc. cit.

[2] Ibid., p. 33. The description of the inhabitants of the island(s) fits what is still believed about the low-caste Fuga of the region. Cf. Shack, W. A., *The Guragé* (1966), pp. 9–10.

[3] *Gädlä Fīlipos*, pp. 231–4. *Gädlä Anoréwos*, pp. 88–9. Abba Sīnoda (d. before A.D. 1433), founder of Däbrä Ṣimona in Gojjam, went to school in Lake Zway, and he was given the monastic habit by one Indryas, at the island monastery, 'Gädlä Sīnoda', MS. Dīma, ff. 3ª–5ª. This means that already at the end of the 14th century a monastic community flourished there. Since then we have continuous references to it in both Christian and Muslim documents, Alvarez, *The Prester John of the Indies*, pp. 435–6. *Futuh al-Habasha*, tr. Basset, p. 371. Almeida, *Some Records*, p. 36. Antoine d'Abbadie, *Géographie d'Éthiopie*, pp. 60–7. Blundell, H. W., 'Exploration in the Abbay Basin, Abyssinia', in *GJ*, xxvii, no. 6 (June, 1906), p. 531.

[4] *Gädlä Fīlipos*, p. 235. *Gädlä Anoréwos*, p. 89. The place is said to be Gämasqé in Damot, which seems to indicate a general direction towards the upper Omo and Gibé rivers. Cf. also *Gädlä Bäṣälotä-Mīka'él*, pp. 34–5.

shortly after his accession to power. A fourteenth-century note relates the king's victories over the king of Gojjam soon after the year 1316/17.[1] His chronicler mentions in addition successful campaigns against Gojjam and Wägära some time before 1332.[2] It is probably to one of these early expeditions that we also have a reference in a hagiographical tradition:

> The king sent [his men] to bring him a *tabot* from the monastery of Ṣana because he wished to set out on an expedition. They took for him a *tabot* consecrated in the name of Qīrqos. Having taken this, he went to war and defeated the rebels (who were) his enemies . . .[3]

The first Christian influence in Gojjam came from the direction of the south-eastern corner of Lake Ṭana. The island church of Ṣana Qīrqos has the earliest tradition. Its alleged foundation in the fourth century A.D. is almost certainly apocryphal.[4] There seems to be no doubt, however, that a Christian community existed in the area before the end of the Zagwé dynasty.[5] About the end of the second decade of

[1] Taddesse Tamrat, 'The Abbots of Däbrä Hayq', pp. 95–6. Cf. also Guidi, I., 'Le canzoni Ge'ez-Amarina in onore di re abissini', in *RRAL*, v (1889), pp. 62–3.

[2] Perruchon, op. cit., p. 309.

[3] *Gädlä Yafqirännä-Igzī*, ed. and tr. by Wajnberg, I., in *OCA*, no. 106 (1936), pp. 18–22. Conti Rossini, 'L'agiografia etiopica e gli atti del santo Yafqiranna-Egzi' in *ARIV*, xcvi (1936–7), pt. 2, pp. 414–15, 424. The early date of this incident is quite clear from a close examination of the *Gädl*: Yafqirännä-Igzī was still a young member of the community as he is referred to as 'my brother' by the king's messenger who is described as a mere 'deacon', p. 20. This tallies very well with the chronological notes we have about the saint who died at an advanced age in 1376, Conti Rossini, op. cit., p. 420. He was born one year before the arrival of Abunä Yohannis in Ethiopia. This bishop is also mentioned in the note commemorating the king's success in Gojjam. Yohannis came as a result of Yagba-Ṣiyon's letters to Egypt in 1290, Quatremère, *Mémoires*, ii (1811), pp. 268–73. He apparently only reached Ethiopia in the reign of Widim-Rä'ad (1299–1314), when we have the earliest references to him, Budge, *The Life of Takla-Haymanot*, p. 84 (text). *Gädlä Qäwisṭos*, f. 68ª. He was accused of simony by Bäṣälotä-Mīka'él in the early part of Amdä-Ṣiyon's reign, *Gädlä Bäṣälotä-Mīka'él*, pp. 22–4.

[4] *Mäṣhafä-Kidanä-Mihrät*, extract ed. and tr. by Conti Rossini in 'Il convento di Tsana in Abissinia e le sue laudi della Vergine' in *RRAL*, ser. v, vol. xix (1910), pp. 602–3 (text), 617–18 (tr.). Cheesman, R. E., *Lake Tana and the Blue Nile* (1936), p. 172.

[5] It seems that Amdä-Ṣiyon's success was only a culmination of earlier attempts at Christian expansion in this direction. We have early traditions about Christian activities already in the Aksumite period, Conti Rossini, 'Il convento di Tsana', pp. 581–2. Id., 'Il libro delle leggende', pp. 706–7. The Zagwé kings also seem to have had contact with Gojjam in this direction, Perruchon, *Vie de Lalibela*, p. 117. Conti Rossini, *Gli atti di Nä'akuto-Lä'ab*, (1943), pp. 37–8. The traditions of some churches in the Lake Ṭana region also connect them with Amdä-Ṣiyon's grand-

the fourteenth century Amdä-Ṣiyon had firmly consolidated his power in the region between the river Täkäzé in the east and Lake Ṭana, and the stage was set for the expansion of the Church further afield.

Yafqirännä-Igzī joined the community of Ṣana Qīrqos in the first years of Amdä-Ṣiyon's reign.[1] On his arrival there the community was fairly well established. But its reputation as an important centre of monastic activities and Christian learning was a relatively recent development. The modest position occupied by Ṣana at the time is suggested in the stories of the early life of Yafqirännä-Igzī. On his advent to the lake region the activities of the monastery were still firmly controlled by the ruler of Gojjam whose special permission was required to admit the young monk from Tigré into the island.[2] It was only after Amdä-Ṣiyon's successful campaigns that the position appears to have changed. Ṣana Qīrqos became the natural recipient of the king's favours,[3] and soon asserted itself by gradually extending its supremacy over all the other islands. The local rulers of Gojjam and Dämbya now seem to give some protection to the monks living in the islands.[4] This was apparently followed, however, by the monks of Ṣana Qīrqos venturing into the mainland and the still unoccupied islands in the lake.

Local opposition to the expansion of the Church was still considerable on the mainland south of the lake. On his first attempt to establish himself in the district of Bäda, Yafqirännä-Igzī was forced to return to the islands:

And then came the messengers of Widim, king of Gozam and said to him, 'Why are you staying in the district of Bäda? Return to your place . . .'

father, 'The Book of Miracles of St. Mary', MS. Daga, beginning of the MS. Cheesman, op. cit., pp. 107–9.

[1] The saint was born in Tigré, *Gädlä Yafqirännä-Igzī*, pp. 14, 16. For the place of his birth, cf. Conti Rossini, 'L'agiografia etiopica', pp. 412 n. 3 and p. 413 n. 1. He was already ordained monk by one Adhanī in Tigré. He is elsewhere said to have been the disciple of Mädhanīnä-Igzī, id. *Gädlä Filipos* (Bīzän), table, p. 156. Basset, *Études*, p. 10.

[2] *Gädlä Yafqirännä-Igzī*, p. 16. The ruler is called 'Žankimir, King of Gojjam'. Cf. Guidi, I., 'Le canzoni', pp. 62–3. 'Gädlä Täklä-Haymanot', MS. (17th-century) Kibran, end of MS. Here 'Zīnkimir' is king of Gojjam about A.D. 1323/4. Conti Rossini, *Gli atti di Nä'akuto-Lä'ab*, pp. 37–8 (text), where he is called Ṣara-Qämis, 'the enemy of God'. From all these it appears that a notorious ruler of that name strongly resisted the expansion of the Christian kingdom into Gojjam. The indications seem to show that he was Amdä-Ṣiyon's contemporary.

[3] *Gädlä Yafqirännä-Igzī*, pp. 20, 22.

[4] Cases of such co-operation are reported in the early part of the saint's career at Lake Ṭana, ibid., pp. 26, 28.

Having heard the message, the saint refused to go . . . and they wanted to take him back by force . . .[1]

This local opposition appears to have been even stronger in the region north and north-west of the lake. The most serious resistance to the Christian advance here seems to have come from the Fälasha, who were predominant in the mountainous districts between the lake and the Täkäzé river. The early campaigns of Amdä-Ṣiyon had resulted in the consolidation of his power in Gojjam and in the districts immediately to the north and east of the lake. But his conquest of the mountain Fälasha tribes had apparently been only temporary and, probably also provoked by the resultant activities of the Church in the area, the Fälasha rose in an open rebellion against the king on the eve of his campaigns in Adal in 1332:

He sent other contingents called Damot, Säqält, Gondär, and Hadya [consisting of] mounted soldiers and footmen and well trained in warfare . . .; their commander [was] Bägämdir Ṣäga-Kristos. He sent them to the country of the rebels to fight . . . [the people of] Simén, Wägära, Ṣälämt, and Ṣägädé. Originally these people were Christians but now they denied Christ like the Jews who crucified him. For this reason [the king] sent an army to destroy them . . .[2]

This did not represent a 'Révolte de Bagamdir'. Perruchon reached this conclusion by a casual misunderstanding of the term *Bägämdir* which was only part of the title of Ṣäga-Kristos, who seems to have been the governor of the district of that name at the time.[3] Only the

[1] *Gädlä Yafqirännä-Igzi*, p. 24. *Bäda* seems to be the district which today bears the name Bäd on the mainland just opposite, and south of the island of Kibran. In a 16th-century land grant 'the chief of Bäd' is mentioned together with 'the king of Gozam', '*The Four Gospels*', MS. Kibran, f. 238b. Widim seems to be the successor of Žankimir as king of Gojjam. The same name was borne by an officer who commanded Amdä-Ṣiyon's cavalry contingent called Gojjam in 1332, Perruchon, *Histoire des guerres d'Amda-Seyon*, pp. 289, 383.

[2] Ibid., pp. 293, 339–40. It is curious that the chroniclers of both Amdä-Ṣiyon and Zär'a-Ya'iqob considered the Fälasha as Christian apostates, cf. *Les Chroniques de Zar'a Ya'eqob et Ba'eda Maryam*, pp. 96–7. The hagiographical traditions are, however, unanimous in attributing Jewish religious practices to them, *Gädlä Yafqirännä-Igzi*, p. 56. Conti Rossini, 'Appunti di storia e letteratura Falascia', in *RSO*, viii (1920), p. 571. Id., 'Note di agiografia: Gabra Iyesus', in *RSO* xvi (1938), pp. 446–8. In this latter work their origin is taken to the time of the destruction of Jerusalem. Some information about their existence in Ethiopia seems to have reached medieval Europe, cf. Conti Rossini, 'L'itinerario di Beniamino da Tudela e l'Etiopia', in *ZA*, xxvii (1912), pp. 360–3. Cerulli, *Etiopi in Palestina*, i (1943), pp. 234–6.

[3] It is consistently used as such in the documents, Perruchon, *Histoire des guerres*, loc. cit., and p. 281. This is further confirmed by two land grants of the early 15th century where a Princess held the title Bägämdir (or Mägämdir),

Fälasha rebelled against the Christian kingdom in 1332, and Bägämdir Ṣäga-Kristos was sent to suppress them with an army which included Gondar, a contingent of local extraction still loyal to the king. The expedition was apparently successful, and the Fälasha revolt was put down for a time. The king's success in his Muslim campaigns further enhanced his power throughout his kingdom, and we have no case of major Fälasha risings on record for at least fifty years. It seems, in fact, that those years saw a speedy development in the establishment of the Church in this direction.

The island monastery of Ṣana Qīrqos had been the major centre of Christian activities in the lake region. In the reign of Amdä-Ṣiyon its influence at the royal Court was apparently considerable. Abba Ya'iqob, the second abbot of the community since Yafqirännä-Igzī's arrival in Ṣana, seems to have had very good connections at the court and was probably appointed from there. He was later sent to Egypt as a member of the delegation to fetch a new bishop, apparently Abunä Ya'iqob, in about 1337.[1] It is not clear what part the community of Ṣana played in the conflicts between Abunä Ya'iqob and his monastic allies on the one hand, and Amdä-Ṣiyon and Säyfä-Ara'd on the other. But the series of exiles which Amdä-Ṣiyon imposed upon the monks in 1341 eventually led to the establishment of monastic centres in the lake region, other than Ṣana Qīrqos, and considerably strengthened the Christian mission work in Gojjam and in the Fälasha country. The activities of the followers of Abba Aron and Fīlipos of Däbrä Asbo were particularly significant in these developments.

We have already seen how, after some wandering in Tigré and Lasta, Aron finally established himself at Däbrä Qäṭīn.[2] The site was on a hill overlooking the western bank of the Täkäzé on its upper course immmediately west of Lalībäla. Aron and his followers built a church and settled in what is today the south-eastern corner of Bägémdīr.[3] Their influence was soon felt around the country and many of the local people seem to have joined them:

'The Four Gospels', MS. Kibran, ff. 3ª–238ª. The province of Bägémdir now covers the whole area west of the Täkäzé and north of the lake and borders with the Sudan. In the medieval context, however, it only referred to the area between the river Bashilo and the upper course of the Täkäzé on the east and the south-eastern shores of the lake.

[1] *Gädlä Yafqirännä-Igzī*, pp. 26, 38. For the date of the bishop's arrival see Taddesse Tamrat, 'The Abbots of Däbrä Hayq', n. 57.

[2] See p. 187 n. 3.

[3] It seems that the church was hewn out of the rock, *Gädlä Aron*, p. 136. Cf. also A. Caquot, in *AÉ*, v (1963), p. 272, no. 65.

[The reputation of Aron] spread in all the districts of Mäqét, Asasa, and the countries of Wadla and Dawnt. The whole of Bägémdir was full of his news from Amhara to Wägära . . . and many received the monastic habit from his hands and he taught them the ways of God . . .[1]

The district of Gaynt, west of the river Bashilo and south of the monastery, was apparently still pagan, and Aron baptized many of the inhabitants there. His work was interrupted by another period of exile, this time south of the river Awash.[2] On his return from there about seven years later, Aron's activities were redoubled and his influence was felt even more widely. He travelled to his own native land of Gämbya, further west, and built churches and established communities.[3] His own seat remained at Däbrä Qäṭīn where he built a new rock-hewn church[4] on a nearby hill called Däbrä Darét which became the centre of his activities. The monastic community of Abba Aron had a great reputation, and even a daughter and a brother of King Säyfä-Ara'd were among its residents.[5]

The dispersal of the leading members of Däbrä Asbo also contributed to this vital process of the expansion of the Church in this direction. Some of them are said to have settled eventually in the districts of Dämbya and Bägémdir, and on the islands of Lake Ṭana.[6] Abba Zäkaryas, a disciple of Fīlipos, established his community on the island of Gälīla, about the end of the reign of Amdä-Ṣiyon.[7] There, fresh reinforcements increased Christian activities in the area and further advances were made in the pagan districts south of the lake. This new development comes out very clearly in the story of the

[1] *Gädlä Aron*, loc. cit.

[2] See pp. 188–9.

[3] *Gädlä Aron*, pp. 152–3.

[4] It is quite clear here that it was a rock church: 'He finished hewing the rock in three years.' For identification of this site cf. Caquot, op. cit., p. 274, no. 64.

[5] *Gädlä Aron*, pp. 137–8, 140. His refusal to give up these princes was one of the reasons for Aron's conflict with the king. Aron gave the Princess the monastic name of Barbara, and her career is confirmed by a contemporary note of 1390/1, in a MS. of the Four Gospels belonging to herself, S. Grebaut, 'Note sur la princesse Zir-Ganela' in *JA* (1928), pp. 142–4. The identity of the king's brother is, however, still obscure. A son of Amdä-Ṣiyon, Abba Yasay, is the traditional founder of Mandabba on the northern shore of Lake Tana, Cheesman, op. cit., p. 199. But it is not certain where he first received his monastic ordination.

[6] Basset, R., *Études sur l'histoire d'Ethiopie*, pp. 10 (text), 100 (tr.). The date of the MS. he used is mid 18th century, ibid., pp. 5–6; and as such it has some chronological errors of which the most conspicuous is its mention of Täklä-'Alfa (16th century) among the 14th-century monastic leaders.

[7] Ibid., pp. 10–11 (text), 100 (tr.). This is also confirmed by *Gädlä Yafqirännä-Igzī*, pp. 104–8, 112. Gälīla was 'uninhabited' when Yafqirännä-Igzī first visited it, ibid., p. 28. Zäkaryas seems to have come many years later. But he appears to be the senior of the two in terms of age and monastic experience.

life of Abba Zäyohannis, who settled on the island of Kibran apparently in the reign of Säyfä-Ara'd.

Zäyohannis originally came from the district of Märhabīté in north-western Shäwa. He joined the monastery of Däbrä Asbo and was professed a monk by Hizkyas, who became abbot in 1341 when Fīlipos was exiled to Tigré.[1] It is not clear why he left Däbrä Asbo; the traditions about his life state that, after moving about in the country for some time, he went to the region of Lake Ṭana.[2] He first stopped in the district of Dära on the south-eastern shore of the lake where the people were already Christians. He is said to have made friends with a Christian family of fishermen who helped him cross over to Kibran: 'There are no people [his friends told Zäyohannis] living on that island. But we often spend the night there when we [intend to] catch many fish.'[3] This contradicts the tradition in the Life of Yafquirännä-Igzī, according to which some clerics were already settled on the island, and were part of the community of Ṣana Qīrqos.[4] The hagiographers of Zäyohannis also indirectly imply elsewhere that some hermits were already living on the island before him.[5] These hermits may have originally been members of Ṣana. It is also most probable that Zäyohannis himself was first connected with the same community when he started his career in Kibran.[6]

The most interesting part of the story of Zäyohannis's life is the tradition about his attempts to evangelize the mainland south of the lake. With the unsuccessful attempts of Yafqirännä-Igzī to settle

[1] 'Gädlä Zäyohannis', MS. Kibran, ff. 3^{a}, 12^{a}, Basset's text makes him a disciple of Fīlipos, loc. cit.; together with other traditions it also makes him settle in Kibran in the reign of Amdä-Ṣiyon, cf. 'Gädlä Zäyohannis', ff. 20^{b}–21; *Gädlä Täklä-Haymanot*, MS. (17th-century), Kibran, end of the MS. But this contradicts his accepted monastic ordination by Hizkyas, and it seems doubtless that his advent to the island was in Säyfä-Ara'd's reign (1344–71). Säyfä-Ara'd is in fact the earliest king mentioned in early (15th-century) historical notes at the monastery, 'The Four Gospels', MS. Kibran, ff. 3^{a}, 235^{b}–237.

[2] It is interesting that the *Gädl* does not mention his alleged exile with Fīlipos given in Basset's text. His itineraries are uncertain and the usual hagiographical story of the saint's 'flight in the clouds' makes his alleged visit to Tigré, Hamasén and Jerusalem very suspect, 'Gädlä Zäyohannis', ff. 13^{b}–14^{a}.

[3] Ibid., f. 16^{a}.

[4] *Gädlä Yafqirännä-Igzī*, p. 24. The island is here called 'Kobra' and differs from the etymology given in 'Gädlä Zäyohannis', loc. cit.

[5] Ibid., f. 18^{a}.

[6] Many of the land grants to Kibran since the early 15th century clearly show that the *Niburä-Id* of Ṣana still held a position of considerable authority on the community of Kibran, 'The Four Gospels', MS. Kibran, ff. 3^{a}, 235–237^{a}, 238^{b}–239^{a}.

in the district of Bäd[1] before him, this tradition seems to offer another stage in the gradual expansion of the Church in Gojjam. The pagan people 'south of the island' are said to have been under 'the ruler of Agäw' called Jan-Chuhay. Zäyohannis crossed over to the mainland and began preaching in Zägé and the adjoining districts. When Jan-Chuhay heard of the religious activities of the monk in his territory, he put him in prison, from which he was only freed by the intervention of the officials of the Christian kingdom:

> [Jan-Chuhay] ordered his men to arrest him and beat him . . . And Zäyohannis remained a prisoner in Amädamīt. Then King Amdä-Ṣiyon heard [this] and sent many soldiers [to Jan-Chuhay] saying: 'If you do not release this monk, there shall be no peace between you and me.' The king ordered [his messengers] to kill Jan-Chuhay if he refused . . . and they killed him . . . and released Zäyohannis.[2]

This seems to suggest that local resistance to the new religion was persistent, and the power of the Christian state was once again required to suppress it. As in the other frontier areas, the degree of political control which the Christian kingdom possessed always determined the speed of advance of the Church. In the case of the rich kingdom of Gojjam, the end result of these early efforts was particularly successful. But as we shall soon see, the vital process of the complete integration of Gojjam in the Christian kingdom was further promoted by evangelical activities conducted from other directions, accompanied by considerable Christian settlement from Shäwa and Amhara. We must now turn to the area north and north-east of the lake, where the Fälasha were becoming restive once again, after more than fifty years of apparent calm.

The evangelization of the Fälasha

This period of about fifty years had been one of continuous Christian pressure on the ancient habitat of the Fälasha. During the first half of the fourteenth century this pressure came from Bägémdir in the south, and the fertile plains of Dämbya north of Lake Ṭana. During the whole of this period, no major traffic seems to have been opened directly between the district of Shiré in Tigré and the lake region.

[1] See pp. 191–2.

[2] 'Gädlä Zäyohannis', ff. 20^{b}–21^{a}. The people are said to have worshipped a serpent which Zäyohannis killed by praying to his God. The conflict with Jan-Chuhay started from this, ff. 19–20. The ruler is elsewhere given as being the king of Gojjam, Žīnkimir, 'Gädlä Täklä-Haymanot', MS. (17th-century), Kibran, end of MS.

The whole region between Dämbya and Bägémdir in the south, and the Täkäzé river in the east and north, was Fälasha country, and a forbidden ground for the Christian movement. The itineraries of Yafqirännä-Igzī, on his way from Tigré to Ṣana Qīrqos at the beginning of Amdä-Ṣiyon's reign, are not given in his *Gädl*; but it is probable that they followed the ancient route from Tigré to Lalībäla, and then went westwards across the upper course of the river Täkäzé to Lake Ṭana, via Bägémdir. This was exactly the route followed by Abba Aron of Däbrä Darét towards the end of the same reign.[1]

The energetic campaigns of Amdä-Ṣiyon pushed this Fälasha frontier considerably northwards into the heart of Wägära, and into the mountain districts to the immediate north of Bägémdir. This increasingly impelled the Fälasha to retire into the inaccessible mountain districts of Ṣägädé, Ṣälämt, Simén, and northern Wägära.[2] An active process of religious expansion followed the conquests of the Christian king. In the early part of Yafqirännä-Igzī's career in the Lake Ṭana region, the areas immediately to the north and east of the lake were already Christianized.[3] Towards the end of the reign of Amdä-Ṣiyon, the Christian pressure on Fälasha country was increased. Unlike the extensive areas south of Amhara, where all the mission work is attributed to the descendants of Īyäsus-Mo'a, both Tigré and Amhara clerics worked side by side in the Christian mission among the Fälasha. In the reign of Säyfä-Ara'd we have references to the intensive activities of Tigré clerics in the area, particularly at the monastic centres of Zazo and Wäyna.[4] But it was the advent of Abba Gäbrä-Īyäsus in Infraz that represented a new factor in the history of monastic development in Ethiopia.

Gäbrä-Īyäsus was one of the early disciples of Éwosṭatéwos, and he is said to have accompanied his master to Egypt, the Holy Land, and Cyprus.[5] Éwosṭatéwos had left Ethiopia soon after the arrival

[1] *Gädlä Aron*, pp. 133–6. The traditions about early Aksumite missions to Bägémdir and Amhara point to the same route. In the Zagwé period when Lalībäla was the seat of government this was probably the main route.

[2] It is interesting that Almeida was told that Dämbya was originally part of Fälasha country, *Some Records of Ethiopia*, p. 54. It may also be that Wägära in the 14th century extended much more to the south than the present district of that name.

[3] *Gädlä Yafiqirännä-Igzī*, pp. 28, 30. The Käntība of Dämbya and his people helped the saint during his self-exile in the island of Gälīla; pp. 66, 80, 94, 108, Fogära, Gämbya, Wido, and Infraz, all on the eastern side of the lake, are mentioned as having Christian communities.

[4] *Gädlä Yafqirännä-Igzī*, pp. 50–8. *Gädlä Samu'él* (Waldibba), pp. 3–7.

[5] Conti Rossini, 'Note di agiografia etiopica: Gäbrä-Īyäsus', pp. 441–3.

of Abunä Ya'iqob about 1337, and many of his surviving followers returned home on his death in Armenia about 1352. The story of his eventful life belongs to another chapter and will be fully considered later.[1] But the 'house of Éwosṭatéwos', which he founded in Säraʼé and Hamasén, also played a significant part in the expansion of the church. In Fälasha country the role of his disciple Gäbrä-Īyäsus was very considerable.

Gäbrä-Īyäsus was apparently born in Wag, a frontier district between Tigré and Lasta.[2] He travelled to Tigré, and eventually joined the growing community of Éwasṭatéwos, whom he accompanied on his self-exile abroad. On his departure, Éwasṭatéwos entrusted his community to the leadership of one of his senior disciples, Absadī, who made his centre at Däbrä Maryam of Qohayīn.[3] It was probably here that Gäbrä-Īyäsus and his colleagues first stopped on their return from Armenia. They have a tradition that, some time before his death, Éwosṭatéwos had assigned them to teach in different places in Ethiopia.[4]

According to this arrangement, Gäbrä-Īyäsus is said to have been allocated the district of Infraz, east of Lake Ṭana. After some unsuccessful attempts to establish himself in Tigré, he moved south wards probably via his district of Wag and Lasta to Infraz. From the story of his activities in this district it is quite clear that Infraz was inhabited by the Fälasha. He established his centre at Däbrä San among them. Of all the traditions we have about the fourteenth-century effort to spread the Christian teaching in this region, the story of Gäbrä-Īyäsus is unique in its explicit mention of direct mission work among 'the Jews of Ethiopia': 'Even the sons of the Jews believed, received baptism and entered into his teaching.'[5] The

[1] See pp. 206–9.

[2] His conscientious hagiographer discloses that the original *Gädl* of Gäbrä-Īyäsus was lost during the Gragn wars. His origin, as well as the rest of the story of his life are based on traditions collected from memory, Conti Rossini, op. cit., p. 441.

[3] *Gädlä Éwosṭatéwos*, pp. 73–6, 115–17, 135–6, 176. *Gädlä Fīlipos* (Bīzän), p. 157, note on f. 17ʳ.

[4] Conti Rossini, op. cit., p. 443. The assignments are said to have been given to his 'twelve disciples'. This arrangement is not mentioned in *Gädlä Éwosṭatéwos*. According to this *Gädl* many followed him on his travels abroad, but only two are mentioned by name, Téwodros, p. 97; and Bäkīmos, p. 113. Bäkīmos later settled at Ṣärabī where he ordained Fīlipos, the famous founder of Däbrä Bīzän, *Gädlä Fīlipos*, pp. 78–9. Märqoréwos, who is also believed to have travelled with the master, later established himself at Däbrä Dimah, *Gädlä Märqoréwos*, pp. 32–3.

[5] Conti Rossini, op. cit., p. 446.

cultural impact of the Christian church on the Fälasha went even deeper, and we have a report in precisely this period that a renegade Christian monk called Qozīmos left his monastery in Wäyna, joined the Fälasha community in Simén, and copied the Old Testament for them.[1] Quite apart from the conversion of some of the Fälasha to Christianity, their close contact with the Ethiopian Church began to enrich their own religious legacy, and much of their literary and organizational borrowings may date from the mid-fourteenth century.[2]

Apart from some territorial gains in Dämbya and in the districts north of Bägémdir, Amdä-Ṣiyon's repressive measures against the Fälasha in 1332 did not result in a complete annexation of the Fälasha country. The only important result appears to have been the withdrawal of the centre of Fälasha resistance further north. It was in the district of Simén that a serious rising took place some time in the reign of King Dawīt (1380–1412).[3] The revolt appears to have been a general reaction to the growing Christian domination, and both secular and monastic leaders were conspicuous among its victims. Qozīmos, the renegade monk mentioned above, is particularly mentioned as having led the movement:

> [The Fälasha rebels] left, and held their positions against the Käntība of Dämbya: they fought and they defeated him. [The Käntība][4] made an agreement with them. Then [Qozīmos] went out [of Simén], he burned numerous churches, came to the road of Infraz, and killed Abba Qérlos, Abba Yohannis Käma, and Abba Tänsi'a-Mädhin with thirty-six of their disciples. The others who died then were innumerable throughout Infraz, monks and nuns . . . He further killed many chiefs and officials. . . .[5]

The new Fälasha resurgence overpowered the local Christian troops,

[1] *Gädlä Yafqirännä-Igzī*, p. 56.

[2] Conti Rossini, 'Appunti di storia e letteratura Falascia', pp. 577–8, 584–93. For the striking similarities which the organization of the Fälasha religious institutions displays with that of the Ethiopian Church see Leslau, W., *Falasha Anthology* (1951), pp. xxi–xxvi, and xxxvi-xliii.

[3] The story of this revolt is told in *Gädlä Yafqirännä-Igzī* (text) pp. 50–8. Conti Rossini also published the extract in his 'Appunti di storia e letteratura Falascia', pp. 567–77. From the text, the revolt seems to have taken place not very long after Yafqirännä-Igzī's death in 1376. It is most likely that it belongs to the last years of the 14th century.

[4] Here Conti Rossini substitutes the pronoun in the Ge'ez text with 'Käntiba', and thus suggests that the ruler of Dämbya had co-operated with the Fälasha after his first defeat. This seems to me very arbitrary, and the pronoun clearly refers to Qozīmos who is the chief concern of the whole extract.

[5] Ibid., pp. 571–2 (text), pp. 576–7 (tr.). *Gädlä Yafqirännä-Igzī*, p. 5 (text).

and King Dawīt had to send fresh auxiliaries to them under the command of Akhadom, governor of Tigré. The expedition was successful, and the Fälasha revolt was once again suppressed. There are very clear indications that, after this incident, serious attempts were made to integrate the Fälasha country into the characteristic feudal system of the Christian kingdom. This was particularly the case in the reign of King Yishaq (1413–30). We have seen earlier in the last chapter how a policy of 'divide and rule' was successfully directed towards the Wälasma family of Īfat by Amdä-Ṣiyon and Säyfä-Ara'd. Yishaq pursued an exactly similar policy towards the local chiefs of the Fälasha country.[1]

The king appointed a strong Fälasha chief, Bét-Ajir, as governor of Simén and part of Dämbya. Under Bét-Ajir he appointed the chief's own nephew Bädagosh to serve as a liaison officer with the royal Court. Bädagosh regularly visited the Court and his special responsibility was to ensure that his uncle duly paid the tributes of the king. On one occasion he went to his uncle to remind him to send his tributes. Bét-Ajir refused to obey, and mistreated his unpatriotic nephew. When he was summoned to appear at the king's Court he declined to come. On this open act of revolt King Yishaq personally led an expedition against him: 'And the king came and struck his tent in Wägara. Bét-Ajir did not notice his arrival. They made war from morning to evening. After that Bét-Ajir escaped; but the soldiers of the king surrounded him, and cut off his head.'[2]

After this victory the king generously compensated Bädagosh for his loyalty, and granted him a large fief in Wägära. Friendly groups among the Fälasha chiefs were similarly rewarded for their co-operation during the hostilities.[3] Nevertheless, Yishaq fully realized the essentially religious nature of the Fälasha question. For him the only solution to this chronic problem lay in bringing an end to the

1 'Tarīkä-Nägäst', paper MS., Däbrä Ṣigé, pp. 53–4.

2 Ibid., p. 54. Cf. also Basset, R., *Études sur l'histoire d'Ethiopie*, pp. 11, 101. For the name of the chief, see Conti Rossini, 'Appunti di storia . . .', p. 567 n. 2.

3 The 24 elders of *Bäläw Amba* are particularly referred to as having been rewarded by the king for their co-operation against the Fälasha, 'Tarīkä-Nägäst', loc. cit. 'The Book of the History of the kings', MS. Däbrä Ṣigé, p. 45. Also Basset's short text reports the same, although he altered it in the translation by changing the word *Ṣar'o* to *Sä'aro*. The spearhead of the ancient Christian [originally Béja] people, the *Bäläw*, had apparently been established in the region of Wälqayit, Conti Rossini, 'Schizzo etnico e storico delle popolazioni Eritree', pp. 76, 84. They probably had old rivalries with the local Fälasha, and may have been willing to help Yishaq against them.

religious difference and in imposing Christianity on the 'rebelling infidels'. With this in mind he passed a decree from which the Fälasha are sometimes said to have derived their name: ' "He who is baptized in the Christian religion, may inherit the land of his father; otherwise let him be a *Fälasī*." Since then, the House of Isra'el have been called *Fälashoch* [= exiles]. And the king built many churches in Dämbya and Wägära.'[1] This seems to have served as another stage for further Christian expansion in Fälasha country. But the 'Jews of Ethiopia' continued their hostilities to the Church, and the Fälasha question was still alive to the end of our period.[2]

The establishment of the Church in Gojjam

The reigns of Dawīt and Yishaq were also marked by a similar expansion of the Ethiopian Church in eastern Gojjam. We have seen above the pioneer work of Yafqirännä-Igzī and Zäyohannis in the districts immediately south of Lake Ṭana. These activities were conducted among the Agäw population who appear to have constituted the medieval kingdom of Gojjam.[3] It is impossible here to estimate how far inland the power of this kingdom extended; but it seems clear that its centre lay between the lake and the central highlands of Agäw-midir. The earliest attempts at Christian expansion in Gojjam[4] came from the direction of the lake. This is fairly well confirmed by the lack of any acceptable clerical traditions in eastern Gojjam which refer to a period earlier than the reign of Dawīt. The Christian troops of Amdä-Ṣiyon in his early expeditions against Gojjam seem to have never crossed the middle Abbay from the direction of Amhara in the west. They were probably conducted through the Christian district of Bägémdir to the south-eastern corner of the lake, north of the Nile, which was also probably controlled by 'the king of Gozim' at first.[5] It was probably in this region

1 'Tarīkä-Nägäst', loc. cit. Basset, op. cit., pp. 12, 101. 'Mar Yishaq', MS. Dīma, ff. 171^{b}–112^{a}.

2 This is fairly well documented, *Les Chroniques de Zar'a Ya'eqob*, pp. 96–7, 172–3. Halévy, J. *La Guerre de Sersa-Dengel contre les Falashas* (1907), pp. 17, 54–5. *Gädlä Täklä-Hawaryat*, ed. and tr. Conti Rossini, pp. 103–7 (text). Kolmodin, *Traditions*, A25, A32. *Futuh al-Habasha*, tr. Basset, pp. 456–9.

3 'Jan-Chuhay, the ruler of Agäw' is elsewhere mentioned as 'Žīnkimir, King of Gozam' in the traditions of Kibran, cf. 'Gädlä Zäyohannis', ff. 19–21. Cf. 'Gädlä Täklä-Haymanot', MS. Kibran, end of the MS. Elsewhere, the same area south of the lake, and the islands in the southern half of the lake, are said to have been under 'the king of Gozim', *Gädlä Yafqirännä-Igzī*, pp. 16, 24, 26.

4 See Ch. IV.

5 See p. 191 n. 2.

on both sides of the Nile that the first hostilities were conducted, leading to the eventual recognition of Amdä-Ṣiyon as the overlord of the kingdom of Gojjam. The attempts of the Church to extend its influence on the eastern shores of the lake, on the islands of the lake, and further inland to the south of it, followed precisely the same direction. But the Agäw population south of the lake continuously resisted these religious activities. The mountain of Amädamīt is the furthest point inland where *even* hagiographical traditions take Zäyohannis as a prisoner of 'the ruler of Agäw'.[1] The 'kings of Gozim' were probably still pagan at least until the end of the reign of King Dawīt.[2] Until the advent of Christian clerics in eastern Gojjam across the Abbay, the missionary activities of the island monasteries could not penetrate the Agäw barrier. This is clear from a close study of the traditions of Däbrä Dīma,[3] Däbrä Ṣimmona,[4] and Däbrä Wärq,[5] which have been the principal monastic centres in the area.

[1] See p. 196 n. 2. Amädamīt is still the name of the high mountain range about 32 miles south of the lake.

[2] In a land grant of King Dawīt dated July, A.D. 1412, we have 'M'ata-Goné' as king of Gozam, 'The Four Gospels', MS. Kibran, f. 3[a]. Before him, in the reign of Amdä-Ṣiyon we have Žankimir and Widim as successive kings of Gojjam. The names of these officials gradually become clearly Semitic, and Christian: Anbäsa Dawīt, *Chronique de Ba'ede Maryam*, ed. and tr. Perruchon, pp. 160–1; Särṣä-Maryam and Täklä-Ṣiyon, both in the reign of Libnä-Dingil, 'The Four Gospels,' MS. Kibran, ff. 5[b], 236[b]–238. From a comparative study of Agäw dialects Conti Rossini has also concluded that the 'Semitic' influence on the Awīya and Damot dialects is most recent, *Etiopia e genti d'Etiopia* (1937), p. 136.

[3] The traditions about Täkästä-Birhan, founder of Dīma, derive his origin from Däbrä Asbo, 'Täkästä-Birhan', paper MS. Dīma, f. 2[a]. He is said to have followed Fīlipos in exile to Tigré whence his master sent him to Gojjam, 'Gädlä Fīlipos', MS. Däbrä Dīma, ff. 35[b], 37[a]. Here, his original name is given as Bäkīmos which also appears in the text edited by Turaiev, but in quite a different context, *Gädlä Fīlipos*, ed. Turaiev, pp. 222–3. Basset's short text mentions one Täkästä-Birhan of Däbrä Ṣot as Fīlipos's fellow exile, *Études*, p. 10. A place called Ṭot is also included in the very uncertain itineraries of the founder of Dīma, 'Täkästä-Birhan', ff. 3[b]–4[a]. He is said to have been still active in the reign of Dawīt, and his successor Tomas ruled for 20 years, apparently in both Dawīt and Yishaq's reigns, *ibid.*, ff. 7[a], 16[b]–17, 'Zéna-Mämhiran', in Qäléminṭos, MS. Dīma, f. 2[a].

[4] Abba Sinoda, its founder, was born in Wäj, in Shäwa and studied at the island monastery of Lake Zway. He had already been in Gojjam, and he established Däbrä Ṣimmona in the reign of Yishaq, and died on an island of Lake Ṭana, where he was exiled for political reasons in the reign of Hizbä-Nagn (1430–33), 'Gädlä Sīnoda', MS. Dīma, ff. 2–3, 5[a], 17[b], 20–25.

[5] The traditions of Däbrä Wärq have been affected most by relatively recent monastic rivalries in the region: and Aksumite foundation is claimed, Cohen, 'Dabra Warq', in *Mélanges René Basset*, i (1923), p. 150. 'Gädlä Särṣä-Péṭros', f. 13. Its later building in Dawīt's reign by Särṣä-Péṭros is said to have only been a restoration, ibid., ff. 13–16. Särṣä-Péṭros is then said to have lived until the reign

The most interesting element in these traditions is that they represent two new directions of Christian activities in Gojjam, from Bägémdir in the north (across the Nile), and from Amhara in the west. Since the reign of King Dawīt these communities on the eastern edge of the Gojjam plateau definitely represented the advance points of Christian expansion into the interior. This movement seems to have been considerably promoted by some Christian families beginning to settle in eastern Gojjam. Apart from the monastic leaders themselves,[1] we also have some indications that secular Christian families were beginning to settle in the area.[2] These early settlements ushered in a vital process which would soon result in the almost complete transformation of eastern Gojjam into a distinctively Christian and Amhara country.[3]

The settlement of Īyäsus-Mo'a at the island church of Däbrä Hayq in 1248 took place at an opportune moment. Immediately followed by the rise of the new dynasty, which had its centres in Amhara and Shäwa, the establishment of the earliest monastic school at Däbrä Hayq provided an essential factor in the process of Christian expansion in the Ethiopian region. Compared with the previous nine centuries of Ethiopian Christendom, the achievements of the new dynasty were particularly remarkable in this respect. At the beginning of our period, during the last quarter of the thirteenth century, the Christians south of Lasta had only occupied a long and very narrow crescent running from the south-eastern corner of Bägémdir to the

of Bä'idä-Maryam (1468–78), f. 28^{b}. In his monastic genealogy he is also made at least three generations younger than Abba Sīnoda of Däbrä Ṣimmona, 'Tarīkä-Mänäkosat', in *Compendium of Homilies*, MS. Däbrä Wärq, ff. 1^{b}–2^{a}.

[1] For Täkästä-Birhan and Sīnoda we have traditions of their Shäwan origin. Särṣä-Péṭros is said to have been born from a Christian family in Inäbsé a district in Gojjam north of Däbrä Wärq and his monastic ancestry is traced back to Gäbrä-Īyäsus of Infraz in Bägémdir, 'Gädlä Särṣä-Péṭros', ff. 5^{b}, 18^{b}. 'Tärīka-Mänäkosat', loc. cit. He is also associated, however, with a certain community of Miskabä-Qidusan in Amhara, 'Gädlä Särṣä-Péṭros', f. 32^{b}. He died in Shäwa, ibid., ff. 61–3; cf. also 'Mäzgäbä-Gädam', MS. Däbrä Wärq, see under his name. The Abbot I met insisted that Särṣä-Péṭros's parents were Christian settlers from Mänz in Shäwa.

[2] *Gädlä Täklä-Alfa*, ed. and tr. E. Cerulli (1943), p. 10 (text). The saint's father was originally from Shäwa, and the family settled at Wäsän Amba in Gojjam in Yishaq's reign.

[3] The process was already complete in the beginning of the 16th century. It probably started with the conversion of the 'Nägasé-Gozim', and the close association of his family with the central Christian Court afterwards. This is fairly clear from the reign of Zära-Ya'iqob onwards; cf. Alvarez, op. cit., pp. 425–8, 458–9. See also p. 202 n. 2.

upper waters of the Mugär, along the high ridge forming the watershed of the Nile and Awash basins. At its Shäwan end, the crescent was much broken by intervening pagan communities. Täklä-

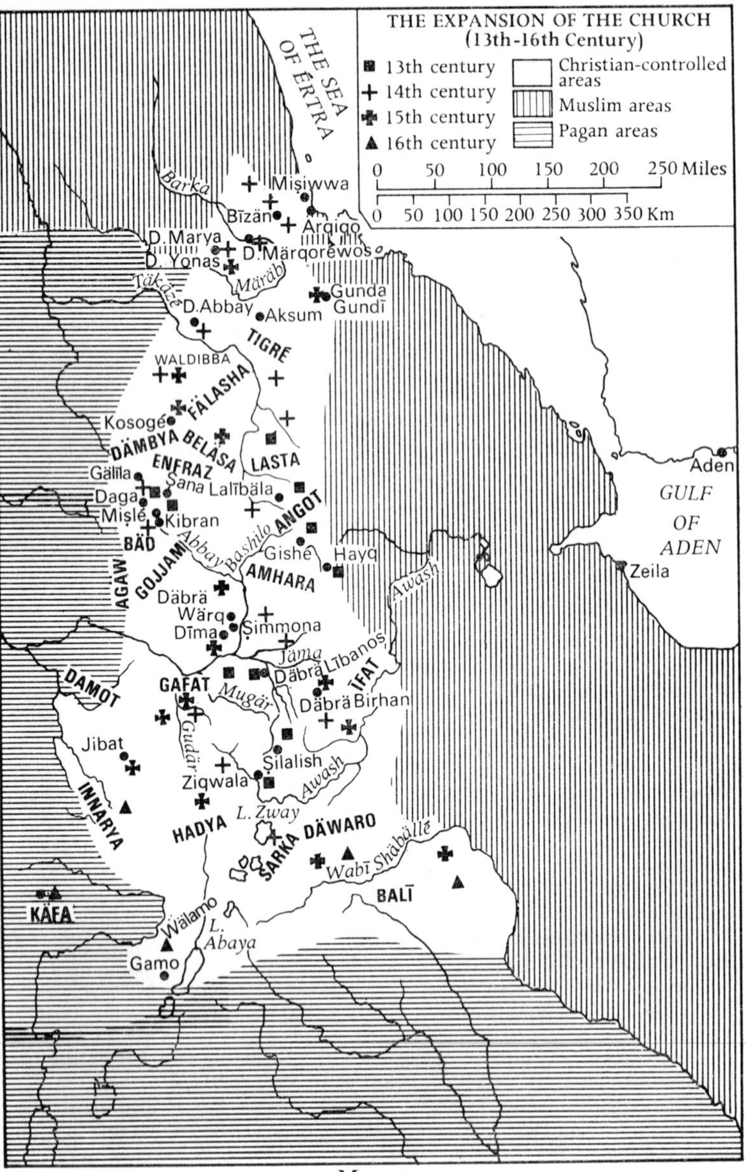

MAP 5

Haymanot's career helped fill up these gaps in the central Shäwan plateau, and with the reign of Amdä-Ṣiyon this crescent became elongated at its two ends, spreading into yet wider areas which had previously been non-Christian. The achievements of his immediate successors lay in widening this narrow Christian corridor, extending to the heart of Fälasha country in the north-west, and medieval Damot in the south-west. The Church played a significant role in the development, and by the beginning of the fifteenth century the central part of the kingdom, south of the provinces of Tigré and Lasta, had grown into a circle consisting of Shäwa, Amhara, and eastern Gojjam. The political boundaries of the kingdom extended much further than the frontiers of the Church. This reflected both the relative strength of the non-Christian communities, and the internal weakness of the Ethiopian Church. Zära-Ya'iqob's religious and administrative reforms were particularly aimed at solving these important problems.

CHAPTER VI

Zär'a-Ya'iqob, and the Growth of Religious Nationalism

(1380–1477)

THE descendants of Yikunno-Amlak, until the last quarter of the fourteenth century, were primarily engaged in the establishment of the dynasty, and the expansion of the kingdom. This afforded them little time for serious thought on the internal organization of the church and its relations with the monarchy. In the meantime, monasticism underwent a rapid development which found ample expression in the evangelization of the Ethiopian region, which has been considered in the last chapter, and in the reform movements which were particularly active in the reigns of Amdä-Ṣiyon (1314–44) and Säyfä-Ar'ad (1344–71).[1] Another outcome of this development was the emergence of strong monastic groups of which the 'house' of Éwosṭatéwos is of great significance to the theme of this chapter.

Éwosṭatéwos

The traditions about the origins of Éwosṭatéwos (*c.* 1273–1352)[2] are not very clear, but he is said to have been a nephew of Abba Daniél of Gär'alta, under whom he later studied.[3] He was professed monk by his uncle, probably in the community of Gär'alta. He apparently left this community soon afterwards and established his own in Sära'é.[4] There, he was joined by many students[5] and taught vigorously

[1] See pp. 114–18.

[2] *Gädlä Éwosṭatéwos* has been edited by B. Turaiev in his collection *Monumenta Aethiopiae Hagiologia*, fasc. iii (Petropoli, 1905). A Latin translation is available in *CSCO*, Script. Aeth., series altera, vol. 21 (1906), pp. 1–97. My references below are to the edited text.

[3] Ibid., p. 7. Here Daniél is only mentioned by name and the place where he had his community is not stated. In the spiritual genealogies, however, he is consistently referred to as Daniél of the community of St. Mary in Gär'alta, cf. *Gädlä Fīlipos* (Bīzän), ed. and tr. Conti Rossini, p. 156 (table).

[4] 'And then he went out to preach . . .', *Gädlä Éwosṭatéwos*, p. 26. Following this, the centre of his monastic activities is said to have been in Sära'é, pp. 35, 38–41, 58, 62–3. *Gädlä Fīlipos* (Bīzän), pp. 71–3.

[5] Of these the principals were Absadī, Bäkīmos, and Märqoréwos, ibid., pp. 78,

until the arrival of Abunä Ya'iqob whom he met on his way to the king's Court in about 1337. Soon after this, Éwosṭatéwos left the country, visited Cairo where he met Patriarch Benjamin (1327–39), and passed via the Holy Land to Cyprus and Armenia, where he died fourteen years later.[1]

It is quite clear from the traditions about his career that Éwosṭatéwos left the country as a result of religious controversies in Ethiopia. Immediately before his departure, there was an attempt on his life, organized by a rival group of the clergy in Sära'é.[2] At the court of the patriarch in Cairo, he was accused by his fellow Ethiopian pilgrims of refusing to communicate with them and of observing the Sabbath as well as Sunday.[3] The question of the Sabbath was central in the conflict, and Éwosṭatéwos admitted the charge. He defended his position by resorting to the Ten Commandments and to the Apostolic Canons.[4] He bitterly complained to the patriarch, who apparently asked him to be reconciled with his countrymen:

> I came to your country . . . so that I may die for the word of God, for I have found no rest in this World. In Ethiopia they said to me, 'Break the Sabbath and the [other] rest Days like us' and I refused. And here you say to me 'Be one with us in prayer' while you do not observe the rest Days.[5]

His reception in Egypt was clearly unfavourable, and he passed on to Jerusalem, apparently suffering some acts of persecution on the way.[6]

When he left Ethiopia, Éwosṭatéwos was accompanied by some of his followers, but he entrusted the leadership of the rest of the community to his senior disciple, Abba Absadī.[7] However, his absence

84, 88; *Gädlä Éwosṭatéwos*, pp. 31, 68, 113. Gäbrä-Īyäsus came from Lasta or Tigré, and joined him, Conti Rossini, 'Note di agiografia etiopica', in *RSO*, xvi (1938), pp. 441–2.

[1] *Gädlä Éwosṭatéwos*, pp. 79–129. The duration of his stay abroad is given in *Gädlä Fīlipos* (Bīzän), p. 99. Conti Rossini, 'Note di agiografia etiopica', p. 443. He must have visited Cairo between 1337, the date of Ya'iqob's arrival in Ethiopia, and 1339, the date of the end of Patriarch Benjamin's reign. He was still alive when Amdä-Ṣiyon died in 1344, *Gädlä Éwosṭatéwos*, p. 108. It seems, therefore, that he died in about 1352. Another tradition states that he died at 79.

[2] Ibid., p. 57.

[3] Ibid., p. 89.

[4] Ibid., pp. 90–1. Conti Rossini, 'Il "Senodos" etiopico', in *RRAL*, ser. viii, vol. iii (1942), pp. 44–7.

[5] *Gädlä Éwosṭatéwos*, p. 91.

[6] At the monastery of Scete, where Éwosṭatéwos and his followers had called on their way to Jerusalem, he is said to have been put in fetters and '(these) cruel people opposed him for the Law and Commandments (of God)', ibid., p. 96.

[7] Ibid., pp. 73–6. Conti Rossini, 'Un santo eritreo: Buruk-'Amlak', in *RRAL*

greatly weakened the community and, on the eve of his departure, some of his followers are said to have already defected from him.[1] Absadī had a difficult task in keeping the small group intact, and only on the return of some of Éwosṭatéwos's companions from abroad did his efforts begin to bear fruit. Bäkīmos,[2] Märqoréwos,[3] and Gäbrä-Īyäsus[4] went with their master to Armenia and returned home only after his death. An Armenian monk who had joined Éwosṭatéwos abroad came with them and became an active member of the community in Ethiopia.[5] According to their hagiographical traditions, all the followers of Éwosṭatéwos soon gathered around Absadī and established the community of Däbrä Maryam in Qohayīn.[6] Other communities were also founded by the leading members, and a chain of monastic groups, collectively known as the 'Seven Disciples of Éwosṭatéwos', was soon established.[7] Apart from that of Gäbrä-Īyäsus, who proceeded to Infraz in Bägémdir,[8] two of the communities were in northern Tigré and the remaining four in Sära'é and Hamasén. Thus, the geographical distribution of the 'house' of Éwosṭatéwos was more heavily represented in the northern provinces of the kingdom. This regional character of the movement gave a greater homogeneity to the 'house' of Éwosṭatéwos, and for the same reason too, the kings were more deeply concerned about it. A recent tradition about Éwosṭatéwos and Anoréwos of Shäwa puts this in good relief. The two monastic leaders, we are told, once met at the royal Court of King Amdä-Ṣiyon. They began to discuss the question of the Sabbath in violent terms, and this was reported to Amdä-Ṣiyon. The king summoned his fellow Shäwan, Anoréwos, to his presence and had him flogged because 'you will divide my kingdom by your religious disputes'.[9]

ser. vi, vol. xiv (1938), pp. 21–2. According to a tradition collected by Ellero, Absadī originally came from Agamé and was buried at Inda-Mäsqäl at the present site of Inda Mädhané-Aläm in Mäqalé, 'Note sull'Enderta', in *RSE*, i (1941), pp. 157–8. Conti Rossini apparently had a copy of *Gädlä Absadī*, which is still unpublished, op. cit., p. 7 n. 1.

1 *Gädlä Éwosṭatéwos*, p. 69.

2 Ibid., p. 113, *Gädlä Fīlipos* (Bīzän), p. 70.

3 *Gädlä Éwosṭatéwos*, p. 68, *Gädlä Märqoréwos*, ed. and tr. Conti Rossini, pp. 32–3 (text).

4 Conti Rossini, 'Note di agiografia etiopica', pp. 443–4.

5 *Gädlä Éwosṭatéwos*, pp. 112–13. Another member of the community, Buruk-Amlak, is also given a foreign origin, Conti Rossini, 'Un santo eritreo', pp. 10, 22.

6 *Gädlä Éwosṭatéwos*, pp. 116–17, 136.

7 Conti Rossini, op. cit., pp. 1–3.

8 See pp. 198–9.

9 Mäl'akä-Birhan Ṣigé, 'Mäshafä-Tarīk', MS. B. 30, National Library, Addis

It is probable that the controversy over the Sabbath in the Ethiopian Church was much older than the fourteenth century. In a report on Ethiopia, Bishop Sawīros once requested Patriarch Cyril II (1077–92) to write to the Ethiopians 'forbidding them to observe the customs of the Old Testament'.[1] Apart from the customs of circumcision[2] and marriage,[3] the bishop may also have had the Sabbath in mind. However, the early position of the Alexandrian Church itself is not very clear on this point, and the Sabbath seems to be held with a great deal of honour in its Coptic and Arabic literature. But in Ibn al-Assal's Collection of Canons compiled in 1238 the observance of the Sabbath is clearly rejected as a Jewish custom.[4] At least from this period onwards, it is quite evident that the Egyptian bishops were determined to impose the official Alexandrian line on the Ethiopians.

The 'house' of Éwosṭatéwos.

Éwosṭatéwos taught against the Alexandrian position on the Sabbath. It seems that at first he could gather little active support for his cause, and he left the country in self-exile. When his disciples returned fourteen years later, they apparently came with even stronger views on the subject, and with new ideas of better organization. During

Ababa, pp. 45–6. Cf. also 'Tarīkä-Nägäst', MS. Däbrä Marqos, ff. 29^{b}–31^{a}. Another tradition, which also appears to be of recent formulation, reports that Éwosṭatéwos had visited Shäwa and met Amdä-Ṣiyon there, G. Ellero, 'Note sull'Enderta', p. 166. Another only takes him to Lasta, *Gädlä Märqoréwos*, p. 21. Cf. Conti Rossini, 'Il libro delle leggende', p. 709.

[1] Sawirus, *History of the Patriarchs of Alexandria*, ii, part 3, p. 330.

[2] As early as the reign of Patriarch Yoséf (830–49) there is a reference to Ethiopian insistence on circumcision. In an attempt to explain St. Paul's point on circumcision (1 Corinth. 7: 8) Bishop Yohannis apparently created local suspicions about himself and was forced to leave the country for some time. On his return to Ethiopia after some negotiations, trouble started once again and a petition was submitted to the king that the bishop should be circumcised: 'for all the inhabitants of the country are circumcised except him'. When he was examined later, it was found that he was properly circumcised, Sawirus, *History of the Patriarchs*, in *PO* x (1915), pp. 508–11. At a Council held in 1238, Patriarch Cyril III ruled that 'customs established in Coptic churches shall not be changed, such as circumcision before baptism', Khs-Burmester, O. H. E., 'The Canons of Cyril III ibn Laklak', pp. 106–7. Maqrizi also reports that 'Les Coptes, contrairement aux autres Chrétiens, ont l'usage de la circoncision', *Les Fêtes des Coptes*, ed. and tr. Griveau, R., in *PO* x (1915), p. 325. Wansleb, *L'Histoire de l'Église d'Alexandrie* (Paris 1677), pp. 78–9.

[3] Bäṣälotä-Mīka'él's parents planned for him to marry his (late?) brother's wife, *Gädlä Bäṣälotä-Mīka'él*, p. 12 (text). Cf. Alvarez, op. cit., p. 108; cf. also, *Liber Aksumae*, ed. Conti Rossini, pp. 71–2.

[4] Muyser, J., 'Le Samedi et le Dimanche dans l'Église et la littérature Copte', appendix to Togo Mina, *Le Martyre d'Apa Epima* (Cairo, 1937), pp. 89–111.

their sojourn in the Levant they probably had much access to the literature of the early Christian Church, and they may have brought their own copies of religious books back with them. The traditions of great love for books which we have about the leading members of the movement probably arise from this.[1] An active literary development appears to have taken place among them during this period,[2] and not only did it strengthen their own position but also seems to have served in time as a decisive landmark in the cultural renaissance of the whole of the Ethiopian Church. The memory of the exile and death of Éwosṭatéwos gave his followers a strong sense of unity, and they continued to defend his position on the Sabbath, for which they were excommunicated:

> The disciples of Ma'iqäbä-Igzī observed the Sabbaths, Saturday and Sunday; but they did not enter in the residence of the king nor in the house of the metropolitans. And they did not receive the Holy Orders because the observance of the Sabbath was not in force in the kingdom, and the Sabbath was abolished in the realms of the patriarchs [of Alexandria]. They considered it just like the other five working days [of the week]. They also considered all those who observed the Sabbath as Jews, they excommunicated them, and did not give them permission to enter the churches.[3]

The opponents of Éwosṭatéwos among the local clergy actively persecuted his followers and expelled them from the settled areas. The difficulties which they had to face in this early period are evident from their traditions. On one occasion, the first companions of Éwosṭatéwos, Absadī and Märqoréwos, are said to have met at a place called Midrä-Goda'i and to have prayed together for God's guidance about whither to proceed. On another occasion Fīlipos (*c.* 1323–1406), who later founded Däbrä Bīzän, accompanied Absadī on a visit to his aged father, Tomas, who advised them to go

[1] Conti Rossini, 'Un santo eritreo: Buruk-Amlak', p. 7 n. 1.

[2] *Gädlä Fīlipos* (Bīzän), p. 104. They co-operated among themselves to bring this about, and there seems to have developed a healthy sense of competition among the leaders. According to a tradition preserved here, Absadī once copied *Anqäsä-Birhan* for Fīlipos. The latter wanted more and requested Absadī to copy for him another work, *Bihérä-Yohannis*. When Absadi hesitated to do it some hard feeling was created between the two. Another tradition has it that Fīlipos had all the Books of the Old Testament copied in 1378/9, Kolmodin, *Traditions*, A23.

[3] Zär'a-Ya'iqob, *Mäṣhafä Birhan*, ii (tr.), ed. and tr. Conti Rossini and L. Ricci, in *CSCO*, vol. 262, Script. Aeth., t. 52, p. 82. Ma'iqäbä-Igzī was the name of Éwosṭatéwos before his ordination as monk by his uncle Daniél, *Gädlä Éwosṭatéwos*, pp. 6, 23.

PLATE 3

The monastery of Däbrä-Bīzän on the edge of the Hamasén plateau overlooking the Sea of Értra. It was founded by Abba Fīlipos in

in different directions and to start, each of them, a community of his own.[1] It is apparent that, in their search for suitable places, they were forced to withdraw into frontier areas. This seems to have determined the location of the first major communities established by the followers of Éwosṭatéwos: Däbrä Maryam and Däbrä Dimah in Qohayīn and Dämbälas respectively,[2] Däbrä Bīzän on the eastern edge of the Hamasén plateau, and Gäbrä-Īyäsus's community of Däbrä San among the Fälasha in Infraz.[3] Once established in these peripheral areas, however, they soon evolved a meticulous organization of their own in complete defiance of the rest of the Ethiopian Church.

Zär'a-Ya'iqob provides us with an excellent contemporary description of their curious organization.[4] They consisted of three major communities, namely Däbrä Maryam, Däbrä Bīzän and Däqī Yīta.[5] Each of these had a number of smaller monasteries and convents under its supervision and the total number of their inmates was considerable.[6] Since all the members of the 'house' of Éwosṭatéwos were debarred from receiving Holy Orders at the hands of the Egyptian bishop,[7] these communities lived in an almost complete

[1] *Gädlä Fīlipos*, p. 88.

[2] In about the same period as the establishment of these two communities, these frontier areas were being gradually occupied by the Christian tribes of Adkämä-Mälga, Conti Rossini 'Studi su Populazioni dell'Etiopia', pp. 89, 92 (extract). The itineraries of Fīlipos before his settlement at Bīzän also indicate that the disciples of Éwosṭatéwos were forced to wander in distant forests and uninhabited areas. Only a little to the west of the present site of Däbrä Maryam, which Conti Rossini calls 'il selvaggio distretto di Cohain', Fīlipos is said to have once visited Dubäné, described as '. . . a barren land . . . where there are no people, no food or water, and no cattle are seen in it', *Gädlä Fīlipos*, p. 81. Fīlipos was met by a hostile group of people there, and Conti Rossini identifies these with the Kunama, ibid., p. 154, note on f. 14ʳ. Cf. also p. 157, note on f. 17.

[3] In the traditions about him he is said to have first established himself at a site in Tigré, where he had a revelation that the site was not assigned for him and that he should travel to Infraz, Conti Rossini, 'Note di agiografi aetiopica Gabra-Iyesus', p. 444. This is probably an allusion to a hostile reception in Tigré.

[4] *Mäṣhafä Birhan*, ii (tr.), pp. 83–4. Cf. also Dillmann, *Über die Regierung, insbesondere die Kirchenordnung des Königs Zara-Jacob* (Berlin, 1884), pp. 45–7.

[5] Cf. *Liber Aksumae*, p. 26 (text).

[6] Zär'a-Ya'iqob gives a short statistical survey: Däbrä Maryam consisted of 81 monasteries and 23 convents; Däbrä Bīzän had 8 monasteries and 3 convents with a total number of 1146 nuns; and Däqī Yīta, 6 monasteries, op. cit., p. 84. Twenty-five churches are elsewhere said to have been built by Fīlipos and administered together with Bīzän, *Gädlä Fīlipos*, p. 107.

[7] Éwosṭatéwos himself was duly ordained, apparently before he established his distinctive school, *Gädlä Éwosṭatéwos*, p. 22, 25. Zär'a-Ya'iqob, op. cit., pp. 82–3. No traditions of such ordinations are given about Fīlipos and his successor

independence from the rest of the Church. However, they apparently needed a small number of ordained priests, whom they admitted into their group only after giving them penance for having been members of other communities. These priests were mainly required to celebrate mass for the group. In all other matters, however, each of the communities was headed by a lay brother with absolute powers over the religious conduct of the members. Despite his lack of sacerdotal powers, he fully exercised the authority of an ordinary abbot. He conferred the monastic habit on the novices in the community; confessions had to be individually reported to him and he fixed all penances given by the priests. Däbrä Bīzän also had additional rules of its own for its dependent convents. The head of this community appointed a Mother Superior for each convent and invested her with full powers, almost similar to his own. She had powers of conferring the monastic habit on the novices in her convent and confessions were made through her. She was in regular communication with the head of Däbrä Bīzän through a lay brother, who reported all the confessions back to his master, and penances were fixed by the latter as in the case of the dependent monasteries.

This structure of the organization of the followers of Éwosṭatéwos had already taken shape towards the end of the fourteenth century. Despite the official excommunication pronounced against them, they had already obtained a firm footing in the outlying districts, where the direct influence of the Church was minimal. Just like any other monastic group, they had gradually acquired much prestige among the local people. They probably got an increasing number of recruits from among the Christians in the area, especially from the poor and orphaned.[1] They may also have gained some converts from among their pagan neighbours.[2] It seems quite clear, however, that in the last decade of the fourteenth century their influence in what is today the heart of the Eritrean plateau had already been securely established along a widening crescent between Däbrä Maryam of Qohayīn, Däbrä Märqoréwos of Dämbälas, Imba Därho,[3] and Bīzän.

Yohannis, whose *Gädls* have been published by Conti Rossini. Zär'a-Ya'iqob simply refers to the head of Däbrä Bīzän as a lay brother, ibid., p. 84.

[1] *Gädlä Fīlipos*, pp. 91–3.

[2] Such conversions are claimed among the pagan Barya pastoralists, ibid., pp. 107–8, 162, note on f. 43ʳ.

[3] One of the earliest sites, remembered as having been the place where Fīlipos was welcomed by the local Christians on his way to Bīzän, is Gäramī in Hamasén, which Conti Rossini identifies as being a little north of Imba Därho, ibid., pp. 91, 158. Another community established by a contemporary of Fīlipos,

The anti-Sabbath party within the Ethiopian Church was greatly alarmed by this rapid success. As the champion of the official Alexandrian doctrine on the Sabbath, this party had the full support of the kings, and the great majority of the monasteries belonged to it. Moreover the Egyptian bishop himself personally led the onslaught against the followers of Éwosṭatéwos. Indeed, it was not a mere accident that the greatest advance of the fortunes of the 'house' of Éwosṭatéwos coincided with the vacancy of the episcopal seat for a period of ten years.

Abunä Sälama (1348–88)[1] was not succeeded until 1398/9, when Bärtälomévos came as the new metropolitan of Ethiopia.[2] The defiance of the followers of Éwosṭatéwos was clearly the most important issue in the Ethiopian Church at the time, and the first public act attributed to the new bishop is his energetic attempt to bring an end to the problem. The anti-Sabbath faction had no doubt awaited his arrival with much eagerness, and they provided him with up-to-date reports on the growing influence of the followers of Éwosṭatéwos in northern Ethiopia. The dangerous implications of this for the unity of his diocese were clearly understood by Bishop Bärtälomévos, and he asked for the help of King Dawīt (1380–1412) in bringing the recalcitrant 'house' of Éwosṭatéwos back to strict Alexandrian discipline. In 1400,[3] not long after the arrival of the bishop, Dawīt sent messengers to fetch the leading figures of the Éwosṭatéwos party:

> There came to us men with handsome looks, and they are finely dressed. We have never seen their like since we ascended this Mountain . . . They said to us: 'We have a message from the king and the bishop.' They look strange and their language is incomprehensible.[4]

These were the king's messengers to Däbrä Bīzän, and some of them were probably Amhara courtiers whose language the Hamasén monks

Abba Matyas, was at Shimagillé, also identified by Conti Rossini as being a small village a little north of Asmara, ibid., pp. 120, 163.

[1] For the brilliant career of this Egyptian bishop to Ethiopia see Lantschoot, A. Van, 'Abba Salama métropolite d'Éthiopie (1348–88) et son rôle de traducteur', in *Atti del Convegno di studi etiopici* (Rome, 1960), pp. 397–401. Cf. also Taddesse Tamrat, 'The Abbots of Däbrä Hayq, 1248–1535', pp. 102–3.

[2] He seems to have ruled as bishop of Ethiopia until after 1431. For these dates see ibid., notes 88, 92, and 101.

[3] The year given is 52 Year of Grace = A.D. 1399/1400, but Fīlipos is said to have gone to Amhara in April, so that 1400 is preferable, *Gädlä Fīlipos*, p. 117. Kolmodin, op. cit., A23.

[4] *Gädlä Fīlipos*, p. 111.

could not easily understand. Their orders were to summon Abba Fīlipos for a theological discussion on the Sabbath. Similar envoys were apparently sent to all the Éwosṭathian communities as well, and a number of other 'Disciples of Abunä Ma'iqaba-Igzī accompanied Fīlipos to the metropolitan's court in Amhara'.[1]

King Dawīt was evidently anxious to avoid a direct personal involvement in the matter, and fully authorized the metropolitan to deal with Fīlipos and his fellow Éwosṭathians: 'Punish him [i.e. Fīlipos] as you see fit, until he accepts [your instructions].'[2] The bishop as well as his principal courtiers were the declared opponents of the 'house' of Éwosṭatéwos, and the outcome of the religious discussion was a foregone conclusion. Nevertheless, Fīlipos and his colleagues courageously defended the Sabbath at the Assembly in much the same way as Éwosṭatéwos had done at the court of Patriarch Benjamin over half a century earlier.[3] They persistently refused to accept the bishop's ruling that they should cease the observance of the Sabbath, and they were all put in fetters at his orders. They were told that they would be freed only when they changed their views. The anti-Éwosṭathian party among the clergy in Amhara was led by the powerful *Aqabé-Sä'at* Säräqä-Birhan of the island monastery of Hayq.[4] He was a great friend of King Dawīt and he used all his influence at the Court to support Bishop Bärtälomewos against Fīlipos and his followers. When the Éwosṭathians finally refused to accept the orders of the bishop, Säräqä-Birhan detained their

[1] Kolmodin, loc. cit. Their number is here given as having been 12, besides Fīlipos. His own hagiographer raises the number to 120, *Gädlä Fīlipos*, p. 112. The names in Kolmodin's list are exactly similar to those of 'the twelve teachers of Ethiopia' who are elsewhere said to have called at Bīzän in search of Fīlipos's instructions and spiritual guidance, ibid., p. 107. It is clearly a case of internal rivalry among the Éwosṭathians for primacy. It is apparent that the early companions of Éwosṭatéwos had died by this time, and only the second generation of Éwosṭathian leaders are represented in this tradition. Conti Rossini has, however, estimated that Absadī died in *c.* A.D. 1405, and Märqoréwos in *c.* 1419, ibid., p. 157, note on f. 17. Both dates seem to be too late. This is certainly so in the case of Märqoréwos who, according to his very late (17th-century) hagiographer(s), was already 33 years old in 1318, and died in the seventh year of the reign of Yishaq, in 1419, *Gädlä Märqoréwos*, pp. 20–1, 27, 34–5, 37, 39, 47 (text). Absadī was also represented at the Council of 1399/1400 by Täwäldä-Mädhin of Däbrä Maryam, most probably a reference to the same monk remembered elsewhere as his disciple, Conti Rossini, 'Un santo eritreo: Buruk Amlak', pp. 37–8.

[2] See *Gädlä Fīlipos*, pp. 112–14.

[3] The whole story of this Assembly is related in *Gädlä Fīlipos*, pp. 111–20.

[4] On the career of Säräqä-Birhan see Taddesse Tamrat, 'The Abbots of Däbrä Hayq', p. 103.

leader, Fīlipos of Bīzän, and kept him under close guard on the island of Hayq.[1]

Fīlipos was detained in Amhara for a period of four years. His hagiographer complains of some defection among the followers of Éwosṭatéwos in the period, and Matyas of Shimagillé and Zäkaryas of Bärbäré are specially mentioned in this connection.[2] It is apparent that, from the start, there had been no complete unanimity among the Éwosṭathian leaders. And, faced with the hardships of detention in Amhara, some of them probably took the earliest opportunity to have their excommunication lifted, and to live on peaceful terms with the metropolitan. This apparently created a lasting feud particularly among the descendants of Fīlipos of Däbrä Bīzän and Matyas of Shimagillé.[3] But on the whole, the number of defections was very insignificant, and the great majority of his colleagues followed Fīlipos in holding fast to the teachings of Éwosṭatéwos. In fact, Fīlipos's sojourn in Amhara opened a new period for the 'house' of Éwosṭatéwos, and it seems to have won many more allies among the powerful attendants and influential clergy of the royal Court. The Egyptian bishop, on the other hand, lost his most loyal supporter among the Ethiopian hierarchy at the death of *Aqabé-Sä'at* Säräqä-Birhan of Däbrä Hayq in about 1403. Immediately afterwards, orders came to the island monastery of Däbrä Hayq for the release of Fīlipos.[4] The orders presumably came from the royal Court, and it is unlikely that they had the approval of the bishop. It is apparent that Fīlipos's old age[5] and his unswerving leadership had won much respect and admiration in Amhara, and the pro-Éwosṭatéwos lobby at the royal Court had been growing fast. In 1403, the Christian army had been victorious in Adal, killed the Muslim king Sä'adädīn and sacked the distant port of Zeila.[6] The public rejoicings that followed

[1] *Gädlä Fīlipos* (Bīzän), ed. and tr. Conti Rossini, p. 118.

[2] Ibid., pp. 112, 117. Éwosṭatéwos is said to have had a disciple called Matéwos of Däbrä Bärbäré, and Zäkaryas was probably his pupil. The master himself is said to have stayed at Bärbäré for seven years.

[3] On his way back from Amhara Fīlipos met Matyas at Sähart. It was an unhappy encounter, and Fīlipos is said to have solemnly pronounced a curse on Matyas, whose descendants continued to be under its spell ever after, ibid., p. 120.

[4] Fīlipos was released in 56 Year of Grace = 1403/4, Kolmodin, op. cit., A23. This happened shortly after Säräqä-Birhan's death, *Gädlä Fīlipos*, pp. 118–19.

[5] He died in 1406, at 83. Kolmodin, op. cit., A24, A31 n. 2. This takes his birth to about 1323 which tallies with the tradition that he was born in the reign of 'our king Amdä-Ṣiyon, son of Widim-Rä'ad', and before Éwosṭatéwos's self-exile, *Gädlä Fīlipos*, pp. 69, 73.

[6] See p. 153.

no doubt assumed a highly nationalistic and anti-Muslim character, and very little attention was probably given to the wishes of the Egyptian bishop. The presence at Court of military leaders from Sära'é and Hamasén may have also increased the pressure for the release of Fīlipos.[1] His hagiographer reports that, at the time of his release, both King Dawīt and one of the queens, Igzī-Kibra, sent messages of good will to Fīlipos, entrusting themselves to his prayers.[2] Zära'-Ya'iqob substantially confirms this sudden change of heart in favour of the 'house' of Éwosṭatéwos:

> My father Dawit king of Ethiopia . . . sent messengers so that they might bring back the disciples of Ma'iqäbä-Igzī from the areas where they had dispersed, and so that they enable them to re-enter their churches. The king's messengers did this, and the disciples of Ma'iqäbä-Igzī returned to their [former] places. The king further commanded the disciples of Ma'iqäbä-Igzī to observe both Sabbaths as the Apostles had prescribed in the Sinodos.[3]

It is only natural that Zär'a-Ya'iqob should attribute his father's action to a mere feeling of sympathy towards the followers of Éwosṭatéwos—dispersed everywhere in exile, dying of hunger and thirst, and unjustly persecuted solely for the cause of observing the Sabbath. It is, however, quite clear that Dawīt's change of policy towards the 'house' of Éwosṭatéwos was only a result of their strengthening political and religious influence in the kingdom. The political moves of Dawīt at the time were in fact highly characteristic of the relations between the monarch in Ethiopia and the Egyptian bishops on all similar occasions. At the beginning of the controversy, the king did everything to facilitate the public trial and discipline of Fīlipos and his colleagues at the court of the metropolitan. At the same time, however, he systematically avoided a direct involvement in the proceedings, which he left entirely in the hands of the Egyptian prelate. When the Éwosṭathians continued to be unrepentant and local pressures for their freedom became considerable, the king made political capital out of the situation and personally intervened with an act of clemency towards Fīlipos and his followers. He permitted them to observe the Sabbath as they insisted, and decreed that they should not be persecuted for this any longer. They were now free to reoccupy their previous churches and monasteries, and to establish other communities wherever they could. But he maintained, at

[1] *Gädlä Fīlipos*, p. 65. [2] Ibid. p. 118.
[3] *Mäṣḥafä Birhan*, ii, p. 82.

the same time, that both at the royal Court and in all the non-Éwosṭathian churches the official Alexandrian position on the Sabbath should be observed, and that the leadership of the Egyptian bishop should be strictly followed. In doing this, King Dawīt was clearly anxious to please both parties; but his timid approach to the problem did not bring about a permanent solution. Neither the diehards among the Éwosṭathians, nor the anti-Sabbath party, were fully satisfied by his half-measure. The most drastic effect of his intervention was only to undermine the prestige of Bishop Bärtälomewos, and to weaken the position of his ardent supporters who were completely loyal to Alexandria.

The 'house' of Éwosṭatéwos emerged from the struggle with tremendous success. Its status was suddenly transformed from one of an actively persecuted minority sect into that of a respectable school. It was not only tolerated, but also fully protected by a special royal decree. Towards the end of the reign of King Dawīt, the Éwosṭathians seem to have acquired complete freedom of movement throughout the kingdom. This provided them with much scope for expansion, and their traditions attribute much of their internal development to this period. Even the distant community of Däbrä San among the Fälasha, which had been virtually isolated from northern Ethiopia during the conflict, seems to have felt the impact of Dawīt's decree in 1404. Gäbrä-Īyäsus, its founder, is said to have sent out some of his followers to establish themselves further south.[1] A similar expansion of Éwosṭathian communities is also apparent in northern Ethiopia. On his way back from his detention in Amhara, Fīlipos is said to have been welcomed and to have been invited to

[1] From among his disciples, three are remembered in this tradition: Matéwos succeeded him as abbot of Däbrä San; Fīqiṭor went out to Gädamä Baras to live in solitude; and Indryas was ordered by his dying master to move out to a new area and start his own community, Conti Rossini, 'Note di agiografia etiopica: Gabra Iyesus', p. 450. The MS. used by Conti Rossini probably did not mention the name of the area where Indryas was recommended to go and his translation only has 'Vai verso un paese nuovo'. In more recent MSS. the place is given as the land of Niway (= Ziway?), Or. 705, B.M., f. 154; and Ziway, 'Sinksar', MS. Däbrä Wärq, Hamlé 20. This specific identification with Ziway appears to be suspect, and seems to derive from the attempts in Däbrä Wärq traditions to associate the famous Abba Sīnoda of Däbrä Simmona (E. Gojjam) with Indryas, disciple of Gäbrä-Īyäsus. In his own *Gädl*, Sīnoda is said to have been a disciple of Indryas of Ziway, but there is no mention of any connections with Däbrä San at all, 'Gädlä Sīnoda', MS. Dīma, f. 3a. Däbrä Wärq itself derives its origin from a fourth-generation descendant of Gäbrä-Īyäsus of Däbrä San, 'Gädlä Särṣä-Péṭros', MS. Däbrä Wärq, ff. 24^{b}–25^{a}, 30^{b}–31^{a}.

establish new churches. As a result, a chain of small communities seems to have started in the Eritrean region, along the main road from Amhara to Bīzän.[1] It has been said above that even before the advent of Abunä Bärtälomewos, the Éwostathians had been firmly established along the western edge of the Eritrean plateau. Soon after 1404, a number of communities were newly established on the eastern side as well, and the whole Eritrean region became, once and for all, an exclusive domain of the 'house' of Éwosṭatéwos.

The final success of the Éwosṭathians in their conflict with the Egyptian bishop had far-reaching consequences in the whole of the Ethiopian Church. For themselves, their most important achievement lay in their acquisition of complete freedom to observe the Sabbath. But there was no way to ensure that the royal decree protecting the custom only applied to them. Thus, although Dawīt clearly intended the decree to cover only the 'house' of Éwosṭatéwos, his official toleration of the Sabbath was highly subversive of the basic Alexandrian objection to the 'customs of the Old Testament', which the Egyptian bishops claimed were preserved in the Ethiopian Church. As an essential part of the Christian tradition, the Old Testament had always had a great influence on the thinking and religious practice of the Ethiopians. In the absence of much literary development among them in the early Christian centuries, only the Bible provided the Ethiopians with the necessary guide-lines, and from it they drew not only their religion, but also much of their cultural and political inspiration. As regards the Sabbath in particular, both the Apostolic canons,[2] and the monastic rules of St. Pacomius[3] concurred in giving it a special place beside the Lord's Day.[4] This had apparently led to the observance of the Sabbath being an important monastic practice

[1] Mäṭara and Égala are specially mentioned as the sites where new communities were established. Both places are in what is today the district of Akälä-Guzay, *Gädlä Filipos*, p. 120.

[2] *Les Canons des Apôtres*, ed. and tr., J. and A. Perier in *PO* viii (1912), p. 99: Exemption of slaves from work on Saturdays and Sundays: 'it is actually on Saturday that God rested after having achieved [the creation of] the universe; as for Sunday, it is the day of the resurrection of the Lord'; p. 134: Fasting forbidden on Saturdays and Sundays, except on the Saturday of Passion Week; cf. also *The Ethiopic Didascalia*, tr. Harden, J. M. (1920), p. 127. Muyser, J., 'Le Samedi et le Dimanche dans l'Église et la littérature Copte', pp. 89–91.

[3] Ibid., pp. 92, 95–111. For the early introduction of these rules into Ethiopic literature see Cerulli, E., *Storia della letterature etiopica*, pp. 25–6.

[4] For a detailed review of this problem in the Early Church, see articles on the Sabbath in *A Dictionary of Christian Antiquities* (London 1908). *The Jewish Encyclopaedia* (New York, 1935).

in Ethiopia.[1] The Egyptian bishops always campaigned against it, and already at the beginning of the fourteenth century they had succeeded in obtaining the support of the kings, and the obedience of most of their congregations. It is quite clear that, when he started his career, Éwosṭatéwos was only leading a minority group in active protest against what he considered to be the Alexandrian 'innovation'. By then, the great majority of the Ethiopian monasteries—particularly the royal churches and the newly established communities in Amhara and Shäwa—had been brought into line with the Alexandrian ban on the Sabbath. It is apparent, however, that much of this religious conformity was only due to fears of excommunication and to the kings' full support of the Egyptian bishop. But when, in 1404, King Dawīt finally decided to give protection to the Éwosṭathians he dealt a serious blow to the power of the Egyptian bishop in Ethiopia.

Abunä Bärtäloméwos and his successors never recovered from this momentous setback in their position as heads of the Ethiopian Church. Dawīt's decree in favour of the 'house' of Éwosṭatéwos was, in effect, also an official encouragement of other dissenters. It is further apparent that the controversy over the Sabbath was only symptomatic of the divergencies in religious practice that had developed between the Alexandrian and the Ethiopian Churches over the centuries. The literary development which the Ethiopian Church had been undergoing since the thirteenth century[2] had provided the Ethiopians with fresh means of self-expression through which they were beginning to assert themselves. The organized protest and final success of the Éwosṭathians sparked off a restless period of religious controversies, which lasted throughout the reigns of Dawīt and his sons. Nevertheless, only Zär'a-Ya'iqob (1434–68) understood the conflict in its true nature as a national movement, and he readily adopted it in the fabric of the religious nationalism of medieval Ethiopia of which he was the principal author.

[1] The date of the Ethiopian adoption of this and other 'customs of the Old Testament' is still an object of discussion. For a balanced view of the controversy see Ullendorff, E., 'Hebraic-Judaic elements in Abyssinian (Monophysite) Christianity', in *JSS*, i (1956), pp. 216–56. Rodinson, M., 'Sur la question des "influences juives" en Ethiopie', in *JSS*, ix (1964), pp. 11–19. Ullendorff has reaffirmed many of his earlier views on this topic in his recent book, *Ethiopia and the Bible*, the Schweich lectures, 1967, (London, 1968). See also my short review of this book in *Addis Reporter*, i, number 12.

[2] Guidi, I., (*Breve*) *storia della letteratura etiopica* (Rome, 1932), pp. 8–10. Conti Rossini, 'Il "Senodos" etiopico' in *RRAL*, ser. vii, vol. iii (1942), pp. 41–4. Cerulli, E., *Storia della letteratura Etiopica* (Rome, 1956), pp. 67–70.

Zä'ra-Ya'iqob, and the Council of Däbrä Miṭmaq

By a strange coincidence, Zär'a-Ya'iqob was born in 1399, within a few months of the first council called by Abunä Bärtäloméwos to discuss the Sabbath.[1] He was the youngest son of Dawīt and Queen Igzī-Kibra.[2] An interesting tradition about his youth[3] seems to offer a useful background to his extraordinary career of intensive literary and religious activities. However, despite the fresh light it throws on the struggle for succession among Dawīt's sons, the tradition tends to be hagiographical in character. While Zär'a-Ya'iqob was still a little boy, we are told, many saintly monks foretold his future greatness. This aroused against him the jealousy and hatred of his brothers, particularly Téwodros.[4] Greatly alarmed by this and concerned for her son's safety, Igzī-Kibra entrusted him to one of her relatives, a monk of apparently Tigré origin. The monk took the boy away from court incognito, settled in Aksum and began to give

[1] Zär'a-Ya'iqob himself says that he was 50 years old in the 15th year of his reign, 'Mäṣhafä-Ṭéfut', MS. Inst. Archaeol., Addis Ababa. It is also said elsewhere that he 'acceded to the throne when he was 35 years old; others say he was 40', 'Tarīkä-Nägäst', MS. Däbrä Ṣigé, p. 54. Other traditions record his birth in 60 Year of Grace (= A.D. 1407/8). *Liber Aksumae*, p. 67 (text). Kolmodin, op. cit., A24. This is probably affected by the alleged prophecy of Fīlipos (Bīzän) about him, *Gädlä Fīlipos*, p. 118.

[2] It is not known exactly how many queens Dawīt had, but his children were born of different women, 'Yägalla Tarīk', MS. Däbrä Ṣigé, f. 28. The names of three of his queens are available: Dingil-Ṣäwäna, *Gädlä Märqoréwos*, p. 39; Ṣiyon-Mogäsa, mother of Téwodros, *Sinksar*, ed. and tr. Guidi, in *PO*, i (1904), pp. 695–6. Yishaq may have also been her son. Hizbä-Nagn was probably of Lasta origin on his mother's side, 'The Four Gospels', MS. Lalībäla Bétä-Gäbriél, f. 9[a]. Igzi-Kibra was probably Dawīt's youngest queen, and lived as late as 1455, Wright, *Catalogue*, Or. 481, ff. 154[a], 208[a].

[3] 'Tarīkä-Nägäst', MS. Däbrä Ṣigé, pp. 54–5.

[4] Téwodros was Dawīt's first son, 'Mälki'a-Dawīt Nigus', appendix to 'Gädlä Särsä-Pétros', MS. Däbrä Wärq. He succeeded Dawīt in October 1412, but died only nine months later, 'Gädlä Gīyorgīs of Gascha', MS. Hayq, f. 27. He died east of the river Awash, probably during an expedition in Adal, Sapeto, G., *Viaggio e missione cattolica fra i Mensa* (Rome, 1857), pp. 437–8. He is remembered in the Church as a saintly man, *Sinksar*, ed. and tr. Guidi, in *PO*, i (1904), pp. 695–6. Bermudez relates the tradition that Téwodros gave a district called Nazrét in Tigré as fief to the Egyptian bishop, La Croze Veyssière, *Histoire du Christianisme d'Éthiopie et d'Arménie* (1739), pp. 125–6. *The Portuguese Expedition to Abyssinia in 1541*, as narrated by Castanhoso and Bermudez, tr. Whiteway, R. S., Hakluyt Society (1902), p. 160. Probably based on the same tradition, Bruce painted an altogether different picture of the reign, *Travels to Discover the Source of the Nile*, ii (1790), pp. 64–5. Attempts have been made to identify this king with his namesake in an apocryphal work of an unknown date. There are however no convincing reasons for this, Basset, R., *Les Apocryphes éthiopiens*: XI, *Fikare-Iyesus* (1909), pp. 9–12, 25–6.

him a religious training. Soon afterwards the monk died, and Zär'a-Ya'iqob left Aksum on his own, and joined the monastery of Däbrä Abbay in Shiré, still incognito. He remained there until all his brothers had reigned in succession and died. Troops were then sent in search of the hidden prince, who was only discovered with much difficulty. He was then brought back to Court and crowned by force.[1]

This is invaluable as providing a religious background for Zär'a-Ya'iqob's career, but the story is very improbable in its details. The considerable learning which Zär'a-Ya'iqob later displayed, and the depth of his personal involvement in the reorganization of the Church during his reign, are indeed highly indicative that he had very close contacts with the Church before his accession to the throne. He may have even spent much of his early life in monastic surroundings. It is unlikely, however, that he went into hiding. In fact it is apparent that he was very much in the running for the crown particularly after the death of King Yishaq (1413–30). His struggle for the succession with Hizbä-Nagn (1430–33) and his two sons is well remembered in some traditions and will be discussed elsewhere in greater detail.[2] It suffices here to point out that Zär'a-Ya'iqob himself relates that he was brought down from the royal prison of Mount Gishän only on the eve of his accession to the throne.[3]

In many ways the advent to power of Zär'a-Ya'iqob in 1434 was a godsend to the Ethiopian Church. It was almost exactly a century earlier, in about 1337, that Éwosṭatéwos had left his country in self-exile. Since then, his small following in Ethiopia had rapidly grown in strength and had taken full control of the northern part of the kingdom. The issues raised by him and his followers had revealed, much more clearly than ever before, that the Alexandrian and Ethiopian Churches were at variance on many points of religious practice. In an attempt to remove these differences, the Egyptian bishops had insisted on strict disciplinary measures, and their stern action had almost broken the Ethiopian Church into two contending parties. Apart from these internal conflicts, the by-products of its rapid expansion in the Ethiopian region since the thirteenth century had also presented the Church with even more serious problems. As the area under the political control of the kingdom steadily increased, so did the number of churches and monastic communities among the

[1] Cf. also, 'Gädlä Zéna-Marqos', MS. Däbrä Ṣigé, ff. 109^{b}–110^{a}.
[2] See pp. 278–83.
[3] *Mäṣhafä Birhan*, ii (text), p. 157.

newly conquered peoples. An increasing number of people with varied cultural and religious backgrounds began to adopt the Christian religion, and by the middle of the fifteenth century the additional responsibilities of the Church were clearly beyond its educational and organizational facilities. A drastic reorganization of the institutions of the church, and a complete rethinking of its role in the kingdom, had to be made. Zär'a-Ya'iqob came to power at this crucial period, and set himself the vital task of reforming the Ethiopian Church.

His attention was first drawn to the problem of settling the internal conflicts among the Ethiopian clergy and to the creation of a perfect union within the Church. The hottest issue that had divided the clergy for as long as he could remember was that of the Sabbath. Complete freedom to observe it had been granted by his father to the 'house' of Éwosṭatéwos in 1404. Since then the custom had apparently spread among other communities, despite the protests of the Egyptian bishop. It was gaining ground even at the royal Court. This seems to be quite clear from the story of the life of Abba Gīyorgīs of Gascha.[1]

Gīyorgīs was born at Sägla, probably some time before the beginning of the reign of Dawīt.[2] His father, Hizbä-Ṣiyon, was one of the chaplains at the royal Court where young Gīyorgīs apparently spent most of his early days.[3] Hizbä-Ṣiyon sent his son to school in the

[1] 'Gädlä Abba Gīyorgīs of Gascha' MS. Hayq. This is a 19th-century copy of which the original is said to be at Gascha, where a community has been established at the site of his tomb. For the location and short description of the site see Wright, S., 'Notes on some cave churches in the province of Wallo', in AÉ, ii (1957), pp. 12–13. Stephen Wright adopts a 14th-century date for the saint, erroneously said to have been Amdä-Ṣiyon's contemporary in an 18th-century compilation of the royal chronicles, Basset, R., *Études sur l'histoire d'Éthiopie* (1882), pp. 5–6, 10, 99. Gīyorgīs died in the 12th year of the reign of Yishaq, which was also the first year of the 14th Grand Cycle, equivalent to A.D. 1425, 'Gädlä Abba Gīyorgīs' ff. 46^{b}–47^{a}. Cf. also Zotenberg, *Catalogue des manuscrits éthiopiens*, N. 113. It is apparent that the *Gädl* was composed soon after Gīyorgīs's death, not later than the reign of Zär'a-Ya'iqob, the last king mentioned, 'Gädlä Abba Gīyorgīs', ff. 31^{b}, 37^{b}–38^{a}.

[2] According to a late and dubious tradition it is said that 'Abba Gīyorgīs was born in the reign of King Dawīt, . . . son of Säyfä-Ar'ad', 'Mar Yishaq', MS. Dīma, f. 171^{b}. His mother is said to have been from Wäläqa in Amhara where Sägla was located, 'Gädlä Abba Gīyorgīs', f. 4^{a}. The place-name is also given as 'Shägla' which is said to be the same site as Gascha, ibid., f. 15^{a}. Thus the names of Gīyorgīs of Sägla and Gīyorgīs of Gascha are a reference to the same person, cf. Conti Rossini, 'Due capitoli del libro del mistero di Giyorgis da Sagla', in *RSE*, vii (1948), pp. 13–16.

[3] 'Gädlä Abba Gīyorgīs', f. 4^{b}.

island monastery of Hayq where the priests were reputed to be 'very wise, and proficient in (the art of) reading and exposition of books'.[1] The abbot of the monastery was then Säräqä-Birhan, the great anti-Sabbath leader until his death in *c.* 1403.[2] Gīyorgīs apparently stayed at Däbrä Hayq for a long period, and when his father retired into a monastery he replaced him as a secular priest of the royal Court.[3] He was a very talented scholar, and a prolific writer. A number of doctrinal and service books are attributed to him.[4] Both Dawīt and Yishaq admired and respected him. He once held the important post of *Niburä-Id* (= Abbot) of Däbrä Damo in Dawīt's reign,[5] and Yishaq later appointed him head of the community of Abba Bäṣälotä-Mīka'él in Amhara.[6]

Abba Gīyorgīs was thus a prominent ecclesiastical courtier of

[1] Ibid., ff. 4^{b}–5^{a}.

[2] See pp. 214–15.

[3] 'Gädlä Abba Gīyorgīs', f. 15. Zär'a-Ya'iqob makes a reference to 'Gīyorgīs . . . (one of the) priests of the Court', *Mäṣhafä Birhan*, ii (text), p. 131. It was Dillmann who first identified this priest with Gīyorgīs of Sägla, *Über die Regierung, insbesondere die Kirchenordnung* (Berlin, 1884), p. 8 and n. 1. Cf. also Cerulli, *Il libro etiopico dei miracoli di Maria* (1943), pp. 114–15.

[4] Among these are *Arganonä-Widasé* written in the reign of Dawīt; *Widasé-Mäsqäl*, and *Mäṣhafä-Sibhat* (also called *Mäṣhafä-Birhan*), 'Gädlä Abba Gīyorgīs', ff. 18^{b}–19^{a}. Other prayers in the names of the Apostles are also attributed to him, ibid., f. 26^{b}. Cf. also Wright, W., *Catalogue of Ethiopian Manuscripts at the British Museum*, no. 337, section 2. He is even said to have been authorized by the Egyptian bishop to compose anaphoras which the local clergy apparently refused to accept, ibid., f. 21^{b}. His monumental work, however, is his great doctrinal compilation *Mäṣhafä-Misṭīr*, completed in the 10th year of the reign of Yishaq, ibid., f. 33^{a}. 'Mar Yishaq', MS. Dīma, f. 172^{b}. Zotenberg, op. cit., no. 113. Conti Rossini, 'Due capitoli del libro del mistero di Giyorgis da Sagla', pp. 13–16. Another book he is reputed to have composed is *Mäṣhafä-Sä'atat* (= The Book of Hours), *Gädlä Iyäsus-Mo'a*, p. 35 (text). Basset, *Études*, pp. 10, 99. This is different from the *Horologium* apparently translated from the Coptic and Arabic into Ge'ez at a very early date, Cerulli, E., *Storia della letteratura etiopica* (1956), pp. 32–3. The identity of Gīyorgīs's *Mäṣhafä-Sä'atat* is not very clear. I was able to examine an early (15th century) MS. believed to be the *Mäṣhafä-Sä'atat*, and specially brought from Gascha for Līqä-Līqawnt Haylä-Mäsqäl, head of the (Menelik) Memorial Church in Addis Ababa. It is a mere collection of Sunday prayers and doctrinal treatises attributed to Gīyorgīs, but of which the connection with the Book of Hours currently in use is not, I think, apparent. I quote it below as *Mäṣhafä-Ṣälot*.

[5] 'Gädlä Abba Gīyorgīs', ff. 19^{b}–20.

[6] Ibid., ff. 38^{b}–39^{a}. It is here, at Gascha, that his community is still located. It was also here that he received his monastic habit from Abba Téwodros, a spiritual descendant of Bäṣälotä-Mīka'él (d. before 1337). ibid., f. 28^{a}. A monastic genealogy given elsewhere makes him a 7th generation descendant of Īyäsus-Mo'a: Sälama, Anoréwos, Bäṣälotä-Mīka'él, Abél, Éfrém, Téwodros, Gīyorgīs, 'Mäshafä-Ṣälot', MS. Gascha, f. 59^{b}.

Kings Dawīt and Yishaq, and had obtained his education at Däbrä Hayq, the citadel of the pro-Egyptian and anti-Sabbath party until 1404. Within the following two decades, however, he became the most vociferous protagonist of the Sabbath. There can be no better example of the decisive change of public opinion on the subject among the clergy at the time than Gīyorgīs's championship of the Sabbath despite his Hayq background. The observance of the Sabbath had long been deeply entrenched in the religious practice of the Ethiopians, and, when Dawīt's protection of the 'house' of Éwosṭatéwos removed their last fears of Alexandrian discipline, an increasing number of communities readopted the custom without any further inhibitions. Gīyorgis taught the legitimacy of observing the Sabbath together with the Lord's Day, and devoted an important section of his *Mäṣhafä-Mistīr* to it.[1] He rigorously practised what he was preaching, and apparently came into conflict with the community of Däbrä Lībanos of Shäwa on this issue. His hagiographer tells us that Gīyorgīs had made a vow to receive his monastic habit from Yohannis Käma, abbot of the community of Täklä-Haymanot. On one occasion, Gīyorgīs visited Däbrä Lībanos to fulfil his vow. As soon as he reached there, however, he quarrelled violently with the community and returned without receiving his monastic habit because: 'They used to break the First Sabbath, and he found them building a church on it.'[2] The royal Court was effectively infiltrated by the pro-Sabbath faction even before Zär'a-Ya'iqob's accession, and Abba Gīyorgīs was its most influential agent in the reigns of Dawīt and Yishaq. As a promising young scholar, one of his first assignments at Court was to give religious instruction to the royal princes:

> They took [Gïyorgïs] and brought him to the inner enclosure of the royal Court, and made him one of the priests of the Court in place of his father who became a monk. And . . . for some time (after this) he taught the children of the king, Zär'a-Abrham and the others.[3]

One of his doctrinal treatises, *Fikaré-Haymanot*, was specially composed for a certain prince called Téwodros, probably Dawīt's

[1] Zotenberg, op. cit., p. 129, Section z. 'Gädlä Abba Gīyorgīs', ff. 39^{b}–40.

[2] Ibid., f. 27^{b}. This reference to Däbrä Lībanos finds confirmation elsewhere. The abbot at the time was indeed Yohannis Käma, and it was in his time that Yishaq authorized the building of the first big church at the present site of Däbrä Lībanos, 'Gädlä Märha-Kristos' MS. Däbrä Lībanos, pp. 51, 53–4. Cerulli, E., 'Gli abbati di Dabra Libanos', in *Orientalia*, xiii (1944), pp. 141–3.

[3] 'Gädlä Abba Gīyorgīs', f. 15. The king referred to is Dawīt. To my knowledge there is no reference anywhere else to a son of Dawīt's called Zär'a-Abrham.

first son.[1] Probably, too, Zär'a-Ya'iqob's close association with the pro-Sabbath clergy started in the private school at the royal court.

The traditional records of the monasteries have been drastically affected by the need to conform with the later decision of Zär'a-Ya'iqob to enforce the observance of the Sabbath in the Ethiopian Church, and it is very difficult to determine which communities stood firm on the side of the losing party, during the actual controversy. Only few and equivocal indications have survived to show which monastic groups remained persistently loyal to Alexandria, until the Egyptian bishops themselves acquiesced to the entreaties of Zär'a-Ya'iqob. We have already seen above that Däbrä Hayq, particularly when Säräqä-Birhan was the abbot, stood firmly behind Bishop Bärtäloméwos, and it may be that Abba Gīyorgīs did not carry the whole community with him in his defection to the opposite camp. It seems quite clear also that another important community in the pro-Egyptian party was Däbrä Lībanos of Shäwa. Together with the tradition about Anoréwos's disputation with Éwosṭatéwos on this issue,[2] the conflict of Abba Gīyorgīs with Yohannis Käma[3] constitutes an important piece of contemporary evidence for the anti-Sabbath persuasions of Däbrä Lībanos at the time. The relationship between Däbrä Lībanos and Bishop Ya'iqob (*c.* 1337–44) was particularly close, and according to its own traditions the community owed much of its later influence to his reorganization of the monasteries in Shäwa.[4] His immediate successor Abunä Sälama (1348–88) is also remembered with much gratitude for having liberated Fīlipos from the exile inflicted upon him by King Säyfä-Ar'ad (1344–71). Fīlipos later died at the court of the bishop.[5] It is apparent that, largely because of these early associations, Däbrä Lībanos always displayed much readiness to follow the leadership of the Egyptian bishops and, as we shall soon see, it remained a devoted ally of Alexandria, even when relations between the patriarchate and Ethiopia were highly strained. In its opposition to the Sabbath, Däbrä Lībanos probably carried with it all the other communities deriving their monastic origin from Täklä-Haymanot, particularly

[1] Ibid., f. 29^{b}. Gīyorgīs was on very good terms with Téwodros. During one of his doctrinal disputations at Court Abba Gīyorgīs had apparently displeased King Dawīt, who sent him to prison where he remained until the king's death. As soon as he became king, Téwodros released him, ibid., f. 27.

[2] See p. 208 n. 9.

[3] See p. 224 n. 2.

[4] See pp. 175–7.

[5] *Gädlä Fīlipos* (Asbo), pp. 236, 244, 246.

in Shäwa. From some isolated references at our disposal, an interesting pattern seems to emerge about the identity of the conflicting parties in the controversy. Thus, we are told that, on one occasion, Samu'él of Waldibba refused to see Abba Gīyorgīs when the latter deliberately travelled all the way from Damo to Däbrä Abbay to meet the famous ascetic leader. The hagiographer gives an altogether different reason for the refusal of the saint; but it may very well be that Samu'él had some reservations about the religious views of the young scholar from the royal Court, who had just been appointed *Nibura-Id* of Däbrä Damo by King Dawīt. That there was a religious content in the decision of Samu'él is suggested by the hagiographer himself in his description of the reaction of Abba Gīyorgīs. Unaffected by the rebuff he received from the old saint, Gīyorgīs hurried back 'to preach the Faith to the people of Damo'.[1] Another monastic group in Shiré which opposed the Sabbath was probably the community of Samu'él of Qoyäṣa.[2] It was here that Isṭīfanos, the founder of the so-called Stephanite 'heresy', first took his monastic habit. Isṭīfanos was expelled from the community in A.D. 1428/9,[3] and one of the accusations later advanced against him was that 'he observes the Seventh Day and breaks Sundays, and he travels (on them)'.[4] Both Samu'él of Waldibba and Samu'él of Qoyäṣa were students of Mädhanīnä-Igzī of Däbrä Bankol, and they seem to have presented a united front in Shiré against the Sabbath.

It is quite clear that Zär'a-Ya'iqob himself ascended the throne with definite pro-Sabbath convictions. Apart from his own religious convictions, however, his support of the Sabbath party was also a sensible political decision. The only mainstay of the opposite party was the Egyptian bishop, and he could pose no serious obstacles to the will of the king. The monasteries which supported the bishop were politically weak, both as individual units and as an organized group. Unevenly distributed throughout the kingdom, their sole unifying force was their loyalty to the Egyptian bishop, and they displayed no compact regional front. The 'house' of Éwosṭatéwos, on the other

1 The incident is related in 'Gädlä Abba Gīyorgīs', ff. 19b–20. According to the hagiographer, Samu'él refused to see him because of the large number of attendants that Gīyorgīs had taken with him on his visit to Däbrä Abbay.

2 For the location and a short description of the community see Ellero, G., 'I conventi dello Scire', in *BSGI*, iv (1939), p. 838, and his sketch map on p. 837.

3 Taddesse Tamrat, 'Some Notes on the Fifteenth-Century Stephanite "Heresy" in the Ethiopian Church', in *RSE*, xxii (1966), p. 106 n. 2.

4 Ibid., p. 110 with n. 2.

hand, presented an altogether different picture. They had successfully defied the power of the Egyptian bishops for a hundred years and, left to their own resources, they had evolved a superb organization independently of the rest of the Ethiopian Church. The official protection which Dawīt granted them in 1404 had only made them more defiant towards Alexandria. Before this time, it had been the bishops who had taken the initiative to exclude the Éwosṭathians from the Church, and to deny them the sacrament of ordination. This last act had been responsible for the creation of the communities of lay brothers by the followers of Éwosṭatéwos.[1] In his decree of 1404, it is apparent that Dawīt also made it possible for them to receive Holy Orders. By that time, however, their characteristic grouping into communities, completely run and dominated by lay brothers, had become an established tradition among them, and they declined to receive Holy Orders. They simply refused to accept that ordination by the Egyptian bishop was an essential institution for the structure of their monastic organization. Only for the celebration of the mass and for hearing confessions did they require ordained priests, and these they apparently recruited from other communities on their own terms:

> . . . They established rules of their own creation which did not conform with the eighty one books of the law: they abstained from taking Holy Orders; they appointed a lay abbot, who did not have the ordination of a priest, to teach them and to administer them according to their own rules. Anyone from among themselves who received Holy Orders was expelled from their communities, and they would not let him enter into their churches. Any priests or deacons who came to them from other communities were interrogated as follows: 'Why did you come to us?' And if they replied: 'We came to you because we like your rules and community; we shall live or die with you', they gave them penance for having belonged to other communities . . . and they let them enter into their Community and into their churches. And all such ordained priests and deacons and monks were ruled by the lay brother who had been appointed abbot. [This lay brother] . . . fully exercised all sacerdotal powers . . . without being duly ordained a priest . . . thus contravening the law of God . . .[2]

Thus within the three decades between Dawīt's decree in 1404, and Zär'a-Ya'iqob's accession in 1434, the controversy had assumed a much more serious character than at the time of Éwosṭatéwos, and was no longer a mere quarrel over the Sabbath. Excluded from the

[1] For Zär'a-Ya'iqob's description of the organization of these communities, see pp. 211–12.

[2] *Mäṣhafä Birhan*, ii (text), pp. 147–8.

Church for their observance of a 'custom of the Old Testament', the disciples of Éwosṭatéwos had been forced to challenge the most cardinal basis of the organization of the Christian Church, and to dispense with the sacrament of ordination in their organization. It is interesting, however, that nowhere in his description does Zär'a-Ya'iqob accuse the 'house' of Éwosṭatéwos of authorizing their lay brothers to celebrate mass, or to give penance without the intervention of an ordained priest. It is quite clear from this that, although they occupied a subordinate position in the hierarchy of the Éwosṭathian monastic organization, duly ordained priests and deacons always constituted part of the community. Throughout the whole period of the controversy, only this slender channel of communication had remained between the 'house' of Éwosṭatéwos and the rest of their fellow Christians in Ethiopia, and Zär'a-Ya'iqob effectively used it for his complete reunification of the Ethiopian Church.

Bärtälomewos (1399–1436) had been too deeply involved in the conflict, and there was very little chance of a peaceful settlement to the controversy until the end of the bishop's reign. In 1438, he was succeeded by two Egyptian prelates—Bishops Mīka'él and Gäbri'él—whose names have become inseparably connected with that of Zär'a-Ya'iqob in the ecclesiastic traditions of Ethiopia.[1] The king sought their full co-operation in his plans to restore the unity of the Ethiopian Church. He assessed the situation with much clarity and suggested a simple way out of the problem. He believed that the only real opposition to the Sabbath in the country came from the episcopal court. Once this was removed, the traditional affinity of the Ethiopians with the Old Testament would suffice to restore complete unanimity in Ethiopia. This would also remove the only obstacle to the full rehabilitation of the 'house' of Éwosṭatéwos, and would naturally lead to their acceptance of the more important Christian institution of Holy Orders. The alternative to this sensible course of action was the perpetuation of the schism, with all its adverse effects on the strength and unity of the Christian kingdom. Surely, these dark prospects appeared to Zär'a-Ya'iqob too dear a price to pay for the observance of the Sabbath, of which the legitimacy was well attested by the Old Testament and the Apostolic canons.

[1] *Liber Aksumae*, p. 67 (text). Kolmodin, op. cit., A24. Cerulli, E., *Il libro etiopico dei miracoli di Maria*, p. 91. They were also accompanied by a third prelate of a lower rank, Epīsqopos Yohannis, Conti Rossini, 'Pergamene di Dabra Dammo', in *RSO*, xix (1940), p. 52 n. 5.

The two bishops were at first adamant against the king's persuasions. His approach was clearly gentle and tactful, and he gave them ample time to consider the problem. In the meantime, however, he made no secret of his pro-Sabbath feelings, and probably started pacifying the Éwosṭathian communities on his own. He went to the ancient city of Aksum in 1436 for his formal coronation and stayed there for three years.[1] It was probably during his sojourn in Tigré that Bishops Mīka'él and Gäbri'él came to Ethiopia, and they were probably welcomed by the king in the ancient city. It is apparent that, right from the beginning, Zär'a-Ya'iqob's advent to power brought in much relief and expectation among the Éwosṭathians, who received assurances that 'there has come to the throne a king who favours your rules'.[2] The Éwosṭathian communities in northern Ethiopia have a tradition that they made a joint present to Zär'a-Ya'iqob, which probably refers to the time of his coronation and his three-year stay in Aksum. Abba Nob, probably Zär'a-Ya'iqob's *Niburä-Id* of Däbrä Damo,[3] advised them to hand in their present through the abbot of Däbrä Maryam, the most important Éwosṭathian community at that time. This Éwosṭathian leader referred to was called Abba Gäbrä-Kristos, and the king is said to have had 'much good will towards him'.[4]

Zär'a-Ya'iqob had made his peace with the 'house' of Éwosṭatéwos long before his Egyptian bishops could make up their minds. Already in 1442, he sent a book to the Ethiopian community in Jerusalem with the following message: 'I hereby send you this book of *Sīnodos* so that you may get consolation from it on the days of the First Sabbath and on Sundays.'[5] In the meantime discussions were under

[1] 'Tarīkä-Nägäst', MS. Däbrä Ṣigé, p. 55.

[2] *Gädlä Abba Yonas*, ed. and tr. Conti Rossini under the title 'Gli atti di Abba Yonas', in *RRAL*, Sc. Mor., ser. v, vol. xii (1903), p. 199.

[3] On this ecclesiastic see *Les Chroniques de Zar'a-Ya'iqob et de Ba'eda Maryam*, pp. 11–12. Cerulli, E., *Il libro etiopico dei miracoli di Maria*, pp. 107–8, 111–12. *Gädlä Abba Yonas*, p. 180 n. 1.

[4] Ibid., p. 199. The community of Däbrä Hayq in Amhara also seem to have paid the king a similar homage at the time of his accession to power, for which he is later said to have exempted them from some taxes: 'I exempted them because in the first year of my reign they came to see me while I was in the land of Dägo', 'The Four Gospels', MS. (IM), Hayq, ff. 132^{b}–133^{a}. It was at Dägo in Shäwa that he was first crowned, *Les Chroniques de Zar'a-Ya'iqob et de Ba'eda Maryam*, pp. 54, 87.

[5] Ludolf, H., *Commentarius ad Suam Historiam Aethiopicam* (Frankfurt, 1691), p. 303. It is dated in the 8th year of the king's reign, p. 301. Cf. also Tisserant and Grébaut, *Codices Aethiopici, Vaticani et Borgiani, Barberinianus Orientalis 2 Rossianus 865*, Vatican Library (1935), MS. Borg. Etiop. 2, ff. 3–4v.

way at various levels, but it was not until eight years later, in 1450, that Zär'a-Ya'iqob convened a Council at his new church of Däbrä Miṭmaq[1] in Shäwa. The two bishops, the followers of Éwosṭatéwos, and the abbots of the leading monasteries attended the council.[2] The debate had already been exhausted in the previous years, and it appears that the gathering was principally intended for the formal reconciliation of the Éwosṭathians with the Egyptian bishops and their Ethiopian followers. The bishops formally authorized the observance of the Sabbath in the Ethiopian Church, and the Éwosṭathians agreed to receive Holy Orders from the Egyptian prelates:

> And God . . . revealed the honours of the two Sabbaths to our fathers, the reverend bishops Mīka'él and Gäbri'él. He had not made this revelation to the [Egyptian] bishops of Ethiopia who came before them . . . And our fathers Abba Mīka'él and Abba Gäbri'él . . . agreed with us on the observance of the two Sabbaths, and they declared this in their own handwriting . . . And the disciples of Ma'iqäbä-Igzī received the Holy Orders, and many of them were appointed abbots of their monasteries . . .[3]

Unlike his father, Dawīt, who left entirely to the Egyptian bishop the conduct of the anti-Éwosṭatéwos assembly fifty years earlier, Zär'a-Ya'iqob himself presided over the Council of Däbrä Miṭmaq, and played a decisive role in bringing about a definite settlement of the most important controversy that had divided the Ethiopian Church for over a century.[4] This also enabled him to embark on a

[1] This was a church built by Zär'a-Ya'iqob in Tägulat at the news of the demolition of an Egyptian monastery of the same name at the hands of the Muslims, *Les Chroniques de Zar'a Ya'eqob*, pp. 55–7. Cerulli, *Il libro etiopico dei Miracoli*, pp. 124–5, 202–3.

[2] Zär'a-Ya'iqob, *Mäṣhafä Birhan*, ii (tr.) pp. 86–7. *Gädlä Abba Yonas*, pp. 198–200. The place of the Council is not given here. Another tradition of an apparently late composition reports that it was held at Däbrä Birhan, 'Gädlä Zéna-Marqos', MS. Däbrä Ṣigé, f. 107. It is said here that '(all the great) teachers of the country of Ethiopia were assembled, and they entered into the presence of the bishops'. The hagiographer is very anxious to associate the community of Zéna-Marqos with the successful Sabbath party, and paints a very dramatic picture of the proceedings of the Council.

[3] Zär'a-Ya'iqob, loc. cit.

[4] There were also a number of other doctrinal issues discussed at the Council. Zär'a-Ya'iqob mentions the questions of 'the Persons of the Holy Trinity . . . and the Unity of God', ibid., p. 87. These had been hotly discussed, it appears, since the reign of Dawīt (1380–1412). A large part of Abba Gīyorgīs's 'Mäṣhafä-Misṭīr' is concerned with these questions, Zotenberg, op. cit., pp. 127–8. 'Gädlä Abba Gīyorgīs', ff. 2[b]–3. Two notorious Ethiopian priests, Zämīka'él Aṣqä and Gämalyal, as well as Bishop Bärtälomėwos, are accused of denying the Three Persons of the Trinity on different occasions, Zär'a-Ya'iqob, op. cit., pp. 71–6. 'Gädlä Abba Gīyorgīs', f. 38[a]. The Stephanites were also accused of some unortho-

series of religious reforms which characterize the period of his reign.

Religious reforms

Zär'a-Ya'iqob felt, more deeply than any Ethiopian monarch before him, the solitary position of his kingdom in a religious sense: 'Our country Ethiopia [is surrounded by] pagans and Muslims in the east as well as in the west.'[1] This idea haunted his mind throughout his reign, and he attributed the religious imperfections of his own people to the bad influence of their non-Christian environment. It seems that after the Council of Däbrä Miṭmaq his major preoccupation was to reorganize the Ethiopian Church, and to make full use of its resources in an attempt to stamp out alien religious practices among his Christian subjects.

Zär'a-Ya'iqob's energetic activities in the field of religious reform are a serious reflection on how small the impact of the Church had been in the extensive provinces of the kingdom. This was certainly the outcome of the peculiar way in which the Christian teaching had spread in the Ethiopian region. During the great period of Christian expansion, from the last quarter of the thirteenth century onwards, the Church had been carried wherever military colonies were established. It is apparent that, with the exception of Islam, which was given a recognized status in Muslim-dominated areas, the Christian kingdom did not at all respect the religious institutions of its pagan subjects, who were automatically presumed to be a preserve of the Church, as soon as they were conquered militarily. Their land, with all its people and other resources, was divided and distributed as fiefs among the Christian political and military officials, thus constituting a number of administrative units.[2] In each of these units, small secular churches were built for the Christian army of occupation. Particularly in the early years of large-scale conquests and military occupation, the Christian settlers formed a completely separate class of their own. The churches built for them were merely one of the distinguishing features of this dominant class, which alone

dox views on the Trinity, *Das Mashafa Milad*, i, pp. 13–14, 38 (text). But the most important issue for which they were persecuted by Zär'a-Ya'iqob was their refusal to revere St. Mary and the Cross, Taddesse Tamrat, 'Some Notes on the Fifteenth-Century Stephanite "Heresy"', pp. 110–12.

[1] *Mäṣhafä Birhan*, i (text), p. 151.

[2] See pp. 98–103.

they were basically meant to serve. For the most part, the educational standards of the priests and deacons, who staffed these churches in the outlying provinces, enabled them only to officiate at the routine religious ceremonies, and to preserve the liturgical traditions of the church. Apart from this, they were quite incapable of transmitting the spirit of the Christian teaching, even within the Christian settler communities. For them, as well as for their congregations, the Christian Church seems to have had very little content other than the regular and formal services impressively performed on the prescribed days. Under these circumstances, it is apparent that they were unsuited to the task of spreading the Christian teaching among the subjected pagan peoples. We have seen above the attempts of Bishop Ya'iqob (1337–44) to organize the monastic descendants of Īyäsus-Mo'a in Amhara and Shäwa during the reign of Amdä-Ṣiyon.[1] These monasteries no doubt helped to produce many more recruits for the service of the Church, and, wherever the monasteries were established, Christian religious pressure on the conquered peoples was considerably intensified. Nevertheless, although the monastic schools certainly produced a relatively greater number of priests and deacons, their output was much less than could suffice for the needs of the extensive empire. Largely for linguistic reasons, almost all the recruits for the service of the Church, who could obtain religious instruction in Ethiopia, apparently had to be of Tigré or Amhara origin. This eligibility to the divine service also seems to have had some ethnic undertones.[2] These important considerations contributed greatly to limiting the number of candidates for Holy Orders. But, more important still, the training programmes of the monasteries organized by Bishop Ya'iqob do not seem to have brought about any appreciable improvement in the evangelical spirit and educational standards of the churchmen. Only the major monasteries themselves, and the royal churches, seem to have been well provided with clerics of considerable learning. The ordinary member of the clergy hardly made any more progress than reading the regular service books, and

[1] See pp. 175–7.

[2] For the special place given to priestly families even within the Christian communities, see p. 113 n. 4. D'Abbadie also collected an interesting tradition, in this respect, about the reign of Bä'idä-Maryam (1468–78), when 'it was necessary to be a son of Levi to become a priest or a deacon', Conti Rossini, 'Il libro delle leggende', p. 711. The reference to Levi is connected with the legend of the queen of Sheba according to which all the priestly families of Ethiopia are descendants of Zadok, King Solomon's high priest, cf. Budge, *The Queen of Sheba and Her Only Son Menyelek I*, pp. 61–2, 165.

reciting the prescribed prayers; and it was these members of the predominantly secular clergy who represented the Church in the distant pagan provinces.

The pagan peoples looked at the impressive ceremonies of the Church as just another curious religious cult, pertaining to their conquerors. The clergy, as the living agents of this cult, seemed to them not very different functionally from the pagan priesthood who officiated in their own religious practices. In the early stages of Christian conquest and settlement, probably very few among the conquered peoples joined the Church. And whenever such 'conversions' did take place, they probably had little significance other than a simple adoption of an alien cult, without necessarily giving up all the manifestations of their native beliefs and practices. For an ambitious local chief of a pagan community, an association with his Christian conquerors, in their curious religious practices, was a clever political decision, which could only bring him political advancement. On a more personal level, his 'conversion' made few demands on him or on his household. Given little spiritual guidance by the local clergy, who were ultimately and essentially part of the same Kushitic background as himself, the new 'convert' continued in much the same way as before, and lost almost none of his traditional loyalties to his pagan gods and their priesthood. It is apparent that, throughout the early and late medieval period of Ethiopian history, the Christian Church underwent an essentially similar process of expansion; and, although it gradually dispossessed the pagan clergy of much of their political and economic power, the Church seems to have never had a complete claim over the souls and loyalties of the newly 'converted' pagan peoples. It is apparent, too, that the same problems confronted Zär'a-Ya'iqob in the middle of the fifteenth century. According to his own historical diagnoses, '. . . that this should be the case was because there are no priests who preach, and Satan reduces the people into slavery'.[1]

There are numerous references to the pre-Christian religious practices of the Kushitic peoples of the Ethiopian plateau in the hagiographical traditions of the Ethiopian Church.[2] It is, however, impossible to determine in precise terms the religious framework of the life of the people from these references. Enough linguistic evidence is still lacking to make possible the identification of the religious terms preserved in the available traditions. There is an interesting

[1] *Mäṣhafä Birhan*, ii (tr.), p. 29. [2] See pp. 178–9.

reference to a pagan god in a story of the life of a fifteenth century local saint of Mugär (Shäwa): 'And (the saint) said to the witch-doctor . . .: "Whom do you worship; who is your God?" The witch-doctor replied: "Our God is he whom they call *Gor* . . ., he is also called *Diagoror*. . . ." '[1] The name of this object of pagan worship also seems to appear in various forms—*jar*, *dero*, *yaro*—in the Kushitic languages of Bilén, Gonga, and Kafficho respectively.[2] The areas which were gradually taken over by the Christian kingdom were originally the homeland of the Kushites, and there seems to have been a basic uniformity of religious beliefs and practices over the Ethiopian plateau. The general features of Kushitic pagan worship[3] seem to be based on a sky god, with numerous good and bad spirits inhabiting the mountains, trees, rivers, and lakes. Prayers and sacrifices were offered to these spirits, through hereditary priestly families which seem to have shared much of the sanctity of the gods of which they were the intermediaries, and, as such, they seem to have wielded much power over their peoples. They could cause good and evil, in accordance with the wishes of the spirits manifested in various forms of natural phenomena, such as fire, storm, famine, life, and death. The smallest details of the daily life of the people were presumed to be under the control of these spirits, who had to be continuously pacified through the pagan clergy. They were believed to have power of life and death: 'And [Mäqawzay] says to us: "If you fulfil my wishes you shall live, and I shall bless you; if you refuse to obey me you shall die with all your sons, your daughters, and your wives." '[4] This was a world where every family lived in a continuous state of fear and uncertainty, where an angry spirit could strike hard at the slightest divergence from traditional forms of ritual worship. It was largely[5] on this Kushitic religious substratum that Christianity was superimposed in the Ethiopian highlands. According to the books of Zär'a-Ya'iqob in the fifteenth century, the establishment of the

[1] *Gädlä Täklä Hawaryat*, ed. Conti Rossini, in *CSCO*, Script. Aeth., series altera, t. 24 (1910), pp. 117–18.

[2] Conti Rossini, 'Appunti sulla lingua awiya del Dangela' in *GSAI*, xviii (1905), pp. 110–11. He particularly identifies *gor* with the Sīdama form *yero*, *Storia d'Etiopia*, pp. 80–6.

[3] Conti Rossini provides the best description, ibid., pp. 78–89; 'Appunti sulla lingua awiya del Dangela', pp. 108–22; *Etiopia e genti d'Etiopia* (1937), pp. 378–82.

[4] *Gädlä Täklä-Hawaryat*, p. 115.

[5] The rulers of pre-Christian Aksum, and probably also some of their subjects, had adopted the worship of the south Arabian gods, Conti Rossini, *Storia d'Etiopia*, pp. 141–2.

Church does not seem to have removed much of the beliefs and superstitions of the old pagan times. The dichotomy between Good and Evil—God and Satan—in Ethiopian Christian cosmology did not at all rule out the existence, nor the strong arbitrary powers, of evil spirits in the world. All pagan worship, in Zär'a-Ya'iqob's view, was a worship of these spirits, which were only the manifestations of the malign forces of the Fallen Angels. The pagans sought to placate these evil forces through the agency of their religious leaders—the *däsk*, *fäṭänt*, *dīno*, *gwidälé*, whom Zär'a-Ya'iqob considered as mere sorcerers.[1] It was also, apparently, a common practice among the Christians, particularly in the regions south of Angot, to consult these men whose powers to do considerable harm seem to have been widely accepted.[2] More common still, apparently, was the use of magical prayers by members of the Christian community, including the clergy.[3] Zär'a-Ya'iqob was determined to abolish all these practices, and energetically set out reorganizing the Ethiopian Church for the task.

He realized the size of the problem and had apparently drawn up his reform programmes even before his accession to the throne. For the first time since the establishment of the new dynasty in 1270, Zär'a-Ya'iqob asked the Alexandrian patriarchate for more than one Egyptian bishop, and he received Bishops Mīka'él and Gäbri'él in 1438, together with Abba Yohannis who was an Epīsqopos and of a

[1] The precise meaning of these terms, frequently used by Zär'a-Ya'iqob in his writings, and in the hagiographies of his period, is still uncertain and must await future linguistic investigation. It seems, however, that they referred not to the deities or the spirits themselves, but to their human agents. Sometimes the king suggests that each term referred to different regions: 'In Shäwa he who (divines) in this way they call *däsk*, in Angot *dīno*, and in Gojjam *Sigwi*. And there are (other) sorcerers in all Ethiopia', *Das Mashafa Milad und Mashafa Sellase*, ii (text), p. 49. Conti Rossini thinks that the form of the word *Fäṭänt* suggests that it has an Agäw origin, 'Appunti sulla lingua awiya del Dangela', pp. 112–13.

[2] Some of the king's wives and their children were once accused of doing this, *Les Chroniques de Zar'a-Ya'iqob et de Ba'eda Maryam*, pp. 6, 98; *Das Mashafa Milad*, ii, pp. 95–6. Fears of the evil powers of these pagan priests were apparently widespread even among the Christian clergy, and Zär'a-Ya'iqob needed to reassure them, ibid., pp. 44–5; *Mäṣhafä Birhan*, ii (text), pp. 23–4. References to the spirit *Zar* in the reminiscences of a notable scholar of the Ethiopian Church indicate that the current attitude to these matters is still basically the same, Aläqa Lämma, *Mäṣhafä Tizita*, ed. Mängistu Lämma (Addis Ababa, 1967), pp. 32, 50–2, 72.

[3] Zär'a-Ya'iqob refers to clerical members of the court who practised this in the reigns of his brothers, *Das Mashafa Milad*, i, p. 19; see also *Mäṣhafä Birhan*, ii (text), p. 49.

lower rank.[1] The most dire problem of the Church in the extensive Christian kingdom, as has been said above, was the lack of a sufficient number of priests and deacons, and the king assigned his bishops to the two most needy provinces, Mīka'él to Amhara and Gäbri'él to Shäwa.[2] Stationed in their respective posts, they performed the most important task of the Egyptian bishop in Ethiopia, namely ordaining priests and deacons. In itself, the very presence of two bishops in the country created a tremendous sensation among the monasteries, and a strong sense of mission seems to have developed in the Ethiopian Church in general.

The basis of Zär'a-Ya'iqob's policy lay in his success in involving the major monasteries of the country in his religious programme, by a strange combination of economic preferment and legal coercion. This was particularly the case after the Council of Däbrä Miṭmaq, when he could pull together the educational resources of all the established communities throughout his kingdom. In an attempt to make the best use of these communities he apparently divided the kingdom into a number of religious spheres of influence, which he distributed among the principal monasteries. The Éwosṭathian communities in northern Ethiopia, and the flourishing monastery founded by Täklä-Haymanot at Däbrä Asbo, which Zär'a-Ya'iqob renamed Däbrä Lībanos,[3] seem to have been the most important units in this arrangement. Däbrä-Maryam in Sära'é, and Däbrä Bīzän in Hamasén were at the head of the monastic groups of the 'house' of Éwosṭatéwos, and the king gave them large tracts of land 'so that they may preach and teach the orthodox Faith'.[4] It is also apparent that Zär'a-Ya'iqob recruited some Éwosṭathians to teach and establish themselves in southern Ethiopia, and we have references

[1] This was the first occasion on which a patriarch had sent two Egyptian bishops to Ethiopia at one time. Wansleb, who gathered much of his information from the MSS. of the Coptic Church, relates that there were four bishoprics in the kingdom of Niexamiteis, *L'Histoire de l'Église d'Alexandrie* (1677), pp. 29–30. Quatremère sought to identify Niexamiteis with Aksum, *Mémoires*, ii (1811), p. 36. But no other references of any bishoprics headed by Egyptians in Ethiopia are available and the identification is most uncertain. In the *History of the Patriarchs* we always have reports of one metropolitan sent to Ethiopia at a time, cf. Abu Salih, *Churches and Monasteries*, pp. 285–6.

[2] *Mäṣhafä Ṭéfut*, MS. Institute of Archaeology, Addis Ababa; cf. also Cerulli, *Il libro etiopico dei miracoli di Maria*, p. 117. Abba Märha-Kristos (1409–97), abbot of Däbrä Lībanos (1463–97), was ordained priest by Gäbri'él at a place called Bärara, 'Gädlä Märha-Kristos', MS. Däbrä Lībanos, pp. 87–90.

[3] *Les Chroniques de Zar'a Ya'eqob*, p. 91.

[4] Wright, *Catalogue*, Or. 481, f. 208[a].

to Éwosṭathian communities in Indägäbṭan, in south-western Shäwa, hitherto the exclusive domain of the 'house' of Täklä-Haymanot.[1]

For the extensive provinces of Shäwa and Amhara, Zär'a-Ya'iqob utilized the facilities of Däbrä Lībanos. He built new churches in these areas and staffed them with recruits from Däbrä Lībanos.[2] On one occasion the king received reports that the local people of a small district in Mugär practised pagan worship, sacrificing cows and sheep for the serpent god inhabiting a tree. He immediately ordered that a church be built on the site, and Däbrä Lībanos supplied him with priests and deacons, apparently led by Abba Gäbrä-Indiryas, a notable member of the Täklä-Haymanot community at the time.[3] Many other members of the community were also active in the area preaching and establishing churches. It is interesting to note that the earliest tradition of some conversions among the Gafat belongs to this period:

> [Mäb'a-Ṣiyon] had been wondering about the Gafat and he thought 'When will they believe, when will they be baptized? Will it be in my lifetime, or will it be after my death?' And while he was contemplating in this way he met many Gafat men going to our king Zär'a-Ya'iqob to be complimented for their [recent] conversion and their baptism in the name of the Trinity.[4]

[1] *Gädlä Éwosṭatéwos*, pp. 151, 165–7. The traditions related here indicate the hostility of Däbrä-Lībanos to the establishment of the Éwosṭathians in this area. It is most probable that they refer to the reign of Zar'a-Ya'iqob, whose sole preoccupation was to spread the teaching of the Church, and cut across old conventional spheres of influence whenever necessary.

[2] *Les Chroniques de Zar'a Ya'eqob et de Ba'eda Maryam*, pp. 53–4; 'Gädlä Märha-Kristos', MS. Däbrä Lībanos, pp. 153–4.

[3] Ibid., pp. 128–30.

[4] Budge, E. A. W., *The Lives of Maba-Siyon and Gabre Kristos* (London, 1898), pp. 25 (text), 79 (tr.). The Gafat were a Semitic-speaking group, apparently inhabiting the inaccessible district overlooking the Nile gorge between the Jama river and as far west as the Gudar, on the Shawan and Damot side. Zorzi's informants located the Gafat around the sources of the Awash river. Crowfoot, op. cit., pp. 161–83, 187; cf. also Alvarez, *The Prester John of the Indies*, p. 458. Bermudez was detained there by Gälawdéwos, La Croze Veysière, *Histoire du Christianisme d'Éthiopie, et d'Arménie* (1739), p. 197, 223–4; Whiteway, R. S., *The Portuguese Expedition to Abyssinia in 1541*, pp. 217, 232–3. It seems that largely because of the later expansion of the Galla the Gafat gradually moved to southern Gojjam, *Chronica de Susenyos*, ed. Esteves Pereira (Lisbon, 1892), pp. 12, 23, 25–8, 30. Almeida clearly considered them as newcomers to Gojjam, *Some Records*, p. 56. Professor Leslau's valuable linguistic studies are based on information gathered in their new habitat of Wämbärma, in Gojjam. He has recently published a document purporting to be the history of the Gafat, 'A Short Chronicle on the Gafat', in *RSO*, xli (1966), pp. 189–98. The converts to the

The districts of Mugär and Indägäbṭan had been within the kingdom since the thirteenth and fourteenth centuries, but it was apparently in Zär'a-Ya'iqob's reign that a strong offensive against local pagan worship was conducted in these areas. The king personally directed these activities, and apparently encouraged baptism by rewarding new converts, who automatically joined the privileged class of the Christian settlers in their country. The assimilation of his pagan subjects into the Christian community, and the creation of a religiously homogeneous society was Zär'a-Ya'iqob's highest ideal, and he sought to realize it tnrough his own personal direction of the Church. Every little detail of the work and administration of the Church was, for him, an affair of state, and he passed numerous decrees to regulate the religious conduct of his people.

The major part of his decrees underlined the responsibilities of the clergy in teaching and guiding the people.[1] On Saturdays and Sundays, every Christian was expected to go to the nearest church, where the priests had to teach the people 'the Worship of God, his commandments, and the observance of his Sabbaths'.[2] When a church was too far from the settlement of a group of Christian families, a priest had to be sent to them every Friday and spend the weekend there, giving them religious instruction. On these occasions the priest was to be fed and looked after by the community. Every Christian had to have his own Father Confessor who looked after his spiritual well-being, and without whose recommendation participation at the Holy Communion was forbidden.[3] A serious problem in many churches was the lack of a sufficient number of religious books, and the king specially encouraged the establishment of a library in every church.[4] Zär'a-Ya'iqob expected the full co-operation of the clergy in his religious programmes, and enacted strict disciplinary measures against anyone amongst them who failed to follow his directions: 'He ordered the local governors to pillage the houses and to confiscate the property of the priests who do not follow these rules, and who do not give religious instructions in their churches.'[5]

Church in Zär'a-Ya'iqob's time must have been very few, and in the 16th century both Alvarez and Bermudez described the Gafat as a pagan people in general.

[1] *Mäṣhafä Birhan* (text), i, pp. 109–14, 149; ii, pp. 28–30, 48–53; *Das Mashafa Milad und Mashafa Sellase* (text), i, p. 65; ii, pp. 25–6.

[2] *Mäṣhäfa Birhan*, i, p. 149.

[3] Ibid., pp. 48–53; *Das Mashafa Milad*, i, p. 65.

[4] *Mäṣhafä Birhan*, ii, p. 33.

[5] *Les Chroniques de Zar'a-Ya'eqob et de Ba'eda Maryam*, p. 82; cf. also *Mäṣhafä Birhan*, ii (text), p. 28 n. 10.

He declared the abolition of all forms of pagan worship in his kingdom. Consultation with witch-doctors and offering sacrifices to pagan gods were forbidden on pain of death.[1] The use of magical prayers was also made punishable in the same way.[2] Zär'a-Ya'iqob required from his people a clear and an unequivocal expression of their beliefs in the teachings of the Church, and their public rejection of non-Christian practices. Thus, he decreed that every Christian should bear the names of 'the Father, the Son, and the Holy Ghost' branded on his forehead.[3] The sign of the cross also had to be affixed on all the belongings of the Christians—on their dress, their instruments of war, and even on their ploughs. To ensure a complete regimentation of the life of his subjects the king insisted on the strict observance of numerous fasting and holy days.[4]

It is apparent that Zär'a-Ya'iqob entrusted the implementation of his religious programmes to the chief priests of the various districts, and required the abbots of the major monasteries to make round tours of their parishes. On these tours of inspection they were accompanied by the king's troops. This emerges quite clearly from the excellent biography of Märha-Kristos, abbot of Däbrä Lībanos (1462–96):

> Zär'a-Ya'iqob said to [Märha-Kristos]: '. . . go, and look after the administration of the Churches, and preach the Faith in all the land.' . . . [And at that time] the Faith of the people of Mugär was not strong as yet, and for this reason [Märha-Kristos] went down to the country of Mugär with the messengers of the king.[5]

[1] *Das Mashafa Milad*, ii, p. 47 (text.) Cf. also i, p. 42 (text); see also *Mäṣhafä Birhan*, i, pp. 26–7, 118 (text).

[2] Ibid., ii, p. 49 (text).

[3] Ibid., p. 29 (text); cf. also p. 17 (tr.), nn. 4 and 5. Here Zär'a-Ya'iqob reports that the Egyptian Christians bore the sign of the Cross tattooed on their hands; and he argues that his prescription is the more Orthodox, and quotes Revelation 14: 1 and 22: 3–4. His chronicler gives two additional requirements, that everyone was asked to have the words 'I deny the devil' branded on his right arm, and 'I deny the cursed *däsk*; I am the slave of Mary' on his left arm, *Les Chroniques de Zar'a-Ya'eqob*, p. 6.

[4] Ibid., pp. 75–6; *Das Mashafa Milad*, ii (text), pp. 102–5; *Mäṣhafä Birhan*, ii (text), pp. 44–7, 159–61, 167–72.

[5] 'Gädlä Märha-Kristos', MS. Däbrä Lībanos, p. 127. Märha-Kristos (1407–96) was the son of a rich family in Wäj, Shäwa. Ordained deacon by Bishop Bärtälomėwos (1399–1436?), he joined Däbrä Lībanos, where the abbot Yohannis Käma invested him with the monastic habit, while still a very young man. He was made a personal attendant of the abbot, who later died in his care. Bishop Gäbri'él (1438–58?) ordained him priest at the recommendation of the next abbot, Indiryas. When the latter was disgraced and exiled by Zär'a-Ya'iqob in 1462, Märha-Kristos was appointed in his place, ibid., pp. 108–9. He was on very good

The presence of the king's troops in his party enabled the abbot to exercise much authority during his visits. On the occasion of his trip to Mugär, Märha-Kristos is said to have 'burned their books of magic', and when confronted with more serious opposition he sent the leaders to Zär'a-Ya'iqob himself. At the royal court, 'the king . . . ordered his men to flog them'.[1] It seems that this was a general pattern throughout the kingdom, and Zär'a-Ya'iqob's personal involvement in the expansion of the Church tended to give considerable political influence, and arbitrary power, to his ecclesiastical appointees in the provinces. Abba Täklä-Hawaryat, who also preached in Mugär, is said to have flogged a witch-doctor in public, and to have expelled many others from the highland districts overlooking the Blue Nile gorge, by burning down their houses.[2] These acts of violence had the king's blessing, and were apparently committed to demonstrate the powerlessness of the pagan gods and their human agents.

Political unrest in the kingdom

Zär'a-Ya'iqob was a despot. In his enthusiasm to create a uniform religious practice among his subjects, he applied very harsh rules: 'If you see anyone sacrificing to Satan, kill him with a spear, or with a staff, or with stones . . .'[3] This arbitrary disposition characterized the second half of his reign. In his chronicles, and in the hagiographical traditions of the period, many of the punishments inflicted by the king are frequently given religious motives. However, towards the beginning of the 1450s, it is possible to detect that serious political reactions were staged against the king's high-handed rule.

His own *Bihtwäddäd* and son-in-law, Amdä-Mäsqäl, is accused of 'rebellious schemes . . . unbecoming to relate'.[4] Another secular

terms with Bä'idä-Maryam (1468–78), whom he accompanied on his campaigns against the Dob'a; ibid., 158–77; *Les Chroniques de Zar'a-Ya'eqob et de Ba'eda Maryam*, pp. 133, 147. He was still abbot when he died in the second year of the reign of Na'od (1494–1508), 'Gädlä Märha-Kristos', p. 346; cf. also Cerulli, E., 'Gli abbati di Dabra Libanos', pp. 145–9.

[1] 'Gädlä Märha-Kristos', pp. 135–7. It is apparent that the clergy of the provincial churches put up a very strong resistance against the strict control of their activities by the king's direct appointees, and there are reports of violent clashes during these tours of inspection.

[2] *Gädlä Täklä-Hawaryat*, pp. 115–23.

[3] *Das Mashafa Milad und Mashafa Sellase*, ii (text), p. 47. 'Whoever is found in possession of magical prayers . . . shall be punished like an idolator, and his property shall be given to the Church', *Mäṣhafä Birhan*, ii (text), p. 49.

[4] *Les Chroniques de Zar'a Ya'eqob et de Be'eda Maryam*, p. 10. The chronicler

official, *Ṣasärgwé* Amha-Īyäsus, and Abba Nob, *Niburä-Id* of Däbrä Damo are mentioned as his accomplices.[1] A former *Bihtwäddäd*, Īsayiyas, was also committed to prison, and was physically tortured, probably on the same occasion.[2] A more definite story of a high-powered revolt against Zär'a-Ya'iqob is told in one of his own books.[3] Here the leaders of the revolt are naturally kept anonymous, but they are described as being 'from among the chiefs of Ethiopia'. They sought to depose Zär'a-Ya'iqob and enthrone another in his place. It is apparent that the movement had assumed very serious proportions, and the king resorted to a very unusual political act to quell the rising. We are told that the news of the revolt reached Cairo, where the patriarch and his congregations were greatly distressed. Patriarch Yohannis (1428–53) immediately sent messengers to Ethiopia with a letter of excommunication against

> all the army, the chiefs and rulers, big and small, men and women . . . [who] desire to crown another while Zär'a-Ya'iqob . . . is still on his throne; these [men], and whoever wishes to take the crown [from him] . . . or to kill him, or to depose him in open revolt or by secret means and by magic; and whoever joins in an evil league against him.[4]

The Patriarchal letter was read at a public gathering by Bishop Gäbri'él, after which many of the rebels are said to have publicly confessed their sins and reconfirmed their future loyalties to the king.

Nevertheless, it is quite clear that immediately after the incident Zär'a-Ya'iqob introduced a number of changes generally intended to centralize his administrative control of the empire.[5] Apparently,

also tries to avoid the real issue in another passage, 'And they exiled [Amdä-Mäsqäl] for treason against the king. I do not know the secrets of the matter. Publicly, he was accused of taking another woman to wife, while he was married to a princess', pp. 94–5.

[1] Ibid., pp. 11–12, 95. The mention of Abba Nob seems to provide a useful chronological term of reference. A certain *Niburä-Id* Nob is mentioned elsewhere as being involved in Zär'a-Ya'iqob's programme of rehabilitating the 'house' of Éwostatéwos, and Conti Rossini has identified him with the abbot of Däbrä Damo, *Gädlä Yonas*, pp. 180 n. 1, 199. Yet another reference to a man of this name is provided in a story of the miracles of St. Mary where he is accused of a private scepticism towards the new cult of St. Mary, and Cerulli identifies him with the same person, *Il libro etiopico dei miracoli di Maria*, pp. 108, 110, 111–12.

[2] *Les Chroniques de Zar'a-Ya'eqob*, pp. 12–13.

[3] *Mäṣhafä Birhan*, ii (text), pp. 19–22.

[4] Ibid., p. 19.

[5] It is perhaps most expressive of the gravity of the political movement against him that these administrative changes consisted in the appointment of his own daughters to high offices of the court, and as heads of the provinces, *Les Chroniques de Zar'a Ya'eqob*, pp. 9–10, 13–14, 94–5. The princesses probably ran their offices from the court through their local agents who are accused of oppressing

this was accompanied by a great purge of many individuals who previously held high offices in the royal court and in the provinces. The hagiographical traditions about the life of a Shäwan saint, Abba Täklä-Hawaryat, seem to provide an additional piece of evidence both for the nature and the chronology of these political unrests.[1] At one time Täklä-Hawaryat asked for an audience with the king, and wished to speak to him about 'the futile deaths of men, the arrests and the beating which takes place'. When the king was told of this he angrily summoned the monk and said to him: 'Is it true that you insulted me? Whom did you see me kill without legal proceedings; and whom did you see me punish outside the law? And why do you thus slander me while I am the anointed one?'[2] Täklä-Hawaryat was himself beaten and cast into prison where he died some months later. Only thirteen years afterwards, when Bä'idä-Maryam (1468–78) succeeded his father, could his disciples remove the remains of Täklä-Hawaryat to Mugär, where his monastery of Däbrä Ṣimmona is still an object of pious pilgrimage. This chronological reference is particularly interesting as additional confirmation that the abortive rising against Zär'a-Ya'iqob took place about the beginning of 1453.[3]

Zär'a-Ya'iqob: Lasting achievements

Zär'a-Ya'iqob displayed a strong sense of mission throughout his reign, and he set himself very high objectives: 'And God raised Us to

the people, ibid., pp. 95–7. The king then took personal control of all the provinces through a new cadre of local appointees, directly responsible to himself, ibid., pp. 14–16.

[1] 'Gädlä Täklä-Hawaryat', MS. Däbrä Lībanos, ff. 49–50. Conti Rossini has published another version of this *Gädl* in *CSCO*, Script. Aeth., series altera, tome 24 (1910). In this published version the saint's quarrel with Zär'a-Ya'iqob is completely suppressed.

[2] 'Gädlä Täklä-Hawaryat', f. 50[a]. A passing remark in the story of the life of another contemporary local saint, from Indägäbṭan, also indicates that unfavourable sentiments were freely expressed about the king at the time. The saint is shown a vision of the Fires of Hell by St. Michael, who tells him, 'Look, those who are crying here are men who slandered King Zär'a-Ya'iqob', *The Life of Maba'Seyon*, ed. Budge, p. 27.

[3] The incident must have taken place between 1450 and 1453. Abba Nob, who took part in the revolt, was still in favour in 1450. Patriarch Yohannis XI, who allegedly excommunicated the rebels, died on 4th May 1453, Chaine, M., *La Chronologie des temps chrétiens de l'Égypte et de l'Éthiopie* (Paris, 1925), Tables. Täklä-Hawaryat's arrest in 1454 takes the incident nearer to 1453 than 1450. Together with that of Indiryas, abbot of Däbrä Lībanos (d. 1462), Täklä-Hawaryat's death as a 'martyr' is also referred to in 'Gädlä Märha-Kristos', MS. Däbrä Lībanos, p. 102.

this orthodox throne so that we may disperse all idol-worshippers.'[1] Judged against this high ideal, however, his attempts to bring about a radical change in the religious life of his people did not bear substantial results. Perhaps the most telling illustration of this drastic failure is the basic contradiction of his own life. Despite his eloquent commentaries on the Apostolic Canons, and on the constitutions of the early Christian Church, Zär'a-Ya'iqob remained polygamous to the end of his days.[2] His superstitious fears of black magic seem also to have been considerable,[3] and his ruthless judgements convey very little of the sense of justice of a deeply religious man. The most lasting achievement of Zär'a-Ya'iqob certainly lay in his encouragement of Ethiopic literature, in the development of which he actively participated,[4] and in his reorganization of the Church.

Zär'a-Ya'iqob's close association with their religious activities promoted the prestige of the monasteries, and greatly increased their economic and political influence in the kingdom. It is even apparent that the revolt of 1453 was as much against the growing wealth of some of the monasteries as against the king. It is reported by the chronicler that Zär'a-Ya'iqob had granted to Däbrä Lībanos all the revenues collected from the rich province of Shäwa. The

[1] *Das Mashafa Milad und Mashafa Sellase*, ii (text), pp. 95–6.

[2] He had three queens: Žan-Hayla (also called Firé-Maryam), his favourite wife and mother of his eldest daughters, *Les Chroniques de Zar'a-Ya'eqob*, pp. 55, 87; Žan-Zéla (= Žan-Zäyla?), also called Illéni and daughter of the Muslim tributary king of Hadya, ibid., pp. 16, 59; another name of a queen, Bar-Zelay (= bar-Zayla?) is mentioned elsewhere, Guidi, I., 'Le canzoni Ge'ez-Amarigna in onore di Re Abissini', in *RRAL*, ser. iv, vol. v (1889), p. 63. It is not clear whether this represents a different person or Žan-Zéla. His other wife was Ṣiyon-Mogäsa, mother of his successor Bä'idä-Maryam, *Les Chroniques*, pp. 105–7. Zär'a-Ya'iqob refers to his 'queens' in *Das Mashafa Milad und Mashafa Sellase*, ii (text), p. 95. Cf. also Dillmann, op. cit., p. 67.

[3] According to his chronicler, 'This king says in his own words, and it is written in his book, that evil men have cast a spell on him wherever he resides and wherever he travels', *Les Chroniques*, p. 41. To ward off the malign effects of this, prayers were held round the clock at the king's residence by a select group of monks, who sprinkled holy water on the premises at regular intervals, p. 40. The patriarch's letter of excommunication also covered those who would like to get rid of the king 'by secret means and through black magic'.

[4] A number of religious compositions are personally attributed to him, among which are 'Ṭomarä-Tisbi't', 'Kihdätä-Säyṭan', 'Mäṣhafä-Bahriy', 'Egzi'Abher-Nägsä', 'Tä'aqibo-Misṭīr', 'Mäṣhafä-Birhan', and 'Mäṣhafä-Mīlad', *Les Chroniques*, pp. 76–8. Conti Rossini has published an extract from 'Tä'aqibo-Misṭīr' in his 'Il libro di re Zär'a-Ya'qob sulla custodia del Mistero', *RSE*, iii (1943), pp. 148–66. The last two works have recently been published in the excellent series of the *Corpus Scriptorum Christianorum Orientalium*, and we have already made some use of them above.

revenues previously belonged to the Ṣahafé-Lam and a number of military contingents under him.[1] The diversion of their former income to the monasteries was no doubt resented by the troops and their leaders, and probably contributed a great deal to the political unrest of the time. The tone of the patriarch's alleged letter of excommunication against the rebels of 1453 also points to the same conclusion: 'If there is any one who trespassed on the churches and monasteries built by . . . Zär'a Ya'iqob . . . and on their land holdings and all their property . . . [he shall be excommunicated].'[2] Other land grants of considerable size in favour of the major monastic communities in northern Ethiopia are also attributed to Zär'a-Ya'iqob.[3] It is further apparent that compulsory contributions in kind were collected from the Christian peasantry throughout the kingdom for the support of the local churches.[4] Probably to ensure that his religious reforms reached every family, Zär'a-Ya'iqob had instituted the position of the Father Confessor, which still remains one of the most distinctive features of the Ethiopian Church. Despite the modest efficacy of this institution in bettering the spiritual life of the people, the close personal and economic relationships between the Father Confessor and the individual family remained intact: 'Love [your Father Confessor] like the pupil of your eye . . . and give him from the fruits of your labour . . . and share with him whatever you have.'[5] The end result of these measures was the creation of a huge clerical aristocracy living almost entirely on the services of their congregation. Many of the monastic communities, which had started their religious pursuits by collecting wild fruits and cultivating their own little terraces,[6] had become owners of large tracts of land as *Gults* by the middle of the fifteenth century.[7] This development naturally gave the monasteries much secular power and administrative responsibility over their tenant farmers, and they began to exercise a considerable political patronage in the Christian kingdom.[8]

[1] *Les Chroniques de Zar'a-Ya'eqob*, p. 101.
[2] *Mäṣḥafä Birhan*, ii (text), p. 19.
[3] *Liber Aksumae*, ed. Conti Rossini, pp. 25–6. Id., 'L'evangelo d'oro', p. 212. Wright, *Catalogue*, Or. 481, ff. 154, 208[a].
[4] *Mäṣḥafä Birhan*, ii (text), pp. 41–3.
[5] *Das Mashafa Milad*, ii (text), pp. 25–6.
[6] Cf. pp. 110–12, 171–2.
[7] For the nature of the land holding known as *Gult* see pp. 98–103.
[8] Puritanical monastic reactions against this acquisition of an increasing amount of wealth and temporal power were not lacking. The most vehement protest came from the remarkable religious movement of the *Däqiqä Isṭifanos*,

Unlike the great monastic leaders of the fourteenth century who kept strictly to their isolated hermitages, many of the abbots of the principal monasteries became regular visitors at the court of Zär'a-Ya'iqob.[1] It is apparent that the king required their presence around him for religious consultations, and probably also to involve them more actively in his programmes of reform and literary development. Especially towards the end of his reign, and after the abortive revolt of 1453, Zär'a-Ya'iqob was always surrounded by his ecclesiastical officials. Besides enhancing the age-old role of the monarchy as the focal point of the religious and political life of Christian Ethiopia, this concentration of the highest clerical and secular leadership around the person of Zär'a-Ya'iqob particularly made his court the centre for the increasingly articulate national self-expression of the Ethiopians, and for their growing sense of independence, even from the patriarchate of Alexandria. This national development found its highest expression, some years after the death of Zära-Ya'iqob, in the council of 1477, convened by his son and successor Bä'idä-Maryam (1468–78). At this council a radical proposal for the discontinuation of the spiritual dependence on Alexandria was put forward by a large section of the Ethiopian clergy, and was seriously considered.[2]

Zär'a-Ya'iqob's favourite bishops, Mīka'él and Gäbri'él, apparently died before 1458,[3] and it is not known if the king ever asked for their replacement during the remaining years of his reign. The two bishops had been most co-operative in his religious programmes, and, having their respective headquarters in Amhara and Shäwa, they were very active in ordaining priests and deacons. Probably, the number of ordinations in the twenty years of their ministry in Ethiopia was very large, and the effect of the absence of a bishop was not keenly felt in Zär'a-Ya'iqob's last years. Towards the

Taddesse Tamrat, 'Some Notes on the Fifteenth Century Stephanite "Heresy" in the Ethiopian Church', pp. 105–12.

[1] *Les Chroniques de Zar'a Ya'eqob*, pp. 27–8. Here the abbots of the major monasteries are mentioned as the king's regular courtiers. The Aqabé-Sä'at of the island monastery of Hayq was specially required to stay at court with the king, ibid., pp. 7–8, 167. The abbot of Däbrä Bīzän, Abba Péṭros, is elsewhere said to have stayed with the king for two years, Kolmodin, op. cit., A25. Märha-Kristos of Däbrä Lībanos frequently visited Zär'a-Ya'iqob, and even accompanied Bä'idä-Maryam on his Dob'a campaigns, 'Gädlä Märha-Kristos', pp. 149, 158–77. *Les Chroniques*, pp. 133–47.

[2] The story of this Council is told in 'Gädlä Märha-Kristos', MS. Däbrä Lībanos, pp. 237–57.

[3] Alvarez was told that Zär'a-Ya'iqob had no bishop in his court for the last ten years of his reign, *The Prester John of the Indies*, ii, p. 356.

end of the reign of his son, however, the shortage of priests in the kingdom had assumed serious proportions. A distant echo of this is found in a tradition collected by D'Abbadie in Bägémdir about the reign of Bä'idä Maryam: '. . . there were only two priests in the church or the chapel of the king.'[1]

A strong representation was made to King Bä'idä-Maryam to break relations with Alexandria and appoint Ethiopian bishops: 'And they said [to the King] we have heard that [the people of] Egypt have changed their Faith. They eat what is forbidden in the Law. And now let us appoint a bishop from our country as it is said "let him be appointed [bishop] who is chosen by the people". . .'[2] Characteristically, the initiators of this radical view are kept anonymous. It seems quite possible, however, to indicate their identity from the opposite stand adopted by Däbrä Lībanos of Shäwa in whose tradition we have the story of the Council. Märha-Kristos was the abbot of Däbrä Lībanos at the time, and he vehemently opposed the new proposal. He based his arguments on the principle of Apostolic Succession.[3] Märha-Kristos submitted to the king and the assembly his own counter-proposal: 'Let the king send wise men whose words are dependable, to investigate for us. If the Egyptians are still in the Orthodox Faith let them bring us a bishop according to the tradition of our forefathers. If they are not, we shall then pray to God and ask for his guidance of what to do.'[4]

The mild tone of this suggestion was only intended to cover up the basic commitments of Däbrä Lībanos to the continued dependence of the Ethiopian Church on Alexandria. We have already seen that the monastery adopted a similar position in the religious controversies before 1450, and Märha-Kristos was only expressing the traditional

[1] Conti Rossini, 'Il libro delle leggende e tradizioni abissine dell'Ecciaghie Filpos', in *RRAL*, ser. 5, vol. xxvi (1917), p. 711. The reason given here for the shortage is altogether different, viz. that no one could be ordained to the priesthood if he did not descend from the 'house' of Levi, a reference to the legend of the queen of Sheba. Most probably, this is a confusion of two different traditions.

[2] 'Gädlä Märha-Kristos', p. 237. Cf. Duensing, H., 'The Ethiopic Version of the Egyptian Church Ordinance', ed. and tr. in *Abhandlungen der Akademie der Wissenschaften*, Gottingen, Phil.-hist. Klasse, Folge 3, No. 36 (1946), p. 16 (text).

[3] 'Gädlä Märha-Kristos', p. 239. In his contention Märha-Kristos reminded the assembly of the wrath of God that befell Ethiopia in the reign of Patriarch Yoséf (830–49) when the Ethiopians expelled the Egyptian bishop and chose one of their own, ibid., pp. 245–8. Cf. also *History of the Patriarchs of Alexandria*, in *PO*, x (1913), pp. 508–9; Renaudot, op. cit., pp. 273, 283–8.

[4] 'Gädlä Märha-Kristos', p. 240.

loyalty of the community to the Egyptian Church.[1] It is also possible to see a similar consistency in the position of the anti-Egyptian party.

It is most likely that the major protagonists of the radical view belonged to the House of Éwostatéwos. The tradition of Däbrä Lībanos about the council only refers to them as 'the other party'. However, their long-standing opposition to the Egyptian bishops, and their remarkable sense of independence, seem to warrant the proposed identification. Just as in the Council of Däbrä Miṭmaq of 1450, the 'Nationalist Party', as it were, consisted of the majority of the assembled clergy.[2] This time, however, it did not have the royal support. The Däbrä Lībanos party was determined to win the day, and applied all the political patronage at its disposal, outside the assembly. Ras Amdä-Mīka'él, the most powerful official in Shäwa at the time,[3] sided with Märha-Kristos, and arranged a private audience for him with the king. The fate of the Council was decided at this secret meeting, and the king announced his final ruling the next day: 'We have ordered that men who are dependable go down [to Egypt], and we shall send a thousand shekel weights of gold to be given to the Holy Sepulchre, the patriarch of Alexandria, and the sultan of Egypt.'[4]

Despite the numerical superiority of the opposition, Bä'idä-Maryam thus decided in favour of the continued dependence of the Ethiopian Church on the patriarchate of Alexandria. It is impossible to tell what Zär'a-Ya'iqob's position in similar circumstances would have been. It must be said, however, that his stand in the Council of Däbrä Miṭmaq had been decisively nationalistic. He was also apparently reluctant to ask for new Egyptian bishops, after the death of Mīka'el and Gäbri'él, in the last ten years of his reign. The radical issue of independence from Alexandria was no doubt the culmination of the religious nationalism so characteristic of the remarkable career of Zär'a-Ya'iqob.

[1] Cf. pp. 225–6 above. It is in fact apparent that the traditions about Täklä-Haymanot's 13th century decision that no Ethiopian should be appointed bishop, and that bishops should always come from Egypt, have their origin in this 15th-century stand of his monastery as a staunch supporter of Alexandria. For these traditions about Täklä-Haymanot see specially Bruce, *Travels to Discover the Source of the Nile*, i (1790), p. 534.

[2] This is attested by the traditions of Däbrä Lībanos itself, '[the supporters of Märha-Kristos] numbered three hundred only . . . and the other party, four hundred', 'Gädlä Märha-Kristos', p. 243.

[3] Ras Amdä-Mīka'él was already a strong provincial governor of Fäṭägar in Zär'a-Yaiqob's reign, *Les Chroniques*, p. 15. For further notes about him see pp. 286–90.

[4] 'Gädlä Märha-Kristos', pp. 248–9.

CHAPTER VII

Early Contacts with Christian Europe
(1380–1460)

THE Council of Däbrä Miṭmaq in 1450 brought an end to the most important schism between northern Ethiopia, increasingly led by the influential 'house of Éwosṭatéwos', and the rest of the Christian kingdom which had persistently followed the leadership of the Egyptian bishops, particularly on the question of the Sabbath.[1] The resolution of this religious controversy, which had considerable regional and political implications, tremendously increased the power of the central Court throughout the realms of Christian Ethiopia. Zär'a-Ya'iqob further promoted this vital development by invoking the highest symbols of Ethiopian Christian traditions to enhance the position of the monarchy in Church and State, and to fortify the unity of his Christian subjects. Perhaps the most dramatic example of this deliberate policy was his revival of the old custom of formal coronation in the ancient city of Aksum. In 1436, two years after he took over as king of Ethiopia in Shäwa, he travelled to Tigré, and underwent the customary rites of coronation in the ancient cathedral city of Aksum.[2] The same formalities of sacral enthronement were probably used every time a new king was proclaimed in the Christian kingdom.[3] The special significance of Zär'a-Ya'iqob's decision was

[1] Cf. pp. 220–31.

[2] *Les Chroniques de Zar'a-Ya'eqob et de Ba'eda Maryam*, pp. 49–52, 83. It is significant that *Mäṣhafä-Aksum* enters the reign of Zär'a-Ya'iqob from this date—89 Year of Grace; *Liber Aksumae*, ed. Conti Rossini, pp. 4–5, 67. Hamasén traditions collected by Kolmodin simply say that the king was there in that year, op. cit., A24; 'Tarīkä-Nägäst', MS. Däbrä Ṣigé, pp. 54–5.

[3] The best description of the ceremony on such occasions is available in Or. 817, MS. B.M., ff. 11^b–12. Cf. also *Chronica de Susenyos rei de Ethiopia*, ed. Pereira, pp. 123–4. According to some traditions similar formalities were undertaken in places other than Aksum. Lalībäla was enthroned in the same way in Bugna, Perruchon, *Vie de Lalibla, roi d'Ethiopie* (1892), pp. 107–8. A slightly different description is given about the coronation of one of his predecessors in Lasta, 'Gädlä Yimriha-Kristos', MS. Lalībäla, f. 28^b. Bä'idä-Maryam, son and successor of Zär'a-Ya'iqob, was crowned in the same way as his father, but in Amhara. Officials from Aksum were specially brought for the ceremony. Later the king planned to reconfirm the ceremony by going to Aksum. But hostilities

his particular insistence that the ceremony of his coronation be conducted at Aksum Ṣiyon.

Ṣiyon, a term figuratively applied to St. Mary, is also used in reference to the kingdom as a symbol of the special identity of Christian Ethiopia, surrounded by a hostile Muslim and pagan world in north-east Africa.[1] It is used in much the same way as the biblical concept of Mount Zion,[2] from which it is derived, and constitutes an integral part of the legend of the queen of Sheba.

The historical connection between the Christian kingdom and the queen of Sheba is still unknown. Cosmas, who visited the kingdom of Aksum on the eve of Kaléb's expedition to south Arabia refers to the queen of Sheba 'of the Homerite country', but he does not at all connect her with the western side of the Red Sea except to say that she obtained many of her rare presents to King Solomon from the land of Ethiopia.[3] About three centuries later, however, a chronicler of the Alexandrian Church makes a reference to 'Abyssinia which is a vast country, namely, the kingdom of Saba from which the queen of the South came to Solomon, the Son of David the King'.[4] Abu Salih who wrote in the beginning of the thirteenth century repeats the same point, but also provides an important addition:

> The Abyssinians possess also the Ark of the Covenant, in which are the two tables of stone, inscribed by the finger of God with the commandments which he ordained for the children of Israel . . . And the Ark is attended and carried by a large number of Israelites descended from the family of the prophet David . . .[5]

from Adal made it difficult, *Les Chroniques de Zar'a-Ya'eqob*, pp. 124–6, 149–50. It is also apparent that a more localized, tribal ceremony was held in Amhara at the accession of the kings. Apart from the secrecy with which it was undertaken, and the sacral use of woollen blankets, nothing is as yet known about this tribal custom, ibid., pp. 167–8.

[1] Amdä-Ṣiyon's accusation against Säbrädīn on the eve of their hostilities in 1332 was that he 'coveted the throne of David and he says "I shall reign in Ṣiyon"', Perruchon, *Histoire des guerres d'Amde Seyon*, p. 281. Amano, who refused to pay tribute to Amdä-Ṣiyon, is referred to as 'a rebel against the king of *Ṣiyon*', ibid., p. 287. Referring to Amdä-Ṣiyon's message of congratulation to his highland Christian subjects following his successes in Adal the chronicler writes, 'he sent messengers to the country of his kingdom which is Ṣiyon', ibid., p. 301.

[2] Johnson, A. R., *Sacral Kingship in Ancient Israel* (1955), pp. 27–9, 61–4.

[3] *The Christian Topography of Cosmas Indicopleustes*, tr. McCrindle (1897), pp. 51–2.

[4] This is in the story of the life of Patriarch Cosmas (*c.* 920–32), *The History of the Patriarchs*, ii, pt. 2, p. 118.

[5] *The Churches and Monasteries of Egypt*, ed. and tr. Evetts, B. T. A. (Oxford 1895), pp. 287–8.

Essentially, the *Kibrä-Nägäst*, which is the Ethiopic version of the legend of the queen of Sheba, also transmits the same tradition. Indeed it is interesting that according to its Ethiopian compilers the Arabic version of the tradition first appeared in Ethiopia in 1225, not much after Abu Salih wrote his book. It is apparent, however, that even before the first compilation of the *Kibrä-Nägäst* in the first years of the reign of Amdä-Ṣiyon (1314–44), the tradition was widely diffused in Christian Ethiopia,[1] and had gradually been transformed, from a mere tradition of the Jewish origin of the Ethiopian state, into an account of the origin of the Christian tribes of the Ethiopian highlands.[2] As the repository of the Ark of the Covenant, also called *Ṣiyon*, the ancient city of Aksum was the focal point of this tradition and its tribal ramifications. Zär'a-Ya'iqob was the first king of the new dynasty who is known to have been formally crowned there, and in doing this he sought to invest the monarchy with all the religious and political symbols of ancient Aksum.

Ethiopia and the Crusades

The pragmatic aspect of Zär'a-Ya'iqob's policy in doing this was of course his intensive programme of strengthening his military and political control of northern Ethiopia. The major routes to Alexandria and the Holy Land ran through these northern provinces, and the rulers of the Christian kingdom had always been anxious to establish a secure and a more direct outlet in this direction. Ever since the new dynasty came to power the kings had been highly sensitive to any problems of security on these routes. Some time between 1270 and 1277 a local rebel in Tigré intercepted Yikunno-Amlak's envoys to Cairo and confiscated the presents sent to Sultan Baybars.[3] It is not clear what Yikunno-Amlak did on that occasion, but it is apparent that, until the advent of Amdä-Ṣiyon (1314–44),

[1] Conti Rossini, 'Aethiopica (ii)', in *RSO*, x (1925), pp. 506–8. *Storia d'Etiopia* (1928), pp. 253–7. Cerulli, E., *Storia della letteratura etiopica* (1956), pp. 45–8. An English translation of the *Kibrä-Nägäst* was made by E. A. W. Budge under the title *The Queen of Sheba and her Only Son Menyelek* (London, 1922). Ullendorff has also incorporated his latest views on the legend of the queen of Sheba in his book, *Ethiopia and the Bible* (London, 1968).

[2] Many of the different tribes, particularly of northern Ethiopia, begin their tribal history by connecting their ancestors with the queen of Sheba, her son, or his companions from Jerusalem, cf. Conti Rossini 'Studi su Popolazioni dell'Etiopia, pp. 59–60 (extract). Kolmodin, op. cit., Tr.3–Tr.5.

[3] Mufazzal, *Histoire des sultans mamlouks*, ed. and tr. Blochet, in *PO*, xiv 1913), p. 387.

his immediate successors had very little power in the northern provinces. Amdä-Ṣiyon personally led a successful expedition in the area, established a non-Tigré military colony at Amba-Sänayata, the native district of the rebel leader Ya'ibbīkä-Egzī, and conducted his troops as far as the coast of the Red Sea.[1] He appointed a new set of local chiefs in the highland districts and, to ensure that they maintained a direct contact with his Court, he placed first his Tigré Queen, Bilén-Saba, and some time later one of his own sons, Bahir-Sägad, at the head of the administration of the northern provinces. He inaugurated a new period for the complete reunification of the Christian kingdom and his successors embarked on a more aggressive policy on this front. Amdä-Ṣiyon is the first among the Ethiopian kings whose names are recorded as benefactors of the library collection of the Ethiopian community in Jerusalem,[2] and from the reign of his son and successor, Säyfä-Ar'ad (1344–71), we begin to have very clear reports of Ethiopians residing in Egyptian monasteries.[3] But together with their need to strengthen their traditional contacts with the patriarchate and the Holy Land, the Ethiopians were now looking at a much wider horizon and had begun to entertain strong hopes of establishing relations with the Christian nations of Europe. Although they have left no traces on the traditions of the kingdom, the Wars of the Crusades could have hardly been unknown to the Christians of Ethiopia. Only the relative weakness of the kingdom before the thirteenth century, and the need to maintain friendly relations with the new and strong Ayyubid dynasty in Egypt, had precluded the Ethiopians taking a close interest in the religious struggle of the eastern Mediterranean. Thus, even the daring

[1] *Liber Aksumae*, pp. 30–1. Taddesse Tamrat, 'The Abbots of Däbrä Hayq', notes 43 and 44.

[2] Tisserant and Grébaut, *Codices Aethiopici, Vaticani et Borgiani, Barberinianus Orientalis 2 Rossianus 865*, Vatican Library (1935), MS. Borg. Etiop. 3; cf. Cerulli, E., *Etiopi in Palestina*, p. 130.

[3] A MS. of the New Testament donated by Säyfa-Ar'ad to the Ethiopian Community at the monastery of Qusqwam is among the Ethiopic collections of the Bibliothèque Nationale, Zotenberg, op. cit., no. 32. During their flight to Egypt the Holy Family are said to have resided at the site, Abu Salih, op. cit., pp. 224–6; Wansleb, op. cit., p. 22. As such, it is the centre of many Ethiopian religious traditions, Cerulli, *Il libro etiopico dei miracoli di Maria*, pp. 206–12. It seems that in Egypt the Ethiopian monks resided mainly at Qusqwam, Har Zuwaila (in Cairo), and the monastery of Scete (Asqēṭis). At each of these places they had an Ethiopian head, but it is apparent from a short note belonging to the reign of Patriarch Yohannis (1484–1524) that the Jerusalem group had supremacy over the rest, Zotenberg, op. cit., no. 35.

maritime expedition of Reynald of Chatillon in the Red Sea, and his sacking of Aydab on the African coast, has not obtained a place in the traditional recollections of the highland Christians of Ethiopia.[1] However, with the revival of the Christian kingdom, and particularly after the brilliant career of Amdä-Ṣiyon, the position was drastically changed. News of the Christian expansion and conquest in the Ethiopian region no doubt percolated through to Europe. Not only did European geographic notions about the Christians, south of Egypt, considerably improve as a result, but the Christians of Ethiopia also began to be thought of as possible allies in the preparation for another Crusade, after the fall of 'Akkah in 1291.[2] One of the proposals for such an alliance was made by a man who knew the conditions of the region from very close quarters. Guillaume Adam, a Dominican monk who was later archbishop of Sultaniyyah, had been in the island of Socotra for many months, and had been making unsuccessful attempts to travel to Ethiopia on many occasions. His plans for 'exterminating the Saracens', first submitted in 1317, were very ambitious, and envisaged the blockade of the eastern trade at the Gulf of Aden, with the military co-operation of the Christians of Ethiopia. In another report presented to King Philip of France in 1332 he mentions a strong Christian people 'who are now living enclosed by mountains in the direction of Egypt', no doubt a reference to the Christian subjects of Amdä-Ṣiyon.[3] The desire to establish contacts was not only a European concern, but Ethiopian pilgrims in Palestine also expressed their unreserved enthusiasm for breaking the long isolation of their country from the Christian world. Niccolo da Poggibonsi, who travelled in the east in the years 1345–7, met a number of Ethiopians in Jerusalem and has this to say about their readiness to communicate with Christian Europe: '[The Christians of Ethiopia] . . . would have willingly communicated with us Latins, but the sultan of Babilonia [i.e. Egypt] never lets a single

[1] Cerulli, *Etiopi in Palestina*, i, pp. 20–6. Cf. also Newbold, D., 'The Crusaders in the Red Sea and the Sudan', in *SNR*, xxvi, pt. 2 (1945), pp. 220–4.

[2] Cerulli, op. cit., pp. 91–8.

[3] Ibid., pp. 95, 97, 99–100. Crawford, O. G. S., *Ethiopian Itineraries*, pp. 4–5. A short biographical note on Adam is given in *Recueil des historiens des Croisades, documents arméniens*, ii (1906), p. 523, note *a*. A much fuller account is given in Kohler, C., 'Documents relatifs à Guillaume Adam, Archévêque de Sultanieh, puis d'Antivari et son entourage (1318–46)', in *Revue de l'Orient Latin*, x (1903–4), pp. 16–17. In 1329, the date given for his death in the *Recueil* and adopted also by Crawford, he was only transferred to Antivari where he was still ruling in 1346, ibid., pp. 47, 49–56.

Latin pass towards their country, so that they do not enter into a treaty to make war against him.'[1]

The vigilance of the Mamlukes in keeping out European Christians from Ethiopia is a constant theme in the reports of travellers of the fourteenth and fifteenth centuries.[2] There was real concern in Cairo about the possible damage Christian Europe could do to the commercial and territorial interests of Egypt, with the use of the growing power of the kingdom. These fears were fully confirmed by the increasingly aggressive attitude that Amdä-Ṣiyon's successors had begun to assume on their nothern frontiers. Traditions of uneasy relations with Egypt are available for the reign of Säyfä-Ar'ad. The last forty-two years (1340–82) of the Bahri Mamluke dynasty were a period of general decline and internal conflict in Egyptian history.[3] During these years the Copts were an object of a widespread persecution, particularly in the reign of Al-Salih (1351-54).[4] According to one tradition,[5] Patriarch Marqos (1348–63) sent word to Säyfä-Ar'ad announcing his imprisonment by the sultan and soliciting his help. Säyfä-Ar'ad at once mobilized a huge army and began moving towards upper Egypt. At the news of the impending attack of his southern frontiers by the Ethiopian army, the sultan released the patriarch, and made him send a delegation to Säyfä-Ar'ad asking him to return to his country. A high-powered delegation was accordingly sent, consisting of a certain Abba Yohannis and another bishop accompanied by some priests and Muslim officials, who carried the sultan's presents to the Ethiopian king. The latter welcomed the envoys, accepted peace on condition that no more persecutions should be conducted against the Christians, and marched back to his kingdom, taking with him Abba Yohannis whom he forced to remain in Ethiopia. Another version of the same story[6] attributes the delegation to quite a different reason. Ethiopian Muslims, persecuted by

[1] Golubovich, G., *Bibliotheca bio-bibliografia della Terra Santa e dell'Oriente Francescano*, tom. v (1929), p. 18. Cerulli, E., op. cit., 133.

[2] Ibid., pp. 150–1, 163–4, 249. Potvin, ch., *Œuvres de Ghillebert de Lannoy, voyageur, diplomate, et moraliste* (Louvain, 1878), pp. 129–30.

[3] Hitti, P., *The History of the Arabs* (ed. 1961), pp. 681–2.

[4] Renaudot, *Historia Patriarcharum Alexandrinorum* (Paris, 1713), pp. 607–11. Quatremère, *Mémoires géographiques et historiques sur l'Égypte*, ii (1811), pp. 251–4. Atiyah, A. S., *The Crusade in the Later Middle Ages* (London, 1938), p. 350.

[5] 'Tarīkä-Nägäst', MS. Däbrä Ṣigé, pp. 50–1, 58.

[6] Perruchon, 'Notes pour l'histoire d'Éthiopie', in *RS*, i (1893), pp. 177–82. Budge, E. A. W., *The Book of the Saints of the Ethiopian Church* (1928), i, pp. 177–9. For the text see 'Sinkisar', Or. 667, MS. B.M. (17th C.), f. 52. Here the patriarchal envoys are identified with Abba Yohannis, Egyptian bishop of

Säyfä-Ar'ad, had appealed for Egyptian intervention, and it was in response to this call that the envoys went to Ethiopia. However, it is quite possible that the two incidents were not completely unconnected, and there are other traditions indicating that the king was in northern Ethiopia at the time with a very large army.[1] It is also interesting to note, that these traditional accounts of Säyfä-Ar'ad's expedition towards the Nile valley find an invaluable confirmation in the reports of a relatively contemporary European traveller. In 1432, Bertrandon de la Brocquière met a Neapolitan called Pietro at the port of Pera, near Constantinople. Pietro had just been to Ethiopia on a mission there from the Duke of Berry in France. Pietro had stayed in Ethiopia for some years and had married an Ethiopian lady. His reports on Ethiopia during the reign of Yishaq (1413–30) are remarkably authentic. Pietro gave the following account of the expedition led by the grandfather of Yishaq, i e. Säyfä-Ar'ad, in the direction of the Nile valley:

> . . . When the king of Cyprus conquered Alexandria, the grandfather of the present king left his country to come to Jerusalem, and he had with him three million people. And when he reached the river Nile, he received reports that the king of Cyprus had abandoned Alexandria . . . He then asked his councillors how many of his troops had survived the heat of the desert route; and, discovering that he had lost two million of his followers, he decided to return to his kingdom.[2]

The invasion and seven days' occupation of Alexandria by Pierre de Lusignan, king of Cyprus, took place in 1365,[3] towards the end of the reign of Säyfä-Ar'ad. Historians of the Crusades tell us that the Christians of Egypt paid very dearly for the adventures of Pierre de Lusignan, in the form of exorbitant taxes and popular persecution.[4] It is interesting, therefore, that precisely such popular persecutions of

Jerusalem, and Qérilos, *Episqopos* of Annas. Yohannis later died in Ethiopia in October 1390. In the Däbrä Ṣigé MS. he is simply referred to as Abba Yohannis, 'of the country of Ethiopia'.

[1] The army was so large that an epidemic broke out in Aksum where they had camped. The king then led his men to Däbrä Lībanos of Shīmäzana further north, Conti Rossini, 'L'evangelo d'oro di Dabra Libanos', p. 177 n. 2. The king is elsewhere said to have visited the old monastic leader, Mädhanīnä-Igzī at Däbrä Bankol, Basset, *Études sur l'histoire d'Éthiopie* (1882), p. 100. Cf. also *Liber Aksumae*, pp. 21–2 (text), and p. 24 (tr.) n. 4.

[2] Schefer, C., *Le Voyage d'outremer de Bertrandon de la Brocquière* (Paris, 1892), p. 148.

[3] Atiyah, Aziz Suryal, *The Crusade in the Later Middle Ages* (1938), pp. 349–76. See also Runciman, S., *A History of the Crusades*, iii (Penguin edition), pp. 441–8.

[4] Atiyah, op. cit., p. 377.

the Copts should be given as the reason for the traditional expedition of Säyfä-Ar'ad towards the frontiers of Egypt.[1]

More reliable sources indicate that King Dawīt (1380–1412) took the offensive against Egypt much further than his father ever did. Maqrizi[2] reports that in 1381 news arrived in Cairo that 'an army sent by Dawīt, son of Säyfä-Ar'ad, king of Ethiopia, had entered in the territory of Aswan, had defeated the Arabs, and committed frightful ravages on the lands of Islam'. The Amir sent for Patriarch Matéwos (1378–1408) and ordered him to write at once to the Ethiopians to stop their hostilities against Egypt. The Patriarch at first refused to co-operate. Finally he agreed to send the letter required by the sultan, who also sent his own delegation, led by the Amir of the important Mediterranean port of Damietta. A whole cycle of traditional accounts is available about Dawīt's attempt to attack Mamluke Egypt, and, freed from their hagiographical trappings, these traditions essentially agree with Maqrizi. Some of these traditions indicate that Dawīt's aim was to go to Jerusalem.[3] Others report precisely what Maqrizi says, that Dawīt's army had reached the territory of Aswan.[4] There seems to be little or no doubt that, on the eve of the advent of the Burji dynasty of Mamluke Egypt, King Dawīt had in fact led his troops beyond the northern frontiers of his kingdom, and created much havoc among the Muslim inhabitants of the area who had been within the sphere of influence of Egypt since the thirteenth century. The effect of this action was

[1] See p. 253 nn. 5 and 6.

[2] Extract in Quatremère, *Mémoires*, ii, pp. 276–7.

[3] 'And then Dawīt II, King of Ethiopia, went to Jerusalem', 'Mar Yishaq', MS. Dīma, f. 171^{b}. 'And then Dawīt II thought, and wished to go to Jerusalem. He looked for men who knew the way, and who would guide him there', 'Gädlä Särṣä-Pétros', MS. Däbrä Wärq, f. 47^{a}. This Dawīt was the first Ethiopian king to bear the name. He is called Dawīt II in deference to the legend of the queen of Sheba and the first Dawīt is King David of Isra'el. Perruchon did not apparently realize this when he attributed a document about this Dawīt (1380–1412) to the reign of Libnä-Dingil (1508–40), who also bore the name Dawīt II, 'Notes pour l'Histoire d'Éthiopie', in *RS*, vi (1898), pp. 157–71.

[4] One version has it that the Egyptian sultan sent the patriarch to persuade Dawīt to march back, and they met at Aswan, 'which is the frontier between Ethiopia and Egypt', 'Mäṣhafä-Ṭéfut', MS. Institute of Archaeology, Addis Ababa. His itineraries are given elsewhere as follows: Hagärä-Nagran, 'on the borders of the Sudan', the Nile valley, 'and he reached the land of Kusa which is in Upper Egypt and camped there', 'Gädlä Särṣä-Péṭros', f. 48. According to a 17th-century version, Dawīt's huge army passed through Sära'é, Hamasén, and into Sinnar where the patriarch's message of peace reached them, *Gädlä Märqoréwos*, ed. Conti Rossini, pp. 42–4.

certainly felt in the Nile valley, and as far north as the Egyptian frontiers. Five years after the campaign, when Barquq (1382–9), the founder of the new dynasty, was well on the saddle of power, peaceful relations were re-established, and Dawīt sent a rich gift to the sultan, consisting of twenty-one camel loads of Ethiopian curiosities.[1]

The readiness displayed by Säyfä-Ar'ad and Dawīt to come to a direct military confrontation with Egypt increased Mamluke determination to isolate Ethiopia from Christian Europe. But it also seems to have made a strong impact on European travellers in Palestine, and the attempts to create relations with the kingdom became particularly active from this period onwards. Ethiopian pilgrims were found in the monasteries of Egypt, in the Holy Places of Palestine, and in Cyprus,[2] and they served as an important link between Ethiopia and the rest of the Christian world. European travellers in Palestine transmitted exaggerated notions of the decisive role which the kingdom could play in a united Christian front against the Muslim powers of the eastern Mediterranean. But even these exaggerated notions were based on authentic reports which the travellers collected among the Ethiopians they met during their sojourn in the east.[3] The Mamluke 'iron curtain' was never completely closed, and

[1] According to Maqrizi this gift 'consisted of all kinds of precious objects which could be found in Ethiopia. There were, above all, many candlesticks full of gold grains of the size of peas', Quatremère, op. cit., p. 277.

[2] In Ethiopic traditions the presence of a community in Cyprus is represented in *Gädlä Éwosṭatéwos*, ed. B. Turaiev, pp. 101–19. See also Conti Rossini, 'Sulla communita abissino di Cipro', in *RSE*, ii (1942), pp. 98–9. Cerulli, E., *Etiopi in Palestina*, i (1943), pp. 33–7. In the second half of the 15th century a small Ethiopian community was also formed in Lebanon, ibid., pp. 325–33.

[3] A constant theme in the accounts of European travellers since the 14th century is the absolute control which the Ethiopians were believed to have over the flow of the Nile, ibid., pp. 116–19. This early tradition, was current both among the Ethiopians themselves and the Egyptian Muslims, Al'-Umari, *Masalik*, tr. Gaudefroy-Demombynes, p. 30 and n. 1. Ethiopic hagiographies insist that one of the strategies used by Dawīt during his campaign against Egypt was to divert the flow of the river Nile, 'Gädlä Särṣä-Péṭros', f. 48[a]. 'Mäṣhafä-Ṭéfut', MS. Institute of Archaeology, Addis Ababa. 'Tarīkä-Nägäst', MS. Däbrä Marqos ff. 31–2. Pietro, who was in Ethiopia in Yishaq's reign, reported in 1432 that 'if it pleases the Prester John, he could very well make the river flow in another direction', Schefer, op. cit., p. 146. Even Zär'a-Ya'iqob refers to the same point in a letter he wrote to Jaqmaq, Al-Sakhawi, *Al-Tibr al-Masbuk* (Cairo, 1896), p. 70. This tradition was seriously considered by the strategists of the later Crusades, Hayton, 'La Flor des Estoires de la Terre d'Orient', in *Recueil des historiens des Croisades*: *Documents Arméniens* vi (1906), pp. 232, 241, 247. Blochet, E., ed., 'Neuf Chapitres du "Songe du viel Pélerin" de Philippe de Mézières relatif à l'orient', in *ROC*, iv (1889), pp. 373–4. Cerulli, op. cit., pp. 92–9, 155–61.

by the turn of the fourteenth century, when the Christian kingdom began to show a favourable response, isolated individuals from Europe could also penetrate the Ethiopian highlands.

The earliest known message to Ethiopia from a European monarch is the letter of King Henry IV, dated 1400, and addressed to the 'king of Abyssinia, Prester John'.[1] Before his coronation as Henry IV, the earl of Derby had been to the Holy Land in 1392–3, and had apparently heard of the Ethio-Egyptian hostilities in the early part of the reign of King Dawīt (1380–1412). In fact, he complimented Dawīt on his desire to liberate the Holy Sepulchre from the Muslims, and expressed his own hope of returning once again to Palestine. Apparently for security reasons, the bearer of the letter was instructed to convey in person Henry's real intentions, and it seems that he aimed at concluding an alliance for Dawīt's participation in a crusade. It is not known if Henry's letter ever reached Ethiopia.[2] However, Ethiopian traditions attribute very active external relations to the reign of King Dawīt: 'And the people of Rome, and Constantinople, and Syria, and Armenia, and Egypt, sent to Dawīt II, king of Ethiopia, saying ". . . the rulers of the Muslims rose against us, to destroy (our) Faith in Christ so that we may not call his Name and that we may not worship his venerable Cross. . . ." '[3] Soon after King Henry's letter, the first Ethiopian embassy to Europe is reported, in 1402.[4] Led by a Florentine called Antonio Bartoli, the embassy

[1] The Latin text of the letter is published with a short description in *Royal and Historical Letters during the Reign of Henry IV, King of England and of France, and Lord of Ireland*, ed. Hingeston, F. C., i, (*1399–1404*) (London, 1860), pp. 419–22. Cerulli, op. cit., pp. 201–2. For the European legend of the Prester John, see Marinescu, C., 'Le Prêtre Jean, son pays, explication de son nom', in *Bull. Sect. Hist. Acad. Roumaine*, t. x (1923), pp. 25–40, and also t. xxvi (1945), pp. 203–22. La Roncière, C. de, *La Découverte de l'Afrique au Moyen Âge*, in *Mém. Soc. Géog. Egypte*, t. v (1925), pp. 57–60. Slessarev, V., *Prester John, The Letter and the Legend* (Minneapolis, 1959). Beginning in the 14th century the name Prester John has been applied by European writers to the kings of Ethiopia, Cerulli, E., 'Il volo di Astolfo sull'Etiopia nell "Orlando Furioso" ', in *RRAL*, ser. 6, vol. viii (1932), p. 21. Id., *Etiopi in Palestina*, i (1943), pp. 77–9, 97–8.

[2] Apparently to avoid its possible interception by the Mamlukes the letter was entrusted to Archbishop John of Sultaniyyah, on the eastern land route. Another reason for the choice of this route seems to be the king's attempt to facilitate the reception of Dominican preachers from the diocese of Sultaniyyah in which Ethiopia seems to have been included by the Papal Bull of John XXII. According to the archbishop himself, however, the missionary programme was still unfulfilled in 1402, ibid., pp. 207–8. Cf. also Conti Rossini, 'Sulle Missioni domenicane in Etiopia nel secolo XIV', in *RRAL*, ser. 7, vol. i (1940), pp. 71–98.

[3] 'Mäṣhafä-Ṭéfut', MS. Institute of Archaeology, Addis Ababa.

[4] Cerulli, op. cit., p. 208. An itinerary dated in Dawīt's reign and believed to

also included some Ethiopians and thus began a new chapter of intermittent, but direct, contact with Europe which was given a particular impetus in the reigns of Yishaq and Zär'a-Ya'iqob.

Maqrizi accuses King Yishaq of writing to Europe proposing a grand Christian alliance against Islam.[1] According to Taghri Birdi (1409–70), Yishaq sent his envoys on the occasion of the Mamluke conquest of the kingdom of Cyprus.[2] Soon afterwards, in 1427, Alphonso V of Aragon received a delegation from Yishaq in the city of Valentia.[3] Probably the same envoys also called at other European courts. King Dawīt had already received some Italian craftsmen consisting mainly of Florentines.[4] Yishaq also had at his court a former Mamluke official in Upper Egypt and an Egyptian Christian with whose help he was reorganizing his army and the administration of his kingdom.[5] It is apparent that, more than anything else, the purpose of the delegations sent out to Europe was to ask for more artisans and military experts. In a letter (September 1450) addressed to Zär'a-Ya'iqob Alphonso refers to the men he had already sent to Ethiopia: '. . . those thirteen men, masters of the different arts, who were requested from us many years ago by you great brother. We sent them, and they died on the way being unable to pass [through the Muslim lands].'[6] The embassy of the Duke of Berry was much

have been the work of this embassy is published, with Prof. I. Guidi's introduction, by Jorga, N., 'Cenni sulle relazioni tra l'Abissinia e l'Europa cattolica nei secoli XIV–XV', in *Centenario delle nascita di Michele Amari* (Palermo, 1910), i, pp. 142, 144–50. La Roncière, op. cit., t. vi (1925), pp. 113–15. Crawford, *Ethiopian Itineraries*, pp. 28–37. In 1407 five Ethiopian pilgrims were in Bologna, Jorga, N., 'Notes et extraits pour servir à l'histoire des croisades', in *ROL*, iv (1896), p. 291.

[1] *Historia Regum Islamiticorum in Abyssinia*, ed. and tr. Rinck (Leiden, 1790), p. 8.

[2] *History of Egypt (1382–1469)*, tr. Popper, W., part 4, p. 60. The date of this conquest is 1424–6, Hitti, op. cit., pp. 697–9.

[3] La Roncière, op. cit., pp. 115–16.

[4] Conti Rossini, 'Un codice illustrato eritreo del secolo XV', in *Africa Italiana*, i (1927), p. 88. Cerulli, E., *Il libro etiopico dei miracoli di Maria* (1943), pp. 87–93. Pietro Rombulo, who was later sent by Zär'a-Ya'iqob on a mission to Rome and Naples, first went to Ethiopia towards the end of Dawīt's reign, Trasselli, C. 'Un Italiano in Etiopia nel secolo XV', in *RSE*, i (1941), p. 176.

[5] Maqrizi, op. cit., pp. 7–8.

[6] Creone, F., 'La politica orientale di Alfonso di Aragone', in *Archivio storico per le Provincie Napolitane*, vol. 27 (1902), p. 40. Alphonso's embassy to Yishaq was led by his own confessor, Joanne Boniae, who spoke Arabic. Their instructions were to proceed first to Jerusalem then to Ethiopia via Egypt, studying in the meantime the routes and military conditions of the country, La Roncière, loc. cit.

luckier. Consisting of the Neapolitan Pietro, a Spaniard, and a Frenchman, they apparently succeeded in reaching Ethiopia through Egypt in the reign of Yishaq. In 1432, two years after his companions had lost their lives on the way, Pietro was at Pera telling his story to Bertrandon de la Brocquière.[1] He was apparently busy recruiting craftsmen, and he even persuaded Bertrandon to go back with him to Ethiopia.[2] Pietro had already been in the country for some time before, and it seems that his mission was a result of Yishaq's embassy to Europe in 1427. It was probably this embassy of King Yishaq that the Mamlukes intercepted in 1429 on its way back to Ethiopia.[3] It was led by a Persian merchant, Al-Tabrizi. Before his mission to Europe Al-Tabrizi had settled in Ethiopia for some time and had attracted the king's attention for his resourceful pursuit of a mixed commercial enterprise. He kept a jeweller's shop and was also engaged in long-distance trade importing arms and other goods from Egypt and Arabia. Yishaq had apparently taken him into his confidence, and entrusted to him his vital mission to the Christian princes of Europe. Two Ethiopian monks accompanied him. It is apparent that on their way out they avoided the lower valley of the Nile and proceeded, according to Maqrizi, 'across the desert, beyond the oases . . .', and took a boat from a north African port. This was a long and arduous route, and they decided to return through Egypt in disguise. But, betrayed by one of Al-Tabrizi's slaves, they were arrested while disembarking in Alexandria. All their goods were confiscated, and Al-Tabrizi executed at a public square in Cairo, with the herald crying: 'This is the punishment of those who carry arms to the enemy, and who play with two religions.'[4]

Zär'a-Ya'iqob and his foreign relations

Like Dawīt and Yishaq before him, Zär'a-Ya'iqob pursued an active foreign policy. An essential part of this programme was his attempt to strengthen his control of northern Ethiopia, and to secure a direct

[1] Schefer, op. cit., pp. 142–8. [2] La Roncière, op. cit., p. 117.

[3] Maqrizi, extract in Quatremère, *Mémoires géographiques et historiques sur l'Égypte*, ii (1811), pp. 277–8. Taghri Birdi, *History of Egypt (1382–1469)*, tr. Popper, pt. iv, pp. 59–61. Wiet, G., 'Les relations égypto-abyssines sous les sultans mamlouks', in *BSAC*, iv (1938), pp. 127–8. Vacca, V., 'Le relazioni dell'Abissinia con l'Egitto nel secolo XV', in *Atti del 3° Congresso di studi coloniali* (1937), vi, pp. 218–23.

[4] Maqrizi describes the goods confiscated from the Ethiopian delegation at the time, '. . . a large number of uniforms on which were embroidered [the symbols of] the cross, and the name of the *Haty*, written in golden letters. These were uniforms for the soldiers', Quatremère, loc. cit.

outlet to the Red Sea. For over a century before his advent to power, the Christian tribes of Hamasén and Sära'é had undergone an active period of territorial expansion in what is today the Eritrean plateau. This had also been accompanied by the religious movement of the monastic centres in the outlying areas.[1] One of these monasteries was Däbrä Bīzän, first built in 1390/1[2] 'at a day's distance from the [sea] of Értra'.[3] Situated on the eastern edge of the Eritrean plateau, and overlooking the major route between the Dahlak islands and the highland provinces, Bīzän represented the movement of Christian expansion characteristic of the fourteenth century. In the early period of its development, its dependence on the kingdom for protection against its non-Christian neighbours was probably minimal. This seems to explain the hagiographical tradition that peaceful relations with the Muslims of the coastal areas could only be achieved through a bilateral agreement between Abba Fīlipos, its founder, and 'the ruler of the sea who resides in the country of Delk'.[4] During the whole period of the excommunication of the Éwosṭathians, who gradually took control of the Eritrean region, their religious influence was an ominous force, and a potential danger to the unity of the Christian kingdom. It seems quite possible to discern this delicate situation, not only in Dawīt's revision of his early anti-Éwosṭatéwos policy,[5] but also in Zär'a-Ya'iqob's complete identification with their religious views.

His pacification of the Éwostathian monasteries, and his re-unification of the Church in 1450, placed Zär'a-Ya'iqob in an excellent position to undertake a more radical policy in the Eritrean region than any of his predecessors. In 1448/9 he established military colonies in the districts of the Eritrean plateau. The colonists were recruited from a Shäwan tribe called Maya,[6] and their reception by the local people was clearly hostile. A hagiographical tradition of the late fifteenth century puts this in very good relief: '. . . the earth trembled on their arrival, and those who inhabit (the earth) were distressed . . . All the people left the country and fled out of fear . . .'[7] This was part of a

[1] See pp. 210–11.
[2] Kolmodin, *Traditions*, A23.
[3] *Gädlä Fīlipos* (Bīzän), ed. Conti Rossini, p. 91.
[4] Ibid., p. 106.
[5] See pp. 213–19.
[6] Kolmodin, op. cit., A24. The Maya were a pastoral people in the Shäwan district of Wäj. Armed with poisoned arrows their warriors were formidable among the Christian army in the Wars of Gragn, *Futuh al-Habasha*, tr. Basset, p. 82 n. 3; *Gädlä Yonas*, ed. and tr. Conti Rossini, pp. 181–3.
[7] Ibid., p. 244; cf. Kolmodin, op. cit., Tr.20–1.

general policy adopted by Zär'a-Ya'iqob throughout his empire, and was aimed at strengthening the defence of his kingdom and ensuring a more direct military control of the provinces.[1] In the Eritrean plateau, however, it was closely connected with his militant foreign policy and assumed a particular importance. He grouped together the districts of Shiré, Sära'é, Hamasén, and Bur, and placed them under one administration entrusted to the Bahir-Nägash.[2] These administrative and military rearrangements were only a prelude to a more aggressive move against the formerly independent Muslim rulers of the islands of Miṣiwwa and Dahlak. In 1449/50, only one year after the establishment of the military colonies in the highland districts, Zär'a-Ya'iqob started building his own sea-port at Girar, on the mainland opposite the island of Miṣiwwa.[3] It is apparent that Yishaq had also made a similar attempt before him.[4] Zär'a-Ya'iqob intended, however, a more permanent and effective occupation of the coastal districts. No doubt, this Christian activity was looked at with much hostility by the local Muslims, and it probably led to armed conflicts. In the end, it is reported that the islands of Miṣiwwa and Dahlak were pillaged in 1464/5, and that the Qadi lost his life in the encounter.[5]

An exactly similar pattern of development characterized Zär'a-Ya'iqob's relations with the Mamluke sultans of Egypt. It appears that, towards the beginning of his reign, he made a serious attempt to be on good terms with them. According to Maqrizi,[6] Zär'a-Ya'iqob wrote to Sultan Barsbay (1422–38) in the year 1437/8. The letter expressed friendly sentiments towards the ruler of Egypt, whom he entreated to protect his Christian subjects, and to respect their churches. This friendly message was also accompanied with a present 'consisting of gold, civet-cats, and other precious objects'. Only three years later, however, Patriarch Yohannis XI (1428–53) wrote to Zär'a-Ya'iqob announcing the demolition of the famous church of Miṭmaq (al-Magtas) on the orders of the same sultan.[7] When the news reached

[1] *Les Chroniques de Zar'a-Ya'eqob et de Ba'eda Maryam*, pp. 45–8.

[2] Ibid., pp. 47–8.

[3] Kolmodin, op. cit., A25, A32 n. 5.

[4] Miṣiwwa is mentioned among numerous other places where the king seems to have conducted military campaigns, Guidi, I, 'Le canzoni Ge'ez-Amarina in onore di re Abissini', in *RRAL*, ser. 4, vol. v (1899), p. 57.

[5] Kolmodin, op. cit., A25.

[6] Extract in Quatremère, *Mémoires*, ii, pp. 278–9.

[7] Cerulli, E., *Il libro etiopico dei miracoli di Maria*, p. 124; Perruchon, *Les Chroniques de Zar'a Ya'eqob*, p. 56.

him, Zär'a-Ya'iqob held a public mourning with his bishops, and immediately provided for the building of a new church, to be named Däbrä Miṭmaq (after the demolished Egyptian church), at Éguba in Tägulät, where he was camping at the time.[1] He then sent envoys to Sultan Jaqmaq (1438–53) with a strongly worded letter. The message reached Cairo in November 1443.[2] Zär'a-Ya'iqob declared to the sultan that the current persecutions against the Copts were a breach of the complete freedom of worship granted them by previous Muslim rulers. He complained strongly of the general insecurity of the Christians, whose possessions were unjustly taken from them, and whose churches were openly desecrated by the populace, with the full knowledge of the government officials. He reminded the sultan, too, that he had himself many Muslim subjects, and he was very kind to them. Unlike the restrictions on the Christians in Egypt, Muslims in Ethiopia dressed as they wished, rode well-harnessed horses and mules, and lived in peace. Not even the *Jiziya* was levied on them.[3] This Zär'a-Ya'iqob declared, was a great sacrifice to his treasury for, if he collected *Jiziya* from his Muslim subjects, his wealth would have been considerably increased. Zär'a-Ya'iqob also made a reference to the Nile, which, he said, rose in his realms, and it was within his power to divert its course. He desisted from doing it, only for the fear of God, and in consideration of the human sufferings that would result from it. Finally, he reminded Jaqmaq that his father Dawīt had corresponded with Barquq, and they had established peace and friendship between them.[4] He now asked for the preservation of the traditional amicable relations between the two countries based on mutual respect.

In reply to this message Jaqmaq sent an envoy to Ethiopia, with complimentary gifts to the king.[5] The envoy also carried a letter which rejected Zär'a-Ya'iqob's demand for the building and renewal of the churches in Egypt as extravagant. Disappointed at this reply, the king detained the envoy in Ethiopia. Relations between the two countries were at this low ebb when Zär'a-Ya'iqob's final victory over the Muslim king of Adal, Ahmad Badlay, in 1445, further increased Jaqmaq's fury against his Christian subjects. The inter-

[1] Ibid., pp. 56–7, 87–8.

[2] Al-Sakhawi, *Al-Tibr al-Masbuk* (Cairo, 1896), pp. 67–72. Wiet, G., op. cit., pp. 124–5.

[3] It is not clear what Zär'a-Ya'iqob meant by this.

[4] A reference, no doubt, to Dawīt's message in 1386; cf. p. 256 n. 1.

[5] The envoy's name is given as Yahya b. Ahmad b. Shadibek, Al-Sakhawi, op. cit., pp. 71–2.

mittent struggle with Badlay had started in earnest in 1443,[1] and was not completed until Badlay was defeated and killed in 1445, at the battle of Gomit in Däwaro.[2] Characteristically, Zär'a-Ya'iqob fully exploited the propaganda value of this success and, incorporated in the compilations of the miracles of St. Mary, it has become perhaps the best-known military campaign in the history of the Christian kingdom.[3] The Egyptian envoy was still in detention at the time of the Christian victory, and apparently suffered a number of indignities on the occasion. In retaliation, Jaqmaq called Patriarch Yohannis, and had him severely beaten, and threatened him even with death. He then sent another message to Ethiopia demanding the release of his envoy. Probably, the patriarch was also made to send his own request on behalf of the Muslim diplomat. After 'nearly four years' as Al-Sakhawi has it, Zär'a-Ya'iqob finally agreed to send his detainee back to Egypt.[4]

The news of Zär'a-Ya'iqob's success over his Muslim adversary in Adal, and his quarrel with the Mamluke sultan, reached Europe, and was received with much satisfaction. In a letter dated 3 July 1448, Jean de Lastic, the Grand Master of Rhodes, told Charles VII, King of France:

According to what has been reported to us by some Indian priests here in Rhodes, on the basis of veritable testimonies, the Prester John of the Indies has greatly demonstrated [his powers] over the Saracins, his

[1] This early conflict is not mentioned in the king's chronicles, and is very little known. It took place 9 years and 2 months after the advent of Zär'a-Ya'iqob to the throne. It apparently consisted of a surprise attack by Badlay on an unspecified Christian district where churches were burnt and many spoils carried away. It was a Muslim success, Cerulli, 'L'Etiopia del secolo XV in nuovi documenti storici', in *Africa Italiana*, v (1933), pp. 83–4, 88, 96.

[2] This is widely known, *Les Chroniques de Zar'a Ya'eqob*, pp. 57–67, 88–90; *Das Mashafa Milad und Mashafa Sellase* ed. Wendt, K., i (1962), pp. 15–20; Conti Rossini, 'Il convento di Tsana' in *RRAL*, ser. 5, vol. xix (1910), pp. 594–5; Cerulli, op. cit., pp. 84–7, and 96 n. 2.

[3] All the above stories on the campaigns published by Cerulli, quoted above, were taken from the Miracles of St. Mary, *Il libro etiopico dei miracoli di Maria*, p. 94. According to the chronicler the remains of Badlay's mutilated body were displayed in public in various parts of the country and his personal possessions distributed among the major royal churches, to be kept as souvenirs and displayed in public on the anniversaries of the victory, *Les Chroniques de Zar'a-Ya'eqob*, pp. 65–6, 117. The visitor to Däbrä Wärq is shown a finely worked shirt in iron chain, and a helmet which local monastic traditions claim belonged to Badlay, and were sent there by Zär'a-Ya'iqob, 'Gädlä Särṣä-Péṭros', f. 40^{b}.

[4] Al-Sakhawi, op. cit., p. 72; Wiet, op. cit., p. 125. It was probably after the return of this envoy that Jaqmaq forbade the patriarch to have any direct communications with Ethiopia except with special permission. The order was given in 1448, Al-Sakhawi, op. cit., p. 210; Wiet, op. cit., p. 122 n. 2.

neighbours, and he has killed many among them, above all those who claim descent from Muhammad . . .[1]

The 'house' of Wälasma, from which Badlay derived his origin, claimed Quraish or Hashemite descent from the Hijaz,[2] and the last phrase quoted above seems to refer to his defeat in 1445. The Grand Master also recounts Zär'a-Ya'iqob's quarrel with the Mamluke sultan, and gives some of the contents of the king's letter to Jaqmaq in 1443 with a remarkable degree of exactitude. But, carried away by his Crusader's spirit, and probably also by the patriotism of his Ethiopian informants, he declares that the Prester John would soon devastate Egypt, Arabia, and Syria. More important still, he also refers to the long detention of an Egyptian ambassador in Ethiopia. In reprisal against this, Jaqmaq had also arrested, we are told, an Ethiopian envoy,[3] on his way back from the Holy Land. Jean Germain, bishop of Chalon-sur-Saône probably had the same information from similar sources, and he repeated many of the Grand Master's points about the Prester John, in 1452.[4]

The Ethiopian informants of the Grand Master of Rhodes were probably isolated individuals who had crossed over to Rhodes from the Holy Land. But their report of Christian military success in Ethiopia greatly facilitated Zär'a-Ya'iqob's official mission to Europe in 1450. This time, the Ethiopian mission was entrusted to a Sicilian, Pietro Rombulo, who had been in Ethiopia since the last years of Dawīt's reign.[5] He had previously carried out a successful trade mission to India on behalf of the king, and he was now sent back to Europe as Zär'a-Ya'iqob's ambassador. He was accompanied by an Ethiopian priest, Firé-Mīka'él, and two other individuals.[6] The

[1] Marquis de Lastic, *Chronique de la Maison de Lastic*, i (1919), pp. 329–30; La Roncière, op. cit., p. 119.

[2] Maqrizi, *Historia Regum Islamiticorum in Abyssinia*, p. 17; Cerulli, E., 'Documenti arabi per la storia dell'Etiopia', in *MRAL*, ser. 6, vol. iv (1931), pp. 42–3.

[3] According to Al-Sakhawi Jaqmaq detained for a short time Zär'a-Ya'iqob's official who had accompanied Yahya back to Egypt, op. cit., p. 72.

[4] Schefer, C., 'Le discours du voyage d'outremer au très victorieux roi Charles VII, prononcé en 1452 par Jean Germain, évêque de Chalon' in *ROL*, iii (1895), p. 326; Cerulli, E., *Etiopi in Palestina*, i (1943), pp. 247–9.

[5] Trasselli, C., 'Un Italiano in Etiopia nel secolo xv: Pietro Rombulo di Messina', in *RSE*, i (1941), p. 176.

[6] Creone, F., 'La politica orientale di Alfonso di Aragone', pp. 71–2, 75–6. Alphonso's letter only mentions one other member of the delegation, Anomer Jandi, elsewhere referred to as 'Baumer Moro'. A third delegate, probably an Ethiopian Christian, called Demetrio is mentioned in an entry of Alphonso's financial aid to the mission, Minieri, R. C., 'Alcun fatti di Alfonso di Aragone dal

A fifteenth-century Madonna by an Ethiopian painter, Firé-Ṣiyon, who lived in the reign of Zär'a-Ya'iqob (1434–68)

principal object of the mission was apparently Pietro's own homeland where Alphonso of Aragon, who had already established good relations with Yishaq, also ruled as king of Naples and Sicily.

In his letter to Zär'a-Ya'iqob, Alphonso says that the Ethiopian mission came to his court 'having at first visited our lord, the Pope'.[1] This itinerary is fully confirmed by two short but valuable documents recently published by Charles-Martial de Witte. Pietro, Firé-Mīka'él, and 'Abumar Elzend' were given an audience by Pope Nicolas V (1447–55), and they proceeded to Naples with a papal escort and a letter of safe conduct.[2] But the purpose of the visit to Rome is not clearly known. Zär'a-Ya'iqob's strong monophysite stand rules out any theological and doctrinal reasons for his envoys calling at the papal court.[3] Right from the beginning of their contact with European Christians, the Ethiopians had always been impressed by the political and military aspects of an over-all Christian solidarity against the Muslim powers of the Near East, and the advantages of sharing in the superior technical advancement of European nations. This had been the underlying motive of the policies of both Dawīt and Yishaq, who sent their embassies to Europe asking for technical aid. Zär'a-Ya'iqob was only doing the same thing in 1450. With the advice of his Italian ambassador, Pietro Rombulo, the king did not hesitate to appeal for technical assistance even through the papacy, which was a strong European state in its own right.[4]

15 Aprile 1437 al 31 Maggio 1458', in *Archivio storico per le Province Napolitane*, vi (1889), p. 257.

[1] Creone, op. cit., p. 64.

[2] Ch.-M. de Witte, 'Une ambassade éthiopienne à Rome en 1450', in *Orientalia Christiana Periodica*, xxi (1956) pp. 295–7. The letter of safe conduct is dated 20 May 1450. Abumar Elzend is the Anomer Jandi or 'Baumer Moro' of the Neapolitan documents; de Witte reconstructs the name as Abu Omar al-Zendi, and suggests that he may have been a Muslim business associate of Pietro Rombulo, ibid., pp. 288–9.

[3] After a close investigation of the chronicles and the writings of Zär'a-Ya'iqob, Dillmann had already concluded in the last century that the king could not have had a favourable attitude towards the Council of Florence, *Über die Regierung, Insbesondere die Kirchenordnung, des Königs Zar'a Jacob*, (Berlin 1884), pp. 69–70. More recent studies of the history of the Council of Florence have only confirmed this conclusion, and they show that no official delegation of the Ethiopian Church took part in the Council, Creone, op. cit., pp. 56–64; Cerulli, E., 'L'Etiopia del secolo XV nel nuovi documenti storici', in *Africa Italiana*, v (1935), pp. 58–80; id., 'Eugenio IV e gli Etiopi al Concilio di Firenze nel 1441', in *RRAL*, ser. 7, vol. ix (1933), pp. 347–68; Hofmann, G., 'Le "Chiese" Copta ed Etiopica nel Concilio di Firenze', in *La civiltà cattolica*, ii (1942), pp. 141–6, 228–35; Gill, J., *The Council of Florence* (1959), pp. 321–7.

[4] Creone, op. cit., pp. 72–3, 87–8.

Zär'a-Ya'iqob's mission to Alphonso was apparently successful. Although he was himself in dire need of more skilled labour, Alphonso wrote to Zär'a-Ya'iqob and informed him that he was sending him the artisans and masons he requested, to please 'his dearest friend and brother'.[1] Pietro and his companions are also said elsewhere to have taken to Ethiopia 'many of our artisans who adorned Ethiopia with their art'.[2] Evidence for their safe arrival in Ethiopia is almost completely absent, and, neither his own writings, nor his chroniclers, make any reference to Zär'a-Ya'iqob's relations with Europe. But, according to the invaluable Vatican sources published by Charles-Martial de Witte, a certain George Sur was given a letter of safe conduct from Pope Nicolas V to go to Ethiopia. This happened soon after the departure of Zär'a-Ya'iqob's delegation from Rome, and the papal letter was dated January 1451.[3] Two other missions are also reported as having been sent to Zär'a-Ya'iqob from King Alphonso: the first led by one Michele Desiderio with a letter dated 18 January 1452; and the second under one Antonio Martinez with another letter dated 3 July 1453.[4] There is no trace of these missions in Ethiopia, or in Ethiopic documents known to us so far. Nevertheless, Giovanni Battista da Imola, who came to Ethiopia in 1482 and returned safely to Jerusalem in 1483, reported that he met there ten Italians who had been in the country for twenty-five years. This takes the date of their arrival in Ethiopia to about 1457, in the reign of Zär'a-Ya'iqob. One of the people thus reported, a man called Lujas Bartuto, is particularly said to have gone to Ethiopia with a papal letter.[5] It is not clear what this message was all about. But King Libnä-Dingil (1508–40), in the letter he sent to the Pope in 1526, refers to *a book* sent to Zär'a-Ya'iqob from the Vatican. Libnä-Dingil sent this document back to Rome, together with his other presents.[6] It has been surmised that this document could have been the Bull of Union signed by the Conferees of the Council of Florence.

[1] Ibid., p. 40.
[2] Trasselli, op. cit., p. 176.
[3] Ch.-M. de Witte, op. cit., pp. 290–1, 297–8.
[4] Creone, op. cit., pp. 76–80. La Roncière, op. cit., p. 121.
[5] Suriano, F., *Il Trattato di Terra Santa e dell'Oriente*, ed. Golubovich, G., (Milan, 1900), p. 86. Somigli, T., *Etiopia Francescana nei documenti dei secoli xvii e xviii*, pt. 1 (1928), p. lxxxviii. The Franciscan mission of 1482 to Ethiopia is the last significant event in the early contacts between Ethiopia and Christian Europe in the period under review. But it will be considered in another context in the next chapter, see pp. 290–2.
[6] Cf. Ramusio, *Navigazioni e viaggi*, i, p. 259.

PLATE 5

A fifteenth-century painting by the famous Brancaleone, also called Märqoréwos. The inscription below the picture of St. George reads: 'I, Märqoréwos, the Frank, drew this painting'

Despite the almost complete certainty that Union with Rome could not have been entertained in Ethiopia at the time, least of all by Zär'a-Ya'iqob,[1] it is nevertheless possible that the unofficial Ethiopian observers sent from Jerusalem may have reported the results of the Council to King Zär'a-Ya'iqob. And there is nothing to preclude even a copy of the Bull of Union from having reached the Ethiopian royal Court.

In the traditions of the Ethiopian Church, the reigns of Dawīt and Zär'a-Ya'iqob are particularly noted for the arrival in Ethiopia of numerous relics, including a piece of the True Cross. These relics are believed to have been deposited at Gishän, the mountain prison of the royal princes. Zär'a-Ya'iqob is said to have entrusted the safe keeping of these treasures to the local clergy with the following message: '[The kings of the Franks] sent Us a piece of the True Cross. Enclosed within a golden box, it is placed inside another cross of gold of marvellous workmanship, and which can stand erect on a golden stand, provided for it by the wise men of the Franks.'[2] It is probable that the story of the importation of these objects from Christian Europe in the reign of Zär'a-Ya'iqob largely refers to the mission led by Pietro Rombulo.

Although the advent of Europeans in Ethiopia in this period has left very little trace in Ethiopian documents, there can be no doubt that in the first half of the fifteenth century, precarious, but none the less continuous, relations were established between Europe and Ethiopia. The most authentic pieces of evidence for this are the map known as *Egyptus Novelo* (*c.* 1454) and Fra Mauro's *Mappomondo* of 1460, which could only have been the outcome of many years of geographical knowledge about the Ethiopian highlands.[3]

[1] Cf. p. 265 n. 3.

[2] Wright, *Catalogue*, Or. 481, ff. 208^{b}–209^{a}. Together with the piece of the True Cross the king is said to have sent to Gishän many other relics from the remains of the saints of the early Christian Church. A whole cycle of hagiographical traditions has developed around these relics, allegedly brought in the reigns of Dawīt and Zär'a-Yaiqob, and the possession of which is claimed by various monasteries, 'Gädlä Täkästä-Birhan,' MS. Däbrä Dīma, ff. 1^{a}, 16^{b}–17; 'Gädlä Särṣä-Péṭros', MS. Däbrä Wärq, ff. 47–50; M. Cohen, 'Dabra Worq', in *Mélanges René Basset*, i (1923), pp. 148–50; 'Mäṣhafä-Ṭéfut', MS. Institute of Archaeology, Addis Ababa; cf. also Basset, R., *Études*, p. 95; Cerulli, E., *Etiopi in Palestina*, i (1943), pp. 267–8.

[3] Berchet, G., 'Lettera sulle cognizioni che i Veneziani avevano dell'Abissinia', in *BSGI* ii (1869), pp. 151–70; La Roncière, op. cit., pp. 123–35; cf. also Conti Rossini, 'Un Codice illustrato eritreo del secolo XV', in *Africa italiana*, i (1927), pp. 83–97.

CHAPTER VIII

Fifty Years of Decline

(1477–1527)

THE internal struggle for royal succession among the descendants of Yikunno-'Amlak had been one of the major factors in the weakness of the dynasty in the first decade following the death of its founder.[1] The problem had never been entirely absent during the history of the next two centuries, and there were frequent signs of political unrest on the accession to power of many of the kings, even during the fourteenth century and in the first half of the fifteenth. By the last quarter of the fifteenth century, however, problems of succession assumed a very serious character, and in the end precipitated the decline of the Christian kingdom—a decline which served as an essential prelude to the remarkable military success of Ahmad Gragn.

We have already looked briefly at the constituent parts of the royal Court during the reign of Amdä-Ṣiyon.[2] Much of the struggle for succession was conducted there, and, to be able to appreciate the anatomy of medieval Ethiopian politics, we must now consider the development in the organization of the mobile Court.[3] The life and

[1] Taddesse Tamrat, 'The Abbots of Däbrä Hayq', pp. 91–3.

[2] See pp. 103–6.

[3] Material for this reconstruction has been obtained from isolated references in the chronicles and the abundant hagiographical traditions. Short unpublished accounts entirely devoted to the organization of the Court and the description of royal officials are available in the MS. collections of the British Museum, the Bodleian, and the Cambridge University Library: perhaps a copy of the earliest version is found in MS. Bruce, 88, Bodl., ff. 30^b–34^b, described in Dillmann, A., *Catalogus Codicum manuscriptorum Bibliothecae Bodleianae Oxoniensis*, pars vii. *Codicis aethiopici* (Oxford, 1848), no. 29. The same version is also available at the British Museum, Wright, W., *Catalogue of the Ethiopic Manuscripts in the British Museum* (1877), Or. 821, ff. 99–108^b. What appears to be a more recent version is given in the same MS., ff. 30^b–35. At the Cambridge University Library, Or. 1873, ff. 3–11^b also contains this later version, and is described by Ullendorff, E., *Catalogue of the Ethiopian Manuscripts in the Cambridge University Library*, pp. 62–3. It is also this later version that has been published according to different copies available in European libraries: Varenbergh, J., 'Studien zur abessinischen Reichsordnung (Sir'ata Mangist)', in *ZA*, xxx (1915–16), pp. 1–45; Guidi, I., 'Contributi alla storia letteraria di Abissinia', in *RRAL*, ser. 5, vol. xxxi (1922),

person of the monarch constituted the focal point of the vast Christian empire of medieval Ethiopia. This was true in more than a literal sense, and the concentric arrangement of the royal camp was only its physical expression.

The organization of the Court

The private quarters of the king and his family consisted of two concentric enclosures at the heart of the huge conglomeration of people assembled at the court.[1] The inner enclosure, separated from the outer one with curtains, or with a fence in cases of a longer sojourn at the site, was exclusively set aside for the use of the king, and all the tents pitched there served his personal convenience. The king's special confidants, literally called 'inner pages', officiated here and provided for his personal needs. Thirteen separate exits, each with its own name, led to the outer enclosure. The principal exit, *Widinäsh Däj*, probably opened in a westerly direction,[2] in a straight line with the residence of the king at the centre. On either side of this principal gate were six others, equidistant from each other, and thus constituting the remaining twelve exits of the inner

pp. 65–89. It is apparent, however, that what we have in these short accounts is only a small section of a much fuller treatise on the subject, now probably lost to us for ever. In Wright, op. cit., Or. 821, ff. 3^b–5^a, and Varenbergh, op. cit., pp. 12–15, we only have what appears to be a list of contents of a more complete description of the Court, and the institutions of the kingdom. Contemporary accounts which have come down to us intact are the description of Zär'a-Ya'iqob's court, *Chroniques de Zar'a-Ya'eqob*, pp. 23–45; and Alvarez's valuable description of Libnä-Dingil's royal camp, *The Prester John of the Indies*, i, pp. 267–72; ii, pp. 437–45.

1 See the accompanying figure. A distinction between the two enclosures seems to be implied in the inconsistent use of the terms *Jägol* and *Mäggaräja. Jägol*, used in general terms, apparently referred to the royal enclosures as a whole, but in the specific description of the arrangement of the Court it clearly indicated the outer enclosure only. *Mäggaräja* is what Alvarez calls 'mandilate' (= Mänṭola'it) and referred to the curtains drawn all around the royal tents. Here again there are inconsistencies in the use of *Mäggaräja* which sometimes also seems to be applied to the outer enclosure. The difficulties of the scribe in giving a consistent usage to these terms probably arose from what Alvarez describes as follows: '. . . they surround (the tents) all with (tall) curtains, which they call *mandilate*; . . . If (the king) is going to remain several days they surround these tents with a big hedge, which will be half a league round', op. cit. ii, p. 437.

2 The Ethiopic descriptions do not give any directions. There was probably no hard and fast rule about this, and the terrain of the particular site where they camped at any particular time may have affected the arrangement. Here, for purposes of clarity, I have adopted Alvarez's direction, 'the principal (gate) is to the *west*', loc. cit.

Key to the Gates
1. Widinàsh Dàj
2. a: Right) Sàrgwan Dàj
   b: Left)
3. a: Màbi'i Dàj
   b: Shilimat Dàj
4. a: Right) Màggaràja Dàj
   b: Left)
5. a: Màsqal Dàj
   b: Willaj Dàj
6. a: Gimja Maryam Dàj
   b: Iyasus Dàj
7. a: Qulf Dàj
   b: Màr'id Dàj

Key to the Tents
Q₁ = Qàgn Bà'altèhat (Queen of the Right)
Q₂ = Gira Bà'altèhat (Queen of the Left)
Q₃ = Bà'alta-Shihna (Junior Queen of the Right)
QM = Queen Mother
AQ = Aqabè-Sà'at
B₁ = Qàgn Bihtwàddàd
B₂ = Gira Bihtwàddàd
EB = Egyptian Bishop

N

Camps

Open space: Guards

PRISON

Court of Justice △

Chief Justice △

△ 'Church of Justice'

Chief △ Justice

Court of Justice △

PRISON

Open space: Guards

Camps

△ 'Church of the Market Square'

LIONS' CAGE ⊠

THE KING

SAQALA

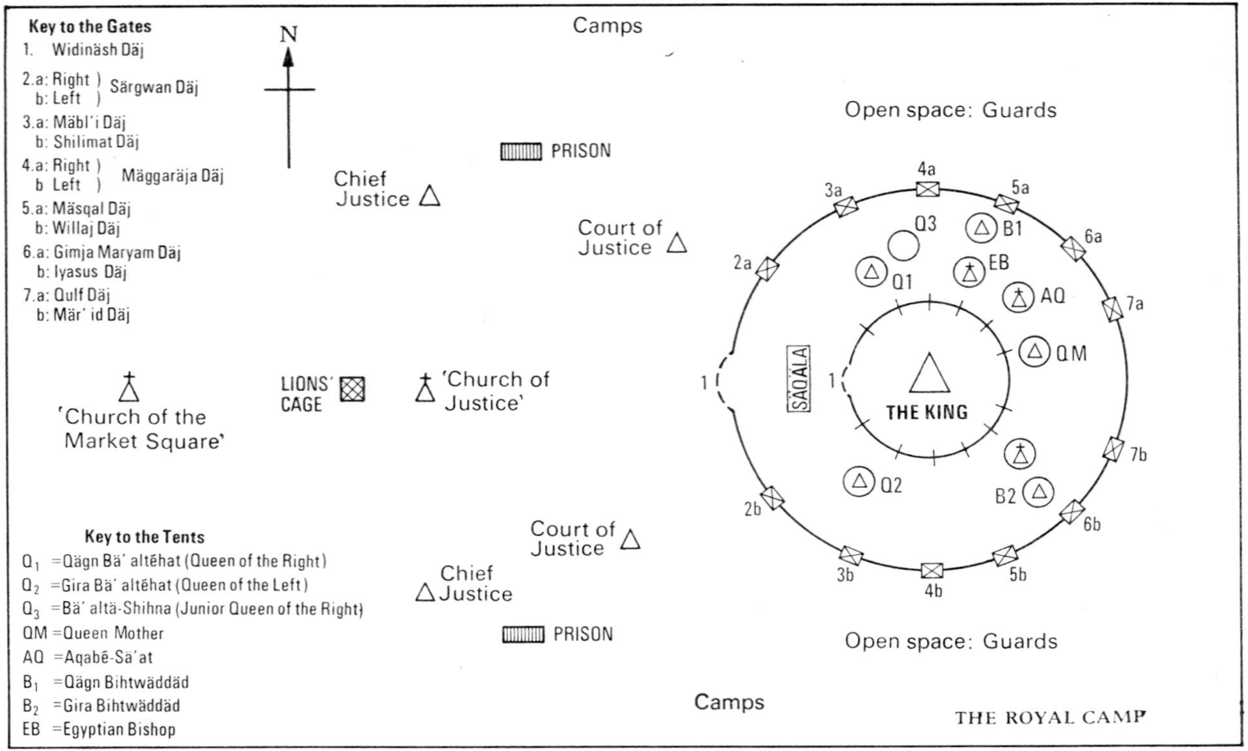

THE ROYAL CAMP

enclosure.[1] The twin organization of the royal court, and of the king's officials, into those of the Right and of the Left is basically derived from this characteristic arrangement of the six gates on either side of the principal *Widinäsh Däj*. Each of these exits of the inner enclosure was closely guarded by high-ranking officials of the royal guard. Admittance to the royal presence was by sole permission of the king, and the use of each entrance was prescribed for particular members of the royal Court from the outer enclosure.

The outer enclosure itself was a direct duplicate of its inner counterpart. It had thirteen gates corresponding to those described above, and followed the same twin arrangement of the Court into Right and Left. All around the fence of the outer enclosure, and particularly at the gates, were stationed numerous guards,[2] specially assigned to cover particular sides of the Court. The area within the enclosure between the *Mäggaräja* and the *Jägol* was very extensive,[3] and in it were pitched many tents on either side. The treasure houses of the king, guarded and administered by a special group of officials, formed a prominent part of the collection of tents.[4] More important still were the tents of the Queen Mother, and those of the queens of the Right and of the Left. Normally, the number of the king's wives was three.[5] Each with her own title: the *Gira-Bä'altéhat*, the queen of

[1] Alvarez was told that the royal enclosures had a total number of 12 gates. He only saw four, 'for they let no one pass (behind)', loc. cit. The existence of a principal gate, *Widinäsh Däj*, at the front of the court, besides the twelve other gates, is however very clear from the available Ethiopic descriptions, cf. Bodl., MS. Bruce 88, f. 32^{b}; Or. 821 (B.M.), f. 104^{b}.

[2] A partial list of the royal guards gives a total number of over 13,000 Bodl., MS. Bruce 88, f. 33^{b}.

[3] Alvarez estimated the circumference as one league, loc. cit. The editors of his work have taken the Portuguese league as equivalent to '3.2 geographical miles', op. cit., i, p. 56 n. 4.

[4] Bodl. MS. Bruce 88, f. 32^{b}. Here the various tents are collectively said to belong to the *Mängist Bét*, a name used by the apparently later versions for a group of tents in the outer enclosure, together with others which had similar functions such as *Bäräkät Bét*, and *Mär'id Bét*, ibid., f. 33^{b}. Zär'a-Ya'iqob's chronicler also gives them considerable prominence, *Chroniques*, pp. 37–8. Alvarez gives a vivid description of how they were transported, op. cit. ii, pp. 447–8.

[5] Amdä-Ṣiyon had one principal queen and many wives and concubines, *Histoire des guerres d'Amde-Siyon*, ed. and tr. Perruchon, J., pp. 325–6; Conti Rossini, 'L'evangelo d'oro', pp. 202–6, and here his principal queen is given the title of *Bä'altä-Bīhat*. His son Säyfä-Ar'ad is accused of marrying three wives, *Gädlä Fīlipos* (Asbo), ed. Conti Rossini, pp. 224–5, (text). For Dawīt and Zär'a-Ya'iqob see p. 220 n. 2 and p. 243 n. 2. During his visit Alvarez only noticed Libnä-Dingil's queen who camped on the left side of the court, and he believed that the king was strictly monogamous, op. cit., p. 193. His acquaintance was probably with the king's favourite queen Säblä-Wängél, a Tigré princess, whose

the Left, who camped just outside the *Shilimat Däj* of the inner enclosure, and used this gate to communicate with the royal tents at the centre; the *Qägn-Bä'altéhat*, the queen of the Right, and the *Bä'altä-Shihna*, a junior queen of the Right, had their tents just outside the *Mäbl'i Däj*. The tents of the Queen Mother, who apparently kept some of the king's children with her, were much more in the rear and were significantly pitched near the so-called *Qulf Däj* (lit. = locked gate).[1] Within the enclosure, the retainers of these queens only included their special guards, the *Žandäräba*, their ladies in-waiting, and their household servants.[2] Besides the royal kitchens, pitched within the *Jägol* on both sides of the court, which were responsible for the daily banquets, each of the queens also prepared food for the king's table in her own quarters.[3]

The royal chapels were also pitched within the *Jägol* on both sides.[4] It is apparent that the leading members of the clergy serving each of these chapels also camped around them. But the most important ecclesiastical official in court was the *Aqabé-Sä'at*, the titular head of the island monastery of Däbrä Hayq,[5] and his tents were often

courageous activities during the Muslim wars are attested by the chronicles, and the Portuguese writers, and who was the mother of Gälawdéwos and Minas, both of whom reigned after the war. But a document about the pre-Gragn part of the reign speaks of the deaths of a *Bä'altä-Shihna* (a junior queen of the Right), and another Queen Qafo, *Liber Aksumae*, ed. Conti Rossini, p. 69 (text). It is difficult, however, to tell whether these were queens of his father Na'od, or of Libnä-Dingil.

[1] These locations of the tents of the Queens of the Right and of the Left are given in Bodl., MS. Bruce 88, f. 33. Or. 821 (BM.), f. 106[a]. As to the tents of the Queen Mother, however, no explicit mention of the site is given. But it is said that she made use of the *Qulf-Däj*, where I assume her tents were pitched.

[2] Cf. also Alvarez, op. cit. ii, p. 443.

[3] This is clearly brought out by Zär'a-Ya'iqob's chronicler, where it appears that additional contributions to the royal banquets were also supplied from other quarters, *Les Chroniques*, pp. 38–9; cf. also Alvarez, op. cit., pp. 437–8.

[4] The number of the royal chapels at the Court increased through the years. Amdä-Ṣiyon, and probably also the kings before him, only had a chapel dedicated to Jesus, and this was taken along even on military expeditions, Perruchon, J., *Histoire des guerres d'Amde-Siyon, roi d'Éthiopie*, in *JA*, ii (1889), pp. 389, 408; *Gädlä Yafqirännä-'Igzī'*, ed. Wajnberg, i., pp. 18–22 (text). Dawīt established the Chapel of the Cross, and Zär'a-Ya'iqob that of St. Mary, Cerulli, E., *Il libro etiopico dei miracoli di Maria*, pp. 121–2. Säyfä-'Ar'ad's other chapel is not attested anywhere else. In the early 16th century, Alvarez does not mention the Chapel of Jesus, and adds another in the area of the royal kitchens, 'a church of St. Andrew and it is called the cook's church', op. cit. ii, pp. 437–8. Outside the enclosure in a straight line with the royal tent but very far from it he mentions 'the church of the justices', and further still 'the market square church', ibid., p. 442.

[5] Hagiographical traditions, probably of the 15th century, claim that the title was given to Īyäsus-Mo'a's descendants by Yikunno-Amlak himself, in return

pitched near the chapel of St. Mary, on the Right. The Egyptian bishop used the *Mäsqäl Däj*, and probably kept an official tent near the Chapel of the Cross.[1] Some of the highest military and court officials could also camp within the *Jägol*, though unaccompanied by their respective followers who had to camp far away, outside the enclosure, on the same side of the court as their masters. Among these were the two highest military officials of the kingdom, the *Bihtwäddäd* of the Right and of the Left.[2] These officials were thus given official premises within the *Jägol* and, outside, on the outskirts of the whole royal camp, their numerous troops pitched their tents and protected the kingdom.[3] Both for their admittance into the royal presence as stated above, and for their communication outside the *Jägol*, each of these camping units within the enclosure utilized corresponding gates specially assigned for it.

The king's numerous vassals, his district and provincial governors who camped in the extensive field outside, each with his large following, were also admitted into the *Jägol* through particular gates prescribed for them—either on the Right or on the Left. The two front gates—each called *Särgwan Däj*—on either side of the principal *Widinäsh Däj* were the most important, and were apparently in frequent use on solemn occasions. Admittance through them is explicitly said to have been possible by sole permission of the king.

for the monk's spiritual help in the dynastic struggle of 1270, *Gädlä Īyäsus-Mo'a*, ed. and tr. S. Kur, pp. 23–6. It is, however, with *Aqabé-Sä'at* Säräqä-Birhan (d. 1403), an intimate friend of King Dawīt, that the political significance of the title emerges. Zär'a-Ya'iqob enhanced its importance by making *Aqabé-Sä'at* Amha-Īyäsus, his most trusted courtier, *Les Chroniques de Zar'a Ya'eqob*, pp. 7–8, 27–9. At the time of Alvarez's visit the office had considerable influence and he calls the *Cabeata*, 'the second man in these Kingdoms', op. cit. i, p. 270. For a complete review of the importance of the office of the *Aqabé-Sä'at* from the thirteenth century onwards see Taddesse Tamrat, 'The Abbots of Däbrä Hayq 1248–1535', in the *Journal of Ethiopian Studies*, viii, no. 1 (1970).

[1] Alvarez reports that during his visit the bishop's camp was outside the enclosure, and suggests that his camp was on the left, loc. cit. His particular use of the *Mäsqäl Däj* is however given in the Ethiopic description, Bodl., MS. Bruce 88, f. 33[a].

[2] The earliest time we have a mention of these twin officials is in the reign of Zär'a-Ya'iqob, *Chroniques*, pp. 9–10, 12. This should not be taken, however, as suggesting that he was the first to institute them. The context in which they are mentioned clearly indicates that they were of a much older origin. Their respective duties are described as follows, 'One (of them) conducts military campaigns, and the other protects the kingdom, and he camps at the outskirts of the royal camp', Or. 821 (B.M.), f. 32[b]. Alvarez reports precisely the same thing, op. cit., pp. 270.

[3] Ibid., pp. 336–7, 443–4.

The tributary vassals of the king and his provincial governors passed through these gates to present their tributes, or whenever they needed to see their sovereign. Once admitted through, however, another permission was specially required to leave the enclosure.[1]

The royal Court maintained its meticulous rules and characteristic organization wherever it moved, and had exactly the same functions as a fixed city.[2] Despite its mobility,[3] it was deeply rooted in the country. Whereas its own movements brought it to the different parts of the Christian empire, the diverse elements of the king's subjects were also represented in the vast crowd always assembled around the royal enclosures. This ethnic and linguistic diversity is clearly brought out by Zär'a-Ya'iqob's chronicler in his description of ceremonious acclamations of the royal troops in the presence of the king: 'And they sing (his glory) each in the language of his country.'[4] The king and his family formed the nucleus of this complex assortment of

[1] 'They shall be admitted through the left *Särgwan Däj* by permission of the king; and they shall not leave without his orders . . . they may not enter or leave through the right *Särgwan Däj* without the king's will', Bodl., MS. Bruce 88, ff. 32^{b}–33^{a}. Or 821 (B.M.), ff. 104^{b}–105^{a}. It is most likely that Alvarez's most scrupulous report of the formalities of admittance into the royal enclosure is a reference to this rule, op. cit. i, pp. 282–3.

[2] Cf. ibid., pp. 335–7, 442–4.

[3] The mobile character of the Court has already been referred to above in Chapter III. Yet particular sites are specially associated with some of the medieval kings, and a general southward movement of these sites can be detected from the beginning of the 14th century onwards. At one time Widim-Rä'ad (1294–1314) seems to have had his Court in the region of Gishé, northern Mänz. Cf. *Gädlä Bäṣälotä-Mīka'él*, p. 9. Both his chronicler and Al-'Umari locate Amdä-Ṣiyon's Court at Mär'adé, where Abba Samuél (Waldibba) later visited Dawīt, apparently in Shäwa, *Gädlä Samu'él*, p. 14. Amdä-Ṣiyon is also said to have held Court at a place called *Säwan* in Shäwa, according to one tradition 3 days' journey from Däbrä Asbo, *Gädlä Filipos*, p. 209; *Gädlä Bäṣälotä-Mīka'él*, p. 25. A hundred years later the same place is mentioned as the winter resort of King Yishaq, 'Gädlä Abba Gīyorgīs of Gascha', MS. Hayq, ff. 38^{b}–39^{a}. His father, Dawīt, is also said to have resided at *Ṭobya*, somewhere east of Däbrä Sīna, *Chroniques de Zar'a-Ya'eqob*, p. 152. Cf. also *Futuh al-Habasha*, tr. Basset, p. 272. He also had another residence further south at Ṭilq in Fätägar, where Zär'a-Ya'iqob was born, *Chroniques*, p. 67. La Roncière has identified this name with the 'pian de Tich' of Fra Mauro's map, *La Découverte de l'Afrique au Moyen Âge*, ii (1925), p. 128. Both Zär'a-Ya'iqob and his son Bä'idä-Maryam also resided there at times, and Iskindir (1478–94) was born there, *Chroniques*, pp. 155–6. Zär'a-Ya'iqob frequented *Tägulät*, ibid., pp. 55–7; he spent the last 14 years of his reign in his newly built residence at Däbrä Birhan, ibid., pp. 78–9. A list of the wintering areas of Na'od (1494–1508) and Libnä-Dingil (1508–40) also shows that there were particular sites favoured by these kings, *Liber Aksumae*, ed. Conti Rossini, p. 69 (text).

[4] *Chroniques de Zar'a-Ya'eqob*, p. 36.

PLATE 6

The only gate to the mountain top

A view of the south-western side of the mountain

The Royal Prison of Amba-Gishän

ethnic and religious communities. But the geometric unity imposed on the royal Court by its concentric arrangement belied the divergent interests of which it always consisted. Each of the camping units within the royal enclosure[1]—particularly the tents of the Queen Mother—represented a separate community of political interests, which were reflected from the royal tents at the centre, right down to the outermost reaches of the royal camp as a whole. Essentially, this was the basis of the chronic struggle for royal succession in medieval Ethiopia.

Amba Gishän, and problems of succession to the throne

A king was normally succeeded by one of his own sons. Except in cases where he died without male issue, this was almost always the case in the whole period covered by this study.[2] Normally too, the eldest son appears to have had priority of succession over his younger brothers. But although this was generally the outcome, it was only reached after serious dynastic conflicts among the princes, and their respective supporters. For all its unique importance in the constitution of medieval Ethiopia, the well-known institution of the Royal Prison of Mount Gishän[3] was only effective in excluding the distant

[1] Each of these units is represented by a small circle in the graphic illustration of the royal camp on p. 270.

[2] One major exception, of which the true story is still unknown, stands out against this rule: It is not clear whether Widim-Rä'ad (1299–1314) assumed power on the deaths of all his nephews (= brothers?), or if any of the latter had left any successors at all, cf. Taddesse Tamrat, 'The Abbots of Däbrä Hayq 1248–1535', pp. 92–3. Another doubtful case is the accession of Yishaq (1413–1430) on the death of his brother Téwodros. Téwodros was a grown man at the time of his death, and it is unlikely that he did not have sons of his own to succeed him, cf. p. 220 n. 4.

[3] For a description of this place see Alvarez, op. cit., i, pp. 237–48; Almeida, *Some Records of Ethiopia 1593–1646*, extracts tr. by Beckingham and Huntingford (1954), pp. 97–102. Almeida's is a much better (probably eyewitness) account. According to him Lalībäla built the first church on the top of the mountain. Alvarez was, however, told that one of Lalībäla's predecessors, King Yimrha, first instituted the Royal Prison, by divine inspiration. Although from the rest of his account Alvarez seems to have had extracts of the king's *Gädl* read for him, Yimrha's connection with Gishän is not mentioned in the copy of the *Gädl* I was able to consult at Lalībäla. Considering the frequent succession problems in the Zagwé period it seems unlikely that the institution of a Royal Prison had ever occurred to the Zagwé kings. But the idea of a mountain prison was not new, and Yitbaräk is said to have once detained Yikunno-Amlak on a mountain top at Mäloṭ, in Wadla, *Gädlä Īyäsus-Mo'a*, p. 20 (tr.). The organization of Gishän as a Royal Prison probably dates from the troubled days following the death of Yikunno-Amlak, Ludolf, H., *A New History of Ethiopia* (1684), pp. 195–7. Although there are many references to the detention of 'Isra'elites' on Mt.

relatives of a deceased monarch from taking active part in the struggle for his succession. His sons, his surviving brothers, and their immediate descendants were each a rallying point for conflicting political groups in the royal Court, who vied for a handsome share in the political and economic preferment of the next reign. There is a general tendency in the official chronicles to play down such conflicts. Despite this, however, many isolated notes strongly indicate that a major struggle for power often preceded the accession of a new monarch in medieval Ethiopia.[1]

Of all the descendants of Yikunno-Amlak, in the male line, only the reigning monarch and his sons lived outside the Royal Prison of Mount Gishän. The children of a king spent the early part of their childhood in the royal Court, in the care of their own mothers and the Queen Mother. When they became older, the sons were apparently sent to one of the royal estates in the country, where they were entrusted to an important official who was also governor of the area. Closely guarded, the young princes grew there, undergoing a period of training in the art of warfare and horsemanship: '. . . And in this period [of his youth, Libnä-Dingil] completely preoccupied himself with riding horses, throwing arrows, and hunting, because this is the way in which the sons of kings were brought up until they were well versed at the art of Government.'[2] The site where the princes were kept probably varied according to the wishes of the king. Bä'idä-Maryam grew up at Zängo near Yäläbash in Fäṭägar, a frontier site just established by his grandfather, Dawīt (1380–1412), and where his father, Zär'a-Ya'iqob, was also born.[3] It is apparent, however, that

Gishän, I have not been able to obtain an Ethiopic description of the Royal Prison as such. From the days of Dawīt and Zär'a-Ya'iqob onwards the place is specially noted for the many relics—a piece of the True Cross included—which these kings are believed to have received from abroad and deposited at Gishän, cf. p. 267 n. 2. This religious legend has since completely replaced the historic importance of the site as a Royal Prison, of which neither the local elders nor the officials of the churches, to whom I spoke there, seem to have any recollections at all.

[1] Traditional signs of such conflicts—in the available sources—are completely absent only in the case of Amdä-Ṣiyon (1314–44) and his son Säyfä-Ar'ad (1344–71). A hagiographical note about the life of Patriarch Matéwos (1378–1408) seems to indicate that Säyfä-Ar'ad's sons—Niwayä-Maryam and Dawīt—had both contested the succession. Niwayä-Maryam (1371–80) took the throne, but already before the end of his reign, the Patriarch is said to have had a revelation that Dawīt would soon take over, Budge, E. A. W., *The Book of the Saints of the Ethiopian Church*, ii, p. 454.

[2] 'La storia di Libna Dingil, re d'Etiopia', ed. and tr. Conti Rossini, in *RRAL*, iii (1894), pp. 622, 630–1.

[3] *Chroniques de Zar'a-Ya'eqob*, pp. 67, 91, 155.

later in the fifteenth century the guardianship of the royal princes was assigned to the governor of Gänz[1]—the *Gänz Gärad*. Bä'idä-Maryam's sons were brought up there, and *Gänz Gärad* Matéwos was responsible for them.[2] The young boys regularly visited the royal Court with him, and there they had a special camping site reserved for them, apparently in the neighbourhood of the tents of the Queen Mother and those of the *Aqabé-Sä'at*.[3] Small private schools were run for them in the royal enclosure, where they received religious instruction, and were taught how to read, and probably also how to write. During their stay in the country too, their retinue included prominent churchmen who continued the religious and literary instruction of the young princes. This assignment of educating the king's children was apparently given to the best scholars of the day, and this probably accounts for the persistent tradition of considerable religious learning reported about many of the medieval kings and other members of their family.[4] Abba Giyorgis of Gascha, the author of many religious works, started his career as a teacher of the children of King Dawīt, at the royal Court.[5] One of Bä'ida-Maryam's chroniclers was also entrusted with the care of the king's sons, and resided with them in Gänz.[6] Probably, too, a prince could sometimes be sent to an ordinary monastic school, where he studied as long as his father lived. For security reasons and to avoid embarrassment, his identity would only be known to the abbot and the local officials,

[1] *Gänz* was apparently a district between the headwaters of the rivers Gudru, Awash, and Gibé, to the north-west of Hadya, and east of Damot, cf. *Gädlä-Mäb'a-Ṣiyon*, pp. 25 (text), 79 (tr.). Alvarez, op. cit., p. 454; *Futuh al Habasha*, tr. Basset, pp. 83 n. 2, 377–98. Zär'a-Ya'iqob's town of Jībat was probably in *Gänz*.

[2] 'Histoire d'Eskender, d'Amda-Seyon II, et de Na'od', ed. and tr. Perruchon, in *JA*, ser. 9, vol. iii (1894), pp. 345–7. It is most likely that this Matéwos was the same official—elsewhere called Žandäräba Matéwos—who brought the good news of the birth of his first son, Iskindir, to King Bä'idä-Maryam, *Chroniques*, pp. 155–6. Apparently he was a personal attendant of Queen Romna at first, and was later promoted to the more prestigious office of *Gänz Gärad*.

[3] Bodl., MS. Bruce 88, f. 33ª.

[4] The case of Zär'a-Ya'iqob is well known. The authorship of two prayers *Mälki'a-Mīka'él* and *Mälki'a-Qurban* are attributed to his son, and successor Bä'idä-Maryam. The latter's son, Na'od, is also represented as a deeply religious man who composed *Mälki'a-Maryam*, and *Täfäsihī Maryam*, Conti Rossini, 'Il libro delle leggende e tradizioni abissini', p. 711. Na'od is particularly said to have excelled in the well-known Ethiopic religious poetry, *Qiné*, and to have actively participated in the religious songs and chanting of the church, 'Gädlä Märha-Kristos', pp. 289–94. 'Tarīkä-Nägäst', MS. Däbrä Ṣigé, p. 57.

[5] See p. 224 n. 3.

[6] Perruchon, 'Histoire d'Eskender', loc. cit.

and as soon as his father, the king, died troops would be sent to fetch the young prince to the Royal Prison of Amba Gishän. This last pattern seems to emerge from the story of the early life of Zär'a-Ya'iqob at the schools of Aksum and Däbrä Abbay.[1]

Zär'a-Ya'iqob was the youngest son of King Dawīt. During the lifetime of his father, and so long as all his elder brothers were alive, there was probably little prospect of his eventual accession to the throne. This may have helped his mother, Igzī-Kibra, in obtaining Dawīt's permission to send the young boy to monastic schools in Aksum and Däbrä Abbay,[2] under the care of her clerical relatives or protegés. But it does not seem that he enjoyed this freedom of movement for a long time. His father died soon afterwards, when he was only fourteen, and his brother Téwodros apparently ordered his detention at the time of his accession to power. The chronicler insists that Zär'a-Ya'iqob remained in his monastic school of Däbrä Abbay incognito for the whole period of twenty years, until his own accession to power. Many historical considerations make this most unlikely. Zär'a-Ya'iqob himself speaks of '. . . the mountain where we were imprisoned', and from which he was only brought down on the eve of his accession in 1434.[3] The particular mention of Téwodros's hostility also indicates that it was at the accession of his eldest brother, in 1413, that he was taken to Amba Gishän.

As has already been said above, Téwodros only ruled for nine months and was succeeded, with no apparent difficulty, by his brother, Yishaq (1413–30). Yishaq was in turn succeeded by his own son, Indiryas, who however died after a few months. Yishaq probably had another son (or sons), and Maqrizi mentions a certain 'Salmun ibn Ishaq', as having ruled after Hizbä-Nagn.[4] But at the time of the death of Indiryas, he may have been too young to obtain strong support from his father's army. Thus the crown passed to Yishaq's brother, Hizbä-Nagn. Such a transfer of power from the family of a monarch to that of his brother was always a dramatic event. It involved selecting one of the princes detained at Amba Gishän, and crowning him instead of his nephews, who immediately replaced him at the Royal Prison. Thus it marked an important occasion, and

[1] See p. 220 n. 3.

[2] It is interesting to note that according to a modern traveller Däbrä Abbay was also known as Addi Shäwa, Faitlovitch, J., *Notes d'un voyage chez les Falashas, Juifs d'Abyssinie* (1905), p. 14.

[3] *Mäṣhafä Birhan*, ii (text), p. 157.

[4] *Historia Regum Islamiticorum in Abyssinia*, p. 39.

was not settled without a serious contest among the supporters of the sons of the deceased king, and the partisans of his surviving brothers. This seems to have been the case at the time of Hizbä-Nagn's accession to power.

It is apparent that Zär'a-Ya'iqob, although younger than Hizbä-Nagn, was a serious contender for the succession of Indiryas. The conflict between his supporters and those of Hizbä-Nagn probably continued, even after the succession was settled in favour of the latter. This political situation is suggested by a hagiographical tradition about a contemporary monastic leader in eastern Gojjam:

> A certain man accused Abba Sīnoda at the Court of King Hizbä-Nagn saying: 'Sīnoda declares that another King, called Zär'a-Ya'iqob, shall rise' . . . and [Hizbä-Nagn] was exceedingly angry . . . and ordered [Sīnoda] to be brought . . . and to be beaten . . .; he also ordered [his men] to imprison him . . . and take him to [the island of] Däq . . . and [the king] sent his soldiers [there] . . . to cut off his hands and his feet.[1]

Four other men suffered similar treatment together with Abba Sīnoda, and all died of the mutilation.[2]

The crisis of the royal succession flared up once again when Hizbä-Nagn died, and his army raised one of his sons to the throne. Hizbä-Nagn ruled for not more than three years,[3] which was too

[1] 'Gädlä Sīnoda', MS. Dīma, ff. 20–1. For the life and work of Sīnoda, see p. 202, n. 4.

[2] 'Gädlä Sīnoda', f. 25[b].

[3] The chronology of the kingdom, particularly between the beginning of the reign of Dawīt and the accession of Zär'a-Ya'iqob, has been very uncertain. The traditional dating of these reigns is represented by Wright, W., *Catalogue*, pp. vi–ix; Perruchon, J., *Les Chroniques de Zar'a-Ya'eqob*, p. 206, Table. It seems possible now to propose a fresh chronology of these years with the help of many additional historical notes. Dawīt began his reign in 32 Year of Grace (= A.D. 1379/80), Kolmodin, *Traditions*, A23. He was still king in 65 Year of Grace (= A.D. 1412/13), 'The Four Gospels', MS. Kibran, f. 237[b]. Immediately following this, there is a land grant by King Yishaq dated 66 Years of Grace (= A.D. 1413/14), 'in the sixth month of my reign', ibid., f. 238[a]. Téwodros's short reign indicated by other sources (see p. 220, n. 4) is also confirmed by these notes on Dawīt and Yishaq. Maqrizi says that Yishaq was killed in the month of Dulkada in A.H. 833 (= August A.D. 1430). There is no good reason to reject Maqrizi's report on this date, nor on the circumstances of Yishaq's death. The date goes perfectly well with many Ethiopic traditions which give Yishaq, and his son Indiryas a joint reign of 17 years, cf. Bodl., MS. Bruce 92, f. 54[b]. Indiryas ruled for six months according to Basset, R., *Études*, p. 12; and only four months according to Maqrizi, op. cit., pp. 9, 39. It is at this point that Hizbä-Nagn began his reign. Most of the available Ethiopic chronological notes either give him 4 years on his own, or 5 years with his two sons, cf. Basset, loc. cit. But this is too long for the interregnum of only four years between Yishaq's death and the accession of Zär'a-Ya'iqob in 87 Year of Grace (= A.D. 1434/5), which seems to

short a period for the consolidation of his newly acquired power in his family. This seems to have precipitated a serious conflict among three distinct political groups at the time of his death. The first apparently consisted of a section of the Christian army, still loyal to the family of King Yishaq, who made a strong bid for a come-back to political power in the kingdom with one of the king's sons as their candidate. Maqrizi's invaluable mention of the short interregnum of 'Salmun ibn Ishaq', on the death of Hizbä-Nagn, strongly indicates at least the existence of this third party. The second group, and probably the strongest at the time, consisted of the officials of Hizbä-Nagn who defended the continuation of the rights of his family to the crown. They apparently won the first round of the political struggle, and Mihrka-Nagn ascended the throne for a time. But he died soon afterwards, and his followers immediately crowned his younger brother, Bädl-Nagn, who was only a very small child. It is at this stage that the supporters of Zär'a-Ya'iqob became particularly strong in the conflict, and finally succeeded in bringing him to power:

> And [the wicked slaves of Hizbä-Nagn] . . . crowned a small child, Bädl-Nagn, because they wanted to rule [the country] themselves. And when God perceived their arrogant intentions, he brought forth Zär'a-Ya'iqob, the Orthodox, to the throne; and those rebels and wicked slaves were jailed and fastened with iron bars and chains . . .[1]

Maqrizi also ends his contemporary account of Ethiopia with the accession of a 'small boy',[2] and the tradition just quoted above does

be a very secure date, cf. Grébaut, S., 'Table de comput et de chronologie', in *ROC*, i (1918–19), p. 326. From all these notes the following table of Dawīt's succession is obtained:

1. Dawīt (1380–1412)

2. Téwodros (Oct. 1412–June 1413)

3. Yishaq (1413–30)

4. Indiryas (Aug.–Nov. 1430)

5. Hizbä-Nagn (1430–33)

6, 7. His two sons (to July 1434)

8. Zär'a-Ya'iqob (1434–68)

[1] 'Istigubu'i', MS. Däbrä Wärq, f. 3.

[2] Op. cit., p. 41. This is almost certainly a reference to Bädl-Nagn, and the prince whom he succeeded and who is said to have died in an epidemic, may be his brother Mihrka-Nagn. Maqrizi collected his notes about the period while he was staying in Mecca in A.H. 839 (= A.D. 1435/6), ibid., p. 1. Cf. also Guidi, I., 'Sul testo dell'*Ilmam* d'Al-Maqrizi', in *Centenario della nascita di Michele Amari*, ii (1910), p. 388 n. 2. Maqrizi dates the accession of the 'small boy' in 1435/6. But since he does not mention Zär'a-Ya'iqob, it seems that the Arab

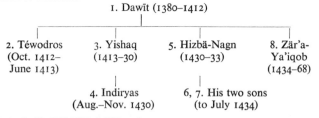

not specify what actually happened to Bädl-Nagn himself. But most Ethiopic sources and king-lists assign to him a short reign of eight months.[1] Nevertheless, the great feud between Zär'a-Ya'iqob and the family of Hizbä-Nagn, of which the tradition was also recorded by Almeida in the seventeenth century,[2] strongly indicates that the whole period of the reign of Bädl-Nagn—the last prince of that family—was specially marked by a protracted political struggle within the Christian kingdom.

Despite the conflicts between the supporters of rival princes, however, it is apparent that careful consultation among the high-ranking (secular and ecclesiastical) officials of the kingdom was also an important factor in the determination of a successor. This no doubt accounts for the definite rules that one can detect in the available king-lists.[3] A tradition about the tenth century describes the process in the following terms: 'When the king died, the bishop, and the governors, and the generals of the royal army took counsel together, and it was said among them: "The younger son will be far better for the kingdom than the elder".'[4] The reports attributed to European travellers in Ethiopia in the fifteenth century,[5] and the more authentic accounts of Alvarez[6] and Almeida,[7] all describe

historian was not aware of the latest developments in Ethiopia, and he simply dated the last king he had heard of to the time of his own sojourn in Mecca. Nevertheless, his information about the troubled years following the death of Yishaq are remarkably accurate. The number of kings he gives within this period, until the advent of the 'small boy', is fully confirmed by the Ethiopic sources, except in the case of 'Salmun ibn Ishaq', for whom Maqrizi is certainly preferable to the Ethiopic scribes who tend to suppress such information. The chronological imperfections, which Maqrizi's account of these years displays, appear to have been largely due to the uncertainties of the political situation in Christian Ethiopia itself.

[1] Cf. Basset, *Études*, p. 12.

[2] *Some Records*, pp. 101–2.

[3] Almeida gives an interesting account of how the election of a new monarch was undertaken, and describes the general ceremony of coronation, *Historia de Ethiopia a alta*, bk. ii, Ch. 21, in Beccari, C., *Rerum Aethiopicorum Scriptores Occidentales inediti*, v (1910). Prof. Cerulli has published a translation of a short extract from a story of the miracles of St. Mary regarding the life of the princes on Mt. Gishän, *Storia della letteratura etiopica* (1956), pp. 127–30.

[4] *The Book of the Saints of the Ethiopian Church*, tr. Budge, E. A. W., (1928), p. 667.

[5] Trasselli, C., 'Un Italiano in Etiopia nel secolo XV: Pietro Rombulo di Messina', in *RSE*, i (1941), pp. 190–1. The account of Pietro of Napoli, one of the messengers of the Duke of Berry to King Yishaq, is to be found in *Le Voyage d'outremer de Bertrandon de la Brocquière*, ed. Schefer, C., (Paris, 1892), pp. 146–7.

[6] Op. cit., pp. 241–3.

Loc. cit.

essentially the same process. Particularly in the fourteenth and fifteenth centuries, the security of the Christian kingdom as against its Muslim and pagan neighbours was always an overriding factor in the choice of a monarch, and provided an important restraint to the extent of the political disputations among rival groups. It is indeed remarkable that, in precisely the same period in which he reports rapid successions to the throne, Maqrizi also describes the continued success of the Christian army in the wars against Adal.[1]

The most valuable contribution of Mount Gishän to the stability of the medieval kingdom consisted in the fact that most of the rival princes themselves were not at large, and could not take an active part in the conflict. During such a crisis of royal succession, only the sons of the deceased monarch were outside the Royal Prison, in the protection of their father's army, and with all the political patronage of his reign still in their hands. It was in fact largely due to this tactical advantage that the family of the deceased monarch always seems to have won the day, at the initial stage of the political struggle The interests of the other princes were only represented by a section of the Christian army and the royal Court which had special family or other connections with them. It is most significant that, in a hagiographical tradition, Zär'a-Ya'iqob is made to say the following words about his advent to power: 'The troops of my relatives raised me to the throne of my father . . .'[2]

Zär'a-Ya'iqob's succession, like that of all other kings of medieval Ethiopia, may have certainly been promoted by his relatives in particular. But other factors also seem to have been working in his favour in 1434. He was the only surviving son of King Dawīt, and he was about thirty-five years of age,[3] no doubt much older than any of his nephews living at the time. Probably too, his reputation as a scholar prince had already spread among both the secular and clerical officials of the kingdom. Moreover, the internal political situation in the preceding years had been particularly unstable, and this may have induced much of the Christian army and the royal Court to favour a strong leadership. It also seems that there was a closing of ranks between the former supporters of Yishaq's family,

[1] Op. cit., p. 9. This was particularly the case towards the end of the reign of Jamal ad-Din, and immediately after his assassination, ibid., pp. 45–36. Cerulli seems to envisage a possible Christian hand in this last act, 'Documenti arabi per la storia dell'Etiopia', in *MRAL*, ser. 6, vol. vi (1931), p. 47 n. 2.

[2] 'Gädlä Zéna-Marqos', MS. Däbrä Ṣigé, ff. 109^b–110^a.

[3] See p. 220 n. 1.

and those of Zär'a-Ya'iqob against the descendants of Hizbä-Nagn. While this explains the lasting enmity between the families of Zär'a-Ya'iqob and Hizbä-Nagn,[1] it probably also accounts for the absence of 'Salmun ibn Ishaq'—remembered by Maqrizi—from the Ethiopic list of the princes who contested the succession. 'Brought down from the mountain', in his own words, 'where we were imprisoned',[2] Zär'a-Ya'iqob was crowned king of Ethiopia, and he more than succeeded in providing the personal leadership of a strong monarch which the country had lacked so much since the death of Yishaq in 1430.

The death of a monarch was not the only occasion which brought about a struggle for the crown. There are a number of cases in which attempts were made to usurp power while the king was still alive. Apart from many instances in the early days of the dynasty,[3] attempts to replace the monarch are evident even in the reigns of Dawīt and Zär'a-Ya'iqob, who were perhaps the most powerful kings of medieval Ethiopia. The incident in the reign of Dawīt is preserved in a story of the miracles of St. Mary.[4] A group of local saints are said to have received a revelation that Dawīt should retire and abdicate in favour of his son. They sent word to the king about their vision which troubled him a great deal. He summoned his former teacher and confidant, *Aqabé-Sä'at* Säräqä-Birhan of Däbrä Hayq, and one of the commanders of the army. He broke to them the sad news, and they all agreed to appeal to St. Mary for help. She heard their prayers and promised the king that he would retain his crown for the rest of his life. *Aqabé-Sä'at* Säräqä-Birhan died in 1403, and therefore the incident must have taken place before this date. Although the king's son in whose favour the abdication was proposed is kept anonymous, the particular mention of the *Aqabé-Sä'at* and 'the commander of the king's forces' certainly implies that it was a high-powered political event. But this apparent movement against King Dawīt was a failure, and the king kept his throne for at least 10 years after this incident.[5]

[1] Almeida, *Some Records*, pp. 101–2.
[2] *Mäṣhafä Birhan*, ii, p. 157 (text).
[3] See Taddesse Tamrat, 'The Abbots of Däbra Hayq', pp. 91–3.
[4] Cerulli, E., *Il libro etiopico dei miracoli di Maria* (1943), pp. 79–86.
[5] It is most likely that this was the origin of the story that Dawīt did actually abdicate, and his son Téwodros took over. Cerulli accepts this, op. cit., p. 86. But the chronology of the reigns of both Dawīt and Téwodros (see p. 279 n. 3) make it impossible.

Zär'a-Ya'iqob's reign was also marked by some attempts to replace him. We have already made a reference to the abortive revolt of 1453.[1] It was apparently led by high-ranking officials of the kingdom and, as indicated above, it seems to have been motivated by political and economic grievances. But towards the end of the reign Zär'a-Ya'iqob was led to believe that even members of his own family at the royal Court were plotting against him. The report involved many of his own children and their mothers. After an ostentatious public trial held at the Court, the king ordered them all to be flogged, as a result of which many lost their lives.[2] The witnesses produced against them testified that they consulted witch-doctors and offered sacrifices to pagan gods,[3] and the king's verdict is therefore said to have been given on religious grounds. However, the victims of this latest purge in Zär'a-Ya'iqob's reign included 'high-ranking officials, governors, monks . . .', and Abba Indiriyas, the Abbot of Däbrä Lībanos, was one of them.[4] The religious façade of the story does not stand a close examination. The political nature of the king's preoccupation is even implied in the cautious writing of the chronicler: 'They accused them of many other things. Only the king knows the [true] story. They did not make public [the charges] other than that [the accused] worshipped *däsk*. . . .'[5] Zär'a-Ya'iqob himself discloses a more acceptable reason for his wild fury against the princes. After describing how their mothers misled them into pagan worship and black magic, the king singles out one of his sons, Gälawdéwos, for having ceremoniously burned copies of 'Ṭomarä-Tisbi'it' and 'Mäṣhafä-Birhan'[6] at a witchcraft ceremony. Gälawdéwos did this, the king tells us, in return for a promise by the witch-doctor of an eventual succession to the throne.[7] The chronicler also gives a similar story about the death of Queen Ṣiyon-Mogäsa, mother of King Bä'idä-Maryam (1468–78). Zär'a-Ya'iqob once accused her of trying to depose him in favour of

[1] See pp. 240–2.

[2] *Les Chroniques de Zar'a-Ya'eqob et de Ba'eda Maryam*, pp. 4–7, 97–100, 105–7; *Das Mashafa Milad und Mashafa Sellase*, ii (1963), pp. 95–6.

[3] For the king's decrees forbidding these practices, see pp. 233–5.

[4] *Les Chroniques*, pp. 99–100.

[5] Ibid., p. 98.

[6] These are two of the religious writings attributed to Zär'a-Yaī'qob himself.

[7] *Das Mashafa Milad*, ii (text), pp. 95–6. Gälawdéwos was probably the eldest son of Zär'a-Ya'iqob. Immediately before his disgrace and imprisonment, Abba Täklä-Hawaryat of Gäbärma (Mugär) was invited to court by Gälawdéwos's mother to bless and edify her young son, 'Gädlä Täklä-Hawaryat', MS. Däbrä Lībanos, f. 49ª. At that time, which was probably soon after the abortive revolt of 1453, the prince seems to have been on good terms with his father.

her son. He had received reports, he told her, that she had been soliciting the help and prayers of many local saints for the success of her rebellious schemes. And despite her protestations of innocence, Queen Ṣiyon-Mogäsa was ordered to be flogged, as a result of which she died some time later. Her young son, Bä'idä-Maryam, was also detained for a time with his favourite slave, Mäharī-Kristos for having privately celebrated the anniversary of her death.[1] It is apparent that these palace recriminations took place in about 1462.[2] Bä'idä-Maryam's later revenge on Gäbrä-Kristos, whom 'he had stoned . . . to death'[3] strongly implies that they all took place as a connected series of political incidents.

Zär'a-Ya'iqob lived on, and continued to rule with an iron hand for another period of six years. In terms of the concentric organization of the medieval Court, the conflicts between a reigning monarch and the rest of his family can best be described as a tug-of-war between the inner and the outer enclosures of the royal camp. At times when the kingdom was ruled by powerful monarchs—Dawīt and Zär'a-Ya'iqob for instance—the inner enclosure always had the upper hand, and the country was thus assured of a strong leadership. When the king was weak or a child, however, the diverse elements and political interests of the outer enclosure asserted themselves, and the Christian nation lacked the unity of purpose so essential for the defence and administration of its extensive empire. This characterized the reigns of Zär'a-Ya'iqob's grandsons after 1478. Between this year and the end of the period covered by this book, the average age of the princes at the time of their accession was only eleven years. And except in the case of Na'od (1494–1508), who was already twenty when he took over, the nation was ruled by a council of regents for the first part of each of the reigns.

[1] *Les Chroniques*, pp. 105–7.

[2] The date is obtained from the story of the life of Märha-Kristos, who succeeded Indiryas as abbot of Däbrä Lībanos. Märha-Kristos died in January, in the second year of the reign of Na'od (1494–1508), after 33 years and 5 months rule, 'Gädlä Märha-Kristos', MS. Däbrä Lībanos, pp. 115–17, 246. This is equivalent to A.D. 1496, and Indiryas must have been deposed and exiled in 1462. For short notices about the life of Indiryas see ibid., pp. 102, 106–7, 112; *Les Chroniques*, pp. 90, 100, 130; *Sinkisar* (Hamlé), ed. and tr. in *PO* vii, pp. 345–6; Cerulli, E., 'Gli abbati di Dabra Libanos', pp. 143–5.

[3] *Les Chroniques*, p. 100. Gäbrä-Kristos was one of the three most trusted officials of Zär'a-Ya'iqob at the time. These officials are said to have given the king false reports about the princes and other personalities including Indiryas. Bä'idä-Maryam's later fury against Gäbrä-Kristos most probably indicates that he also had a hand in the death of Queen Ṣiyon-Mogäsa.

The palace struggle for power (1478–94)

Iskindir (1478–94), the eldest of Bä'idä-Maryam's baby sons, was crowned at six years of age, with no apparent problem of succession. At first, his mother Queen Romna, *Aqabé-Sä'at* Täsfa-Gīyorgīs, and *Bihiwäddäd* Amdä-Mīka'él jointly assumed power as regents.[1] Amdä-Mīka'él was an elderly official who had held considerable power since the days of Iskindir's grandfather. Zär'a-Ya'iqob had invested him with much authority, particularly as governor of the whole of the frontier district of Fäṭägar.[2] Towards the end of Bä'idä-Maryam's reign, we still find him wielding great influence in the royal Court, and he played a decisive role in the council of 1477 as an ally of Däbrä Lībanos.[3] Of the members of the council of regents, he was certainly the strongest and the most experienced hand in the government. It is most likely that Romna and Täsfa-Gīyorgīs were at first included in the council largely because of the traditional importance of the high offices they held as Queen Mother and *Aqabé-Sä'at*, respectively. From the start, however, both of them seem to have been overshadowed by the greater influence of Amdä-Mīka'él, and the Queen Mother soon disappeared from the political scene altogether. Even in the Court of Bä'idä-Maryam, Romna was not one of the principal queens,[4] and her position had only been enhanced by giving the king his two favourite sons, Iskindir and Inqo-Isra'él.[5] She probably felt more important after this, and apparently became quarrelsome among the queens in Court: the king was forced to exile her to Amhara, where she remained until recalled on the coronation of her son.[6] Some time later, however, she abandoned the world and entered a small convent near Däbrä Lībanos where she died, apparently not very long afterwards.[7]

Unmatched by any of his colleagues, Amdä-Mīka'él ruled the kingdom almost single handed. This unprecedented position of personal power held by the old man aroused an outcry against him.

[1] 'Histoire d'Eskender, d'Amda-Seyon II, et de Na'od', ed. and tr. Perruchon, in *JA*, ser. 9, vol. iii (1894), pp. 338–9.

[2] *Les Chroniques de Zar'a Ya'eqob*, p. 15.

[3] 'Gädlä Märha-Kristos', pp. 223, 245–9. Here he is referred to as 'the head of the governors, the great (man), called Amdä-Mīka'él'.

[4] The more prestigious titles of Gira-Bä'altéhat, Qägn-Bä'altéhat, and Bä'altä-Shihna were borne by three other princesses, Žan-Säyfa, Illénī, and Dawīt-Éra respectively, *Les Chroniques*, pp. 125, 149, 176.

[5] Ibid., pp. 155–6, 161.

[6] 'Histoire d'Eskender', pp. 338–9.

[7] 'Gädlä Märha-Kristos', pp. 256–8.

The movement was predominantly led by members of the influential clergy, but Amdä-Mīka'él had little difficulty in suppressing it:

> And after some time Abba Hasbo, Abba Amdu, and Manbäṣidqu quarrelled with *Bihtwäddäd* Amdu when they saw him ruling all Ethiopia on his own. For this reason [the troops] arrested all those who quarrelled with him, and flogged them many times. And they imprisoned them and sent them to exile. There are some who died on the way, and some who survived.[1]

Thus the *Bihtwäddäd* won the first round of the personal challenge organized against him. But the opposition seems to have gathered momentum over the years. As the young king grew up, he apparently began to be surrounded with new officials, who increasingly looked at the old *Bihtwäddäd* as the greatest obstacle to their own advancement. His ruthless suppression of his opponents had made him the most formidable figure in the kingdom, and a large number of Court officials seem to have combined to bring an end to his power. From the confused traditions about this incident, it is impossible here to specify exactly the reasons for his downfall. But it is clear that his enemies alienated him from the young king who finally ordered his arrest, and exiled him to an unknown place. Sometime later he was secretly brought back to the royal Court and executed.[2]

A list of the officials of King Iskindir—probably dated 1486[3]—seems to suggest the identity of the personalities who promoted the movement against Amdä-Mīka'él. At the head of the list appears Illénī as the Queen Mother, and immediately next to the three wives of the king is mentioned a certain Täsfa-Gīyorgis. Täsfa-Gīyorgīs holds the unusual title of *Mäkbibä Bétä-Kristīyan* and is listed prior to a new *Aqabé-Sä'at*. Most probably this Täsfa-Gīyorgis was the same official who, as *Aqabé-Sä'at*, was a member of the council of regents, together with Romna and Amdä-Mīka'él, at the beginning of the reign. Given little share in the exercise of power by his fellow regent Amdä-Mīka'él, Täsfa-Gīyorgīs was probably sympathetic to the predominantly clerical movement against him. On the overthrow

[1] 'Histoire d'Eskender', p. 339.

[2] The accounts we have about him are mostly short, and hagiographical, Zotenberg, *Catalogue*, no. 126, Hidar 3, and Sene 29. Wright, *Catalogue*, Or. 667, f. 60. *Le Synaxaire éthiopien*, ed. and tr. Guidi, I., in *PO*, i (1904), pp. 697–8.

[3] Wright, *Catalogue*, Or. 481, f. 208. This land grant only bears Megabit 7 as its date, and the year is not given. But the land grant was probably made in the same year as another one, given in the 7th year of the king's reign, ibid., f. 92[a]. Two officials—Péṭros and Bishilé—appear in both land grants, and they held the same appointment in each.

of the old *Bihtwäddäd* the former *Aqabé-Sä'at* probably assumed the more dignified title *Mäkbibä Bétä-Kristīyan* [=the Crown of the Church (lit.)], and was succeeded in his original office by Täklä-Iyäsus-Mo'a.[1]

The new Queen Mother was a more formidable character in the political scene. Illénī was originally a Hadya princess, married to King Zär'a-Ya'iqob as early as 1445, some years before Bä'idä-Maryam was born.[2] When Zär'a-Ya'iqob died, Illénī retained her old title *Qägn-Bä'altéhat* in the Court of his successor.[3] Her position appears to have been purely ceremonial, and she was not numbered among the four wives of the new king.[4] Bä'idä-Maryam had lost his own mother before he took power, and it was this role that the talented Illénī was particularly intended to play:

And as for the *Qägn-Bä'altéhat*, whose name was Illénī, the king loved her exceedingly, for she was accomplished in everything: in front of God, by practising righteousness and having strong faith, by praying and receiving the Holy Communion; as regards worldly matters she was accomplished in the preparation of food [for the royal table], in her familiarity with the books, in her knowledge of the law, and in her understanding of the affairs of state. For all these qualities, the king loved our Queen Illénī very much, and he considered her like his own mother.[5]

[1] On Täsfa-Gīyorgīs and Täklä-Īyäsus-Mo'a, see Taddesse Tamrat, 'The Abbots of Däbrä Hayq', pp. 109–11.

[2] *Les Chroniques de Zar'a Ya'eqob*, pp. 16, 59. No doubt the marriage was a political one and Illénī must have been very young. The king of Hadya had obliged King Dawīt by his loyal services against his co-religionist Sä'adädīn, ruler of Adal, Maqrizi, op. cit., p. 23. This and the increasing importance of the southern regions probably motivated the marriage. Although we have no other references to similar unions, it is probable that less notable princesses may have followed Illénī to the Christian Court. One of the complaints of the Hadya Muslims to Ahmad Gragn was that these marriages were forced on them, *Futuh al-Habasha*, tr. Basset, p. 371. Cf. also Alvarez, op. cit., p. 427.

[3] *Les Chroniques*, p. 125.

[4] Altogether, Bä'idä-Maryam had four wives: Žan-Säyfa to whom he gave the title of *Gira-Bä'altéhat*, a title reserved for the king's most favoured queen, ibid., pp. 125, 174–5; Dawit-Éra, who bore the other title of *Bä'altä-Shihna* reserved for the junior queen of the Right, ibid., p. 149; Romna, who gave him his sons Iskindir and Inqo-Isra'él (= Na'od), ibid., pp. 155–6, 161; and Irésh-Gäzét who bore him his other son Téwodros, ibid., p. 156.

[5] Ibid., pp. 175–6. It is very clear from this that Illénī was not Bä'idä-Maryam's wife. But, in deference to his father Zär'a-Ya'iqob, and to her own apparently remarkable capacity, he let her retain the title of *Qägn-Bä'altéhat* which she already held in Zär'a-Ya'iqob's court, ibid., pp. 59, 125. According to the Vatican MS. described by Prof. C. Beckingham, Alvarez also confirms this point. He describes her as 'Queen Illénī who had been the wife of the Prester John [who ruled] before the grandfather of the present Prester John', Beckingham, C., 'Notes

Illénī occupied this position of great influence throughout the reign of Bä'idä-Maryam, and apparently gathered a huge political patronage in the whole kingdom. It is interesting that she was at first left out of the council of regents on the accession of Iskindir. She probably had a hand in the disgrace and exile of Iskindir's mother, Romna, during the lifetime of Bä'idä-Maryam. When Romna was recalled to assume the regency, there simply could not be any place for Illénī in the council. Most likely too, there was an old misunderstanding between her and *Bihtwäddäd* Amdä-Mīka'él, who ensured that she was excluded from all positions of authority. Certainly, Illénī's sudden re-emergence as Queen Mother in Iskindir's Court, soon after the disappearance of both Romna and Amdä-Mīka'él, is very indicative of her decisive role in the political conflicts following the death of Bä'idä-Maryam. Another sign of Illénī's hostile attitude towards Amdä-Mīka'él and his protégés is the systematic silence which the dominant traditions of Däbrä Lībanos maintain about her. As has already been said above, Amdä-Mīka'él was a great patron of the monastery of Täklä-Haymanot. His relationship with the abbot of the day, Märha-Kristos, was very affectionate, and the hagiographer once refers to the *Bihtwäddäd* as 'the (spiritual) son of Märha-Kristos'.[1] After his execution, Amdä-Mīka'él was first buried at Däbrä Lībanos, and the opposition of the monastery to his unjust treatment at the royal Court is still preserved in the canonization which has been conferred upon him. Probably the same reason motivated the diplomatic silence the scribes of Däbrä-Lībanos observed about Illénī, even after her return to power in 1486. It is also significant that not long after Illénī's death King Libnä-Dingil restored the memory of Amdä-Mīka'él to a place of honour by transferring his remains from Däbrä Lībanos to the royal cemetery of Atronisä-Maryam in Amhara.[2]

on an unpublished MS. of Francesco Alvarez', in *AE*, iv (1961), pp. 150–1. It is clear that Zär'a-Ya'iqob is meant here. Illénī was certainly not Bä'idä-Maryam's wife, and the general view about her in this respect is based merely on the ceremonial title she retained in the king's court, cf. Conti Rossini, 'La storia di Libna Dingil', p. 631 n. 1. Huntingford's notes on her are specially arbitrary, cf. Alvarez, op. cit., p. 14 n. 3, and p. 425 n. 1.

[1] 'Gädlä Märha-Kristos', p. 223.

[2] This is said to have been done 40 years after his execution, Wright, op. cit., Or. 667, f. 60. This places the date at *c.* 1525. Illénī probably died in 1522, Alvarez, op. cit., p. 425 n. 1. The restoration of Amdä-Mīka'él's honour was probably part of the political changes following her death, of which Alvarez was a personal witness, ibid., p. 434.

Apart from its disastrous effects on frontier defence, which will be discussed later, the removal of the strong personal rule of *Biht-wäddäd* Amdä-Mīka'él resulted in an intensive political struggle at the royal Court, and in serious insubordination among the troops. Even the official chronicler could not avoid writing about the royal guards of the young king in the following terms: 'His soldiers destroyed the whole world. They afflicted the poor, and (the King) did not reprimand them.'[1] For quite a long period after their takeover, Illénī and the new officials of the kingdom were not in complete control of the situation. There were even some religious undertones in the partisan political clashes of the time.

One of the earliest acts of Amdä-Mīka'él as a regent was to implement the decision of Bä'idä-Maryam at the council of 1477, in which he himself had played a significant role.[2] A delegation was sent with rich gifts to the patriarch and Sultan Qait-bay (1468–95), and they returned in 1480/1, bringing with them two bishops (Yishaq and Marqos), two ecclesiastics bearing the title of Épīsqopos (Mīka'él and Yohannis), and one Qomos (Yoséf).[3] This was the first time for the country to have Egyptian bishops since the death of Mīka'él and Gäbr'él, twenty-three years before. The occasion produced a great sensation throughout the Christian provinces, and numerous candidates flocked towards the main road to Shäwa to be ordained by the bishops on their way to the king's Court.[4] The great relief which was then felt in the Christian kingdom by the arrival of the bishops is described by the chronicler: 'And in his [Iskindir's] reign came bishops from Holy Jerusalem. The priests became many, the Churches were restored, and happiness filled all the land.'[5] Some time later, probably in 1482, a Franciscan, Fr. Ioane de Calabria,

[1] 'Histoire d'Eskender', p. 342.

[2] See p. 247.

[3] 'Gädlä Märha-Kristos', pp. 251–2. Here the names of the leading delegates are given as Ṣägga-Zä'ab and Gäbrä-Birhan. Ibn Iyas also describes this delegation which was in Cairo in A.H. 886 (= A.D. 1481/2). It was led by a high-ranking dignitary and carried rich gifts to the sultan, Quatremère, *Mémoires*, ii (1811), pp. 279–83. For the date see Kolmodin, op. cit., A53–4. Conti Rossini, 'Pergamene di Dabra Dammo', in *RSO*, xix (1940), pp. 50–1.

[4] Yishaq was the senior bishop and we have some traditions of such ordinations by him on the way to Shäwa. The candidates were already advanced in years, and well known for their monastic pursuits, Conti Rossini, 'Besu'a Amlak e il convento della Trinità' in *RRAL*, ser. 5, vol .xi (1902), pp. 409–10; 'Gädlä Gäbrä-Mäsīh', MS. 40, Inst. of Archaeology, Addis Ababa. The Stephanite leader was already 63 when he was ordained by Yishaq.

[5] 'Histoire d'Eskender', p. 340.

arrived in the country with a lay companion, Giovanni da Imola.[1] They sought an audience with the king, but they were kept waiting for eight months without any success. Finally, Giovanni da Imola returned and reached Jerusalem in 1483. He reported that the regents of the young king were unfavourable to the mission and had denied them an interview with him. At this news the head of the Franciscans in Jerusalem is said to have sent another message to Ethiopia in 1484.[2] It is not known if this message ever reached there. But an interesting document seems to indicate that there was a change of heart towards Fr. Ioane de Calabria at the court of King Iskindir: 'And in those days there came Franks from Rome. One of them was a priest called Yohannis. And [the king] received them with honour. When the priests saw this they grumbled and spoke ill of him saying "The king has joined the religion of the Franks."'[3] The similarity of the name of the foreign priest, Yohannis, and that of Fr. Ioane de Calabria is particularly significant. As to the Franks referred to, both Giovanni da Imola[4] and Alvarez[5] report the presence of many Europeans in the country at the time. No definite conclusions can as yet be drawn from this, but it may be that after having stayed in the country for some years Fr. Ioane may have gained sympathy from one of the Court officials. This may have enabled him to see the young king, which could no doubt have produced an outcry among the local clergy. Alvarez was told by Bishop Marqos that Iskindir had tried to change the traditional practice of the Ethiopians, particularly regarding the Sabbath and prohibitions of food.[6] All these isolated notes tend to show that there was a religious aspect to the political strife in the days of Iskindir. They may also explain the hagiographical traditions of hostile relations between the king and some of the local clergy: 'There came an order from Iskindir, king

[1] For this mission to Ethiopia see Suriano, F., *Il trattato di Terra Santa e dell'Oriente*, ed. Golubovitch, G. (Milan, 1900), pp. 80–7; Somigli, T., *Etiopia francescana nei documenti dei secoli XVII e XVIII*, i (1928), pp. lxiii-xci. For the confused background of this mission, and for the alleged Ethiopian mission to Pope Sixtus IV, see Ghinzoni, P., 'Un' ambasciata del Prete Gianni a Roma' in *Archivio storico lombardo*, vi, Anno XVI (1889), pp. 145–54; Creone, F., 'La politica orientale di Alfonso di Aragone', pp. 91–2; Lefevre, R., 'G. B. Brocchi da Imola, diplomatico pontificio e viaggiatore in Etiopia nel 1400', in *BSGI*, iv (1939), pp. 641–3; de Witte, Ch.-M., 'Une ambassade éthiopienne à Rome en 1450', p. 293 n. 1.

[2] Suriano, op. cit., pp. 81–3.

[3] 'Tarīkä-Nägäst', MS. Däbrä Sigé, p. 56.

[4] Suriano, op. cit., p. 86.

[5] Op. cit., pp. 278–9.

[6] Op. cit., p. 357.

of Ethiopia, asking all the priests of the Tabernacle of Wala (?) to be assembled [at the Court] . . ., and the king became angry on a trivial point and he had them flogged.'[1] Iskindir was still young, and all these official acts were certainly looked at as the work of his most influential courtiers. This only aggravated the rivalries and internal divisions among the officials of the royal Court.

The antagonistic feelings in the kingdom simmering under the surface suddenly erupted at the unexpected death of Iskindir, at the early age of twenty-two. The chronicler[2] singles out two officials—Zäsillus and Täklä-Kristos—as the leading figures in the conflicting groupings that emerged at the time. Zäsillus was at the royal Court when the king died. As soon as he realized this, he commanded his followers to keep the king's body at the Court for as long as possible, and he swiftly marched towards Mount Gishän in Amhara. There, he apparently took one of the princes—probably Iskindir's younger brother, Na'od—and declared him king of Ethiopia. Back at the royal Court, in the meantime, Zäsillus's secret disappearance and his orders regarding the remains of Iskindir had been discovered. Täklä-Kristos who was apparently the most powerful official at Court at the time immediately crowned as the next king Iskindir's little son, Amdä-Ṣiyon, a boy of only seven years of age or even younger.[3] Having done this he sent Iskindir's body to Atronisä-Maryam[4] for burial, and he marched with the king's army to fight Zäsillus and his partisans. Zäsillus probably had only a small force at his disposal, and Täklä-Kristos triumphantly marched back to the royal Court, where all the followers of Zäsillus were made prisoners and blinded.

This did not end the civil war in the country, which apparently continued throughout the short reign of the infant king. According to a contemporary observer,

Amdä-Ṣiyon, Iskindir's son, was crowned, but he was an infant. For this

[1] 'Gädlä Īyasu', MS. Däbrä Lībanos, f. 4.

[2] 'Histoire d'Eskender', pp. 340–1, 343–4.

[3] That he was seven is given in Basset, *Études*, p. 13. Conti Rossini, 'Il libro delle leggende e tradizioni dell'Etiopia', p. 711. This would mean that he was born when his father, Iskindir, was only 15!

[4] Many of the late compilations of the chronicles place the tomb of Iskindir at Däbrä Wärq, in eastern Gojjam, where the visitor is still shown what is believed to be the king's mausoleum. If there is any truth in this, the body must have been transferred there only later—from Atronisä-Maryam just across the Nile, probably during the Gragn wars. A similar problem arises in the case of Dawīt, whose remains are said to be at Daga with Zär'a-Ya'iqob's, Basset, op. cit., pp. 11–13. Zär'a-Ya'iqob's body was transferred there in 1498, 'Histoire d'Eskender', p. 350.

reason . . all the troops of the king killed one another, and they had no one to stop them. There was mourning [for the dead] in every province. The holy objects of the church were sacked. The officials of [the kingdom of] Ethiopia destroyed one another like the fish of the river, and they became like beasts with no shelter.[1]

Amdä-Ṣiyon's reign lasted for only six months, and even the hagiographer betrays a sense of great relief at the announcement of his death.[2] But the early part of the next reign did not bring any immediate comfort. For Na'od, who now succeeded to the throne, was the same prince who was brought forward by Zäsillus as his candidate, only six months before. The prince was the second son of Bä'idä-Maryam and Queen Romna, only two years younger than Iskindir.[3] It seems that, right from the beginning, the struggle for Iskindir's succession had also assumed some regional undertones. Zäsillus had declared Na'od king of Ethiopia, in Amhara, and Täklä-Kristos had to march from Shäwa (where the Court was established) to suppress the movement. An exactly similar pattern is evident during Na'od's successful accession to the throne six months later. He was crowned in October, 1494, in Amhara. When the news reached them, many of the officials, who had opposed his candidature in favour of Amdä-Ṣiyon, apparently fled into the country and prepared themselves for armed conflicts. One of them called by the chronicler Täkka-Kristos (which is probably a misprint for Täklä-Kristos) remained in the district of Īfat, and openly rebelled against the new king.[4] To suppress these movements in the region as early as possible, Na'od marched to Shäwa for Christmas, and in January, 1495, he made a formal visit to the monastery of Däbrä Lībanos.[5]

Besides calling at his mother's tomb and paying homage to Täklä-Haymanot, Na'od's visit to the monastery had a strong political motivation. This is quite evident from the tradition about the speech he is said to have made in the midst of the assembled monks: 'Pray in earnest so that Ethiopia is not made waste. You know [what

1 'Gädlä Märha-Kristos', p. 285.

2 'In six months the sacrifice of the Holy Qurban ascended into heaven, and King Amdä-Ṣiyon died', ibid., p. 286.

3 Romna is said to have had two sons: Iskindir and Inqo-Isra'él, *Les Chroniques de Zar'a-Ya'eqob et de Ba'eda Maryam*, pp. 155–6, 161. The second name was probably an early appellation for Na'od, who was certainly her son, 'Gädlä Märha-Kristos', p. 256. Cf. also Cerulli, *Il libro etiopico dei miracoli di Maria*, p. 24.

4 'Histoire d'Eskender', pp. 348–9.

5 The impressive story of this visit is told in 'Gädlä Märha-Kristos', pp. 289–94.

happened in] the last reign, and how the kingdom was ruined. [And now pray] so that the sheep that have gone astray may return under one shepherd.'[1] The king's message was very clear. He was requesting the help of the clergy to influence as many of the rebels in the Shäwan region to accept him as the legitimate king. With the complete support of the clergy on his side, Na'od began military operations against his opponents in the area. The rebel leader in Īfat, Täkka-Kristos, was captured and blinded.[2] Many others were similarly arrested and speared to death.[3] It is apparent that Na'od put an end to the revolts against him soon afterwards. The king seems to have been anxious to restore normal conditions in the kingdom, and to bring to a close the atmosphere of discord that had reigned in the country, particularly after the death of Iskindir. But public recrimination and litigation about wrongs committed during the confused period probably continued to be made among the people, and Na'od had to pass a special decree forbidding them. Only land disputes, arising from the conflicts during the civil war, were permitted.[4]

The weakness of the frontier defences

Na'od's reign promised more calm and tranquillity within the Christian kingdom itself. But serious damage had been done to the frontier defences, particularly in the direction of Fäṭägar, where the united command of the local troops was disrupted with the downfall of *Bihtwäddäd* Amdä-Mīka'él.[5] The last decisive battle against the Muslim kingdom of Adal was fought in 1445, when Zär'a-Ya'iqob defeated and killed Ahmad Badlay on the Däwaro frontiers.[6] The military success of the kingdom at that time was apparently effective for many years, and we find the son and successor of Ahmad Badlay, Muhammad (1445–71), sending a message of submission, as soon as Bä'idä-Maryam succeeded his father.[7] On the death of Muhammad, however, Adal apparently resumed hostile activities, and Bä'idä-Maryam had to drop his intended visit to Aksum to hurry back to the frontiers in the south.[8]

1 'Gädlä Märhä-Kristos', pp. 291–2.
2 'Histoire d'Eskender', p. 349.
3 'Gädlä Märha-Kristos', p. 297.
4 'Histoire d'Eskender', p. 350.
5 'Tarīkä-Nägäst', MS. Däbrä Ṣigé, pp. 56–7.
6 See pp. 262–3.
7 *Les Chroniques*, pp. 131–3. Cerulli, E., 'Documenti arabi per la storia dell'Etiopia', in *MRAL*, ser. 6, vol. iv (1931), p. 48 with n. 3.
8 *Les Chroniques*, p. 150. Cerulli, op. cit., p. 48 n. 5.

It is apparent that at this stage of the conflict it was particularly in the provinces of Däwaro and Balī that the Muslim pressure was increasing. Revolts among the local troops stationed in Balī are reported, and the king suppressed them by resettling the rebels *en masse* in Gojjam.[1] Following this, Bä'idä-Maryam directed successive campaigns to Adal from Däwaro and Balī. The first two of these campaigns were a complete success.[2] The third and the last, conducted in 1474, was however a great setback to the Christian army, which lost both its highest commanding officers and was practically decimated.[3]

It is interesting to note that all this time Bä'idä-Maryam directed his offensives against Adal with his Court established in the Wäj and Guragé area, south of the Awash. He seems to have had no fears about the Fäṭägar frontiers. There, Amdä-Mīka'él had continued in the office, first given to him by Zär'a-Ya'iqob, as governor of the province.[4] It seems that, over the years, he had established a great reputation as a general, and he had set up a strong united command for the defence of the kingdom in this direction. His downfall, in about 1485, seriously disturbed this effective system of defence. It is apparent that, with the removal of the old man, the province was divided into smaller units and distributed among petty officials who may have co-operated in bringing about his downfall. Even the chronicler of Ahmad Gragn refers to this basic change in the defence of the province: 'In the reign of the grandfather of the king of Ethiopia there was only one governor in Fäṭägar who was the chief commander [of the Christian forces there].' He goes on to say that in Libnä-Dingil's time, however, the province of Fäṭägar was divided into seven different commands.[5]

Iskindir's first campaign into Adal had a mixed result. At first he successfully marched as far east as Dakar,[6] but suffered serious military reverses on the long way back, when he lost most of his army.[7] It is specially significant and highly indicative of the great

[1] *Les Chroniques*, pp. 157–9. [2] Ibid., pp. 159, 165–7.

[3] Ibid., pp. 180–2. 'Histoire d'Eskender', p. 345. [4] Ibid., p. 15.

[5] *Futuh al-Habasha*, tr. Basset, p. 83. The Muslim chronicler considered this, however, as a point of strength, since each unit tried to excel the other in military actions.

[6] For this site see Cerulli, op. cit., pp. 42 n. 1, 50 n. 1. It was to the south-east of Harär.

[7] 'Histoire d'Eskender', p. 343. Ricci, L., 'Le vite di Enbaqom e di Yohannes', in *RSE*, xiii (1954), p. 100. Cerulli, op. cit., p. 49 n. 1. Id., 'L'Etiopia del secolo XV', pp. 90–100.

harm done to the Christian army by the internal political conflicts that after this major defeat, Iskindir could not send even a single successful expedition to Adal.[1] The civil war during the succession of Amdä-Ṣiyon II and Na'od considerably aggravated the weakness of the army, and the political discord among the Christian officials.

Compared with the records of his two predecessors, Na'od's achievements in the defence of his kingdom were certainly much better, and even Gragn's Muslim chronicler attributes to him many successes in Balī and Däwaro.[2] However, defections from the Christian army stationed on the frontiers were rife, and the Muslim attacks, particularly on the frontier districts of Īfat and Fäṭägar, were considerably increased.[3] Na'od himself lost his life while on his way to repulse a Muslim invasion in the district of Īfat.[4] The first years of Libnä-Dingil's reign were also marked by continuous Muslim military successes in the eastern frontiers. Even the official chroniclers do not report any Christian victory until Libnä-Dingil had been on the throne for eight years.[5]

1 He died during an expedition to an unknown place, 'Gädlä Märha-Kristos', pp. 281–4. His chronicler attributes his death to a pastoral people called 'the people of the Ar'iho', against whom he had marched to revenge an official, 'Histoire d'Eskender', p. 343. Later compilations have identified these people with the Maya, Basset, *Études*, p. 12.

2 *Futuh al-Habasha*, tr. Basset, pp. 164–8.

3 'Tarīkä-Nägäst', MS. Däbrä Ṣigé, pp. 57–8.

4 Ibid., p. 58.

5 'La storia di Libna Dingil', ed. and tr. Conti Rossini, pp. 622, 632. Cf. also Alvarez, op. cit., pp. 410–15.

CHAPTER IX

Epilogue

HALF a century of political strife among the warlords of the Christian kingdom provided the immediate, favourable background for the swift Muslim conquest under the remarkable leadership of Imam Ahmad ibn Ibrahim or Gragn. But the more basic reasons for the sudden disintegration of the Christian empire transcended the events of those fifty years with which we were concerned in the last chapter.

Despite the extensive conquests in the fourteenth and fifteenth centuries[1] and the resultant expansion of the Church,[2] the Christian empire was still very heterogeneous on the eve of the disastrous conflict with Ahmad Gragn. A large number of diverse linguistic, ethnic, and religious communities had been brought under the control of the Christian kings. But the process of cultural assimilation and political integration had not been completed. Of the territories conquered and annexed since the days of Amdä-Ṣiyon, only Shäwa north of the Awash, eastern Gojjam, Dämbya, and Wägära had been intensively Christianized and Semitized. The remaining vast dependencies to the west, south, and south-east of the river Awash were only minimally affected by the presence of the Church. It appears that most of the areas south of the Awash—places like Hadya and the other smaller Sīdama principalities—were controlled by the central royal Court only through an old system of indirect rule. The Christian kings still appointed for these places members of the old hereditary families who ensured the regular payment of the annual tributes and the continued loyalties of their people to the Christian empire. The same policy was pursued towards the Fälasha of Simén, and the pagan Agäw south of Lake Ṭana. All these peripheral people consisted of small segmentary societies and they could hardly pose any serious challenge to the continued Christian domination. As long as the Christian kingdom was militarily superior and could maintain its garrisons in the outlying territories, these weak tribal communities continued to pay forced allegiance to their Christian overlords. But when Imam Ahmad Gragn overran the Christian empire, these

[1] See Chapter IV. [2] See Chapter V.

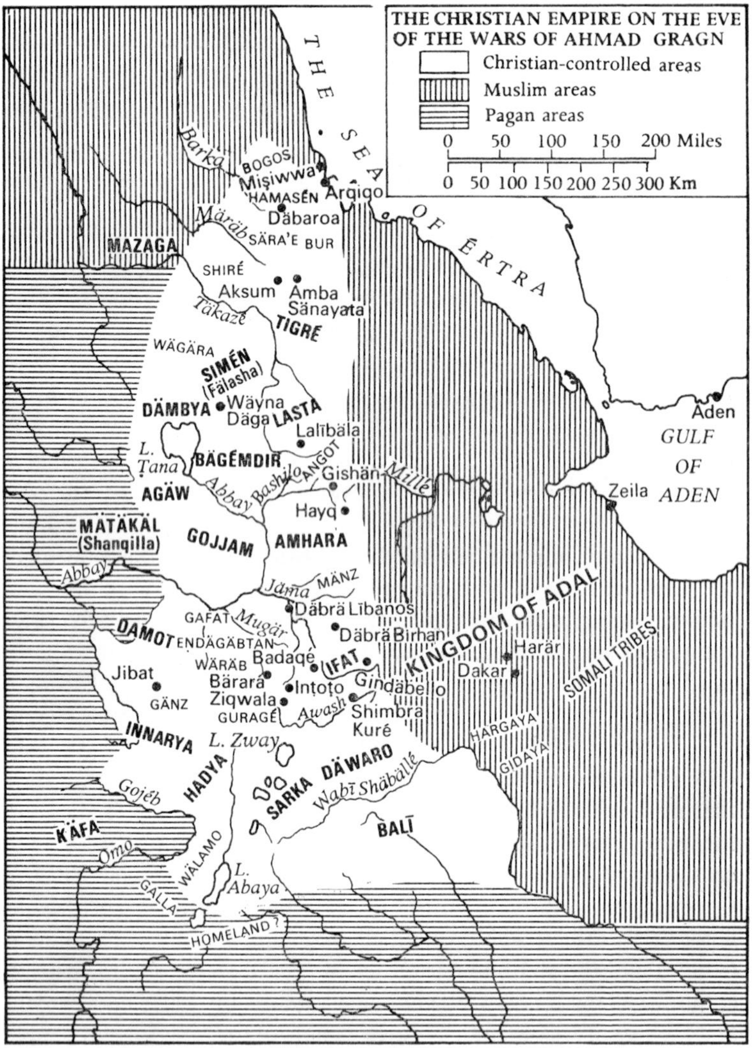

Map 6.

subject people spontaneously rebelled and thus rendered invaluable services to the Imam from within the Christian frontiers. The Fälasha easily submitted to him, and they became his best guides during his campaigns between the river Täkäzé and Lake Țana.[1] The pagan

[1] *Futuh al-Habasha*, pp. 456–9.

Agäw looted and destroyed Christian villages adjoining their tribal areas.[1] The people of Hadya and Gänz actively supported the Muslim conquerors and established excellent terms of friendship with the Imam and his army.[2] But it was in the eastern frontier provinces of Īfat, Däwaro, and Balī that Ahmad Gragn scored his earliest and most decisive victories.

We have already seen that these territories were conquered from a series of Muslim rulers in the fourteenth century.[3] At first, the Christian kings were content to entrust the local administration of these areas to the more loyal members of the Muslim ruling families. There was apparently constant rivalry among the local Muslim princes, and this made the task of their Christian conquerors tremendously easier. When a Wälasma prince was disgraced, for example, many members of his own family were always at hand to replace him as governor of Īfat.[4] It appears from Al-'Umari's statements[5] that similar conditions also obtained in all the conquered Muslim territories. These internal feuds weakened the Muslim position and greatly facilitated the military successes of King Amdä-Ṣiyon and his successor Säyfä-Ar'ad.

In the last quarter of the fourteenth century, however, a very militant branch of the ruling Wälasma family of Īfat moved its headquarters to somewhere near the present location of Harär, and established the kingdom of Adal.[6] The new Muslim state took the place of the large number of small disunited sheikdoms against whom Amdä-Ṣiyon led his famous campaigns of 1332. The Christian–Muslim struggle was then resumed with renewed vigour, and the new kingdom of Adal provided a strong leadership against the expanding Christian empire. However, both Christian and Muslim sources indicate that the Christian army preserved its supremacy until the last years of the fifteenth century.

Yet, the very existence of a viable Muslim state beyond its eastern borders considerably limited the chances of the Christian empire to

[1] This is confirmed by an interesting reference in the hagiographical traditions about a local saint in eastern Gojjam. Abba Täklä-'Alfa, the abbot of Däbrä Dīma during the wars of Ahmad Gragn, once took refuge in a district, apparently in central Gojjam. The Christian families there told him that 'the *Agäw* people had surrounded them, and confiscated all their belongings . . . There were also many of [the Christians] whom the *Agäw* killed . . .' The incident had taken place shortly before the saint's arrival at the locality, and 'he praised God who saved him from the face of the Muslims and the Agäw', *Gli atti di Tekle 'Alfa*, ed. and tr. Cerulli, E., p. 37.

[2] *Futuh al Habasha*, pp. 377, 381, 387–90.

[3] See Chapter IV.

[4] Cf. Chapter IV, pp. 142–8.

[5] Cf. *Masalik*, p. 19.

[6] Cf. Chapter IV, pp. 150–5.

integrate the frontier provinces of Īfat, Däwaro, and Balī. Despite their annexation in the fourteenth century, the inhabitants of these provinces were still predominantly Muslim on the eve of the wars of Ahmad Gragn. The Christian kings recognized the risk that Adal would undermine their position in this region; and unlike most other non-Christian provinces, Īfat, Däwaro, and Balī were placed under the direct rule of the Court. Governors for these areas were carefully recruited from among the most loyal warriors, and they were often closely related to the royal family. Strong military colonies were established at selected places in these provinces, and they were under an almost constant state of emergency. But this military occupation could not dispel the divided loyalties of the Muslim majority. The kings of Adal were in regular contact with these frontier areas and they always encouraged the spirit of independence of the Muslim inhabitants. Sometimes, this subversive propaganda from Adal affected even the Christian military colonies stationed along the frontiers. There were many cases of defection to Adal, and, sometimes, whole units of the Christian frontier troops deserted *en masse*.[1] The Christian kings deeply suspected their Muslim subjects in this region, particularly during active military conflicts with Adal.[2] Thus, the eastern frontier provinces were never fully integrated, and only the military prowess of the Christian empire continued to give a façade of tranquillity to the whole region. These adverse feelings between the Christian kings and the majority of their Muslim subjects continued until Ahmad Gragn led his forces into the Ethiopian highlands.

The brilliant successes of Imam Ahmad ibn Ibrahim against Christian Ethiopia must be seen within the context of the sixteenth-century history of the Near and the Middle East. The Ottoman conquest of the Arab countries also had a great impact on the whole of the Red Sea area. There was a definite revival of Islam in these regions under the protective umbrella of imperial Istanbul. New techniques of warfare and fire-arms trickled through the peripheral districts of the Ottoman empire, and reached the Red Sea and the hinterland of the Gulf of Aden including the Horn of Africa. This tremendously increased the bellicose attitude of the Muslim communities in Adal

[1] Cf. Perruchon, J., *Les Chroniques de Zar'a Ya'eqob et de Ba'eda Maryam*, pp. 45–6, 157–9.

[2] Ibid., pp. 17–21, 58–9; cf. also Conti Rossini, 'Storia di Libna Dingil, re d'Etiopia', pp. 623, 628, 633, 639.

towards Christian Ethiopia. Joined by many Turkish and Arab adventurers from the south Arabian peninsula, these communities poured into the frontier provinces of the medieval Christian empire. This process of Muslim resurgence was particularly enhanced by the internal conflict and decline within Christian Ethiopia in the last quarter of the fifteenth century. Thus, the balance of power between the Church and Islam had definitely changed in favour of the latter. It was under these circumstances that Ahmad Gragn led his tribal forces from the semi-desert areas of eastern Ethiopia, and completely overwhelmed the Christian empire.

The Muslim occupation of the Christian highlands under Ahmad Gragn lasted for a little more than ten years, between 1531 and 1543. But the amount of destruction brought about in these years can only be estimated in terms of centuries. Ahmad Gragn and his followers were dazzled at the extent of the riches of the Church, and at the splendour of Ethiopian Christian culture at the time. And, as the most important repository of the cultural heritage of Christian Ethiopia, the Church was a special target for the destructive furies of the Imam. His chronicler outlines in the *Futuh al Habasha* a large number of cases in which beautiful churches were pulled down, their riches plundered, the holy books burnt to ashes, and the clergy massacred. In this way, the rich material and spiritual culture attained by medieval Ethiopia was almost completely destroyed in not more than a decade. Today, only a short glimpse at the splendour of cultural life in medieval Ethiopia can be had in the remote libraries of some island and mainland monasteries, and in the fast growing collection of the Institute of Ethiopian Studies in Addis Ababa.

Christian Ethiopia was never the same again after the wars of Ahmad Gragn. Indeed, many of the difficulties which befell the Christian kingdom in the sixteenth and seventeenth centuries can be attributed, directly or indirectly, to the disastrous effects of the Muslim wars. The Galla expansion could never be contained in the sixteenth century largely because Ahmad Gragn's forces had effectively disrupted the system of frontier defence of the medieval Christian empire. The Christian kingdom suffered from a long period of dynastic conflicts and political instability—particularly between 1559 and 1607—mainly because the Royal Prison of Amba Gishän had been destroyed by Ahmad Gragn, and many of the contending princes had been left at large. Even the religious conflict with the Jesuit mission was a by-product of the Muslim wars, since direct

European involvement in Ethiopia only started after the Portuguese military assistance in 1541.

Yet, the best key for the swift victories of Imam Ahmad ibn Ibrahim seems to be the heterogeneous character of the medieval Christian empire of Ethiopia. Among the rulers of the fourteenth and fifteenth centuries, King Zär'a-Ya'iqob stands out as the only monarch who made a serious attempt to grapple with the overriding problem of creating a nation out of the manifold communities which constituted his extensive empire. In doing this, however, he sought to superimpose a religious nationalism on his subjects, and his efforts ended in a substantial failure. And when, in the reign of his great grandson, Imam Ahmad Gragn broke into the frontier provinces, the Christian nation could outlast the trying years of the Muslim invasion only where a very long history of ethnic and religious fusion had been effected, namely, in Tigré, Lasta, Amhara, Bägémdir, eastern Gojjam, and in small isolated pockets in Shäwa.

Ethiopian history has a particular tendency to repeat itself. The military exploits of King Amdä-Ṣiyon strongly remind one of the great achievements of the Aksumite kings Ezana and Kaléb on whom he seems to have modelled himself. More recently, in the nineteenth century, the extensive conquests and expansion of Amdä-Ṣiyon were dramatically re-enacted by Emperor Minīlik who, just like his fourteenth-century predecessor, had the Shäwan plateau as the centre of his military activities. It remains to be seen, however, whether Minīlik and his successors have been more successful than their medieval counterparts in the essential task of building an Ethiopian nation.

SELECT BIBLIOGRAPHY

PRIMARY SOURCES

ETHIOPIC: UNPUBLISHED

1. 'Gädlä Yimrha-Kristos', MS. Lalībäla, Bétä-Maryam. Yimrha was the third Zagwé king, but his hagiography seems to have been composed after 1270. Nevertheless, it is a useful compilation of Zagwé customs and traditions.
2. 'Gädlä Abba Bägi'u', MS. Hayq. Bägi'u died before 1292, and his hagiographer claims to have been his contemporary.
3. 'Gädlä Zéna-Marqos', MS. Däbrä Ṣigé. Zéna-Marqos was a disciple of Täklä-Haymanot, and he flourished in the fourteenth century, when he seems to have founded Däbrä Bisrat in Morät. The hagiography was first composed before the wars of Ahmad Gragn, when the community was dispersed. Däbrä Bisrat was re-established in the seventeenth century, when the above MS. was apparently copied with many additional miracles.
4. 'Gädlä Qäwisṭos', MS. Däbrä Lībanos. He was a disciple of Täklä-Haymanot, and the founder of Nibgé Maryam in Bulga, eastern Shäwa. The *Gädl* is said to have first been composed in the reign of Dawīt (1380–1412) and when Bishop Sälama (1348–88) was in the country. It seems, however, that many recent re-editions of it have been made.
5. 'Gädlä Samu'él of Wägäg', MS. Däbrä Lībanos. Another disciple of Täklä-Haymanot, Samu'él is the traditional founder of Däbrä Asäbot on the road to Harär. The last personalities mentioned in the *Gädl* are Bishop Sälama (d. 1388) and King Dawīt (d. 1412).
6. 'Gädlä Zäyohannis', MS. Kibran. A former novice at Däbrä Lībanos in the fourteenth century, Zäyohannis later founded the island monastery of Kibran in Lake Ṭana. M. Schneider of the Institute of Archaeology, Addis Ababa, has just completed editing and translating this *Gädl* into French for her Diploma under Prof. Rodinson of the École des Hautes Études, IVème Section, Sorbonne.
7. 'Gädlä Abba Gīyorgīs of Gas<u>ch</u>a', MS. Hayq. Gīyorgīs is the famous author of *Mäṣhafä-Misṭīr*, and his *Gädl* seems to have been written not much after his death in 1426.
8. 'Gädlä Abba Sīnoda', MS. Däbrä Dīma. A former student at an island monastery in Lake Zway, he later moved to Gojjam and founded Däbrä Ṣimmona there. He died in the reign of King Hizbä-Nagn (1430–3).
9. 'Gädlä Täklä-Hawaryat', MS. Däbrä Lībanos. There is a different version of the same *Gädl* edited and translated by Conti Rossini in the *CSCO* series.
10. 'Gädlä Märha-Kristos', MS. Däbrä Lībanos. Märha-Kristos (1407–96)

was the abbot of Däbra Lībanos in the years 1462–96. This *Gädl* has all the characteristics of an ordinary biography, and it was written under the auspices of Märha-Kristos's immediate successor. The MS. at Däbrä Lībanos has some archaic forms of the Ethiopic alphabet and seems to be of an early date.

11. 'Gädlä Īyasu', MS. Däbrä Lībanos. Īyasu lived in the reigns of Iskindir (1478–94) and Na'od (1494–1508). He was the founder of the famous monastery of Jär Sillassé to the north-east of Däbrä Lībanos.

12. 'Gädlä Särṣä-Pétros', MS. Däbrä Wärq.

13. 'Gädlä Isṭīfanos', MS. no. 2, Institute of Archaeology, Addis Ababa. Isṭīfanos was the founder of the remarkable 'Stephanite' community, and the *Gädl* seems to have been written before 1499.

14. 'Gädlä Yishaq', MS. no. 36, Institute of Archaeology, Addis Ababa. A colleague and follower of Isṭīfanos, Yishaq was the founder of the Stephanite monastery of Gunda-Gundī in Agamé. He died some time before 1475.

15. 'Gädla Gäbrä-Masīh', MS. no. 40, Institute of Archaeology, Addis Ababa.

16. 'Gädlä Habtä Sillassé', MS. no. 40, Institute of Archaeology, Addis Ababa.

17. 'Gädlä Täklä-Näbīyat', MS. no. 43, Institute of Archaeology, Addis Ababa.

18. 'Gädlä Īsayiyas', MS. no. 36, Institute of Archaeology, Addis Ababa.

19. 'Gädlä Gäbrä-Kristos', MS. no. 42, Institute of Archaeology, Addis Ababa.

ETHIOPIC: PUBLISHED AND/OR TRANSLATED

Bähaylä-Mīka'él, *Mäṣhafä Mistiratä-Sämay Wämidr*, ed. and tr. in part by J. Perruchon in *PO*, i (1904), pp. 1–97. Later it was ed. and tr. in full by E. A. W. Budge in his *The Book of the Mysteries of Heaven and Earth*, London, 1935.

Basset, R., *Études sur l'histoire d'Éthiopie*, Paris, 1882. [Extract from *JA*, ser. 7, vol. xvii, 1881.]

—— 'Vie d'Abba Yohannī', in the *Bull. de correspondance africaine*, Algiers, 1884, pp. 433–53.

Budge, E. A. W., *The Life of Maba'Seyon*, ed. and tr., London, 1898.

—— *The Life and Miracles of Takla Haymanot*, ed. and tr., London, 1906.

—— *The Queen of Sheba and Her Only Son Menyelek*, tr., London, 1922.

—— *The Book of the Saints of the Ethiopian Church*, tr. in 4 vols., Cambridge, 1928.

Caquot, A., *Gadla Ezra*, ed. and tr. in *AÉ*, iv (1961), pp. 69–121.

Cerulli, E., 'L'Etiopia del secolo XV in nuovi documenti storici', in *Africa Italiana*, v (1933), pp. 57–112.

—— 'La sconfitta del Sultano Badlay ibn Sa'ad ad-din in due inediti Miracoli di S. Giorgio etiopici', in *Aethiopica*, ii, no. 4 (1934), pp. 105–9.

—— *Gli atti di Tekle Alfa*, ed. and tr. in *Annali*, ii (1943), pp. 1–89.

—— *Il libro etiopico dei miracoli di Maria e le sue fonti nella letteratura del Medio Evo latino*, Rome, 1943.

—— *Gli atti di Zena Maryam, monaca etiopica del secolo XIV*, tr., in *RSO*, xxi (1946), pp. 122–56.

—— 'La festa del Battesimo e l'Eucarestia in Etiopia nel secolo XV', in *Analecta Bollandiana*, lxviii (1950), pp. 436–52.

—— *Atti di Krestos Samra*, ed. and tr. in *CSCO*, vols. 163, 164, Script. Aeth., tom. 33, 34, 1956.

—— *Scritti teologici etiopici dei secoli XVI–XVII*, in *Studi e Testi*, no. 198, 1958.

Conti Rossini, C., 'La storia di Libna Dingil, re d'Etiopia', in *RRAL*, ser. 5, vol. iii (1894), pp. 617–40

—— *Il 'Gadla Takla Haymanot' secondo la redazione Waldebbana*, in *MRAL*, ser. 5, vol. ii, pt. i (1896), pp. 97–143.

—— *L'Omelia di Yohannes, vescovo di Aksum, in onore di Garima*, in *ctes Adu XIe Congrès intern. des orient.*, Paris, 1897, pp. 139–77.

—— 'L'evangelo d'oro di Dabra Libanos', in *RRAL*, ser. 5, vol. x (1901), pp. 177–219.

—— *Il 'Gadla Filipos' ed il 'Gadla Yohannes' di Dabra Bizan* in *MRAL*, viii (1901), pp. 61–170.

—— *Besu'a Amlak e il convento della Trinità*, in *RRAL*, ser. 5, vol. xi (1902), pp. 389–429.

—— *Gli atti di Abba Yonas*, in *RRAL*, ser. 5, vol. xii (1903), pp. 178–201, 236–62.

—— *Gadla Marqorewos seu Acta Sancti Mercuri*, in *CSCO*, Script. Aeth., ser. altera, t. xxii, pp. 1–51 (text), 1–64 (tr.), 1904.

—— *Acta Yared et Pantalewon*, in *CSCO*, Script. Aeth., t. xvii, pp. 1–60 (text), 1–56 (tr.), 1904.

—— *Acta S. Basalota Mika'el et S. Anorewos*, in *CSCO*, Script. Aeth., t. xx, pp. 1–110 (text), 1–98 (tr.), 1905.

—— *Historia regis Sarsa Dengel (Malak Sagad)*, in *CSCO*, Script. Aeth., t. iii, pp. 1–191 (tr.), 1907.

—— *Liber Aksumae* in *CSCO*, Script. Aeth. ser. altera, t. viii, pp. 1–86 (text), 1–104 (tr.), 1910.

—— *Acta Sancti Abakerazun et Sancti Takla Hawaryat*, in *CSCO*, Script. Aeth., ser. altera, t. xxiv, pp. 1–135 (text), 1–120 (tr.), 1910.

—— 'Il libro delle leggende e tradizioni abissine dell'ecciaghie Filpos', in *RRAL*, ser. 5, vol. xxvi (1917), pp. 699–717.

—— 'La caduta della dinastia Zague e la versione amarica del Be'ela Negest', in *RRAL*, ser. 5, vol. xxi (1922), pp. 279–314.

—— 'Note di agiografia etiopica ("Abiya-Egzi, Arkaledes e Gabra Iyesus")', in *RSO*, xvii (1938), pp. 409–52.

CONTI ROSSINI, C., 'Un santo eritreo: Buruk Amlak', in *RRAL*, ser. 6, vol. xiv (1938), pp. 1–48.

—— *Gli atti di re Nä'akuto Lä'ab*, in *Annali*, ii (1943), pp. 105–232.

—— 'Il libro di re Zara Ya'qob sulla custodia del Mistero', in *RSE*, iii (1943), pp. 148–66.

—— 'Due capitoli del libro del Mistero di Giyorgis da Sagla', in *RSE*, vii (1948), pp. 13–53.

CONZELMAN, W. E., *La Chronique de Galawdewos, roi d'Éthiopie*, Paris, 1895.

FOTTI, C., 'La cronaca abbreviata dei re d'abissinia in un manoscritto di Dabra Berhan di Gondar', in *RSE*, i (1941), pp. 87–123.

GUIDI, I., 'Le canzoni Ge'ez-Amarina in onore di re abissini', in *RRAL*, ser. 4, vol. iv (1889), pp. 53–66.

—— *Il Gadla Aragawi*, in *MRAL*, ser. 5, vol. ii, pt. 1 (1896), pp. 54–96.

—— *Il Fetha Negast o legislazione dei re*, ed. and tr., Rome, 1897–9.

—— *Le Synaxaire éthiopien*, ed. and tr., Guidi (Säné, Hamlé, Nähasé, and Pagumé); and Grébaut, S. (Tahsas), in *PO*, vols. i, vii, ix, xv, xxvi, 1904–45.

PEREIRA, F. M. ESTEVES, *Historia de Minas, rei de Ethiopia*, Lisbon, 1887–8.

—— *Chronica de Susenyos, rei de Ethiopia*, Lisbon, 1892–1900.

PERRUCHON, J., *Histoire des guerres d'Amda Seyon, roi d'Éthiopie*, in *JA*, ser. 8, t. xiv (1889), pp. 271–363, 381–493.

—— *Vie de Lalibala, roi d'Éthiopie*, Paris, 1892.

—— *Les Chroniques de Zar'a Ya'eqob et de Ba'eda Maryam*, Paris, 1893.

—— *Histoire d'Eskender, d'Amda-Seyon II et de Na'od, rois d'Éthiopie*, in *JA*, ser. 9, t. iii (1894), pp. 319–66.

RICCI, L., *Le vite di Enbaqom e di Yohannes, abbati di Dabra Libanos di Scioa*, in *RSE*, xiii (1954), pp. 91–120; xiv (1955–8), pp. 69–108; xxii (1966), pp. 75–102; xxiii (1967/8), pp. 79–219; xxiv (1969/70), pp. 134–232.

SANTIS, R. DE, *Il Gadla Tadewos di Dabra Bartarwa*, in *Annali Lateranensi*, vi (1942), pp. 1–116.

TURAIEV, B., *Acta S. Aronis et S. Philippi*, in *CSCO*, Script. Aeth., ser. altera, t. xx, pp. 111–261 (text), 99–234 (tr.), 1905. I have quoted these as *Gädlä Aron* and *Gädlä Filipos* respectively.

—— *Acta S. Eustathii*; the text is edited in Turaiev's collection *Monumenta Aethiopiae Hagiologica*, fasc. iii, Petropoli, 1905. A Latin tr. is available in *CSCO*, Script. Aeth., ser. altera, t. 21, 1906, pp. 1–97. I refer to the edited text which I quote as *Gädlä Ēwosaṭéwos.*

—— *Acta S. Fere Mika'el et S. Zar'a Abraham*, in *CSCO*, Script. Aeth., ser. altera, t. 23, 1905.

VARENBERGH, J., 'Studien zur abessinischen Reichsordnung (Sir'ata Mangist)', in *ZA*, xxx (1915–16), pp. 1–45.

WAJNBERG, I., *Das Leben des hl. Jafqerena' Egzi'*, in *OCA*, no. 106, 1936. I only refer to the edited text quoted as *Gädlä Yafqiränna-Igzi'*.

ZÄR'A-YA'IQOB, *Mäṣhafä Mīlad*, ed. by K. Wendt under the title *Das Mashafa Milad und Mashafa Sellase des Kaisers Zar'a Ya'qob*, in *CSCO*, Script. Aeth., t. 41 and 43. The translations of these two parts are provided in the same series, Script. Aeth., t. 42 and 44. I have only made use of the text.

—— *Mäṣhafä Birhan*, ed. and tr. by C. Conti Rossini and L. Ricci in *CSCO*, Script. Aeth., t. 47 and 48 (1964); and Script. Aeth., t. 51 and 52 (1965).

ARABIC AND OTHERS

ABOUL FEDA, *Géographie*, tr. M. Reinaud, t. ii, pt. 1, Paris, 1848.

ABU SALIH, *The Churches and Monasteries of Egypt and some Neighbouring Countries*, ed. and tr. by B. T. A. Evetts, with notes by A. J. Butler, Oxford, 1895.

ALVAREZ, F., *The Prester John of the Indies*, tr. C. F. Beckingham and G. W. B. Huntingford (Hakluyt Society, ser. 2, vols. 114–15), Cambridge, 1961.

ARAB FAQIH [CHIHAB EDDIN AHMED B. 'ABDEL QADER], *Futuh al-Habasha*, tr. R. Basset, Paris, 1897–1901.

CERULLI, E., 'Documenti arabi per la storia dell'Etiopia', in *MRAL*, ser. 6, vol. iv (1931), pp. 37–101.

—— 'Il sultanato dello Scioa nel secolo XIII secondo un nuovo documento storico', in *RSE*, i (1941), pp. 5–14.

—— 'L'Etiopia medievale in alcuni brani di scrittori arabi', in *RSE*, iii (1943), pp. 272–94.

—— *Etiopi in Palestina*, 2 vols., Rome, 1943–7.

DIMASHQI, *Manuel de la cosmographie du Moyen Age*, tr. M. A. F. Mehren, 1874.

IBN HAUKAL, MUHAMMAD, *Configuration de la terre*, tr. J. H. Kramers and G. Wiet, 2 vols., Paris, 1964.

IBN IYAS, MUHAMMAD IBN AHMAD, *Journal d'un bourgeois du Caire: chronique d'Ibn Iyas*, tr. G. Wiet, i (1500–16), 1955, and ii (1516–22), 1960.

IBN KABAR, ABU'L-BARAKAT, *Livre de la lampe des ténèbres et de l'exposition (lumineuse) du service (de l'Église)*, tr. and ed. L. Villecourt, E. Tisserant, and G. Wiet, in *PO*, xx (1929), pp. 579–733.

IBN KHALDUN, *Histoire des Berbères et des dynasties musulmanes de l'Afrique septentrionale*, tr. de Slane, new edition, P. Casanova, ii, Paris, 1927.

IBN SABA, JEAN IBN D'ABOU-ZAKERIYA, *La Perle précieuse traitant des sciences ecclésiastiques*, ed. and tr. J. Perier, in *PO*, xvi (1922), pp. 593–760.

AL-KHAZRAJI, ALI IBN AL-SUSAIN, *History of the Resuliyy Dynasty of Yemen*, ed. and tr. J. W. Redhouse, 1906–8.

AL-KHOWAYTER, ABDUL AZIZ, 'A Critical Edition of an Unknown Source of the Life of al-Malik al-Zahir Baibars', 3 vols., Ph.D. Thesis (unpublished), London, 1960.

MAQRIZI, *Historia Regum Islamiticorum in Abyssinia*, ed. and tr. F. T. Rinck, Leiden, 1790. [At the library of SOAS there is an English translation from the Latin version of this work by G. W. B. Huntingford, in typescript.]

—— *Les Fêtes des Coptes*, ed. and tr. R. Griveau, in *PO*, x (1915), pp. 315–42.

MUFAZZAL, IBN ABIL-FAZAL, *Histoire des sultans mamlouks*, ed. and tr. E. Blochet, in *PO*, vols. xii, xiv, xx, 1919–29.

PERRUCHON, J., 'Extrait de la vie d'Abba Jean, 74e patriarche d'Alexandrie, relatif à l'Abyssinie', in *RS*, t. vi (1898), pp. 267–71, 365–72; t. vii (1899), pp. 76–85.

QUATREMÈRE, E., *Mémoires géographiques et historiques sur l'Égypte et sur quelques contrées voisines*, 2 vols., Paris, 1811.

RENAUDOT, E., *Historia Patriarcharum Alexandrinorum*, Paris, 1717.

AL SAKHAWI, *Al-Tibr al-Masbuk* (A.H. 845–57), Cairo, 1896.

SAWIRUS (IBN AL-MUKAFFA), Bishop of al-Asmunin, *History of the Patriarchs of the Egyptian Church*, vol. i (to A.D. 849), ed. and tr. by B. T. A. Evetts, in *PO*, t. i, v, x, and xi, 1904–15. Vol. ii (849–1102), tr. by Yassa 'abd Al-Masih, Aziz Suryal Atiya, and O. H. E. Khs-Burmester, 1943–59.

TAGHRI BIRDI, YUSUF ABU-L'MAHASIN IBN, *History of Egypt (1382–1469)*, tr. W. Popper, parts iii and iv, 1957–60.

UMARAH, *Yaman, its Early Medieval History*, ed. and tr. H. C. Kay, London, 1892.

AL-'UMARI, IBN FADL ALLAH, *Masalik al-Absar Fi Mamalik El Amsar: l'Afrique moins l'Égypte*, tr. by M. Gaudefroy-Demombynes, Paris, 1927.

AL-YAQUBI, IBN-WADIH, *Historiae*, ed. T. Houtsma, i, 1883.

—— *Livre des pays*, tr. G. Wiet, 1937.

SECONDARY SOURCES

ABBADIE, A. D', *Géographie de l'Éthiopie*, i, Paris, 1890.

ALMEIDA, *Some Records of Ethiopia 1593–1646*, extracts tr. by C. F. Beckingham and G. W. B. Huntingford (Hakluyt Soc., ser. 2, 107), 1954.

ANNEQUIN, G., 'Notes on "Djibat" and "Adadi Maryam"', in *AÉ*, vi (1965), pp. 13–16.

AZAIS, R. P., and CHAMBARD, R., *Cinq Années de recherches archéologiques en Éthiopie*, 2 vols., Paris, 1931.

BASSET, R., 'Deux lettres éthiopiennes du XVIe siècle', in *GSAI*, iii (1899), pp. 59–79.

—— 'Les inscriptions de l'île de Dahlak', in *JA*, ser. 9, vol. i (1893), pp. 77–111.

BECKINGHAM, C. F., 'Amba Geshen and Asiregarah', in *JSS*, ii (1957), pp. 182–8.

—— 'A note on the Topography of Ahmad Gragn's campaigns in 1542', in *JSS*, iv (1959), pp. 362–72.

—— 'Notes on an Unpublished MS. of Francesco Alvarez', in *AÉ*, iv (1961), pp. 139–54.

—— 'Pantaleao de Aveiro and the Ethiopian Community in Jerusalem', in *JSS*, vii (1962), pp. 325–38.

BERCHET, G., 'Lettera sulle cognizioni che i Veneziani avevano dell'Abissinia', in *BSGI*, ii (1869), pp. 151–70.

BRUCE, J., *Travels to Discover the Source of the Nile in the Years 1768–1773*, 5 vols., London, 1790.

BUDGE, E. A. W., *A History of Ethiopia: Nubia and Abyssinia*, 2 vols., London, 1928.

BUXTON, D. R., 'The Christian Antiquities of Northern Ethiopia', in *Archeologia*, xcii (1947), pp. 1–42.

CAQUOT, A., 'Aperçu préliminaire sur le Mashafa Tefut de Geshen', in *AÉ*, i (1955), pp. 89–108.

—— 'La royauté sacrale en Éthiopie', in *AÉ*, ii (1957), pp. 205–19.

CERULLI, E., 'Note su alcune popolazioni Sidama dell'Abissinia meridionale', in *RSO*, x (1923–5), pp. 597–692.

—— 'Eugenio IV e gli Etiopi al Concilio di Firenze nel 1441', in *RRAL*, ser. 7, vol. ix (1933), pp. 347–68.

—— *Etiopia occidentale*, 2 vols., Rome, 1933.

—— *Studi etiopici*: vol. i, *La lingua e la storia di Harar*, Rome, 1936; vol. ii, *La lingua e la storia dei Sidama*, Rome, 1938; vol. iii, *Il linguaggio dei Giangero ed alcune lingue Sidama dell'omo*, Rome, 1938; vol. iv, *La lingua caffina*, Rome, 1951.

—— 'Gli abbati di Dabra Libanos', in *Orientalia*, xi (1943), pp. 226–53; xiii (1944), pp. 137–82; xiv (1945), pp. 143–71.

—— *Storia della letteratura etiopica*, Rome, 1956.

—— 'Il monachismo in Etiopia', in *OCA*, no. 153, 1958, pp. 259–78.

—— 'Tre nuovi documenti sugli etiopi in Palestina nel secolo XV', in *Studia Biblica ed Orientalia*, iii (1959), pp. 33–47.

—— 'Punti di vista sulla storia dell'Etiopia', in *Atti del Convegno Intern. di Studi Etiopici*, Rome, 1960.

—— 'Gli atti di Zena Marqos, monaco etiopico del secolo XIV', in *Studi e Testi*, nos. 219–220, 1962, pp. 191–212.

—— 'Two Ethiopian tales on the Christians of Cyprus', in *JES*, v, no. 1 (1967), pp. 1–8.

CHAINE, M., *La Chronologie des temps chrétiens de l'Égypte et de l'Éthiopie*, Paris, 1925.

—— 'Un monastère éthiopien à Rome au XVe et XVIe siècles: San Stefano dei Mori', in *Mélanges de la Faculté orientale*, Beirut, t. v (1910), pp. 1–36.

CHOJNACKI, S., 'Day Giyorgis', in *JES*, vii, no. 2, 1969, pp. 43–52.

—— 'Notes on Art in Ethiopia in the Fifteenth and Early Sixteenth Century', in *JES*, viii, no. 2, 1970, pp. 21–65.

COHEN, M., 'Dabra Warq', in *Mélanges René Basset*, t. i (1923), pp. 143–62.

—— *Études d'Éthiopie méridionale*, Paris, 1931.

CONTI ROSSINI, C., 'Note etiopiche', in *GSAI*, x (1897), pp. 141–56.

—— 'Sulla dinastia Zague', in *L'Oriente*, ii (1897), pp. 144–59.

—— 'Tradizione storica dei Mensa', in *GSAI*, xiv (1901), pp. 41–99.

—— 'Lettera a J. Halévy sulla caduta degli Zague', in *RS*, x (1902), p. 373–77; xi (1903), pp. 325–30.

—— 'Per la conoscenza della lingua cunama', in *GSAI*, xvi (1903), pp. 187–227.

——'Al Ragali', in *Boll. Soc. Ital. d'Esplor. Geog. e comm.*, 1903–4, pp. 3–62.

—— 'I loggo e la legge dei Loggo Sarda', in *GSAI*, xvii, pt. 1 (1904), pp. 1–63.

—— 'Appunti sulla lingua Khamta dell'Averghelle', in *GSAI*, xvii, pt. 2 (1905), pp. 183–242.

—— 'Appunti sulla lingua Awiya del Dangela', in *GSAI* (1905), pp. 103–94.

—— 'Sugli Habasat', in *RRAL*, ser. 5, vol. xv (1906), pp. 39–59.

—— 'Racconti e canzoni bileni', in *Actes du XIVe Congrès intern. des Orient.*, ii, Paris, 1907, pp. 331–94.

—— 'Il convento di Tsana in Abissinia e le sue laudi della Vergine', in *RRAL*, ser. 5, vol. xix (1910), pp. 581–621.

—— 'Studi su popolazioni dell'Etiopia', in *RSO*, iii (1910), pp. 849–900; iv (1912), pp. 599–651; vi (1913), pp. 365–425.

—— 'Piccoli studi etiopici', in *ZA*, xxvii (1911), pp. 358–72.

—— *La Langue des Kemant en Abyssinie*, Vienna, 1912.

—— 'Il "Libro del conoscimento" e le sue notizie sull'Etiopia', in *BSGI*, ser. 5, vol. vi (1917), pp. 656–79.

—— 'Popoli d'Ethiopia occidentale', in *RRAL*, ser. 5, vol. xxx (1919), pp. 251–85, 319–25.

—— 'Appunti di storia e letteratura falascia', in *RSO*, vii (1920), pp. 563–610.

—— 'Nuovi appunti sui giudei d'Abissinia', in *RRAL*, ser. 5, vol. xxxi (1922), pp. 221–40.

——'Un codice illustrato eritrea del secolo XV', in *Africa Italiana*, i (1927), pp. 83–97.

—— *Storia d'Etiopia*, Milan, 1928.

—— *Etiopia e genti d'Etiopia*, Florence, 1937.

—— 'L'agiografia etiopica e gli atti del santo Yafqirännä-Igzī (secolo XIV)', in *ARIV*, xcvi, pt. 2 (1937), pp. 403–33.

—— 'Pergamene di Dabra Dammo', in *RSO*, xix (1940), pp. 45–80.

—— 'Sulle missioni domenicane in Etiopia nel secolo XIV', in *RRAL*, ser. 7, vol. i (1940), pp. 71–80.

—— 'Marco Polo e l'Etiopia', in *ARIV*, xcix, pt. 2 (1940), pp. 1021–39.

—— 'Il "Senodos" etiopico', in *RRAL*, ser. 7, vol. iii (1942), pp. 41–8.

—— 'Sul metropolita Yeshaq d'Etiopia (secolo XV–XVI)', in *RRAL*, ser. 8, vol. i (1946), pp. 7–17.

—— *Tabelle comparative del calendario etiopico col calendario romano*, Rome, 1948.

CRAWFORD, O. G. S., *Ethiopian Itineraries*, c. *1400–1524* (Hakluyt Soc., ser. 2, vol. 109), 1958.

CREONE, F., 'La politica orientale di Alfonso di Aragone', in *Archivio storico per le provincie napoletane*, xxvii (1902), pp. 1–93; xxviii (1903), pp. 154–202.

DILLMANN, A., *Catalogus Codicum Manuscriptorum Orientalium qui in Museo Britannico asservantur*, pars tertia, London, 1847.

—— *Catalogus Codicum Manuscriptorum Bibliothecae Bodleianae Oxoniensis*, pars vii, 1848.

—— *Die Kriegsthaten des Königs 'Amda Syon*, Berlin, 1884.

—— *Über die Regierung, insbesonders die Kirchenordnung, des Königs Zar'a Jacob*, Berlin, 1884.

DORESSE, J., *L'Empire du Prêtre-Jean*, 2 vols., Paris, 1957.

DREWES, A. J., *Inscriptions de l'Éthiopie antique*, Leiden, 1962.

ELLERO, G., 'I conventi dello Scire e le loro leggende', in *BSGI*, ser. 7, vol. iv (1939), pp. 835–53.

—— 'Note sull'Enderta', in *RSE*, i (1941).

FUMAGALLI, G., *Bibliografia etiopica*, Milan, 1893.

GARRONE, V., 'Gli Atcheme Melga', in *BSGI*, ser. 4, vol. v (1904), pp. 994–1017.

GERSTER, G., *L'Art éthiopien*, Zürich, 1968.

GHINZONI, P., 'Un ambasciata del Prete Gianni a Roma', in *Archivio storico lombardo*', vi, (1889), pp. 145–54.

GILL, J., *The Council of Florence*, 1959.

GRÉBAUT, S., 'Table de comput et de chronologie', in *ROC*, i (1918/19), pp. 324–6.

—— 'Note sur la princesse Zir-Ganela', in *JA* (1928), pp. 142–4.

—— 'Disciplina alessandrina: II Etiopi', in *Codificazione Canonica Orientale*, ser. I, fasc. 8, 1932, pp. 73–85.

GUIDI, I., 'Le liste dei metropoliti d'Abissinia', in *Bessarione*, vi (1899), pp. 1–17.

GUIDI, I., 'Uno squarcio di storia ecclesiastica', in *Bessarione*, viii (1900), pp. 10–25.

—— 'La Chiesa abissina', in *OM*, ii (1922), pp. 123–8, 186–90, 252–6.

—— *(Breve) storia della letteratura etiopica*, Rome, 1932.

HABERLAND, E., 'The Influence of the Christian Ethiopian Empire on Southern Ethiopia', in *JSS*, ix (1964), pp. 235–8.

—— *Untersuchungen zum äthiopischen Königtum*, Wiesbaden, 1965.

HAMMERSCHMIDT, E., *Studies in the Ethiopian Anaphoras*, Akademie-Verlag, Berlin, 1961.

—— 'Jewish Elements in the Cult of the Ethiopian Church', in *JES*, ii, no. 2 (1965), pp. 1–12.

HASAN, YUSUF FADL, *The Arabs and the Sudan from the Seventh to the Early Sixteenth Century*, Edinburgh University Press, 1967.

JAGER, O. A., 'Some Notes on Illuminations of MSS. in Ethiopia', in *RSE*, xvii (1961), pp. 45–60.

JOHNSON, A. R., *Sacral Kingship in Ancient Israel*, Cardiff University Press, 1955.

JORGA, N., 'Cenni sulle relazioni tra l'Abissinia e l'Europa cattolica nei secoli XIV–XV', in *Centenario M. Amari*, ii (Palermo, 1910), pp. 139–50.

KAMMERER, A., *Essai sur l'histoire antique d'Abyssinie*, Paris, 1926.

KOLMODIN, J., *Traditions de Tsazzega et Hazzega*, in *AÉO*, vol. 5: 1, 2, 3, Uppsala, 1912–14.

LANTSCHOOT, A. VAN, 'Abba Salama, métropolite d'Éthiopie (1348–88), et son rôle de traducteur', in *Atti del Convegno di Studi Etiopici*, Rome, 1960, pp. 397–401.

LA RONCIÈRE, C. DE, *La Découverte de l'Afrique au Moyen Age*, 3 vols., Cairo, 1924–7.

LEFEVRE, R., 'G. B. Brocchi da Imola, diplomatico pontificio e viaggiatore in Etiopia nel '400', in *BSGI*, iv (1939), pp. 639–59.

—— 'Documenti pontifici sui rapporti con l'Etiopia nei secoli XV e XVI', in *RSE*, v (1946), pp. 16–41.

—— 'Presenze etiopiche in Italia prima del Concilio di Firenze del 1439', in *RSE*, xxii (1967/8), pp. 5–26.

LEROY, J., 'La peinture chrétienne d'Éthiopie antérieure à l'influence occidentale', in *Christentum am Nil*, ed. Wessel, K., 1963, pp. 61–76.

—— *Ethiopian Paintings in the Late Middle Ages and under the Gondar Dynasty*, London, 1967.

LESLAU, W., 'The Influence of Cushitic on the Semitic Languages of Ethiopia: a Problem of Substratum', in *Word*, i (1945), pp. 59–82.

—— *Falasha Anthology*, New Haven, 1951.

—— 'The Influence of Sidamo on the Ethiopic Language of Guragé', in *Language*, xxviii (1952), pp. 63–81.

—— 'A Short Chronicle on the Gafat', in *RSO*, xli (1966), pp. 189–98.

LEWIS, B., 'The Fatimids and the Route to India', in *Revue de la Faculté des Sciences économiques Univ. Istanbul*, xi (1949–50), pp. 50–4.

LITTMANN, E., *Deutsche Aksum-Expedition*, t. iv, 1913.

—— 'Arabische Inschriften aus Abissinien', in *ZS*, Bd. iii (1925), pp. 236–46.

LUDOLF, H., *A New History of Ethiopia*, London, 1684.

—— *Commentarius ad Suam Historiam Aethiopicam*, Frankfurt, 1691.

MATTHEW, Canon A. F., 'The Monolithic Church on Yekka', in *JES*, vii, no. 2 (1969), pp. 89–98.

MAURO DA LEONESSA, P., *Cronologia e calendario etiopico*, Tivoli, 1934.

—— 'La versione etiopica dei canoni apocrifici del Concilio di Nicea', in *RSE*, ii (1942), pp. 29–89.

—— 'Un trattato sul calendario redatto al tempo di re 'Amda-Syon I', in *RSE*, iii (1943), pp. 302–26.

MONNERET DE VILLARD, U., *Storia della Nubia cristiana*, Rome, 1938.

MORDINI, A., 'Il convento di Gunde-Gundie', in *RSE*, xii (1953), pp. 29–70.

—— 'Un tissu musulman du Moyen Age provenant de Dabra Damo', in *AÉ*, ii (1957), pp. 75–83.

MUYSER, J., 'Le samedi et le dimanche dans l'Église et la littérature copte', Appendix to Togo Mina, *Le Martyre d'Apa Epima*, Cairo, 1937, pp. 89–111.

RICHARD, J., 'L'Extrême-Orient légendaire au Moyen Age. Roi David et Prêtre Jean', in *AÉ*, ii (1957), pp. 225–45.

RODINSON, M., 'Sur la question des "influences juives" en Éthiopie', in *JSS*, ix (1964), pp. 11–19.

ROSSI, E., 'Sulla storia delle isole Dahlak nel Medioevo', in *Atti del 3º Congresso di Studi Coloniali*, 1937, pp. 367–75.

SADUA, P., 'Un manoscritto etiopico degli Evangeli', in *RSE*, xi (1952), pp. 9–28.

SAUTER, R., 'L'église monolithe de Yaka Mika'el', in *AÉ*, ii (1957), pp. 15–37.

—— 'Où en est notre connaissance des églises rupestres d'Éthiopie', in *AÉ*, v (1963), pp. 235–92.

SCHNEIDER, M., 'Stèles funéraires arabes de Quiha', in *AÉ*, vii (1967), pp. 107–22.

—— 'Deux actes de donation en arabe', in *AÉ*, viii (1970), pp. 79–87.

SERGEW H. SELLASSIE, *Bibliography of Ancient and Medieval Ethiopan History*, HSIU Press, Addis Ababa, 1969.

SHINNIE, P. L., *Meroe, a Civilization of the Sudan*, London, 1967.

SKEHAN, P. W., 'An Illuminated Gospel Book in Ethiopic', in *Studies in Art and Literature for Belle da Costa Greene*, Princeton, 1954, pp. 350–75.

STRELCYN, S., *Catalogue des mss. éthiopiens (collection Griaule)*, t. iv, Paris, 1954.

TADDESSE TAMRAT, 'Some Notes on the Fifteenth Century Stephanite "heresy" in the Ethiopian Church', in *RSE*, xxii (1966), pp. 103–15.

—— 'The Abbots of Däbrä Hayq 1248–1535', in *JES*, viii, no. 1 (1970), pp. 87–117.

—— 'Hagiographies and the Reconstruction of Medieval Ethiopian History', in *Rural Africana*, 1970.

TÄKLÄ ṢADIQ MÄKURYA, *L'Empéreur Zera Yaicob et sa lettre à la communauté éthiopienne de Jérusalem*, 1963.

—— *Les Noms propres, les Noms de baptême et l'Étude généalogique des rois d'Éthiopie (XIIIe–XXe siècles) à travers leurs noms patronymiques*, Belgrade, 1966.

TEDESCHI, S., 'Profilo storico di Dayr as-Sultan', in *JES*, ii, no. 2 (1964), pp. 92–160.

—— 'L'Etiopia nella storia dei patriarchi alessandrini', in *RSE*, xxiii (1967/8), pp. 232–71.

TISSERANT, E., and GRÉBAUT, S., *Codices Aethiopici, Vaticani et Borgiani, Barberinianus Orientalis 2 Rossianus 865*, Vatican Library, 1935.

TRASSELLI, C., 'Un Italiano in Etiopia nel secolo XV: Pietro Rombulo di Messina', in *RSE*, i (1941), pp. 173–202.

TRIMINGHAM, J. S., *Islam in Ethiopia*, 1952.

TUBIANA, J., 'Notes sur la distribution géographique des dialectes Agaw', in *CAA*, no. 5, 1955, pp. 1–12.

ULLENDORFF, E., *Catalogue of Ethiopic MSS. in the Bodleian Library*, Oxford, 1951.

—— 'The Ethiopic MSS. in the Royal Library of Windsor Castle', in *RSE*, xii (1953), pp. 71–9.

—— *The Semitic Languages of Ethiopia*, London, 1955.

—— 'Hebraic-Jewish elements in Abyssinian (Monophysite) Christianity', in *JSS*, i (1956), pp. 216–56.

—— *Catalogue of Ethiopic MSS. in the Cambridge University Library*, 1961.

—— *Ethiopia and the Bible*, London, 1968.

WANSLEB, J. M., *Histoire de l'Église d'Alexandrie*, Paris, 1677.

WIET, G., 'Les relations égypto-abyssines sous les sultans mamelouks', in *BSAC*, iv (1938), pp. 115–40.

—— 'Roitelets de Dahlak', in *BIÉ*, t. 34 (1951/2), pp. 85–95.

—— 'Les marchands d'épices sous les sultans mamelouks', in *CHÉ*, vii (1955), pp. 000–00.

WITTE, C. M. DE, 'Une ambassade éthiopienne à Rome en 1450', in *OCP*, xxi (1956), pp. 286–98.

WRIGHT, S., 'Notes on some Cave Churches in the Province of Wallo', in *AÉ*, ii (1957), pp. 7–13.

WRIGHT, W., *Catalogue of Ethiopic MSS. in the British Museum*, London, 1877.

ZANUTTO, S., *Bibliografia etiopica: manoscritti etiopici*, Rome, 1932.

ZOTENBERG, H., *Catalogue des manuscrits éthiopiens de la Bibliothèque nationale*, Paris, 1877.

INDEX

Abäkärazun, *Gädlä*, 3
Abärgälé, 28
Abbadie, Antoine d', 246
Abbay, river, 20, 170, 201
Abdallah, 128
Abdun, 47–8
Absadī, 198, 207, 208, 210
Abu-Abdallha, Sheikh, 130–1
Abu Salih, 249
Abut, 128
Achäfär, 27
Adäfa, 21, 59, 62
Adal, 92, 105, 128, 138, 140, 141, 142, 185, 192, 215, 263
  kingdom of, 145, 147, 150–5, 282, 294–6, 299–300
Adam, Guillaume, 252
Adamat, 182
Aden, Gulf of, 51, 66, 77, 252, 300
Adhanī, 176
Al-Adid (1160–71), Caliph of Egypt, 57
Adkämä-Mälga, 28, 75
  administration, 94–8
Adulis, 5, 7, 11, 14, 15, 16, 17, 18, 21, 22, 23, 76, 79
Agamé, 34
Agärä-Nagran, 33
Agäw, 5, 8, 20, 25, 34, 37, 53, 68, 132, 196, 201, 202, 297, 298–9
  traditions of migrations, 27–9
Agäw-midir, 27, 155, 201
Ahmad, 146–7
Ahmad Badlay (d. 1445), king of Adal, 262–4, 294
Ahmad ibn Ibraham (Gragn), Imam, 20, 297–302; *see also* Gragn
Akälä-Guzay, 11, 75
Akhadom, 200
Aksum, 5, 11, 13, 14 n., 21, 22, 23, 24, 26, 29, 30, 31, 34, 35, 43, 45, 53, 73, 79, 81, 159, 163, 220, 229, 248–9, 250, 278
Aksumite kingdom:
  alliance with Byzantium, 22–3, 31
  beginnings of, 16
  decline of, 32–4, 45, 89
  early conflict with Islam, 31–2
  expansion of, 28–9
Ali, 145, 146–8
Ali ibn Sallar (d. 1153), Egyptian vizir, 55
Almeida, Manoel de, 281
Aloa, kingdom of, 29
Alphonso V, king of Aragon, 258, 265,
Alvarez, 281, 291
266
Amädamīt, 196, 202
Amano, 106, 136
Amanu'él, 140
Amara, 37–8
Amba Gishän, *see* Gishän
Amba Sänayata, 74, 251
Amdä-Mäsqäl, 240
Amdä-Mīka'él, Ras, 247, 286–92, 294–5
Amdä-Ṣiyon (1314–44), king:
  campaigns in Tigré and Eritrea, 73–4, 76–7, 251
  conflicts with Church leaders, 106, 109–10, 116–17, 178, 186–7, 208
  conquests of Damot, 122, 235; Fälasha, 192–3, 197, 199; Gojjam, 189–90, 196, 201–2; Hadya, 106, 135–6; Īfat, 132–5, 137–45, 153
  dual system of local administration, 94–8
  early contacts abroad, 250–3
  economic motives for his wars, 80–1, 84–5, 87–9, 136–7, 140
  military organization, 89–94
  royal Court of, 103–6, 268
  other references, 4, 20, 42, 104, 112, 173, 174, 175, 179, 180, 194, 200, 205, 206, 232, 250, 297, 302
Amdä-Ṣiyon II (1494), king, 292–4, 296
Amdu, Abba, 287
Amha-Īyäsus, 241
Amhara, 34, 35, 36, 42, 43, 53, 57, 60, 64–5, 66, 67, 68, 72, 75, 77, 80, 81, 82, 85, 86, 90, 98, 107, 109, 110, 112, 114, 115, 120, 121, 138, 142, 152, 154, 156, 157, 159, 160, 167, 170, 173, 174, 175, 177–8, 182, 187, 189, 194, 196, 197, 201, 203, 205, 213, 215, 217, 218, 223, 232, 237, 245, 292, 293, 302
Angot, 35, 37, 42, 53, 66, 82, 138, 142